Studies in the History of Christian Traditions

Founded by

Heiko A. Oberman†

Edited by

Robert J. Bast
Knoxville, Tennessee

In cooperation with

Henry Chadwick, Cambridge
Scott H. Hendrix, Princeton, New Jersey
Paul C.H. Lim, Nashville, Tennessee
Eric Saak, Indianapolis, Indiana
Brian Tierney, Ithaca, New York
Arjo Vanderjagt, Groningen
John Van Engen, Notre Dame, Indiana

VOLUME 132

Narrative of the Anabaptist Madness

Narrative of the Anabaptist Madness

The Overthrow of Münster, the Famous Metropolis of Westphalia

By

Hermann von Kerssenbrock

Translated with Introduction and Notes by
Christopher S. Mackay

BRILL

LEIDEN • BOSTON
2007

Cover illustration: this bird's-eye view of the city was published in commemoration of the treaty that was signed in the council hall of Münster in 1648 to end the Thirty Years' War, and it gives a good idea of the city's massive defensive works (Stadt-archiv, Münster, Germany).

Brill has made all reasonable efforts to trace all right holders to any copyrighted material used in this work. In cases where these efforts have not been successful the publisher welcomes communications from copyright holders, so that the appropriate acknowledgements can be made in future editions, and to settle other permission matters.

This book is printed on acid-free paper.

BX
4933
.G3
K4713
2007
v.1

ISSN: 1573-5664
ISBN: 978 90 04 15721 7

Kellie meae
optimae conuigi de me bene merenti,
quae textui recognoscendo maximas contulerit operas

CONTENTS

LIST OF ILLUSTRATIONS

ACKNOWLEDGEMENTS

My thanks to Annette Gresing and Bernd Thier of the Stadtmuseum of Münster, Anke Wollenweber of the Stadtarchiv of Münster, and Peter Ilisch of the Westfälisches Landesmuseum für Kunst und Kulturgeschicht and to their respective institutions for their assistance in providing me with the illustrations for this book. I would also like to thank Robert Bast for suggesting improvements to the general introduction. And finally I have to say that this translation could not have been possible without the help that my wife Kelly MacFarlane provided in various ways, most notably in the yeoman work she did proofreading. Maximas ago gratias!

NOTE ON THE TEXT AND NOTES

In the margin of the translation are numbers indicating the pagination of Detmer's edition. If the line opposite the number contains the sign "|", then that marks the start of the page. (Since the Latin word order sometimes distributes words rather differently than English, at times a sentence extends over the page break, and a few words may appear on the wrong side of the divide.) If the number appears at the start of a paragraph without the sign, then the page begins with that paragraph. In my introduction and the notes, a reference that ends with the letter "D" (for "Detmer"; e.g. "105D") refers to this marginal numeration.

Much of the discussion of other contemporary sources comes from the extensive German notes in Detmer's *editio princeps* of the Latin text, and anyone interested in further information on such matters should consult Detmer (1899–1900).

GENERAL INTRODUCTION

Undoubtedly, one of the most lurid events of the Reformation was the takeover in 1534 of the city of Münster by a variety of Anabaptists who proceeded to institute polygamy and a form of collective ownership of property and to elect a Dutch tailor as their king. The city had been subject to Lutheran attacks on the traditional Catholic ecclesiastical establishment since the mid 1520s, and by the start of the 1530s the preacher Bernard Rothman came to accept increasingly radical interpretations of religious reform that went far beyond anything that Luther would have approved. In 1532, the previous prince-bishop, who had both ecclesiastical and temporal powers, died, and was replaced by Francis of Waldeck. Just at this time, when the city council was inclined to assert its determination to reform the city's religious practices, a wave of religious enthusiasm inspired by the ideas of Melchior Hofman was spreading in the northeastern corner of the Holy Roman Empire (Hofman combined Anabaptist belief with a millenarian conviction that the end of the world was at hand). By February 1533, the city council had extorted from the new prince-bishop an agreement that guaranteed the city virtual autonomy in its religious decisions, but the influence of the Anabaptists came to be felt. A three-way struggle then ensued in the city between the traditional-minded Catholics, who opposed any reform, the Lutherans, who wished to institute a comparatively limited reform, and the Anabaptists, who had much more wide-ranging reforms in mind, and eventually the arrival of radical preachers from outside strengthened the hand of the radicals. In the new municipal elections of February 1534, the radicals under the leadership of the Dutch prophet John Matthisson took control of the city council, and at the end of the month expelled from the city anyone who refused to be rebaptized. The prince-bishop then undertook to besiege the city to compel its obedience, and when Matthisson fell in battle in April, his place as inspired leader was taken by the Dutch tailor John Bockelson of Leiden. During the initial months of the Anabaptist regime, various radical measures were taken, such as the iconoclastic destruction of religious art, the institution of communal ownership of property and of polygamy, and the replacement of government by the city council with a "council of elders." An attempt to take the city by siege in May failed through flawed execution, and when a second full-scale assault was driven back on August 28, John was crowned as the head of the New Jerusalem that was to lead the battle against the Antichrist in the Last Days (he was assisted in his position by Bernard Knipperdolling, a member of the city's old ruling class who had radical inclinations). Attempts to spark sympathetic revolutions elsewhere and to enlist support from outside the city failed, however, and after the siege was tightened so that no supplies could get into the city, starvation took root in Münster. The new kingdom was then ended when refuges from the city suggested a plan of attack that resulted in the capture of the city in June 1535. Francis was now properly installed in his position as prince-bishop, and the city's privileges were curtailed. John, Knipperdolling and another associate were then executed in the following January. Such in broad strokes were the events that Herman of Kerssenbrock set out to relate.

For differing reasons, the Melchiorite Anabaptists of Münster have been the unloved and unwanted foster children of the Reformation. Catholics could point to them as a clear example of the religious and political excesses which they predicted would be the result of the rejection of the traditional unity of Church and state that preceded the Reformation. To rebut these accusations, mainline (i.e., magisterial) Protestants were equally ready to disown Anabaptists in general and the Melchiorites in particular. For some decades, the Anabaptists have been studied in a much more sympathetic light both by scholars who belong to modern forms of Christianity that are derived from non-Melchiorite strains of Anabaptism and by secular historians without such religious preconceptions. Nonetheless, there remains a strong tendency in modern scholarship to speak of the Melchiorites as being in some way not really "legitimate" Anabaptists.[1]

---

[1] See, for example, the interesting shift in thought in Stayer (2002). On p. 223 of the main text (which repeats verbatim the first edition of 1976), he flatly states that "The line from Hofman to Obbe and Menno [i.e., the line to pacifist forms of Dutch Anabaptism] is the legitimate one; that from Hofman through Jan Matthijs, Jan of Leyden and Jan van Battenberg is a bastard line." (Melchior Hofman is the man who inspired the men who took over Münster; see later in the introduction.) In a passage in the "Reflections and Retractions" section of the second edition of 2002 (pp. xxv–xxviii), Stayer disowns this characterization as "overly quotable, and overwritten" on the basis of an analysis of Deppermann in which the latter discusses the various trains of thought in Hofman's thought regarding secular authority and the implementation of the imminent End of Days. Stayer concludes from this that it is not a question of "legitimate" or "illegitimate" succession but of ambiguity in Hofman's message,

The major contemporary history of the Anabaptist kingdom of Münster is the massive Latin history written by the schoolmaster Herman
of Kerssenbrock, a work that is disparaged more than read by modern
scholars. Kerssenbrock had lived in Münster as a boy at the time of
the kingdom, but he wrote the work some three decades later, and in
any case since he was a committed Catholic, his work can hardly be
called unbiased. As a work of historiography, it has many failings of
overall interpretation and specific detail. Nonetheless, it provides much
information not otherwise preserved and is valuable in its own right
as a contemporary's reaction to such astonishing events. Furthermore,
since its views have had a strong influence on previous scholarship (first
in its initial transmission in manuscript format and then via an inaccurate German translation made in 1771), it is worthwhile for students
of the period to be able to read the work in its entirety. The following
introduction is meant to lay out the religious context of these events,
to explain some of the political and cultural aspects of early sixteenth-
century history that may confuse the modern reader, and to give a short
account of Kerssenbrock's life and his historiographical methods. There
will be no attempt here to examine how Kerssenbrock's account deviates from modern ideas of what took place in Münster (though some
attention is given to such issues in the notes to the text), as this task
would itself constitute a full discussion of the events.[2]

then launches into an extended discussion of the nature of Dutch Anabaptism and
the relationship to it of the leaders of the movement in Münster. It is remarkable
that Stayer conceives of this sort of relationship as comparable to the arguments
in Marxist thought as to who is the "legitimate" heir of Marx (xxvii). This sort of
analysis is fundamentally an engaged and partisan one of sorting out who is "right"
and "wrong" rather than a neutral historical investigation of the development of the
lines of thought of various thinkers during the heady days of the early Reformation.
Naturally, the attempt to distance oneself from the events in Münster is all the greater
on the part of the many writers about Anabaptism who have a direct involvement in
modern forms of Anabaptism.
    [2] Karl-Heinz Kirchhoff has produced a number of important studies on the course
of events; see especially Kirchhoff (1962a) and the collection of essays in Kirchhoff
(1988).

1) *Religious Background*

a) *Lutheran Background*

In October 1517, the Augustinian friar and professor of theology Martin Luther unwittingly launched what came to be known as the Protestant Reformation by circulating his famous ninety-five theses. The immediate issue was a comparatively minor one, but it had extremely serious implications for the logical underpinnings of the universal church of the Middle Ages (the ancestor of the modern Roman Catholic Church).[3] Luther rejected the institution of indulgences, whereby Christians could acquire (generally through purchase, though the theory of indulgences denied this) release from the torments of purgatory, where the souls of sinners who nonetheless were not worthy of eternal damnation were subjected to a temporary sentence of affliction before being purified and admitted to heaven. Luther's major objection was the idea that a human was incapable of redeeming himself from his sins through his own actions, and instead had to rely exclusively on his "faith" that Jesus had redeemed him through his death by crucifixion. Rejection of the idea that the Church could secure the soul's release from purgatory logically led to a broader denial of the medieval church's general claim that there were meritorious acts that earned the believer "credit" in heaven. Control of these works rested with the Church, which in effect served as an intermediary between God and the believer. Furthermore, a large number of the institutions by which the Church acted in effect as God's representative on earth (e.g., auricular confession and purgatory) had no explicit justification in the writings of the Bible, especially the New Testament. These institutions had grown up in various ways during the preceding millennium and a half of Christian life, but the theoretical underpinning that justified them is the Catholic idea that Jesus had delegated the keys to the kingdom of heaven to Peter and that as the first bishop of Rome Peter had passed on this power ("the power of the keys") to his successors (as "the vicars of Christ"), who in turn imbued the Church with the right to institute and validate non-Biblical practices. In more concrete terms, it was held that the long-standing institutions of the Church went back in direct tradition

---

[3] The medieval church was the institutional descendant of the state-sponsored church established in Late Antiquity by the Christian Roman emperors of the fourth century.

to the teachings and practices of the early Church as established in the aftermath of Jesus' crucifixion and resurrection, and thereby received justification through the acts and deeds of both Jesus himself and of his apostles.

Luther appears to have believed (rather naively) that all he had to do was demonstrate the correctness of his rejection of indulgences on the basis of scriptural passages, and then the pope and the Church hierarchy would recognize the error of their ways and abandon the practice. Not surprisingly, this did not happen. And it could not happen, because to do so would lead to the logical necessity of dismantling the entire edifice of what was taken at the time to be the traditional practice of the universal church. As pressure was applied to make Luther recant, the opposite effect resulted. He drew the logical conclusions from his own thought, which turned his rejection of indulgences into a thoroughgoing repudiation of papal authority. This culminated in his refusal to recant before the Diet of Worms in 1521.

In the normal course of events, Luther should have been burned alive as an unrepentant heretic. A number of chance circumstances prevented this result. The Czech critic of the Church Jan Hus had been invited to speak before the Council of Constance in 1415, but the safe conduct granted by the Holy Roman emperor had been disgracefully broken and he was burned. Though specious excuses had been made to justify this act of perfidy, the emperor Charles V was fully aware of the outrage that would result from a repetition. Furthermore, Charles' political position in Germany was comparatively weak, and Luther enjoyed the protection of Frederick III, the electoral duke of Saxony. This protection allowed Luther to disseminate his views in a way that had not been feasible for Hus or any other earlier critic of the Church: through the printing press.

The movable-type printing press was invented around 1450, and the new technology spread swiftly. A large number of the earliest works printed were thoroughly orthodox, but it turned out that the printing press was probably the strongest weapon in the arsenal of the Church's opponents. In the lead up to the Diet of Worms, Luther published three works (*Address to the Christian Nobility of the German Nation*, *Babylonian Captivity of the Church*, and *The Freedom of a Christian*), which spread his views throughout Germany. Conceivably, the death of Luther in the early 1520s might have halted the attack on the traditional Church, but his ideas would have lived on in published form. In any case, Luther lived for two more decades securely in Saxony, and oversaw the establishment

of a new church (the Evangelical or "Lutheran" Church) on the basis
of his ideas. He would find, however, that some were willing to extend
his ideas much further than he was.

There were two major premises for Luther's attack on the traditional
Church. The first was the idea that salvation depended solely upon
faith in the redemptive power of the crucifixion. In Luther's view of
human nature, the individual was incapable of achieving salvation
through his own efforts, and the good works promoted by the Church
were useless in terms of salvation (in Luther's eyes, it was presumptuous to believe that inherently sinful humans could force omnipotent
God to do anything, which was how he viewed the traditional idea that
good works could "earn" salvation, as if this were being bargained for
with God). The notion that faith alone provides salvation is known as
"solafideism" ("faith-alone-ism" in Latin). The second fundamental
premise in Luther's thought was the idea of "Scripture alone" (*sola
scriptura*), that is, that the only guarantee of the validity of a religious
practice was its attestation in the Scriptures, especially the New Testament.[4] To further the propagation of the "evangelical" message (i.e.,
the Gospel or *evangelium* in Latin), Luther in 1522 published the New
Testament in his German translation. Now, his followers could read
the "Good News" in the vernacular without technical knowledge of
the Latin of the Vulgate Bible, which had previously been the form
used by the Church. As it turned out, once people were able to read
the text themselves, they would sometimes come to conclusions of their
own that were quite different from Luther's.

b) *Radical Ideas of Reform Go Beyond Luther's Intentions*

Luther's ideas about solafideism were in themselves extremely radical,
entailing as they did the rejection of traditional ideas about good works
and the entire papal hierarchy. The abandonment of clerical celibacy
and the abolition of monastic institutions were other aspects of Luther's
thought that scandalized the traditionally minded. But once Luther had
worked out the implications inherent in his rejection of indulgences, he
proved to be rather conservative in his acceptance of various medieval
dogmas and practices that seemed to conflict with his injunction to

---

[4] This idea goes back to Erasmus' injunction of returning *ad fontes* ("to the sources"),
though Luther's application of the proposition was rather different from Erasmus'.

follow "*sola scriptura*." He rejected iconoclasm (the seemingly biblical destruction of religious images, especially those of the saints and the Virgin Mary, whose worship was taken by the radically minded to be idolatry), and in 1522 he had been forced to return from the seclusion in which he was writing in order to use his personal authority to suppress an outbreak of iconoclasm in Wittenberg. A leader of this outburst was a university colleague of Luther's, Andreas of Karlstadt, who was eager to push Luther's ideas farther than Luther was. We will come across Karlstadt's influence on Anabaptism. Of the seven sacraments of the traditional Church, Luther ultimately accepted only two, the eucharist and baptism, but even here he interpreted these in a traditional fashion. He accepted a real physical presence of the blood and body of Christ in the wine and bread of the eucharist. The more radically minded took Christ's statement that the wine and bread were his blood and body to be a mere symbol and interpreted the eucharist as a commemoration of Christ's self-sacrifice for humanity rather than a physical transformation of the wine and bread. As for baptism, Luther again accepted the traditional practice of infant baptism. All of these differences became reasons for Luther's more radical followers to reject him because of his continued adherence to practices that in their opinion were merely holdovers from the non-Biblical fabrications of the medieval Church, while Luther himself castigated and repudiated those who disagreed with him on these issues.

One of the most important doctrines under dispute concerned the nature of baptism. Luther advocated the traditional position that infants should be baptized soon after birth. Some of his followers, however, interpreted the Gospels as showing that baptism was the act of a knowing adult, who thereby renounced his previous sinful life, something of which an infant was literally incapable. The arguments against infant baptism are so firmly (and in strict logic compellingly) based in the clear statements of the Gospels that it is hard to see what could have led Luther (and Zwingli and Calvin) to defend the practice just as vigorously as a Catholic would. The very implausibility of the logical arguments used to support infant baptism serves to show that this was no mere example of a personal attachment to traditional practice. Rather, the issue of infant baptism involved the most serious implications for the entire relationship between Church and state, a matter that was of the greatest concern in the attempt of the magisterial reformers to set up an institutional framework for their new understanding of the Church.

c) *Relationship between Church and State, and Magisterial Protestantism*

In medieval ecclesiastical thought, Church and state were the intertwined institutions of God's governance on earth: the Church determined the correct interpretation of God's ordinance for human behavior and the secular state implemented this. Luther at first simply believed that once he convinced the traditional Church of the errors of its ways, a reform would be implemented from within and all would be well. It took some years to disabuse him of this notion, but he eventually came to see that his reforms could be implemented only "from above" by princes who had allied themselves with his religious movement.[5] This implicit alliance of secular and religious power came to be cemented by the tempestuous events of 1524–1525, which are known as the Peasants' War. Already in 1522–1523, some Imperial knights along the Rhine had attempted to overthrow the electoral archbishop of Trier in the name of Lutheran hostility to the established authority. Next, it was the turn of peasants in central Germany, whose own economic grievances were commingled with demands for religious reform.[6] Luther reacted to this attempt to turn his religious views against governmental authority with shrill denunciation, particularly as some of his radical religious opponents such as Thomas Müntzer lent their support to the revolt. Eventually, Luther came to establish a new religious hierarchy in territories controlled by princes who espoused adherence to his doctrine. The reformer Ulrich Zwingli, who in many ways differed from Luther, set up his own form of state-sponsored reformed religion in Zürich.[7] Protestant churches that were established in cooperation with the secular authority and under its auspices are known as "magisterial" (from a false etymology with the Latin *magistratus* or "ruler").

This commingling of ecclesiastical and secular authority had important implications for the nature of the church. For just as in the medieval conception, there had to be an equivalence between the broader society governed by the state and the church as a whole. This in turn meant that every citizen of the state, regardless of his own virtue, necessarily belonged to the new reformed church. And the formal symbol to signify

---

[5] For Luther's role in the establishment of territorial churches, see Holborn (1959) 183–91.

[6] For a discussion of the interpretation of the Peasants' War and of Luther's responsibility for it and attitude towards it, see Blickle (1981).

[7] For Zwingli's reforms and his disagreements with Luther, see MacCulloch (2003) 144–152.

that each member of society was likewise a member of the universal
(if local) church was his baptism soon after birth. In rebutting the
arguments against infant baptism, Luther made a passing remark that
infant baptism took the place in the new covenant (i.e., Christianity)
of the circumcision in the old covenant established between Abraham
and God. Luther did not make much of this comment, but Zwingli
seized upon it as a justification of the old practice, which after all was
hard to justify in terms of the New Testament.

d) *Anabaptism*

All baptisms recorded in the New Testament involved adults. The
Gospel of Mark describes John the Baptist as proclaiming "a baptism
of repentance for the remission of sins" (1:4), and Jesus himself states,
"Whoever believes and is baptized shall be saved" (Mark 16:16).[8] It is
hard to see how an infant could believe, and even if one is inclined to
disjoin the notions of belief and baptism in the second passage (contrary
to the surface sense of the passage), an infant can hardly repent.[9] Thus,
in the 1520s the doctrine arose that baptism is a rite that should be
undergone by an adult in full knowledge of the tenets of the faith, and
the term for this sort of baptism is "believer's baptism." In the context
of the sixteenth century, when everyone who adopted the rite would
perforce have previously received traditional baptism as infants, such
believer's baptism would be a second baptism or rebaptism, and the
term Anabaptist (from the Greek for "rebaptizer") arose to characterize
them. Naturally, since the radicals rejected the validity of the initial
infant baptism, there could be no rebaptism for them, and the term
is in origin one of hostility. Nonetheless, the term is useful to describe
those who adhered to the doctrine of believer's baptism, especially as
in the absence of "Anabaptism" there is no common term to define
this (rather variegated) strain of Protestantism.

   Ulrich Zwingli was a priest in Zürich, and in the years 1522–1523
he oversaw the establishment of a territorial reformed church under the

---

[8] Of course, the absence of any text after Mark 16:9 in the manuscript Sinaiticus
(also called Aleph), the best witness to the ancient text of the New Testament, shows
that this verse is a later addition to the text. No one in the sixteenth century knew this,
and the English here is simply a translation of Luther's rendering of the text.
   [9] The traditional explanation of the remark about the remission of sins in connection with baptism is that this refers to original sin. Even if one grants this theoretical
possibility, the specification of repentance ought to exclude this explanation.

auspices of the local city council. In a number of ways (e.g., hostility to religious art and symbolic interpretation of the eucharist) he was more radical than Luther. But like Luther, Zwingli voluntarily recognized the power of the city council (which happened to be on his side) to decide in matters of doctrinal dispute.[10] Again like Luther, Zwingli also felt it necessary to uphold the practice of infant baptism.[11] There was increasing tension between him and various followers who advocated more radical reforms (for example in the practice of the mass). After an official disputation on the sacraments in 1523, in which Zwingli was declared the winner by the council, a number of the radicals began to conceive of the notion of founding an independent church of believers. The radicals continued to harass Zwingli, and also to counsel parents against the baptism of their infants. By late 1524, the council called for another disputation, and in January 1525, Zwingli again was ruled to have met the objections of his detractors, and an official decree was passed stating that all infants had to be baptized within eight days under penalty of expulsion. A secret meeting was then held in which Conrad Grebel baptized George Blaurock, and they in turn baptized an assembly of about fifteen men. This was the formal birth of Anabaptism, though it arose from a number of strains of previous thought.

The subsequent bloody history of Anabaptism as a whole is not relevant for present purposes. Considered a threat to society as a whole by both Catholic and Protestant authorities, the Anabaptists suffered greatly from official persecution, even as they gained adherents across a broad expanse of territory stretching from present-day Switzerland through southern Germany into Austria. This movement was spread by a number of charismatic proselytizers of the radical conception of Christianity. The movement was never organized into a unitary hierarchically arranged institution, and indeed its very tenets logically prevented such a development. Instead, a number of strains arose and influenced each other. To some extent, the one thing these movements held in common was the practice of believer's baptism, which in turn symbolized the attempt to set up a community of "true" Christians that was separate from the broader society.

---

[10] For a discussion of Zwingli's views on the relationship of church and state, see Stephens (1992) 123–137.
[11] For a sympathetic discussion of Zwingli's views on the matter (including his dispute with the Anabaptists), see Stephens (1992) 85–93.

The attempt to establish a pure "city of God" in this impure world goes back to the beginnings of Christianity. When Christianity was a persecuted religion of a small minority, it must have taken a firm faith to join and adhere to the new religion in the face of the dire consequences of martyrdom, but as Christianity began to spread across the Roman world, especially after the adoption of the new religion by the Emperor Constantine, there would have been people who were Christians by birth, their ancestors having converted generations before. Christianity was no longer a religion composed mostly of enthusiastic new converts. Instead, it encompassed large amounts of society, and many nominal Christians went about leading their normal secular lives without too much overt thought for the doctrines and dictates of Christianity. The solution to the "secularization" of Christian society was the withdrawal from society of ascetics who practiced a solitary devotion to God. Such individual hermits came to gather together in separate communities dedicated to the worship of God. This monastic movement began in the Greek East in the late third century, and spread rapidly in the Latin West in the later fourth and fifth centuries. In effect, monasticism reflects an attempt to lead a purely religious life in the midst of the corruptions of the secular world by withdrawing from the secular world.[12] The Anabaptist world view leads to a similar rejection of the world at large and to a withdrawal into a separate world devoted to God, but with the difference that whereas the (theoretically) celibate monastery posed no threat to society as a whole (and in fact was supposed to set it an example of saintly living), the Anabaptist community was a fully fledged society of married couples who rejected the wickedness of the world around them and by virtue of their believer's baptism set themselves apart from their unredeemed neighbors. In effect, there was a conflict between two Biblical passages. In Romans 13:1, Paul asserts that the secular state is ordained by God, and the Christian subject owes obedience to it. In Acts 5:29, on the other hand, Peter and the other apostles state, in reply to the Sanhedrin's complaint that they have ignored its prohibition against their teaching, that it is necessary to obey God before man. In effect, the view of the Catholics and of the magisterial Protestants globally recognized the claims of the Christian state to loyalty, while the Anabaptists rejected the state's pretensions

---

[12] Of course, there were inherent problems in the concept of leading an ascetic life in a richly endowed institution, but that is not relevant to the issue at hand.

if these conflicted with their interpretation of the Word of God. It is little wonder that those authorities, both Catholic and Protestant, who conceived of a civil society that was coterminous with the established religious community took such violent exception to the exclusivist and separatist claims of the Anabaptists.

And it was not simply the rejection of infant baptism (known by the rather ungainly term of antipedobaptism) that distinguished the Anabaptists from their neighbors. As already stated, there was no uniformity of doctrine among them, but on the basis of their literalist reading of Biblical injunctions, the views that were subscribed to by assorted Anabaptists and that brought them into conflict with the secular authorities were the refusal to pay taxes, to swear oaths, or to perform military service (because of the injunction against killing). As it turned out, these pacifistic tendencies were by no means dominant among the Melchiorite Anabaptists of Münster.[13]

e) *Melchior Hofman*

In his attack on the traditional church's monopoly of access to God, Luther had criticized the traditional order of the priesthood that was formally separate from the full body of believers. He argued that every Christian was in effect a priest, though only those who had been called upon by the community or authority to exercise this function in a formal manner were proper priests. While a number of radical religious leaders were, like Luther, renegade Catholic priests (Zwingli, Hübmaier, Menno Simons), others had no formal religious training before embarking on the propagation of the new faith as they saw it. One such man was Melchior Hofman, whose brand of Anabaptism was to be the ultimate inspiration for the remarkable turn of affairs in Münster.[14] Born in around 1495 in Swäbisch Hall in southwestern Germany, Hofman was a furrier by trade, and he eventually wound up in Livonia on the Baltic in 1522. Already an adherent of Luther's, he got himself into trouble as a preacher in assorted German towns along the eastern Baltic (at one point his preaching resulted in an iconoclastic

---

[13] Kirchhoff (1988) 33–46 argues that the Anabaptists in Münster were pacifist prior to the arrival of the Melchiorites. For a discussion of the Melchiorites in the context of Anabaptist thought on the use of force, see Stayer (2002) 205–280 with the "retraction" of xxv–xxvii.

[14] For a full analysis of Hofman's views (though a chronologically confusing biography), see Deppermann (1987).

riot), and by 1526 he held a position as preacher in Stockholm. In 1527, his preaching yet again caused rioting, and he had to flee. He took up residence in the Baltic port city of Lübeck, but once the municipal authorities became aware of the radical nature of his preaching, they too sent him packing. He then sought to establish himself in Denmark, where the king was attempting a reformation. Hofman soon became embroiled in doctrinal disputes with the Lutheran preachers, and he traveled to Wittenberg to receive a letter of commendation from Luther. Hofman had already gained Luther's approval before (back in 1525) by concealing their doctrinal differences, and now Luther repudiated him. What separated Hofman from Luther was not only his iconoclasm and allegorical interpretation of the eucharist but his apocalyptic eschatology. Already in a work of 1526 Hofman predicted that the cataclysmic war between the chosen of God and the godless that is foretold in the Book of Apocalypse would take place seven years later in 1533.[15] The only element lacking for the program that would cause such turmoil in Münster was Anabaptism. A disputation was set up in the duchy of Schleswig (controlled by the Danish king) in 1529 to "test" Hofman's views, but it was clearly intended to provide an authoritative venue in which to reject those views. In April, Hofman was ordered to recant or leave, and he was duly banished. He moved to East Frisia, which was in religious foment under the influence of Zwinglian ideas, and there he collaborated with Karlstadt, Luther's erstwhile colleague who was now his radical opponent.[16] Once more, Hofman ran into trouble with the Lutherans, and in June he moved to the city of Strasburg, one of the great centers of Reformation thought.

In Strasburg, Hofman at first was welcomed, but he soon earned the enmity of local Zwinglian religious leaders just as he had that of Luther, as Hofman's doctrine had become even more radical. He saw himself as the prophet of God, and added to his apocalyptic views a conviction of the validity of believer's baptism. (Exactly when or under what circumstances this happened is unknown; perhaps Karlstadt had recently influenced him.) Swiss Anabaptists had arrived in the city back in 1526, and although Wolfgang Capito had a certain amount

---

[15] The figure of seven years was apparently reached by adding the forty-two months assigned to the two witnesses in Apocalypse 11:3 to the similar figure given to the Beast in 13:5.

[16] For a discussion of Karlstadt's influence on Hofman (plus an extensive treatment of Hofman in his own right), see Pater (1984) 173–253.

of sympathy for them, the other leaders of reform in Strasburg were implacably opposed to them. After being rejected by the religious authorities, Hofman consorted with the so-called "Strasburg prophets," a group of lower class individuals who claimed to receive visions from God. Hofman was completely convinced of these prophecies, and even published a book about them. Despite the city's rejection of him, however, Hofman officially declared that Strasburg would be the "New Jerusalem" mentioned in the Book of Apocalypse, and would be the center of resistance against the godless in the impending cataclysm that would mark the end of the world in 1533.

In April 1530, Hofman rashly petitioned the Strasburg city council to grant the Anabaptists a church, and was duly expelled. By the next month he was back in East Frisia, where he now began to spread the doctrine of Anabaptism. He acquired several hundred followers in this area, which was riven with strife between Lutherans, Sacramentarians and Catholics, but he was first forced to withdraw from Emden, the main city, in May, and he had to leave the entire territory in the fall. His subsequent movements are somewhat obscure (apart from a visit to Strasburg in December 1531) until his final arrival in Strasburg in 1533, but he seems to be have been successful in spreading his apocalyptic beliefs in the Low Countries and Frisia. In the Low Countries, the Sacramentarian movement, which rejected the actual presence of Christ in the bread and wine of the eucharist, was widespread, and was tolerated by the local magistrates, who were reluctant to uphold the repressive orders of the central government (the regency was held in the name of the absent Emperor Charles V by his aunt Margaret and then by his sister Mary after Margaret's death in November 1530).[17] Hofman's doctrines were propagated in Sacramentarian circles, and it was the prohibited practice of adult baptism that attracted the attention of the (reluctant) local authorities.

A change in Hofman's policy on baptism was brought about by the actions of one of his followers. John Voelkerts had been baptized by him in Emden, and began to act as Hofman's emissary in Amsterdam.

---

[17] For the Sacramentarian setting in the Low Countries, see Houston (2000) 528–535. The term "Sacramentarian" is in origin a hostile one used by Luther to denigrate the more radical reformers who refused to accept his comparatively conservative views about the Eucharist. It is nonetheless a convenient one (and it is hard to see what to use in its place); for the origin and modern usage of the word, see Williams (2000) 85, 95–96.

(Among the first to be baptized by him was Bartholomew Boekbinder, who would later spread the good word to Münster.) Despite the authorities' tolerant attitude, Voelkerts wished a martyr's death, and even though he was all but invited to escape when first arrested, he not only refused to do so but even revealed the names of those whom he had baptized. Eventually, nine others were arrested, and on December 5, 1531, they were beheaded in The Hague. This news shocked Hofman, who thought it pointless to court a martyr's death unnecessarily, and ordered a halt to adult baptism until the end of 1533.[18] For the next year, the temporary succession (*Stillstand* or "standstill") of adult baptism brought a virtual halt to the execution of the Melchiorites (as Hofman's followers may be termed), so that it is hard to track the exact spread of the sect in this period, but it would seem that its message of impending doom proved attractive to Sacramentarians.

In March 1533, Hofman returned from his peregrinations (most recently in East Frisia) to Strasburg, the city that he was sure would be the salvation of mankind in the Last Days. The city council, which had recently been taking a turn towards Lutheranism, was not at all pleased with his faith in it, and when he was accused in May of plotting rebellion, it ordered his arrest. (Hofman welcomed this as part of the apocalyptic Last Days, as he had been predicting since 1526 that a great council would imprison one of the two witnesses mentioned in Apocalypse 11; as it turned out, this was himself.) When he was brought to trial before the city's synod in June, this charge was dropped, and it was his views on various technical theological points for which he was tried. Since there was no proof of any plot to rebel, there was no cause to execute him, yet he had large numbers of followers, and his unshakable faith in his prophesy of the world's demise made him dangerous. He would remain in close and isolated detention until his death (under obscure circumstances, apparently in 1543).

f) *Melchiorite Unrest and Excitement in the Low Countries*

As the end of 1533 approached, and the time predicted for the dreaded events prophesied in Apocalypse came ever nearer, the prohibition

---

[18] Since Hofman predicted that the apocalyptic end of the world would take place in 1533, the rebaptism could wait until then. In any case, he justified his action by analogy with the two-year suspension of the rebuilding of the Great Temple in Jerusalem that is recorded in Ezra 4:24.

against believer's baptism began to chafe among the Melchiorites of the Low Countries.[19] The reason for this was that it was thought that such "real" baptism was the equivalent of the seal that distinguished the pious from the godless in Apocalypse (7:3 and 9:4), and the man who took advantage of this discontent to replace the imprisoned Hofman as the direct leader of the Melchiorites was John Matthisson (or Matthys).[20] A baker by trade, Matthisson had long been involved in the Sacramentarian movement, and he had been sentenced to having his tongue pierced in 1528 for such views. He now proclaimed that he was Enoch, the second of the two "witnesses" mentioned in Apocalypse 11 as the leaders of the godly in the Last Days; Hofman continued to be considered the new Elijah, but previously the role of Enoch had been bestowed upon Cornelius Polderman, another of Hofman's followers.[21] On All Saints' Day (November 1), Matthisson lifted the prohibition against adult baptism, and the same day he met and baptized John Bockelson of Leiden, who eventually succeeded Matthisson as the Anabaptist leader in Münster and would be crowned its king. (Matthisson also decided to abandon his previous wife, and take as his new "spiritual" wife the beautiful young Diewer, whom John of Leiden would in turn marry upon Matthisson's death in battle.) Matthisson sent emissaries (including John) to various Melchiorite communities in the Low Countries in order to assert his authority, which became generally accepted once he managed to overawe the Melchiorites of Amsterdam, who included some of Hofman's earlier adherents, such as Bartholomew Boekbinder and William de Cuiper. At year's end, with his leadership now generally recognized, Matthisson sent off further emissaries, who were not only to proclaim the resumption of adult baptism but to bid the faithful to assemble, as they would constitute the 144,000 pious people who would oppose the Antichrist according to Apocalypse 7:4 and 14:1. Boekbinder and de Cuiper were first sent to Leeuwarden, and after delivering their message there, they continued to Münster,

---

[19] For a general discussion of the Melchiorite ferment in the Low Countries, see Krahn (1968) 80–135 (with 135–164 on the events in Münster from the perspective of the Low Countries).

[20] For Matthisson's usurpation of authority among the Melchiorites, see Deppermann (1987) 333–339.

[21] Strictly speaking, the two witnesses are not named in Apocalypse, but in popular medieval eschatology these two were identified as the Old Testament figures Enoch and Elijah: for the sixteenth century in general, see Petersen (1993); for the broader context in medieval eschatology, see Cohn (1973) 145.

where on January 5, 1534, they baptized Bernard Rothman and the other radical preachers, who were dominant in the city and would soon take it over. Eight days later, another pair of Matthisson's emissaries, John of Leiden and Gerard de Cuiper, appeared in Münster, and in early February Matthisson himself arrived. These Melchiorites would take advantage of the religious discord within Münster to set up that city (rather than Strasburg) as the New Jerusalem that would witness the final conflagration predicted in Apocalypse. This is the point at which the Anabaptist and the specifically Melchiorite background to the events in Münster, of which Kerssenbrock was generally unaware (he never even mentions Hofman), converge with his narrative, and it is best to leave him to narrate the subsequent course of events.

g) *Disputed "Legitimacy" of the Münster Radicals as Followers of Hofman*

There is much talk in modern scholarly discussion of whether the men who seized control of Münster were the "legitimate" heirs of Melchior Hofman. The very question is prejudicial, in that it implies that Hofman had some sort of copyright on his ideas, and those who "infringed" this control through misinterpretation are inherently wrong and misguided. It is preferable to consider the question from the point of view of the internal logic of ideas. The men in Münster seem to have genuinely believed that the Last Days would begin in 1533, just as told in the Book of Apocalypse. Both Hofman and Matthisson shared this belief, but differed on the stance which they, as the prophets who would lead the pious in the coming conflict, should adopt towards this conflict. Hofman took a rather more passive attitude and thought that God should be left to implement the conflict without human intervention.[22] Matthisson, on the other hand, decided that it was necessary to prepare the faithful to take an active role in the events foretold for them. If words like "delusional" are to be used of Matthisson, Bockelson, Knipperdolling and other leaders of the radicals in Münster (and this judgmental tone is still frequently used of them), then it should be pointed out that they were no more deluded than Hofman. They simply acted upon their

---

[22] Or at least without the intervention of the godly. The Turks, who at this time were marauding victoriously in southeastern Europe and had threatened to capture Vienna as recently as 1529, would play the role of Gog and Magog (Apocalypse 20:8).

beliefs, whereas Hofman waited for them to take place of their own accord while he languished in his prison cell.[23]

h) *Radical Views of the Münster Melchiorites*

This is not the place for a full discussion of the theological and other religious views of the Münster radicals, but a few short words about some particularly noteworthy aspects of their beliefs would not be out of order.[24]

1) Lord's Supper. Given the Sacramentarian background of so many of the radicals from the Low Countries, it is not surprising that they rejected the traditional belief in transubstantiation (as well as Luther's modified consubstantiation), which saw a real transformation of the eucharist bread and wine into Christ's flesh and blood.

2) Christology. The nature of the relationship between Christ as the son of God and God himself, a concept that caused much dispute in antiquity but was generally uncontroversial during the Middle Ages, became a matter of great dispute at the time of the Reformation. The notion that had been accepted as orthodox since antiquity held that the three "persons" of God (Father, Son and Holy Spirit) were seen as manifestations of a single God, and this threefold conception of God is called the Trinity. A different line of thought in antiquity known as Monophysitism held that the divine nature of Christ supplanted the humanity of the fetus of Jesus that was conceived in Mary, and Hofman adhered to a similar idea that arose in the 1520s (he famously compared the birth of Christ through Mary to the passage of water

---

[23] The attempt of the radicals to bring about through their own efforts the events that they expected to happen on the basis of their understanding of scripture is in some ways reminiscent of the way in which Lenin "anticipated" the communist revolution. Marx had predicted that the condition of the working classes would grow steadily worse, and that the proletarian revolution would take place in the most industrially advanced countries. By the end of the nineteenth century, it was clear that the first prediction was simply false, and the loyalty of the working classes to their national governments at the outbreak of the First World War demonstrated the fallacy of the second. Instead of waiting for the coming revolution to take place in the predicted manner (which it seemed it would not), Lenin decided to seize power on behalf of the working class through his putatively enlightened party of conspirators, and then to use the compulsive powers of the state institutions which the party had seized to destroy all opposition and to bring about the utopian future that was supposed to result from the revolution, even if the revolution needed a "kick start." Ultimately, the Bolshevik Revolution was no more successful than the one in Münster; it simply took longer to fail.
[24] For a general discussion of the policies of the Münster regime, see Klötzer (1992).

through a pipe). In his final days after his capture, John Bockelson of Leiden (the erstwhile king of the Anabaptist kingdom) showed himself willing to recant a number of his views, but he balked at the notion that God was born of a human.

One interesting side effect of the emphasis on the divinity of Christ is that to some extent he was in turn assimilated to God the Father. A notable aspect of the Münster radicals' conception of God is their constant invocation of "The Father," which for them meant the vengeful and jealous God of the Old Testament.

3) "Inspirationalism."[25] A particularly noticeable trait of Hofman's doctrine was his belief in divine inspiration. (As already noted, he went so far as to publish the prophetic dreams of some of his followers, and it was such a dream that led him to return to Strasburg and court arrest there.) Such divinely inspired prophets were not uncommon among the more radically minded (e.g., the "Zwickau prophets" whose visions threatened the social order back in 1522). While the established Church of the Middle Ages did what it could to suppress or at least check such spontaneous revelations from people who were not in holy orders, it is not surprising that in their careful reading of the Bible some reformers were led by Acts 2:1–21 to think that God would again speak directly to the common man. It is noteworthy that Acts 2:38 connects (seemingly adult) baptism for the remission of sins with the reception of "the gift of the Holy Spirit." The radicals of Münster would not infrequently invoke this spirit.

4) Adherence to Biblical authority/hostility to the past. The Münster radicals often refer to the Reformation notion that Biblical precedent was necessary for any ecclesiastical practice to be considered valid (they often profess to be willing to admit error if this can be demonstrated through citation of the Bible), and concomitantly reject any practices that cannot be validated in this way. The latter brings with it the notion that any "papist" practices from the past which do not pass muster by the standard of the New Testament are mere "human accretions" that are to be eradicated. One form of this eradication is the destruction of the cathedral library, another the destruction of the paraphernalia for traditional service. Towards the end of their control of the city, the radicals even undertook the task of destroying the city's churches.

---

[25] This notion could perhaps be more properly called "spiritualism," but the term would bring with it unwanted and irrelevant associations.

5) Iconoclasm. A very specific form of rejection of the traditional forms of worship is the destruction of the religious art that adorned the churches. Of course, a prohibition against the worship of images is one of the Ten Commandments (Exodus 20:3–4; Deuteronomy 5:8), and in both the Old Testament and in the works of the early Church Fathers idolatry was associated with the worship of false gods. Hence, hostility to traditional religious art was a prominent feature of the early rejection of the Church of Rome. Karlstadt had disagreed with Luther over the issue, and Hofman was forced to leave first Dorpat in Livonia and then Stockholm after his preaching resulted in iconoclastic rioting.

6) Apocalypticism.[26] The events of Münster are incomprehensible without a clear understanding that the main driving force behind the radical leaders was the belief that the events portrayed in the Book of Apocalypse were about to come to pass and that they would play a prominent role as the 144,000 who would do battle with the forces of the Antichrist.[27] Hence, a careful reading of that book is a good preliminary to reading Kerssenbrock.

In the early books of the Old Testament, God seems to promise the Israelites that if they worship him properly, he will assure them of success as a people in the secular world (the *locus classicus* is Deuteronomy 28). The course of history, as the Israelites were dominated and conquered by the Assyrians, Babylonians, Persians and Greeks, seemed to suggest that God was not fulfilling his end of the bargain, and to deal with the unsettling implications, two solutions were found. First, the fault was ascribed to the sinfulness of the Israelites, and if they reformed, God would restore his favor. Second, the prophets, who claimed to be speaking for God, came forth with various visions and dreams in which they described (often in rather obscure "mystical" language) the ultimate humiliation of the Lord's (and the Israelites') enemies and the triumph of his chosen people. The one text from

---

[26] One may also term the ideas associated with the Last Days portrayed in the Apocalypse as "millenarianism" and "chiliasm," but this terminology is not entirely apposite for the situation in Münster. The two terms are based respectively on Latin and Greek expressions for "one thousand years," and refer to the thousand-year rule of Christ that is to follow the first defeat of Satan and at the end of which Satan will be finally defeated and the Last Judgment will take place. Though presumably the radicals in Münster saw themselves as preparing the way for Christ's second coming, the emphasis was naturally on the battles against the godless that will precede his arrival, and the term "Apocalypticism" seems to describe this aspect better.

[27] For a quick overview of the Münsterites' apocalyptic views and the origins of these in the ideas of Hofman, see Kirchhoff (1985) 20–24.

early Christianity written in this tradition that made it into the canon
of the New Testament is the Book of Apocalypse, whose author calls
himself John. This author was identified in antiquity with the Gospel
writer John, though the identification was disputed even then and is
unlikely to be correct.[28] In any case, the bizarre imagery of the book,
with all its beasts and swords and its gripping (if unreal) picture of a
final war between the forces of good and evil, had a strong affect on
the mystically inclined throughout the Middle Ages.[29] The vision in the
Book of Apocalypse of the struggle between the pious and the wicked
could be associated with various statements of Jesus' in the Gospels
which express hostility towards the wealthy (e.g., Matthew 19:23–24,
Mark 10:23–25, Luke 18:24–25) and indicate an eventual inversion of
the social order when people will be judged according to their religious
merits (Matthew 19:30, Mark 10:31, Luke 13:30).

Though the Book of Apocalypse stands on its own as a Christian
work, its imagery calls to mind works of the Old Testament which
either inspired the Apocalypse or were written under the inspiration
of the same models, and the radicals informed their interpretation of
the Apocalypse with such texts as Daniel 7, Ezekiel 9, and 2 Esdras 4.
These violent images of a relentless and savage God (the Father) who
protects his chosen people against their (and his) far more numerous
(and wicked) foes had recently inspired Thomas Müntzer in his support
of peasant attacks on the social order back in the Peasants' War, and
the same spirit infused the radicals of Münster (though the peculiarities
of the situation in Münster would allow their escapades to last a bit
longer than Müntzer's).

7) Mimicry of the Bible. As good reformers who wished to return the
Church to the pristine state of the Apostolic Age, the radicals naturally

---

[28] In the earliest form of Christianity, some "Christians" still felt themselves to be
close to the Jewish tradition, and this strain of Christianity is represented by both the
Gospel of Matthew and the Apocalypse. Other Greek-speaking Christians distanced
themselves from the Jewish background to Jesus and were receptive to Greek culture,
notable examples of this being the Gospels of Luke (this tendency is also noticeable
in Acts) and John. The obscure allegory of the Apocalypse is hardly compatible with
the influence of Greek philosophical thought in the Gospel of John, which sets it apart
from the other three canonical gospels.
[29] The classic treatment is Cohn (1973). (This work is really a sociological study of
the cultural settings that favored millenarian ideas and behavior, but he must perforce
discuss the development of millenarian thought.) The Apocalypse did not appeal to
more rationally inclined religious thinkers such as Erasmus and Luther (though their
dislike of the work was based on rather different reasons: see Backus [2000] 3–11).

found much inspiration in the New Testament. To some extent, this
is a variant on section 4 about accepting as valid only those practices
that could be justified in the text of the Bible. In this case, however, the
point is not to vet current practice against the apparent usage of the
Bible, but to attempt to recreate the state of affairs that were thought
to be laid out in the text. As already noted, Acts 4 seemed to validate
direct inspiration of men through the Holy Spirit. Verses 32–37 were
taken to mean that the followers of Christ should share their goods
communally, and the radicals' undertaking to confiscate the property
of the faithful in Münster was one of the more shocking events to
sixteenth-century (and later) sensibilities.[30]

Inspiration based on the New Testament was not out of the ordinary
at a time when the cry of *ad fontes* led to various efforts to recapture
the spirit of the Primitive Church (however interpreted). What is rather
distinctive in the thought of the Münster radicals is the extent to which
their emphasis on the Apocalypse caused them to dwell upon the Old
Testament. This is perfectly understandable given that the Apocalypse
overtly harkens back to the Old Testament by referring to the pious
144,000 as being raised from the twelve tribes of Israel (7:4–8) and
describes the city that will descend from heaven after the final triumph
over the godless as the "New Jerusalem" (21:2). As already noted, the
Apocalypse is written after the model of various prophetic visions
from the Old Testament, a circumstance that contributed to a natural
inclination to interpret the events predicted by Apocalypse in terms of
the story told of the Israelites in the Old Testament.

The radicals seem to have taken the association of the pious in Apocalypse with the Israelites and their assumption that they were themselves
the pious to its logical conclusion by conceiving of themselves as the
modern embodiment of the Israelites. While it might be reasonable
enough for Christians to view themselves as being comparable to the
ancient Israelites by virtue of the fact that both are portrayed as having a special bond with God, the radicals took the comparison quite
literally. One woman attempted to recreate the biblical story in which

---

[30] And the fallacious notion that this religiously inspired attempt to establish a community without personal wealth was a precursor of modern communism led to much
scholarly misinterpretation in East Germany (similar strains in the thought of Müntzer
were handled in the same vein). For a treatment of the theoretical underpinning of
the policy of communal property in Münster, see Stayer (1991) 123–138.

Judith saved a besieged Jewish town through the crafty murder of the enemy commander by sneaking out of besieged Münster in order to give the prince-bishop a poisoned garment (605–607D).[31] King John also conceived of himself as a new King David and divided the defenders of the city into the "twelve tribes" (773D with notes). The cathedral yard was named Mt. Zion (cf. Apocalypse 14:1). The sign of the covenant that distinguished the 144,000 was equated with believer's baptism.

There was one more element of biblical imitation which undoubtedly went the furthest in branding the radicals as unredeemed perverts in contemporary thought, and this was polygamy.[32] The introduction of the practice may have been motivated by the circumstance that there were far more women than men in the besieged city, and in contemporary thought a woman needed a man to look after her. In any case, the radicals justified it by the example of the Old Testament patriarchs (619D).[33]

2) *Historical Background*

In Kerssenbrock's narrative, the religious views of the radicals are comparatively unimportant (except to the extent that such issues are discussed in the diplomatic correspondence that forms a large part of Kerssenbrock's story). His story concentrates on the political and military developments that led to the Anabaptist takeover in Münster and ultimately destroyed their rule. The following is meant as a short introduction to various aspects of this situation.

---

[31] Citations ending with "D" refer to the marginal numbers in the translation (see the "Note on the text and notes," p. xiii.

[32] Kerssenbrock routinely portrays John of Leiden as a libertine satyr, as if the institution were a fraud concocted to satisfy his lust.

[33] The potential peril of applying Old Testament precedents to contemporary usage had been pointed out a half millennium earlier by the English ecclesiastic Aelfric in his preface to a translation of part of the Book of Genesis that he made at the request of an important layman: "Now it seems to me, my friend, that this work is very dangerous for me or for any man to undertake, since I fear that if some foolish man reads this book or hears it read, he will think that he may live now under the New Law just as the Elder Fathers lived then in the period before the Old Law (i.e., the Pentateuch) was established or just men lived under Moses' Law (another name for the Pentateuch)."

a) *Geography*

It is necessary to erase the borders of the modern (nation) states of
the Netherlands, Belgium, Luxemburg, and Germany. All of these territories were regions within the Holy Roman Empire, and while the
circumstances that would eventually lead to the establishment of these
entities as autonomous states already existed at the time of the events
in Münster, this was certainly not the situation at the time. First, all of
these were basically areas in which Germanic dialectics were spoken.[34]
The low-lying territory along the North Sea and (very roughly speaking)
to the west of the rivers Rhine and Ems may be neutrally described as
the Low Countries.[35] This region achieved some sort of conceptual unity
through the acquisition in the fifteenth century of control over various
counties and duchies in the area by the dukes of Burgundy (a branch
of the French royal family). In 1477, the rash Duke Charles the Bold
was killed in battle, leaving his many territories to his daughter Mary.
Most of the Burgundian territory in what is now eastern France was
lost, but Mary's husband Maximilian, the son and heir of the Habsburg
Holy Roman Emperor Frederick III, retained control of the Burgundian holdings in the Low Countries. Though these territories remained
distinct, there had been attempts to impose centralized oversight of the
various territories under the rule of the dukes of Burgundy, and this
inchoate unity was strengthened when the area remained loyal to Mary
(the representatives would meet in a joint assembly known as the States
General). In 1515, Maximilian's grandson Charles (soon to become the
Holy Roman Emperor) entered his majority in the Low Countries. Upon
Charles' abdication in 1555, his Low Country territories passed to his
son Philip II of Spain, and the effects of the Reformation would lead to
a revolt in the north, where a Calvinist republic was established in 1588.
The south meanwhile remained under Habsburg control (first Spanish
and then Austrian) until 1794. After the vicissitudes that attended the
French Revolution and the Napoleonic hegemony, the old Habsburg

---

[34] With the exception of French-speaking Wallonia at the south of Flanders (in
modern Belgium).

[35] This is basically an English version of the French term *pays bas*. "Netherlands"
is the English equivalent of the Dutch "Nederlands," which has become restricted in
application to the Dutch Republic. The fact that the name of the province of Holland (only the most prominent of the provinces that constituted the new republic) was
adopted in English as a popular designation of the Dutch Republic shows that there
had not previously existed any self-evident term for the area.

territories were united under the king of the Netherlands in 1815, but in 1830 Belgium was established as a separate (Catholic) kingdom, and the grand duchy of Luxemburg was split between the two countries (a personal union with the royal house of the Netherlands ended in 1890 and the grand duchy acquired its own dynasty). Thus, the historical accident of Habsburg control of the area led to the establishment of a separate identity for the region. If not for this, the German speaking areas could today simply be regions of the German state without a distinct literary language of their own.

The term "German language" causes much misunderstanding. The group of the ancient West Germanic languages consisted of a number of related dialects in central and northern Europe. Eventually, a form of southern ("High") German became the accepted literary language of all Germany, and all the other varieties became socially inferior dialects, which are now mostly in the lamentable process of dying out. In the early sixteenth century, High German was beginning to gain its predominant position—this was the dialect of eastern central Germany, and had already begun to gain wide currency elsewhere in German-speaking territory, when Luther's use of it for his influential Biblical translations and for his other writings gave it additional prestige in the Protestant north—but there was still a lively literary form of northern German known as Low German (*Plattdeutsch*), which was spoken (and written) all along the North Sea and the Baltic from the area of the northern Low Countries as far to the east as the German towns of Livonia, where Melchior Hofman began to preach. (Already at this time, written Low German began to adopt High German forms, and by the middle of the seventeenth century it had been supplanted by High German as the language of the educated elite.) One of the dialects of this area was Westphalian, the form of German used in the Münsterland. The modern Dutch language is the descendant of Old Low Franconian (Franconian is the name for the dialects of central Germany). Seemingly, this Franconian dialect intruded to the northwest into the Low Countries, and displaced Frisian (a variety of Low German). Thus, while Dutch had a slightly different origin from the Low German dialect of Westphalia, the Low Franconian language adopted certain characteristics of Low German, and in any case, unlike the other Franconian dialects, it did not participate in the so-called second (or High) German consonant shift, which is the primary distinction between the Low and the High German dialects. Thus, while there were certainly perceptible differences between the Westphalian dialect of Münster and the language of the Low Countries directly to the east, these were comparatively minor, and it is anachronistic to think that the present-day border between Germany and the Netherlands had any significance in the early sixteenth century. To people of the time, there would have been no thought of any inherent difference between the residents of the Münsterland and those of Holland or other Low Country regions where Anabaptist sentiments spread.[36] The future histories of the Netherlands and Belgium lay far in the future, and the notion of the Dutch language as an independent language would have been meaningless.[37] This is not to say that the Low Countries did not have certain peculiarities of their own. They were culturally far more subject to French influence, and the Sacramentarian tendencies of the 1520s that have already been remarked upon were to some extent at least the result of various pietistic movements that were characteristic of the fifteenth century. Nonetheless, in the early sixteenth century, the various territories that constituted the Habsburg possessions in the Low Countries were simply another part of the Empire, and this very similarity would contribute to the ease with which the Melchiorite movement of the Low Countries was so readily received in neighboring Münster.

b) *Decentralized Political Authority in the Holy Roman Empire*

The events of Münster played themselves out against the background of the political decentralization of the Holy Roman Empire. In the budding nation states of England and France and in the kingdoms of the Spanish peninsula, the monarchy had certainly suffered setbacks along the way, but the central authority had established its control over the

---

[36] Note that Kerssenbrock seems to imply (122D) that Holland is a province of Germany.

[37] Of course, the eventual development of Dutch as a national language of education and literature has led to the designation of its late medieval ancestor as "Middle Dutch" rather than "Middle Low Franconian." If the Habsburg association had not led to the distinctive and independent development of the Low Countries, "Low Franconian" would simply be one more "dialect" of German that was being driven into extinction by High German. (Note that the English term "Dutch" is simply a deformation of *deutsch*, the German word for "German," and in the Netherlands the language is known rather neutrally as "Nederlandisch.") Naturally, none of this talk of what would have happened if the Low Countries had not gone their own way should be taken as in any way a disparagement of the present-day countries or their sometimes complicated linguistic situations. The point is that the present independent status of these regions should not be read into the early sixteenth century.

anarchic forces of local feudal territories. In Germany, the prolonged struggle of the house of Hohenstaufen against the papacy had resulted not simply in the destruction of the dynasty but also in the collapse of central control over the vast number of territories—large and small, hereditary and ecclesiastical—into which the Empire was divided. These local authorities assumed responsibility for such government as was exercised, and the emperor had no direct control except to the extent that he himself was a territorial magnate (Charles V held the most expansive collection of territories within the Empire).[38] While the emperor could issue edicts on his own and preside over the Imperial diet (assembly of the princes and cities who were directly subordinate to him) and pass laws through it, he had no ability to enforce such laws without the cooperation of the local powers. It was this situation that first granted Luther protection with the electoral duke of Saxony, then led to the establishment of various forms of reformed religion in the local territories. It also contributed to the unique circumstances that allowed the Melchiorite takeover of Münster. In any case, at the very time when the central monarchies of England, France and the Spanish peninsula were finalizing their suppression of independent feudal powers, the religious strife of the sixteenth and seventeenth centuries would thwart all efforts to establish a central imperial authority and see the powers of the early modern state fall into the hands of the local powers.

Because the various local authorities carried out functions that would be associated with "sovereignty" in modern terms, they engaged in "diplomacy" with each other, and at times met in local assemblies to deal with common affairs and to work out their differences. Kerssenbrock's history is filled with this sort of correspondence between various cities and princes, and with the meetings that were held in order to aid the prince-bishop in his war against Münster.[39]

c) *Ecclesiastical Princes*

One of the peculiarities of Germany was the large number of large territories that were controlled by prelates of the traditional Church.

---

[38] In addition to the original Habsburg lands in the southwest, he was duke of Austria (which was governed by his brother Ferdinand), and from his Burgundian inheritance he received Franche-Comté to the west of modern Switzerland, and the various duchies and counties of the Low Countries.

[39] For a discussion of the impact of the events in Münster on neighboring territories, see Haude (2000).

In the distant past, the emperors had exercised power through bishops and other prelates appointed by them, and this practice had led to the prolonged Investiture Conflict in which the emperors opposed the papal claim to the exclusive right to bestow episcopal positions. The emperors had long since lost control of episcopal appointments, and in the case of Münster, the chapter of the cathedral had the right to appoint the new bishop, who then had to secure confirmation from the pope (at a high price, which had to be paid by his temporal subjects). The cathedral chapter (canons, who were known in German as the *Domherren* or "cathedral lords" but whom Kerssenbrock refers to as *dominici domini* or the "Lord's Lords") was controlled by members of the local nobility, and they would elect someone of the highest noble rank as the bishop, who was entitled "prince-bishop" by virtue of his control over both secular and ecclesiastical jurisdiction. Thus, not only was the central ecclesiastical administration controlled by noblemen, but the prince-bishop himself did not even have to be a priest (Francis of Waldeck did not get around to being consecrated as a priest until 1543, eleven years after his election by the cathedral chapter).

d) *Governmental "Authority"*

There is much talk in documents quoted by Kerssenbrock of what he translates as the "magistrate" (*magistratus*), which is his Latin term for the German "*Obrigkeit*" (*Oberkeit*). The German term is an abstraction meaning "superiority" and signifies the person or persons who in traditional medieval political thought have "authority" over their "subjects" (whether in ecclesiastical or secular matters). The Latin term shares with the German original the peculiarity that it can refer to this position in the abstract ("magistracy") and to the individual who exercises this power ("governor" or "ruler"). The traditional term in English used to render this notion in religious contexts is "magistrate," but since this has elective connotations, the term would cause confusion when used of the prince-bishop (particularly when the elective officials of the city council of Münster are so frequently referred to). "Authority" gives some sense of the German term, but as an abstract term for the persons exercising such authority, it is usually in the plural, which again would cause confusion in reference to the prince-bishop. "Government" is the term used in the translation when the term seemingly signifies the position without specific reference to an individual exercising it. In the latter situation, "governor" would seem the logical translation, but unfortunately this term would be inappropriate for the members of the city council. Hence, it has been necessary to resort to two different translations: "ruler" when it seems clear that the prince-bishop is meant, and "member of the government" when the powers of the city council are intended.

e) *Ecclesiastical Politics under Charles V*

Charles V became emperor in 1517, and as the position of emperor had been created in 800 by Charlemagne to carry on the powers of the later Roman emperors, who among other things were obligated to maintain the orthodoxy of the Christian world, he took his duties to uphold the traditional Church and its practices very seriously.[40] The wave of popularity that swept across Germany when Luther challenged the authority of the pope was due not simply to the immediate issue but was a reflection of a century of German discontent about papal interference in the Church in Germany (and about the funds that flowed from Germany to Rome).[41] Various circumstances prevented Charles from dealing directly with Luther himself, but the result of Luther's appearance at the Diet of Worms in 1521 was that Luther was placed under Imperial ban as a heretic, and an edict was issued that prohibited the further dissemination of his views. Because of the protection extended to Luther by the elector of Saxony, the ban had no effect (apart from obstructing Luther's ability to travel), and the edict did little to thwart the spread of reforming ideas.

Charles himself left Germany in 1521 to secure his tenuous hold on his Spanish crowns and then to engage in a prolonged war against the king of France, and he apparently did not realize the extent to which reformist religious thought was taking root in Germany and undermining the old Church. He wished to convene an ecumenical council of the Church to deal with the admitted faults in the Church while at the same time maintaining its unity. Like his predecessors since the end of the Great Schism in 1417, Pope Clement VII was completely opposed to the convocation of such a council as a threat

---

[40] For a convenient treatment of Charles' religious policy, see Blockmans (2002).

[41] For a short introduction on the broad range of secular issues that contributed to the widespread popularity of Luther's basically religious disputes with Rome and for a collection of contemporary texts illustrating the discontent caused by these issues, see Strauss (1971).

to papal supremacy (the theory of conciliarism held that councils were superior to the pope). Eventually, in 1526 a new diet was convened in Speyer, where it was decided that in anticipation of such a council the various member states of the Empire should behave in such a way as they could justify before God and the emperor. In effect, the attempt to enforce the edict of 1521 against religious innovation was abandoned, since leaving control over the course of religious reform to the local administrations ensured that certain authorities would institute reforms that would be unacceptable to the traditional Church. And so it happened. In 1526, Landgrave Philip of Hesse, who would be a mainstay of Protestant leadership for years and would figure prominently in the disputes between the city of Münster and its prince-bishop, instituted a reform like that of electoral Saxony, and in the late 1520s many cities in southern Germany and princely states in the north followed suit, and further reformations took place in the early 1530s.

When Charles had set out for Spain, he left his brother Ferdinand to act as his regent in Germany (Ferdinand also received direct control over Hapsburg possessions in southern Germany and Austria). A devout Catholic like his brother, Ferdinand was determined to stamp out opposition to the traditional Church, and in 1529, before Charles' return, he convened a new diet at Speyer. Here he demanded that in light of the recent rapprochement of the emperor and the pope and as a means of facilitating the convocation of an ecumenical council, all religious innovation was to be halted, and any bishops whose authority had been undermined by the recent reforms were to be restored to their traditional standing.[42] The Catholic majority in the diet duly passed an appropriate law, but five princes and the delegations of fourteen cities "protested" that the unanimous resolution passed at Speyer in 1526 could not be repealed by a mere majority, and that they were therefore not bound by the new law. This was the origin of the term "Protestant," but any chance of unity on the part of state-supported reformers disappeared in 1529, when a meeting between Luther and Zwingli that had been arranged in Marburg by Landgrave Philip reached agreement on most points but broke down when Luther absolutely refused any compromise on the issue of the Lord's Supper. (Regardless, neither Lutherans nor Zwinglians would have tolerated Anabaptists.)

---

[42] For a summary of the wrangling about religion in the diets of 1529–1532, see Holborn (1959) 208–219.

By the late 1520s, Charles V, who had brought his war against France to an end, turned his attention back to Germany. On the one hand, he wished to have his brother accepted as German King, now that he had himself been officially crowned as Holy Roman Emperor by the pope in 1529, and he also needed assistance against the Turks, who had resumed their depredations in Austria in the same year (they had overwhelmed the kingdom of Hungary at Mohács in 1526, and that crown now fell to Ferdinand). On the other hand, Charles was determined to thwart the astonishing spread of heresy in Germany by reaching an agreement on reform in a narrow sense and thereby restoring the unity of the traditional Church. To achieve his ends, yet another diet was convened in Augsburg in 1530, with the emperor himself in attendance. Melanchthon appeared as Luther's representative and submitted the "Confession of Augsburg," which laid out twenty-eight propositions to represent the Lutheran position. This confession was drawn up in such a way as to minimize the differences between the Lutherans and Catholics (while distinguishing the former from Zwinglians and Anabaptists), but even so it was rejected as unacceptable by Charles' Catholic theologians, who issued a "Confutation." Charles then called upon the Protestants to return to the Catholic fold, and threatened to act against them if they refused. The Protestant princes left, and with two exceptions the Protestant cities refused to acquiesce. The final "recess" (concluding resolution) of the diet then returned to the uncompromising position of the edict of Worms of 1521, banning all innovation of any variety, demanding a restoration of confiscated ecclesiastical property, and instituting censorship. The Protestants had until April 15, 1531 to comply.

In response, the six Protestant princes and ten such cities (soon joined by four more) formed a defensive alliance known as the Schmalkaldic league. There was some friction between the Lutheran adherents and the Zwinglian cities of the south, but the alliance would bring unity to the Protestant side in their conflicts with the emperor and his various Catholic allies over the next fifteen years. Zwingli's death in battle in 1531 weakened the influence of his adherents, and in 1532 John of Wieck tried unsuccessfully to persuade Münster to join the league as a Lutheran city.

At the next diet, which met in Nuremberg in 1532, the emperor was in dire need of help against the Turkish threat, so he was willing to make concessions to the Protestants. But instead of concessions on specific points, the Protestants wanted permanent protection against the

provisions of the Diet of Augsburg of 1530, and now it was the turn
of the Catholic members to object. The upshot was the "Nuremberg
Stillstand (truce)," which suspended all litigation against the Protestant
members who were present (plus the cities of Nuremberg and Ansbach)
until an ecumenical council was convened or the next diet met. This
was the prevailing legal situation when the strife between the city of
Münster and its prince-bishop turned violent in 1533.

f) *Warfare in the Empire*

One aspect of public life of sixteenth-century Germany that may
seem puzzling is the right of the local ruler to raise troops on his own
authority. By virtue of this authority, the prince-bishop of Münster
would gather an army against the rebels in the city. The later fifteenth
and early sixteenth centuries saw a swift development in military
organization, as the spread of small firearms led to semi-professional
infantry armies (in place of the knighthood and ad hoc feudal lev-
ies of the previous period). The extensive use of mercenaries began
when the highly effective infantrymen of Switzerland began selling
their services in the later fifteenth century; soon similar troops were
raised in Germany, and these were known as Landsknechts (termed
simply *milites* or "soldiers" by Kerssenbrock).[43] The prince-bishop
incurred huge expenses maintaining his army (the spiraling costs of
military activity proved to be an ongoing headache for earlier modern
rulers such as Charles V who wished to engage in prolonged cam-
paigning), and he was soon forced to seek the financial support of
neighboring princes, who thereby gained control over the operation
against the city.

g) *Role of the City Councils in Establishing Reformed Churches*

The city of Münster as a corporate institution (i.e., the government
elected by the citizens of the community known as "burghers")
played a prominent role in bringing about the situation that enabled
the Melchiorites to take over the city, and this was the unintended
consequence of the city council's decision to follow the lead of other

---

[43] The classic treatment of the independent officers who raised such troops on behalf
of "sovereigns" who pay them for this service is Redlich (1964). For a handy (if dated)
treatment of the Landsknechts in our period, see Oman (1937) 74–88.

cities in exercising their internal autonomy by setting up their own reformed religious establishments. The political decentralization of the Holy Roman Empire allowed a number of cities to play a crucial role in the establishment of non-Catholic religious practice by instituting reforms under the auspices of the local municipal government. Naturally, these city churches adhered to magisterial beliefs (mainly Lutheran, though also reformed). It was only the Imperial free cities (e.g., Augsburg, Nuremberg, Strasburg) that could act on their own without outside interference. A city that was subject to the jurisdiction of a lord, whether secular or temporal, could act only to the extent that the autonomy granted to it in the past permitted or that its prince allowed. The cities that arose in the later Middle Ages acquired rights to internal autonomy (known as liberties or privileges) that were generally won as a result of prolonged strife with their lords and guarded with jealous tenacity against later encroachment. At the time of the religious foment caused by Luther's dispute with the Catholic hierarchy, there was much resentment against both ecclesiastical privilege, which often entailed the avoidance of municipal taxes and claims to revenue from the community, and the economic activities of monasteries, which were taken to be harmful to the well-being of the burghers. Not only did such feelings of resentment contribute to the popularity of Luther's challenge to traditional religious practices, but these can clearly be seen to play a major role in the early attempts to institute church reform in Münster. Kerssenbrock does recognize the difference between the Lutherans and the radicals who eventually seized control of the city, but in light of his hostility towards the Lutherans and his tendency to view the efforts of the city council to institute a Lutheran reform as merely a precursor to the Anabaptist regime, he does not clearly distinguish the very different motives and aims of the Lutheran city council from the mid 1520s until the Anabaptist takeover on the one hand and those of the radicals on the other. In fact, the city council managed to win the prince-bishop's acquiescence in its internal religious reforms with the settlement that was reached in February 1533, but, as Kerssenbrock gleefully notes (379D), the subsequent takeover of the city allowed the prince-bishop to repudiate the agreement by right of conquest. To some extent, the internal developments in Münster can be seen as a struggle between the Lutherans and the radicals, but Kerssenbrock does not really see things that way. In any case, the cause of reform became intimately connected with that of the privileges and autonomy of the city of Münster.

h) *Role of the Guilds in Municipal Politics*

A very prominent role in the religious strife in Münster was played by
the guilds (and Kerssenbrock's honest portrayal of this role in his history
would cause him much grief). Though the medieval guilds bear some
superficial resemblance to modern labor unions, the differing economic
situation makes them fundamentally different.[44] Whereas unions attempt
to organize a labor force in opposition to the management of large-scale
unitary economic concerns (whether major corporations or governmental institutions), the guilds' main purpose was to organize all levels of a
given economic profession within the framework of artisan production,
with each guild including all the men engaged in a given city. At the
top of the guild were the master craftsmen who had set themselves up
as independent operators, and lower down were the journeymen and
apprentices who had entered the trade and wished to become masters
themselves. The guilds regulated the practice of the trade, and prevented
outsiders from engaging in it. Since the guilds were corporate bodies
that were meant to look after the interests of their members, it is not
surprising that they came to play an important role in the public life
of economically prominent cities. Given the fact that economic grievances formed an element in the objections to the established Church,
the guilds were often enthusiastic supporters of reform. Not only were
these grievances prominent in the earlier attempts at church reform in
Münster, but concerns about such matters are still perceptible in the
decrees of the Anabaptist regime.

i) *Estates of the Bishopric of Münster*

While the story of the Anabaptist radicals centers around the city of
Münster, from the point of view of the prince-bishop it involved his
entire diocese. The wealth and fortifications of the city allowed it to
stand up to the prince-bishop in a way that was not feasible for the
smaller towns, but the latter were affected by the religious turmoil of
the times, and did show a certain inclination to reform (though this was
suppressed without too much difficulty). In any case, the bishop in his
capacity as secular ruler had to deal with the "estates" of the diocese,
that is, with those entities who had traditional claims to direct interac-

---

[44] For a general treatment of medieval guilds and their importance in municipal
politics, see Nichols (1997) 203–257.

tion with their overlord—apart from the diocesan capital in Münster and the other recognized towns, the nobility of the diocese acted as a corporate body in relation to the prince-bishop—and these groups met as separate estates in the assemblies of the diocese. For the most part, the nobility (who had a vested interest in the traditional order through their control of the cathedral chapter) supported the prince-bishop in his efforts to bring the city to heel.

3) *Kerssenbrock and his Historical Work*

a) *Life of Kerssenbrock*

Herman of Kerssenbrock (Hermann von Kerssenbroch/Kerssenbrock) came from a minor noble family that can be traced back to the thirteenth century.[45] His father Gerlach apparently had a certain aversion to marriage, in that he had two relationships of concubinage (i.e., the situation in which a man and woman permanently cohabited and acted as "spouses" without undergoing the ecclesiastical rite of marriage). Of the first concubine were born Herman and his brother Bernard, and of the second (Gerlach's cook) two sons and three daughters (plus two legitimates daughters after Gerlach eventually married his concubine).[46] Kerssenbrock's date of birth is unknown. When relating his participation in the armed resistance to the Anabaptists in February 1534 he was still a boy (*adhuc puer*), but was old enough to follow his landlord into battle (though unfamiliarity with gunfire made him hide after an initial volley).[47] Regardless of his apparently illegitimate birth, Kerssenbrock styles himself at the start of the Anabaptist history as a member of

---

[45] The facts of Kerssenbrock's life are laid out in Detmer (1899–1900) 1*–89* and 200*–264* (the asterisks are used in Detmer's edition for the separate pagination of his introduction).

[46] These familial relationships are laid out in a much later legal case, in which Henry and his brother intervened on behalf of their father's later children (referred to as half-siblings). Upon the death of Gerlach, his brothers dispossessed the children of their father's estate (the males were barred from inheriting by virtue of their illegitimacy, and the females, whether legitimate or not, could not inherit in any case). Nothing is explicitly said of Henry and his brother's legitimacy, but their lack of standing as heirs suggests that they must have born of an earlier concubine. (The upshot of the case was that the uncles were granted possession, and the sons by the second concubine had to settle for some monetary compensation.)

[47] See 491–492D.

the knighthood. Perhaps he was born around 1520, and throughout his life he remained a staunch Catholic.[48]

Nothing is known of Kerssenbrock's boyhood. He was an eyewitness to certain events in Paderborn (a city to the east of Münster) in 1532 (118D); what he was doing there is not stated. By the next year, he was living in Münster (he reports his presence at a number of events involving the Anabaptists). As already noted, he is attested in Münster during the armed resistance to the Anabaptists, when he attended his "landlord" (*hospes*) Dr. John Wesseling. Why Kerssenbrock was residing with the good doctor is not stated, but apparently, his whole family was living with Wesseling. When the Anabaptist Henry Krechting moved to Münster in February, part of Wesseling's residence was commandeered for him (510D), and by the time that the Anabaptists expelled those who refused to undergo believer's baptism on February 28, 1534, Wesseling had already left for Herford and sent a letter advising his wife and "our family" to join him there (539D). What happened to Kerssenbrock in the next few years is unknown, but presumably he returned to the city after its capture by the prince-bishop and resumed his studies.[49]

In 1538, Kerssenbrock matriculated at the University of Cologne, and completed the requirements for a baccalaureate in the arts two

---

[48] Detmar quotes a poem printed in a collection of elegies issued after July 5, 1585 as stating that Kerssenbrock "completed twice eight lustra plus two years" (*annis cum binis supplevit lustra bis octo*). The Latin term *lustrum* signified the five-year period between censuses in the Roman Republic, and thus became simply a designation for that period of time. By this reckoning, the poem would have put Kerssenbrock's age at eighty-two (the use of "twice" to double a number is simply a metrically convenient way of expressing certain figures in Classical Latin poetry), which is clearly too high (he would then have been born in 1503 and thus about thirty-one in 1534, a year in which he later indicated that he was "still a boy"). Detmer (1899–1900) 4* n. 3 merely asserts that *lustrum* "can only signify a period of four years here." This would conveniently reduce the number to sixty-six, which would put his date of birth in 1519 and make him fifteen in 1534. Unfortunately, wishes are not horses, and the significance of a term cannot be changed from its normal meaning for no other reason than convenience. Presumably, the poem is simply wrong.

[49] Detmer (1899–1900) 5* takes it that Kerssenbrock moved to Münster for further education. In n. 1, he supports this idea by noting that Kerssenbrock refers to a friend in an anecdote as his "companion in studies" (*meus contubernalis et in re literaria comilito*, 503D), which presumably means no more than that they were friends at school, but the later reference to the presence of Kerssenbrock's family in the Wesseling residence must mean that the Kerssenbrocks lived in Münster, and that Kerssenbrock's presence in Paderborn the previous year was most likely not the result of any permanent residence there. Records from the University of Cologne concerning Kerssenbrock during the period 1538–1540 describe him as being "of Lemgo," a town to the southeast of Münster.

years later. His activities over the next few years are unknown, but as he styles himself as a master of the arts and of the laws (i.e., civil and canon law) at the start of the Anabaptist history, he presumably acquired these honors at some university (seemingly not Cologne). In 1545, he was (again?) in Cologne when he dedicated a Latin poem about the Anabaptist events of Münster to the prince-bishop. He joined the new school founded in 1546 by the duke of Cleves-Jülich-Berg, but soon left (perhaps because of the school's Lutheran affiliations) to join the faculty of the school at Hamm, where he served from 1548–1550. In 1550, he was appointed as the rector of the cathedral school at Münster (the school of St. Paul, which had been founded in 1500), and he held this post for the next quarter century. A surviving syllabus of the school's program for all grades shows that while instruction concentrated mostly on acquiring Greek and Latin, there was a definite element of Catholic indoctrination. His interest in the religious element of pedagogy is indicated by the fact that when Bishop John III of Hoya was in the process of implementing the reforms instituted by the Council of Trent, he had Kerssenbrock draw up plans for the corresponding educational reforms (no details of these plans are known, and the death of the prince-bishop in 1574 caused the plans for reform to be dropped).[50]

Kerssenbrock's dispute with the city council about his historical work (see below) caused him to move away from Münster in 1575, when he became rector of the cathedral school in Paderborn. There it was unclear whether the Catholic or the Protestant faction in the city would prevail, but by 1578 it was clear that the latter were becoming predominant. Given his staunch Catholicism and his efforts to uphold the Catholic faith in his educational program, it is not surprising that

---

[50] As already noted, Charles V desired an ecumenical council to be called in order to quash religious strife and restore the unity of the Church. As it turned out, a council was eventually summoned to Trent in northern Italy, but its purpose was rather different from Charles' intention. So far from bridging the gaps between Protestant and Catholic thought, the Council of Trent (1542–1564) rejected challenges to traditional dogma and practice and hardened the Catholic position, paving the way for the attempt to regain Protestant territory known as the Counter Reformation. As part of this effort to revitalize the traditional Church, a number of decisions were passed with the purpose of raising the admittedly unsatisfactory training of the secular clergy. Long after the recapture of Münster back in 1535, a considerable Lutheran tendency remained, and Bishop John III instituted a visitation (inspection) of the entire bishopric in the early 1570s. The proposed educational reforms were an element in the effort to implement the reforms laid out in the decisions of the Council of Trent. (It was not until the election of a new bishop in 1585 that this was finally brought about.)

Kerssenbrock felt compelled to move on once more. His new position
was as school rector (1578–1582) in the town of Werl. In 1582, he
became the rector of the cathedral school in Osnabrück. This city had
a strong Protestant element, so that even though the school was run
by the Catholic cathedral, Kerssenbrock's contract specifically provided
that the pupils were free to follow Catholicism or the Augsburg (i.e.,
Lutheran) faith (they were to go to their parish church for worship
during school hours). Presumably, Kerssenbrock was bored in the
small town of Werl, and was willing, despite his strong commitment
to the Catholic Church, to accept restrictions on the religious element
of his educational program in order to work at a large establishment.
He abided by these terms, and there were no Protestant complaints
about the educational program of the school. He was still serving as
rector when his health took a sudden turn for the worse, and he died
on July 9, 1580.

Kerssenbrock was married twice. By his first wife Katharina (last
name not known), he had five sons who survived to adulthood. Katharina was dead by late 1573, and Kerssenbrock next married Elsebein
Judefeld, who was a close relation of the Caspar Judefeld who played
a significant role in the events of 1533 as a Lutheran burgher master.
She had at least one son, and they both survived Kerssenbrock.[51]

b) *Kerssenbrock's Legal Troubles Arising from the Anabaptist History*

By the spring of 1573, Kerssenbrock had decided to publish his work.[52]
The city council had the legal obligation to approve the printing of
books, but he approached a local printer about an edition of the work
without the council's authorization. When the council learned of this,
they explicitly prohibited the printer from undertaking the job. It is not
clear what Kerssenbrock's motives were in this surreptitious procedure
(perhaps he foresaw the sort of opposition to the work that eventually
arose), but his actions certainly suggest a desire on his part to get the
book published without allowing the council to vet it first. Once he was
thwarted in Münster, he sent a copy to a printer in Cologne. When
the council got wind of this, it called him in to ask if he had described
the city's defenses and referred to individuals by name. To satisfy the

---

[51] For the details and evidence, see Huyskens (1904).
[52] The facts of the dispute about the work's publication are laid out in great detail
by Detmer (1899–1900) 90*–200*.

council, he produced one third of a second copy of the work that he had kept in his own possession, and the council soon decided that it did not like what it saw and demanded that he halt the printing in Cologne and produce the manuscript which he had sent there. Now, in addition to the council's objections, the patricians (hereditary municipal office holders) complained that he had insulted them by indicating that they did not belong to the bishopric's knighthood (a point of contention), and the guilds accused him of having defamed them in his unfavorable characterization of their activities in his introduction. Kerssenbrock tried to conceal the Cologne copy by handing it over to Goswin of Raesfeld, a canon of the cathedral, but after prolonged and rancorous negotiations, he finally turned it over to the council in September. (First, however, a copy was transcribed and retained by the chapter.)

The council had promised under surety to return it to him within a month, but kept the work for months, much to Kerssenbrock's indignation (he threatened legal action). By the end of April 1574, the city's syndic (legal advisor and spokesman) turned in a memorandum about the content of Kerssenbrock's work, but the council continued to do nothing. In May, the complaints of the patricians and the guilds were repeated, and the council decided to seek outside legal advice to determine what courses of action were available, and delegated the matter to a commission. In September, Kerssenbrock again requested the return of his manuscripts, which the council had retained for a year, and was once more refused. He then secured from the chapter the loan of the copy that had been made of the Cologne manuscript in the summer of 1573, and surreptitiously began to have further transcriptions made.

On October 31, the city council solicited the legal advice of two jurists of the legal faculty of the University of Marburg.[53] On the basis of the information provided by the council, the jurists in their report of December 15 completely sided with the council in their criticisms of the work (which included those of the patricians and guilds), and rejected any suggestion that it was inappropriate for the council to act as judge in a matter concerning their own interests, on the grounds that the public good of the community was at stake. The jurists indicated

---

[53] With the introduction of the complicated procedures of Roman law in Germany in the fifteenth and sixteenth centuries, it became common practice for local courts (often staffed by officials who lacked legal training) to refer doubtful issues to established legal authorities such as legal faculties at universities.

that Kerssenbrock should be compelled to produce any copies through the imposition of a heavy fine, and advised that to avoid the difficulties involved in his expected appeal, he should be arrested. The council happily paid the fee for this unbiased advice, and asked the jurists the further question of what exact steps the council would be justified in taking against Kerssenbrock.[54] In return for a further fee, the jurists judiciously responded in January 1535 that since Kerssenbrock's actions were tantamount to lèse-majesty (treason)—strictly speaking, as an official of the cathedral chapter, he should have been immune to the city's jurisdiction in this regard—he should be beheaded.[55]

Armed with this daunting weapon, the council summoned Kerssenbrock on February 5, and demanded that he admit to nine points indicating defective passages in his work (this was the first time that the exact charges were laid before him, though he had repeatedly requested this information). He asked for a delay to allow himself to prepare his defense, and when this request was denied, he began to reply to the charges on the spot. With this, he was arrested and imprisoned. The same day, the syndic came to advise him of the possibility of execution, and Kerssenbrock gave way, agreeing to admit to his errors and to oblige himself to return all outstanding copies of the work. He was then released.

The next day, he delivered some unfinished copies, and on February 7, he again appeared before the council and admitted to and retracted the following errors, which were laid out by the syndic:

1) Describing the fortifications of the city, including walls, ditches and bulwarks, with measurements,[56]
2) Revealing the council's secrets, including its method of selection and the distribution and function of various offices,[57]
3) Derogating from the authority and jurisdiction of the city council in his account of the lower secular court in that he ascribed the whole court to the prince-bishop and designated the judges appointed by

---

[54] The jurists had initially received ten thalers for their efforts, but in handing over their duly considered advice they asked for a further seventy on account of the wide-ranging nature of their deliberations. Naturally, there can be no question that in its decision to accede to these requests the city council was influenced by the favorable nature of the advice!

[55] The new consultation cost another forty-five thalers.

[56] See Chapter Four of Kerssenbrock's Introduction.

[57] See 106–107D.

the city as assessors, though the truth was otherwise and the judges were designated as *iudices civitatis* ("city judges"), and the prince of the bishopric had long had a dispute with the council about this and the matter had nonetheless been passed down through long tradition,[58]

4) Similarly misrepresenting the appeals from the lower court to the council, as if these were a method of remitting the matter for consultation rather than proper appeals, and thereby confusing the order of instances,[59]

5) Attributing too much privilege to the cathedral chapter, the Monastery Across-the-River and the Bispinghof, thereby derogating from the authority and jurisdiction of the council, as if the monastery had its own privileges and a right of asylum, though this is undocumented, as if the power over all the property everywhere in Münster were subject to the control of the chapter of the cathedral and the *Wordtgelt* indicated that ownership of the real estate within the city belonged to the chapter, and as if the Bispinghof too possessed an immunity that exempted its owner from all civil impositions,[60]

6) Writing wickedly and at times inaccurately about the restitution of the city (i.e., the attempt to regain the city's traditional privileges, which had in part been abrogated by the prince-bishop upon the city's capture) and about the policy of the council at that time, and reporting that the council opposed the aldermen, the guild masters, and the common citizenry in the attempt to recover their liberty, which could readily cause disturbances in the future,[61]

7) Writing uncivilly and maliciously about the customs of the city, especially carnival, cookie baking, and the horseback procession, which could bring the city into disrepute among outsiders,[62]

8) Offending the government in other passages by describing the practice of the freigrave's court and the presentation of livings and of ecclesiastical benefices, and slanderously naming indiscriminately certain families and clans that are still alive as factious, seditious

---

[58] See 93–95D, 106D.

[59] See 94D.

[60] For the asylum, see 55DK, for the *Wordtgelt*, see 12D, for the Bispinghof, see 61D.

[61] For the dispute about the role of the guilds in the city's constitution after the recapture by the bishop, see 900–947D.

[62] For these customs, see 82–88D.

and criminal, though in fact they should not be held responsible for the Anabaptism if the facts were examined carefully.[63]

As soon as Kerssenbrock agreed to these terms, a spokesman for the patricians appeared and accused him of disparaging the patricians by treating them as a separate body from the knighthood.[64] The council backed up these assertions and told Kerssenbrock that he had to leave any such assertions out of his work. Representatives of the guilds now attacked him for calling the *Schohaus* (guildhall) a "house of Satan" and for asserting that their opinions were sewed together so tightly that even the council could not untie them, which defamed the aldermen and guild masters, who had had no intention of starting a disturbance.[65] Once again, the council upheld the criticisms lodged against Kerssenbrock, and he gave in but claimed that he had been speaking only of the period of Anabaptism. Once he agreed to revision and correction of the work as dictated by the council, the session was over.

In April, the council once more demanded that he deliver copies of the work then in other people's hands, but before the council could deal with his inability to carry out this impossible task (it postponed the matter a few times because of other business), Kerssenbrock left the city (for his new position as rector of the school in Paderborn).

This is not the place for an extensive discussion of the substance of the complaints lodged against Kerssenbrock, but a few comments are in order.[66]

---

[63] For the (to Kerssenbrock) offensive leniency of the court, see 107D, for the giving of ecclesiastical benefices to minors (even infants), see 108D. As for the charge of slandering some members of families as Anabaptists, the council never provided any concrete examples, but presumably the descendants of some of those involved in the events of 1533–34 claimed that while their ancestors may have been on the Lutheran side, they had not supported the Anabaptists, contrary to Kerssenbrock's presentation of events (see below for his inclination to hold the Lutherans responsible for bringing about the situation that allowed the Anabaptist takeover).

[64] See 10–109D.

[65] See 77D.

[66] Detmer (1899–1900) 137*–197* discusses the charges individually at length, examining their historical justification in instances of disputes regarding privileges and jurisdictional conflicts. For what it is worth, Detmer is clearly inclined to give Kerssenbrock the benefit of the doubt and to depreciate the concerns of the council.

1) Kerssenbrock objected that the city council had in fact recently voted an engraver a sum of money as thanks for his copper engraving of the city, which shows the city's defenses, and in any case claimed that he described the defenses in general terms. A perusal of the relevant section shows that he did in fact discuss the fortifications in some detail, and while it is unlikely that some enemy would have drawn up a plan of assault merely on the basis of his description, the very story of the capture of the city in 1535 shows how small pieces of information could be very helpful. The extent to which the safety of the city was still felt in the sixteenth century to depend upon its walls should not be underestimated.

2) The claim about the elections and the functions of the officials seems rather contrived. This information could hardly have been a secret.

3–4) The status of the city court was a longstanding bone of contention between the city and the prince-bishop, and while Kerssenbrock's account is fairly neutral in its presentation of the facts, it could certainly be seen as supporting the prince-bishop's position.

5) The ecclesiastical claims of exemption from municipal jurisdiction were a source of dispute throughout the later Middle Ages, and it is hardly surprising that the city council took offense at Kerssenbrock's statements about such exemptions in Münster, even if his statements were mostly neutral description.

6) It is certainly true that the city council is portrayed as opposing the restoration of the guilds in the city of Münster in the attempts to revive the city's autonomy after its capture by the prince-bishop in 1535, but in this section Kerssenbrock is following his anonymous source virtually verbatim (see below). This seems to be an instance of blaming the messenger for the message, the council wishing to hush up its previous opposition to the guilds.

7) In describing certain raucous local customs, Kerssenbrock exhibits a schoolmasterly disdain for the exuberance of youth, but once again, he hardly deserved censure if his description is accurate.

8) The council took as aspersions on its administration Kerssenbrock's (rather mildly expressed or even merely implicit) complaints that the city court had shown itself to be disinclined to hang convicts, and that the city sometimes appointed minors to ecclesiastical benefices in its control. Again, it boils down to a question of whether Kerssenbrock was accurate, and there seems to be no

reason to doubt him. As for the additional charge that with his blanket condemnations of families he accused of complicity in Anabaptism certain individuals who were in fact opposed to it, the lack of any details makes it impossible to evaluate this charge, but it sounds like another instance of people wishing to hush up what they would prefer not to hear.

9) The patricians had long attempted to associate themselves with the knighthood and to distinguish themselves from the rest of the burghers of Münster, and they felt very strongly about these claims. During the session of the council in which Kerssenbrock recanted his views, a representative of the patricians angrily stated that Kerssenbrock should thank the council for saving his life, because otherwise (presumably if the council were not present) Kerssenbrock would already have had his head split open. Once more, Kerssenbrock rather neutrally noted the patricians' claims, which could be taken by partisans as implicitly rejecting them.

10) As Kerssenbrock pointed out, his remarks about the guilds' obstreperous behavior towards the council and their responsibility for the Anabaptist takeover refer to that period of time specifically and should not be taken as aspersions on their present attitude. Just as the council did not wish to be reminded of its earlier opposition to the restoration of the guilds, so too did the guilds wish to forget their previous behavior.

Overall, it would seem that Kerssenbrock's offenses mainly consisted not of telling falsehoods but of saying things that various people did not wish to hear. The only really substantive charge was that of revealing secrets about the city's defenses, but his account did not say much that would not have been obvious to a casual observer, and in one instance he passes over a detail on the grounds that it would be best not to reveal it (25D). Some of the accusations (such as the objection to his account of local customs) give the appearance of being contrived attempts to justify the council's hostility. In any case, there is nothing in the account that deserves the threat of death.

How then to explain the council's persistent efforts to intimidate and silence Kerssenbrock? In the first place, modern sensibilities about artistic and personal freedom have no place. The council members would have felt themselves justified in suppressing a writing that placed them in a bad light, even if this was deserved. In addition, Kerssenbrock seems to have been an obstinate individual (he records several heated exchanges with council members), and the council may well have decided on principle that he should be brought to heel, especially since he had tried to have the book surreptitiously printed first without the council's approval and then in violation of its prohibition, and had persistently avoided turning in copies of the work when ordered to do so. Furthermore, it must be borne in mind that important members of the patriciate and of the guilds had seats on the council, and no doubt vigorously expressed their opposition to Kerssenbrock's work because they found his point of view regarding certain matters of interest to them uncongenial. Given that in addition some of his statements about various ecclesiastical privileges and jurisdiction within the city conflicted with the city's claims, it is not surprising that the council as a whole came to view Kerssenbrock as an advocate of their ecclesiastical opponents (he was after all an employee of the cathedral chapter), and that they adopted a rather hostile stance towards him and eventually used the full coercive forces available to them in forcing him to bend to their will.

In September 1575, the council of Münster decided to impose upon Kerssenbrock a very large fine (200 thalers, in part justified by the 125 previously spent by the council for its two legal consultations about his case) for his disobedience in initially trying to circumvent the city's right to censure the work and in having the work copied in violation of the council's explicit prohibition. For months, Kerssenbrock tried to get the council to rescind or at least moderate its decision (the cathedral chapter of Paderborn acted as his intercessor). These efforts were in vain, so in February 16, 1576 he finally paid the fine.[67] The council may have thought that this seemingly complete victory on its part would put an end to this dispute, which had been dragging on for more than two and a half years. But no.

For one thing, Kerssenbrock tried in vain later in 1576 and in early 1577 to secure the return of the manuscripts of his work that were still in the council's possession. Furthermore, being embittered by what he took to be persecution at the hands of the council, he could not leave well (or bad) enough alone, and he composed an apology or "self-justification." The original dedicatory letter to the work is dated February 6, 1576, but the content shows that he later revised it to

---

[67] Kerssenbrock complained that in order to harm him further, the council valued a thaler at twenty-six shillings instead of the prevailing commercial rate of twenty-four.

take into account the events down to the spring of the next year. In this work, in which he went over the entire course of events at great length, he threw all restraint to the winds and savagely attacked both the council as a body and certain individuals by whom he felt hard done by in particular (e.g., the city's syndic and Burgher Master Plonies). He began to circulate hand-written copies of this work, and by late 1577 or early 1578, the council was fully informed of what Kerssenbrock was up to, and undertook to seek legal redress.[68]

This took some time (more outside legal advice had to be gotten), so it was not until the fall of 1579 that the city was ready to proceed to court. By this time, Kerssenbrock was in Werl, so the council needed the authorization of the archbishop of Cologne (Werl was in his territory), which took further time to secure since there were men in the archbishop's entourage who supported Kerssenbrock. Eventually, a trial was to take place in Arnsberg, but as a result of the influence of his supporters in the archbishop's entourage, the president of the court (the count of Solms) suggested to the representatives of the city that given Kerssenbrock's advanced age and the services which he had previously performed for the city, it might be best to avoid all the travails and complications involved in legal proceedings by settling the matter with an agreement whereby Kerssenbrock would undertake to destroy the copies of his apology in his hands and to seek to suppress any other copies. The representatives remitted this question to the city council, which eventually agreed with some ill grace to the proposed arbitration. On January 9, 1580, a legal transaction took place in Arnsberg to settle the matter formally. First, a delegation presented the council's complaint, and then Kerssenbrock apologized for any offense he may have given, and bound himself under oath to acquire any copies of the defense that may be in other people's possession and to say nothing detrimental to the council's or to its members' and employees' authority or reputation, on the penalty that if he violated his oath, he would be treated as convicted (of the present accusation). With this, the council expressed its willingness not to proceed with its case. The council was thus able to assert that its position was vindicated, even if Kerssenbrock's supporters prevented the council from exacting any punishment from him. The city council did not, however, relent in its hostility to him. Although it occasionally granted him permission to

---

[68] The council also drew up a pamphlet giving its side of the dispute.

return to Münster for short stays, it continued to ban him on a regular basis from visiting the city.

c) *Kerssenbrock's Writings*

Despite his constant work as an educator during adulthood, Kerssenbrock never composed a work on pedagogy. He did, however, have an affinity for historical writing.[69]

1) In the early 1540s he wrote a Latin poem in dactylic hexameter about the Anabaptist rebellion in Münster, and in 1545 he published it with a dedication to Bishop Francis of Waldeck.[70] The work shows a craftsman-like proficiency at versification, but has little poetical merit. Its first book relates in 755 lines the events from the arrival of Rothman in the city until the expulsion of the opponents of Anabaptism on February 27, 1534, and the second book relates in 1131 lines the events until the capture of the city. The main source is Heinrich Dorp's publication (see below), but Kerssenbrock left out his pro-Lutheran stance, and had to make good Dorp's failure to describe the capture of the city with either Fabricius Bolandus' poem or a common source now lost. He also added some details from his own personal experience.

2) In 1555, he wrote another poem celebrating the new prince-bishop upon his installation. It was to have been recited to him when he visited Münster to receive the town's oath of allegiance. Other business thwarted this plan, but the poem was published under the title "Grieving Mimimgardford's complaint."[71] Another composition in Latin (this time in elegiac couplets), this work portrays Münster as an

---

[69] Detmer (1899–1900) 266*–282* and 449*–462* lays out the evidence for Kerssenbrock's other works.

[70] *Belli Monasteriensis contra anabaptistica monstra gesti brevis atque succincta descriptio nunc primum et impressa et edita, autore Hermanno a Kerssenbrock* ("A short and succinct description of the war waged in Münster against the Anabaptist monstrosities, now printed and released for the first time, by Herman of Kerssenbrock").

[71] *Mymegardevordae lugentis querimonia, quae variis sese erumnis iactari queritur, sed opem et praesidium sperans ad reverendissimum atque amplissimum principem ac dominum D. Wilhelmum suum antistitem confugit eidemque divinum suscepti episcopatus honorem gratulatur, M. Her. a Kerssenbroch authore* ("The complaint of grieving Mimimgardford, who complains that she is being buffeted by various hardships but in the hopes of aid and protection seeks refuge in the most reverend and esteemed lord Lord William, her bishop, and congratulates him on the divine honor of the bishopric entrusted to him, by Master Herman of Kerssenbrock").

48 GENERAL INTRODUCTION

afflicted widow who seeks comfort and succour for her dire situation from the new prince-bishop. The poem's bleak picture of present difficulties is rather general and exaggerated, but Kerssenbrock does find time to lament the lack of respect given to schoolteachers like himself (a point on which he felt sufficiently strong to repeat the passage in his Anabaptist history: see 102D).

3) *Anabaptistici furoris Monasterium inclitam Westphaliae metropolim evertentis historica narratio* (the present work).

4) "Apology".[72] This is the work written by Kerssenbrock in anger at his treatment at the hands of the city council. Though Kerssenbrock did his best to retrieve all copies of this work in order to settle his dispute with the city council of Münster, several manuscripts are extant.

5) *Catalogus episcoporum Padibornensium eorumque acta, quatenus haberi potuerunt.*[73] This was an occasional piece written in 1578 in honor of the newly installed administrator of the church in Paderborn while Kerssenbrock headed the cathedral school there, and it was immediately published.

6) *Catalogus episcoporum Mymingardevordensium, nunc Monasteriensium, per M. Hermannum a Kerssenbroch, nunc scholae Padibornensis et collegii Salentiniani moderatorem, repurgatus.*[74] Completed in 1578 during Kerssenbrock's sojourn in Paderborn, this work was meant to aid the cathedral chapter in Münster in upholding its privileges against the counterclaims of the city council. Not only does this show that the city council was not being capricious in objecting to statements in Kerssenbrock's Anabaptist history that he seemed to take the chapter's side against the city council, but it also illustrates how Kerssenbrock continued

---

[72] *Causarum captivitatis M. Hermanni a Kerssenbroch, scholae maioris D. Pauli Monasteriensis ad annos 25 moderatoris, succincta narratio cum earundem vera et solida confutatione, et quod senatus Monasteriensis magis tyrannum quam bonarum literarum Maecenatem in ea captivitate sese declaravit, ad universam totius Westphaliae nobilitatem et omnes pios lectores* ("Short narrative of the reasons for the arrest of Master Herman of Kerssenbrock, director of the larger school of St. Paul in Münster for twenty-five years, together with a true and solid refutation of these reasons and (a demonstration) that with this arrest the city council of Münster showed itself to be a tyrant rather than a patron of the fine arts, (addressed) to the entire nobility of all Westphalia and to all pious readers").

[73] "List of the bishops of Paderborn and their deeds, to the extent that these can be recovered."

[74] "List of the bishops of Mimimgardford, now (called) Münster, revised by Master Herman of Kerssenbrock, now director of the school at Paderborn (the Salentinian College)."

to take an active interest in this dispute during the years when his conflict with the city council dragged on even in his absence from the city. The work is preserved in a single manuscript that is mainly written by someone else but does contain a few passages written in Kerssenbrock's own hand.

7) *Catalogus episcoporum Monasteriensium carmine conscriptus authore Hermanno a Kerssenbroch.*[75] This poetical work, preserved in a later manuscript, devotes three elegiac couplets each to fifty-four bishops of Münster. None of this poetry appears in Kerssenbrock's prose work on the same subject, so the poem was presumably composed after 1578.

d) *Composition of the Anabaptist History*

Kerssenbrock's introductory poem is dated to 1564, so presumably he resolved to write a prose work on the Anabaptist events in that year.[76] In his later apology, he notes that Bishop John of Hoya, who became prince-bishop in 1566, opened the episcopal archives to him. He also reports without any indication of date that the city council had made its archives available to him (perhaps back in 1564?). He particularly worked on his project when outbreaks of the plague forced the cathedral school to close. The original letter of dedication to the four estates of the city (later suppressed after his long dispute with the city council about the work) is dated January 4, 1573. In his account of the year 1532, Kerssenbrock notes (214D) that John Menneman served as alderman "for many years down to 1570" (*per multos annos ad annum domini 1570*), and a seemingly tagged-on notice records that Menneman was elected to the city council in 1573 (the municipal elections took place on February 20 in that year). Presumably, Kerssenbrock originally wrote his notice about Menneman's activities as alderman in 1570, then added in a reference to his recent election to the council when, at some date after February 20 in the spring of 1573, a clean copy of the text was being prepared for publication, an event which he already anticipated when he composed the original dedication on January 4.

Kerssenbrock's original intent had been not to have the work published but to leave the manuscript in the municipal archives. For one

---

[75] "List of the bishops of Münster drawn up in a poem, by Herman of Kerssenbrock."

[76] Detmer (1899–1900) 282*–439* discusses Kerssenbrock's methods in his work and the sources that he used.

thing, he knew that relatives of men whom he blamed for the ultimate course of events would object to any explicit mention of their activities, but he felt compelled by historical necessity to reveal the relevant names (see his disclaimer on 5–6D, where he goes out of his way to profess no intent to besmirch the relevant families; cf. his reluctance to name some of John of Leiden's wives in 659D). He was impelled to compose and publish the work, however, by certain men whom he never names (3D). Given his pro-Catholic stance, his championing of the spirituality in any jurisdictional disputes with the city council, and the fact that he tried to hide the manuscript that had been sent to Cologne from the city council by entrusting it to the member of the cathedral chapter, which then insisted that he return the manuscript within one month once he got it back from the council, it is a reasonable conjecture that those who wished to see the work published were ecclesiastical supporters of a full restoration of Catholicism in Münster. Such men could argue that the horrors of Anabaptism were the logical result of any deviation from traditional religious practice, since it was the pro-Lutheran attitude of the city council that had undermined the prince-bishop's authority and prepared the way for the Anabaptist takeover.

Kerssenbrock states (3D) that he had three sources of information: his own personal experiences, published accounts written by others, and oral accounts from trustworthy participants. Since the description of the published accounts will take up far more space than the others, it will be treated last.

Kerssenbrock identifies a certain number of striking anecdotes as events that he witnessed himself, and there are some other vivid pictures that may well go back to his personal experience, even if he does not explicitly designate them as such, for instance the adventure of Dr. Wesseling's maid (488D) or the misadventure of the fat Scottish beggar (486D). Even if Kerssenbrock's memory was perfect (and no doubt his recollection of events that had taken place three decades earlier was at times faulty), his perspective at the time would have been restricted. In the first place, since he was only a teenager, his understanding of events would have been comparatively limited. In any case, he speaks mainly of public events and had little sense of the background to what he saw. Finally, he was expelled along with the other opponents of the Anabaptists on February 27, 1534, and thus had no personal experience at all of the subsequent Anabaptist regime.

There seems to have been little scope for the personal recollection of others. Some anecdotes cannot be traced to any written source (e.g., the death scene of the city's syndic Wieck: 515–516D). Kerssenbrock is also happy to report malicious rumors that cast those whom he dislikes in a bad light (e.g., 161D on Rothman's parents, 192D on Herman Bisping's supposed forgery and counterfeiting). In the account of the capture of the city in particular, there are numerous details and episodes that can be traced to no written source, and these may well be reflections of oral traditions to which Kerssenbrock had access.

Far and away the largest proportion of the work can be ascribed to written sources. These can be divided into two categories. The first consists of documents, that is, official correspondence and the records of official transactions such as the summations of decisions that were drawn up at the end of meetings and assemblies. One of the major contributions of Kerssenbrock's work to the study of the Anabaptist incident in Münster is its preservation of a large number of such documents that do not otherwise survive. Comparison with the original documents in instances where the latter survive shows that Kerssenbrock is an accurate translator. He never consciously misrepresents what he does translate, though sometimes he is not full in his description of documents that he paraphrases rather than translates, and occasionally in his direct translations he adds in a short phrase to make the sense clearer or to elaborate on it. The other category of written sources consists of historical works or contemporary broadsheets (i.e., short printed narratives of an ephemeral nature that were issued soon after events, and acted like modern newspapers as a means of disseminating information about important current events).

As already noted, Kerssenbrock had access to both the city's and the prince-bishop's archives, but since the former had suffered damage during the Anabaptist regime, the latter were his main source for the period before the city's takeover. Thus, he had full access to the prince-bishop's correspondence, which provided him both with letters sent to him and ones sent by him. For the period down to the agreement entered into by the prince-bishop and the city council in February 1533, Kerssenbrock had no written narrative that he could follow, and here he was left to his own limited abilities as a narrator. The result was a rather unsatisfying attempt to stitch together a story by adding anecdotes and episodes taken from various sources to the long series of documents that he reproduces. In this portion of his work in particular, Kerssenbrock's lack of historical analysis is shown by his inability to digest information and to make an interpretation of events out of it. Instead, he simply preserves large amounts of documents as if this alone discharged the historian's duty to his readers. When, in the subsequent period of events, he begins to have earlier historical works to give him a sense of narrative, his reliance on documents lessens, though he continues to make use of large numbers of them to supplement his account (and in the process preserves a number of important documents relating to both the conduct of the war outside the city and the Anabaptist regime within it). One somewhat surprising element in this later use of the episcopal archive is Kerssenbrock's comparative neglect of the prince-bishop's dealings with his princely neighbors in his efforts to secure their support for the continuing war effort as the prince-bishop increasingly found himself unable to bear the burdens of maintaining the besieging force through his own resources. Presumably, Kerssenbrock felt that he had enough to narrate merely in relating the events around the city, and decided to restrict his account of the prince-bishop's diplomacy. Another aspect of his reliance on archives is the greatly divergent emphasis on Bernard Rothman. Whereas in the period down to the agreement between the prince-bishop and the city council, disputes involving Rothman and his position in the city played a prominent role in the archival material, Rothman is practically unmentioned in the later correspondence and virtually disappears from the narrative, despite the fact that he continued to play a prominent role in the city until the day of its capture by the prince-bishop.

Kerssenbrock makes little or no effort to discuss the significance of the documents, and simply cites the letters and the replies in chronological order. A notable example of his lack of historical acumen is given by his use of the many confessions of Anabaptists that he found in the archives. At one point (733–736D), he quotes two such confessions (from refugees from the city) at length verbatim, but only for the narrow purpose of illustrating conditions in the city. When it came to the numerous confessions of senior Anabaptists, however, (not just those of the captured "apostles" dispatched from the city in October 1534, but those made by John of Leiden, Bernard Knipperdolling and others after the city's fall), he did little more than extract bits of information about their earlier lives. In particular, he made no use of the elaborate information provided in them about the establishment and the practices of the Anabaptist regime. Perhaps, in this he simply felt that the self-justifications of men whom he took to be lecherous tricksters and charlatans of the worst sort were worthy of no credence and should best be ignored. On the other hand, he nowhere else exhibits much ability to formulate a historical interpretation of the course of events, so it is not surprising that in this instance too he shows no interest in trying to turn the information provided to him by the confessions into some sort of coherent analysis.

When Kerssenbrock made use of other works, it was his constant policy not to name them, but when he did follow earlier accounts, he would do so verbatim, which makes it easy to determine such sources when they survive. His preferred literary account was Henricus Dorpius (Henry Dorp) of Münster's *Wahrhafftigen Historie* ("Accurate history"), which had also been the main source for Kerssenbrock's earlier poem on the Anabaptist events.[77] Kerssenbrock supplemented Dorp's account with excerpts from other sources. One of these is the *Tumultuum Anabaptistarum liber unus* ("Single book on the uproars of the Anabaptists") of Lambert Hortensius (1500/01–1574), though this was not used extensively. More use was made of the Latin poem *Motus Monasteriensis* ("Disturbance in Münster") of John Bolandus, which had also been used to supplement Dorp in Kerssenbrock's youthful poem. It is particularly noteworthy that Kerssenbrock has no knowledge of the *Summarische Ertzelungk und Bericht* ("Summary narrative and report"), an account of the affairs in the city that was written by a burgher named Henry Gresbeck.[78]

In addition to these broad accounts, Kerssenbrock used sources of more limited scope. Specific accounts of the affairs of the city's cloisters provided some details relating to ecclesiastical events. It would seem that in the period from November 1533 until February 11, 1534, he had access to some source that recorded events on a day-to-day basis, as is indicated by the very specific chronological anchoring of his narrative. As already noted, he did make use of Anabaptist confessions, though not in a very systematic way. It would seem, however, that he did make extensive use of some sort of memorandum drawn up by Herman Ramers, who fled the city in June 1534 to inform the prince-bishop

---

[77] The work was published in Wittenberg in 1536. Stupperich (1958/59) and Kirchhoff (1962b) both argue that Dorp was really a pseudonym (he apparently is unaware of things that a man from Münster ought to have known) and that the author was in fact Anthony Corvinus, the Lutheran pastor who interviewed John of Leiden after the city's capture (see below in text).

[78] Gresbeck escaped from the city immediately before its fall, and as his account is the only one written by an eyewitness or by someone who had been within the city, it provides a valuable check on Kerssenbrock's accuracy, though the rather disordered and clumsy nature of Gresbeck's account, which more or less provides only narrative without any explanation, makes it often difficult to follow without consultation of Kerssenbrock.

of a plot to assassinate him and gained the prince-bishop's pardon as a result (609–610D). At any rate, a manuscript in the state archives in Münster, a contemporary broadsheet, and excerpts in the *Chronicle of the Bishops of Münster* contain statements that appear verbatim in Kerssenbrock, and the *Chronicle* overtly attributes the statements to Ramers. Since none of these sources can serve as the source for the others (none gives a complete account), it would seem that they all go back to a more extensive confession of Ramers that does not survive, and this was an important basis for Kerssenbrock's account of the events in the city until Ramers' flight. Kerssenbrock supplemented this information about affairs within the city with a few contemporary broadsheets. The fullness of his account of the events in Warendorf suggests that he had access to some sort of local chronicle that does not survive (contrast his comparative silence about Coesfeld). For the diplomacy of Landgrave Philip of Hesse with the city in early 1535, Kerssenbrock made some use of the published *Acta* of Anthony Corvinus,[79] and for the prince-bishop's interactions with the emperor and the imperial diet, he made use of John Sleidan's diplomatic history.[80]

These sources account for most of Kerssenbrock's information for the period from the expulsion of the "godless" in February 1534 down to the city's capture. For the capture itself and the immediate aftermath, he continued to rely on his usual literary sources (which he follows in ascribing the plan for the capture to Hans of Langenstraten alone, to the exclusion of any role for Henry Gresbeck; see 825–827D with notes), but he adds large numbers of details and episodes that have no known source. For the last days and execution of John of Leiden and his two associates, Kerssenbrock relied on Anthony Corvinus' published account, but supplemented it with a contemporary broadsheet (but even so he adds details that are otherwise unattested). Kerssenbrock's account of the prolonged struggle of the city to regain its previous privileges after the capture is a virtually verbatim reproduction of an anonymous tract on this subject that was published in 1562.[81] Ironically, one of the city

---

[79] *Acta, Handlungen, Legation und schrifffte, so durch…Herrn Philipsen, Landgraven zu Hessen, etc., in der Münsterschen sache geschehen* ("Acts, negotiations, embassies and writings, which were made by Philip, Landgrave of Hesse, in the Münster matter"), which was published in 1536.

[80] *De statu religionis et reipublicae sub Carolo Quinto* ("The condition of religion and of the state under Charles V").

[81] *Eine korte antekunge, was sick binnen Münster nach veraverunge der stadt uit der wedderdoper gewalt in der ersten und lesten restution* (sic) *hefft begeven und togedragen* ("A short indication

council's complaints about Kerssenbrock's account concerned the presentation of the council's opposition to the full restitution of the guilds, but this picture was taken over entirely from the anonymous source. Kerssenbrock also adds in some details from Dietrich Lilie's continuation of Ertwin Ertman's chronicle of the bishops of Osnabrück.[82] (There is some similarity between Kerssenbrock's account and Lilie's for earlier events, but seemingly these are to be attributed to the use of common sources.)

e) *Kerssenbrock's Historical Method*

Kerssenbrock's aims were rather circumscribed. Although he extended his account temporally to include the earlier events that gave the Anabaptists the opportunity to seize control of the city and the endeavors to recover the city's privileges after its capture, it was only when he dealt with the period of Anabaptist control that he made much effort to try to weave together a coherent picture from the various literary sources available and to supplement this picture with archival material. For the most part, in the earlier narrative about the attempts to make the city Lutheran, he relies overwhelmingly on poorly digested documents and gives little in the way of analytical framework, while for the later events he simply follows one main source. Even in terms of the events that do draw his attention, his emphasis is firmly focused on the city of Münster itself, and he makes little attempt to place them in a broader context (as noted above, he tends to shortchange, and at times misrepresent, the prince-bishop's efforts to enlist the support of surrounding communities). In effect, he conceived of himself as a local historian (note how he lovingly relates antiquarian details of the city's earlier history and its physical fabric and institutions in his introduction), who was narrating (in great detail) an important event in local history; hence, the broader circumstances and implications of the events in Münster were not within his remit.

Kerssenbrock wrote as a committed Catholic, and as such he felt nothing but revulsion at the Anabaptist movement and did nothing to conceal the contempt in which he held its leaders in Münster, whom

---

of what took place and occurred in Münster after the city was recaptured from Anabaptist control").

[82] *Beschrivinge sampt den handlingen der hoichwerdigen bisschopen van Osnabrugge* ("Description and activities of the most worthy bishops of Osnabrück").

he considered to be self-serving frauds. Apart from the uniform rejection which believer's baptism in general met with from all adherents
of established state-sponsored churches (that is, from Lutherans and
supporters of Zwingli, no less than from Catholics), the institution
of polygamy by the besieged radicals was enough to ensure that the
Anabaptists of Münster would be treated harshly by all contemporary
writers. Not surprisingly, Kerssenbrock makes no effort to understand
the origin or development of Anabaptist doctrine, which he conceived
of as having been devised by Satan himself (113–114D, 442D), though
he does preserve the occasional reference to such doctrines in the documents that he reproduces.[83]

Kerssenbrock's hostility extends to the Lutherans, since he ascribes
the blame for the Anabaptist takeover of the city to the earlier efforts
of the city council and guilds to establish Lutheran religious practice
in the city. At the start of his introduction, he indicates that among
his purposes in writing the work was to praise Bishop Francis for extir-
pating heresy and to warn the ecclesiastical and secular authorities of
the dangers of not doing their duty to stamp out such threats to the
established order (4D). It is clear that in his mind it was just as much
Lutheranism as Anabaptism that was to be eradicated. He refers to
the "earlier disturbances" (i.e., the efforts to establish Lutheranism) as a
sort of Trojan horse from which emerged the Anabaptist conflagration
(6D), and later makes his distaste for Lutheran reform clear, blaming it
for disturbances both in Münster and in many other cities (114D). He
uses the striking image of comparing the Lutheran movement to some
sort of beast that conceived the monstrous spawn of Anabaptism in its
womb and reared it on the milk of lechery (334D), and even goes so
far as to thank God for allowing the subsequent Anabaptist disaster to
come about in order to put the prince-bishop in a position to repudiate the agreement between him and the city council whereby the city
was basically made Lutheran (379D, where he again states that Anabaptism was given birth to by Lutheranism). This last passage makes
it reasonably clear that while Kerssenbrock was no doubt repelled by
the Anabaptist episode of his youth, he was more directly animated

---

[83] He notes in connection with Rothman's *Restitution*, which he cites without going
into any details of its contents, that it was better to suppress this along with other books
printed at the time in Münster than to allow their pernicious doctrine to be disseminated
(758D). Note also his failure even to paraphrase the content of the important debate
between radicals and conservatives before the council in August, 1533 (424–425D).

by hostility towards Lutheranism, which still found many adherents in Münster at the time when Kerssenbrock was writing his work. His general distaste for Lutheranism is shown by numerous ironic references to "evangelical liberty," which could be taken (by Protestants) to mean "Lutheran liberation (from papist tyranny)," but is meant by him to signify "the impudent licentiousness caused by Luther."[84]

Not surprisingly, Kerssenbrock has no sympathy for those opposed to the traditional Church, and exhibits no sense of what animated them. He merely characterizes them as those who condemned the notion of "good works" (more or less the converse of the concept of salvation by faith alone) and rejected ecclesiastical ceremonies (126D; also 116–117D), and upholds the claims of the traditional Church without any further elaboration. This partisan interpretation of religious developments leaves him with little analytical framework. He attributes the rejection of traditional practices to self-indulgent turpitude and greed (334D). He also conceives of the innovation in religion as a sort of disease that was foretold by God through various omens (115D, 117D), but he has two explanations of what motivated God to allow these calamities.

On the one hand, such misfortunes seem to be the result of some sort of natural tendency, which can be averted only if God is propitiated through prayer and averts what would otherwise take place, seemingly of its own accord (119D). Kerssenbrock has a general sense that the calamity of 1534/35 was God's punishment for the city's sins (6K), but he does not have a clearly defined causality. In one of the most elaborate explanatory passages (112–113D), he argues that the fault responsible for the misfortunes was wealth: the prosperity of the city made the ecclesiastics lazy (a sin which manifested itself in their failure to take vigorous action against the incipient heretical disturbances of the 1520s), and the laity greedy and defiant of authority (both ecclesiastical and secular).[85] In a later passage characterizing those who advocated religious reform (334–335D), he lays much more emphasis on the supposed greed of the reformers than on their religious motives.

---

[84] Note how on 334D he associates those who reject "good works" with the idea of thinking that anything was permissible. Presumably, here he connects Luther's stance with the licentiousness that he thought characteristic of the Anabaptists of Münster.

[85] The language used of the reformers' greed on 334D seems to be based on platitudes in ancient Roman literature, but the notion of the corrupting power of wealth was hardly a novel conception in Christian thought.

On the other hand, however, Kerssenbrock seems to give a different explanation. First, he lays out (14–15D) a sort of geographical
determination of character that is based on the astrological influences
of the heavenly bodies that dominate the area (he shows himself to
be a strong believer in the attenuated theory of astrology that saw the
heavenly bodies as giving an "impulse" towards certain behavior that
could nonetheless be counteracted by the human will).[86] The resulting
natural disposition of the Westphalians was towards a character that
was straightforward and honest, if uncultivated and prone to con-
tentiousness (16D). This pristine character is then said to have been
corrupted through the malign influence of foreigners and through the
locals' hankering after novelty (17D). Kerssenbrock at first seems to be
speaking of fashions in clothing, but it then becomes clear (18D) that
he has in mind the adoption of outside religious practices, seeming to
imply that non-Catholic reforms were taken on in place of the respectable traditions of the past in the same way that frivolous new forms
of attire were picked up from abroad. There is no explanation of how
this interpretation whereby religious reform is presented as a capricious
innovation adopted for novelty's sake relates to the conception that the
urge to reform was born of greed. Presumably, Kerssenbrock had no
clearly thought-out explanation of the exact causalities, since in his
mind the innovations were simply wicked deviations from the proper
rites and beliefs passed on by the past, and he did not go any further
than attributing this unfortunate behavior (and the resulting debacle) to
the corruption of wealth and the perverse frivolity that he considered
inherent to the Westphalians as a whole.

f) *Later Fate of the Anabaptist History*

The two copies of the Anabaptist history that Kerssenbrock turned over
to the city council (i.e., the copy that was intended to serve as the clean
copy for the printer and the copy that he retained) were never in fact
returned to him.[87] There is a note in the minutes of the city council from

---

[86] At first sight, such a conception would seem odd in a convinced Catholic, but the
general (rather than compelling) influence of the heavenly bodies was widely recognized
in late medieval scholastic thought (and the clear modern distinction between astrology
and astronomy did not exist). For a general treatment of medieval and early modern
astrology, see Tester (1987) 98–243.

[87] Detmer (1899–1900) 439*–448* discusses the manuscripts and translations of
the work.

1581 that suggests that the work should be corrected and published, but nothing came of this, and though the two copies of his work are duly noted as present in the relevant archive, they have disappeared. The copy that was made for the cathedral chapter in the summer of 1573 has likewise not survived, but it served as the basis for a number of copies that were made during the period of Kerssenbrock's dispute with the city council. As part of his various agreements with the council, he was obligated to turn over all copies of the work, and while he did so with the copies that he himself had had transcribed, he constantly maintained that the obligation was impossible to fulfill because there were copies that had not been made by him and over which he had no control (for instance, in October 1574, he told the council that he had seen two nicely bound copies at a bookbinder's). In later years, interest in the remarkable events in Münster endured, and as Kerssenbrock's work, which was known to be the most elaborate account, remained unprinted, the work continued to be transcribed into the eighteenth century, and large numbers of manuscript copies survive.

The manuscript used for Detmer's edition is distinctive for the explicit indication of its origin. The title page of this copy, which is preserved in the Pauline Library in Münster, states that it was the property of Nicholas Steinlagen, the prior and vicar of the cathedral, and is dated to 1574. Thus, this manuscript was almost certainly copied directly from the copy that was made from the Cologne manuscript that Kerssenbrock had deposited with Goswin of Raesfeld (i.e., it was two steps removed from Kerssenbrock's clean text). The manuscript is 672 pages (i.e., folio sides) long, and was carefully written by a single hand.

A number of translations were made into German, and one was published in 1771. This work is anonymous, which is just as well, since it is incomplete, inaccurate and unreliable (it was reprinted without corrections in 1886 and 1929).[88]

g) *Assessment of the Historical Worth of Kerssenbrock's Account*

It should be clear that from a modern perspective, Kerssenbrock has many failings as a historian. He has no sense of historical development, and his analysis of events is deeply influenced by his partisanship on behalf of the Catholic Church. As a glance at the notes indicates,

---

[88] *Geschichte der Wiedertäufer in Münster zu Westfalen.*

he is often subject to chronological inaccuracy, and he at times omits crucial information. As a result both of his traditional understanding of historically important information and of the nature of the sources available to him, his account concentrates on "high politics," that is, the behavior and interactions of official bodies and warfare. He has no understanding of what one might broadly call "social history," that is, the way in which common individuals perceived events and participated in them. Indeed, for the most part, he speaks vaguely of an amorphous "mob" (*multitudo*) of Anabaptists, and has no interest in their attitudes or actions (except to the extent that an anecdote of some individual is worthy of note). Nonetheless, his work remains important on several levels.

First, as has been noted, the work is crammed full of large numbers of documents, some of which are not otherwise preserved, and even when they are, these are often not very accessible. Though such documents are for the most part limited to the official declarations of the actors, nonetheless, such statements allow the parties involved to "speak for themselves." Second, his is the most extensive contemporary account and continues to be a major source for the astounding events in Münster. While one need hardly take Kerssenbrock's word for anything, he was a well-informed reporter of events that had happened within his lifetime and made a great impression on contemporaries. He may well not always relate events as a modern historian would prefer, but his account is worthy of consideration. Third, his account has been at the basis of much of later historiographical tradition about the Anabaptist incidents of Münster. But not only did those whose interpretations rested on his work often not have direct access to his thoughts, but much of the opprobrium that is now generally cast upon him is likewise not based on direct consultation of his work. Now, it should be easier to assess Kerssenbrock's strengths and weaknesses. Obviously, one should no more rely unquestioningly on Kerssenbrock than the accounts of Thucydides or Tacitus would be taken at face value in a modern work on ancient history. But it is only through a direct and full consideration of the work as a whole that one can assess the author's methods and intentions, and thereby determine the validity of his version of events. Finally, Kerssenbrock's work has value in its own right as a document of one man's interpretation of events around him. The work is indicative of the views of a committed Catholic on the eve of his Church's efforts to reclaim the lands that had renounced their allegiance to papal authority.

In reading Kerssenbrock's account, two questions should always be borne in mind. First, what really happened and how well does Kerssenbrock's presentation of events fit with that reality? Second, why did he choose to present the matter as he does? So long as one bears both of these questions in mind, his account is both fascinating and informative.

4) *Note on the Translation of Names*

In the early sixteenth century, the development of fixed last names had not yet been completed, and people could be known according to three system. First, the last name could consist of a patronymic. This could take two forms. The person could be known as the "son" (or "daughter") of the father's given name, e.g., Bockelson (i.e., "son of Bockel") as the last name of John of Leiden. Such a name could also be given as an abbreviated genitival form with the word "son" understood, so that the same man could also be called Bockels.[89] I have decided to use the former version (which gives Matthisson instead of Matthys or Matthis for the first Melchiorite leader in Münster). Second, a person could also be indicated by his geographic origin, so that John Bockelson could also be called John of Leiden. If this is indicated with the Latin prepositions *a* or *de*, it is easy enough to render it with "of." (If the Germanic form had the definite article, e.g., von der Tann, I have rather reluctantly omitted it.) As for the practice of indicating present residence with the preposition *to* (High German *zu*), often modified by the contracted definite article, I have left these alone in their Low German form due to the absence of a satisfactory correspondence in English. On the few occasions where Kerssenbrock seems to reflect the German usage of mentioning in the case of certain high-born individuals both his family's original place of origin and the individual's actual residence (the preposition *von* indicates the former and *zu* the latter), I have used the preposition "of" for the first and "from" for the second. Third and finally, a person could be known by the name of his profession. While my practice leads to the occasional difficulty,

---

[89] English has a large number of such forms, such as Williams, Edwards, Andrews, Peters (though they are probably not understood as such, and in any case, they do not vary by generation).

it is consistent and straightforward, and should cause no difficulty of identification.

The linguistic variety in the origins of the characters in this story makes it hard to avoid some doubtful forms. English works about these events often give a miscellany of English, Dutch and High German forms (e.g., John, Jan, and Johann, or Bernard, Bernt and Bernhard; the list could easily be multiplied), and it seemed best to pick a fixed system of rendering the names and to stick to it, even at the cost of the occasional infelicity. To make the dramatis personae seem less alien I have decided to give them the English version of their first names. Last names, on the other hand, have been more or less regularized to give a reasonable rendering of the form used by Kerssenbrock.[90] Since most of the locations referred to by Kerssenbrock are now given on maps in the High German form, this seemed preferable to the Low German forms used by Kerssenbrock (unless there is a standard English version, like Cologne). This procedure led to some uncertainty over the town generally known in English by the French form "Liege" (called "Leodinum" in Kerssenbrock's Latin). According to the map, the Dutch form "Luik" should be used, but since other towns have their High German form, I reluctantly settled on the German "Lüttich." As for the major reformation center in Alsace, the slightly Anglicized "Strasburg" seemed preferably to the anachronistic French version "Strasbourg."

Finally, a brief mention of the adjective "evangelical." In German, this term eventually becomes a synonym for "Lutheran," and at times Kerssenbrock clearly means it in this sense. But the word is literally merely the adjective derived from the Latin word for "Gospel," and thus signifies whatever is associated with the Gospels. In the Reformation context, it refers to the attempt to return to the usages of the Gospels, in contradistinction to the rejected practices of the medieval Church (the sense which gives rise to the meaning "Lutheran"). Sometimes, Kerssenbrock uses the term in this broader sense (especially when translating texts composed by Anabaptists). In a number of instances,

---

[90] Kerssenbrock sometimes wavers between Low and High German phonology in his inconsistent and at times ambiguous rendering of German names into Latin, and I have striven to pick a form that conveys the way the name was probably pronounced. At the least, the same person's name should always appear in the same form. To lessen the feeling of foreignness, I have written the common ending "man" in the English manner with a single "n" (and this practice is continued for consistency's sake in this introduction, even with names like Rothman that are generally written the German way in other works).

however, it is not entirely clear which sense is meant (and conceivably the second is intended with overtones of the first). The problem arises from English orthography, which would demand capitalization in the first usage but not the second. The instances when it is not entirely clear which sense is meant have induced me to avoid prejudicing the interpretation by eschewing capitalization in all cases, even when it is clear that the meaning "Lutheran" is intended. The reader may decide for himself when the word should be capitalized.

BIBLIOGRAPHY

Backus, Irena, *Reformation Readings of the Apocalypse: Geneva, Zurich, and Wittenberg* (New York: Oxford University Press, 2000).

Behringer, Wolfgang, *Shaman of Oberstdorst: Chonrad Stoeckhlin and the Phantoms of the Night*, trans. by H.C. Erik Midelfort (Charlottesville: University Press of Virginia, 1998).

Blickle, Peter, *The Revolution of 1525: The German Peasants' War from a New Perspective* (Baltimore and London: The Johns Hopkins University Press, 1981).

Blockmans, Wim, *Emperor Charles V: 1500–1558* (New York: Oxford University Press, 2002).

Cohn, Norman, *Pursuit of the Millennium*, rev. ed. (Oxford: Oxford University Press, 1973).

——, *Europe's Inner Demons: The Demonization of Christians in Medieval Christendom*, rev. ed. (London: Pimlico, 1993).

Deppermann, Klaus, *Melchior Hoffman*, trans. by Malcolm Wren, ed. by Benjamin Drewery (Edinburgh: T. & T. Clarke, 1987).

Detmer, H. *Hermanni a Kerssenbroch, Anabaptistici Furoris Monasterium Inclitam Westphaliae Metropolim Evertentis Historica Narratio*, two vols. (Münster: Druck und Verlag der Theissing'schen Buchhandlung, 1899–1900).

Hamilton, Alastair, *The Apocryphal Apocalypse: The Reception of the Second Book of Esdras (4 Ezra) from the Renaissance to the Enlightenment* (Oxford: Clarendon Press, 1999).

Haude, Sigrun, *In the Shadow of "Savage Wolves": Anabaptist Münster and the German Reformation during the 1530s* (Boston, Leiden and Cologne: Humanities Press, Inc., 2000).

Holborn, Hajo, *A History of Modern Germany: The Reformation* (Princeton: Princeton University Press, 1959).

Huyskens, Viktor, "Elsebein Judefeld, des Rektors Hermann von Kerssenbroch zweite Gemahlin," *Zeitschrift für vaterländische Geschichte und Altertumskunde* 62 (1904) 246–247.

Kirchhoff, Karl-Heinz, "Die Belagerung und Eroberung der Täfergemeinde zu Münster 1534/35. Militärische Maßnahmen und politische Verhandlungen des Fürstbischofs Fran von Waldeck," *Westfälische Zeitschrift* 112 (1962a) 77–170.

——, "Wer war Henricius Dorpius Monasteriensis? Ein Nachtrag" *Jahrbuch des Vereins für Westfälische Kirchengeschichte* 53/54 (1962b) 173–179.

——, "Die Endzeiterwartung der Täufergemeinde zu Münster 1534/35" *Jahrbuch des Vereins für Westfälische Kirchengeschichte* 78 (1985) 19–42.

——, *Forschungen zur Geschichte von Stadt und Stift Münster: Ausgewählte Aufsätze und Schriftenverzeichnis*, ed. Franz Petri et al. (Warendorf: Fahlbusch & Co., 1988).

Klötzer, Ralf, *Die Täuferherrschaft von Münster: Stadtreformation und Welterneuerung* (Münster: Aschendorff, 1992).

Krahn, Cornelius, *Dutch Anabaptism: Origin, Spread, Life and Thought (1450–1600)* (The Hague: Martinus Nijhoff, 1968).

MacCulloch, Diarmaid, *Reformation: Europe's House Divided, 1490–1700* (London: Allen Lane, 2003).

Nichols, David, *The Later Medieval City: 1300–1500* (London and New York: Longman, 1997).

Oman, Charles, *A History of the Art of War in the Sixteenth Century* (New York: E.P. Dutton and Company, 1937).

Pater, Calvin Augustine, *Karlstadt as the Father of the Baptist Movements: The Emergence of Lay Protestantism* (Toronto, Buffalo, London: University of Toronto Press, 1984).

Petersen, Rodney, *Preaching in the Last Days: The Theme of the "Two Witnesses" in the Sixteenth and Seventeenth Centuries* (New York: Oxford University Press, 1993).

Redlich, Fritz, *The German Military Enterpriser and his Work Force: A Study in European Economic and Social History* (Wiesbaden: Franz Steiner Verlag, 1964).

Strauss, Gerald, *Manifestations of Discontent on the Eve of the Reformation* (Bloomington: Indiana University Press, 1971).

Stayer, James M., *The German Peasants' War and Anabaptist Community of Goods* (Montreal & Kingston, London and Buffalo: McGill-Queen's University Press, 1991).

——, *Anabaptists and the Sword*, new ed. including "Reflections and Retractions" 1976 (Eugene: Wipf and Stock Publishers, 2002).

Stephens, W.P., *Zwingli: An Introduction to his Thought* (Oxford: Clarendon Press, 1992).

Stupperich, Robert, "Wer war Henricius Dorpius Monasteriensis? Eine Untersuchung über den Verfasser der 'Warhafftigen Historie, wie das Evangelium zu Münster angefangen und danach, durch die Widderteuffer verstöret, widder aufgehöret hat. Wittenberg 1536'," *Jahrbuch des Vereins für Westfälische Kirchengeschichte* 51/52 (1958/59) 150–160.

Tester, S.J., *A History of Western Astrology* (Woodbridge and Wolfeboro: The Boydell Press, 1987).

Williams, George Huntston, *The Radical Reformation*, third edition (Sixteenth Century Essays and Studies, vol. 15, 2000).

Fig. 1. This bird's-eye view of the city was published in commemoration of the treaty that was signed in the council hall of Münster in 1648 to end the Thirty Years' War, and it gives a good idea of the city's massive defensive works. Important locations are marked with the following symbols: A) Cathedral of St. Paul; B) College of St. Paul (the Old Church); C) parish church of St. James; D) parish church of the Virgin Mary Across-the-River; E) parish church of St. Ludger; F) parish church of St. Martin; G) parish church of St. Lambert; H) parish church of St. Giles (Aegidius); I) parish church of St. Servatus; K) house of the Brothers of the Fountain; L) Church of St. George (Teutonic Order); M) Church of St. Nicholas; N) Church of St. Michael; O) Church of St. Margaret; P) Church of St. Catherine (Franciscan); R) Church of St. John (Hospitalers); S) College of the Minorites; X) Nitzing's Convent; Y) Rosenthal Convent; Z) Hofrugging's Convent; AA) Reine Convent; BB) Hospital of St. Mary Magdalene; CC) marketplace; DD) Council Hall; EE) public cellar; FF) Gate of the Virgin Mary; GG) Jews' Field Gate; HH) Cross Gate; II) New Bridge Gate; KK) Gate of the Savior/Horst Gate; LL) Gate of St. Maurice; MM) Gate of St. Servatius; NN) Gate of St. Ludger; OO) Gate of St. Giles. (Stadt-archiv, Münster, Germany)

Fig. 2. This not unsympathetic portrait of John of Leiden was made by Heinrich Alder-graver in 1536 after John's execution. It is the source of numerous later portraits. (Stadt-Museum, Münster, Germany; photo: Tomasz Samek)

WAERHAFTICH·GEKONTERFET·BERNT·KNIPPERDOLLICK
DER·XII·HERTOGEN EYN·THO·MONSTER·

IGNOTVS·NVLLIS·KNIPPERDOLLINGIVS·ORIS·
TALIS·ERĀ·SOSPES·CVM·MIHI·VITA·FORET·
HINRICVS·ALDEGREVER·SVSATIĒ·FACI
1536

Fig. 3. This portrait of Bernard Knipperdolling was made by Heinrich Aldergraver as a companion to the previous portrait of John of Leiden. (Stadt- Museum, Münster, Germany; photo: Tomasz Samek)

Figs. 4a.–b. Obverse and reverse of a thaler minted in May–August, 1534 by the Anabaptists in Münster to entice soldiers of the besieging army to defect; cf. 533D. Obverse
inscription: (rim) WE NICHT GEBARE IS UIT DEM WATER VN GEIST; (inner
field) DAT WORT IS FLEISCH GEWORDEN VN WANET VNDER VNS 1534.
Reverse inscription: (rim) MACH NICHT IN GAEN IN DAT RIKE GOIDES; (inner
circle) EIN HER EIN GELOVE EIN DOEPS; (inner field) THO MVNSTER. The
language is a confusion of High and Low German forms. The rim inscriptions (starting
on the obverse and continuing on the reverse) give a rendition of John 3:5 ("Whoever
is not born of water and spirit may not enter into God's kingdom"), but while the corresponding inscription on the companion half thaler (next illustration) mimics Luther's
translation, for some reason the translation of this coin gives an independent translation
of the text that diverges from Luther's phraseology. The legend in the inner field on
the obverse gives a version of John 1:14 (in place of the Luther's "The word became
flesh and dwelt in us," the tenses on the coin give the phrase more immediacy: "The
word has become flesh and resides in us."). Like the half thaler, the inner circle on the
reverse gives the slogan "One Lord, one faith, one baptism." The inner field then gives
the location of mintage ("at Münster"). (Westfälisches Landesmuseum für Kunst und
Kulturgeschichte, Münster, Germany)

Figs. 5a.–b. Obverse and reverse of a half thaler minted in May–August, 1534 by the Anabaptists in Münster to entice soldiers of the besieging army to defect; cf. 533D. The layout of the legends on this coin is comparable to that of the thaler, with a rim legend and an inner field on one side and two circular legends and an inner field on the other, except that while on the thaler the rim legend begins on the side with one the single line of text around the rim, on this coin the rim legend begins on the side with two circular lines of text. Obverse inscription: (rim) ET SI DAT IMADT VPT NIE GEBARE WERDE; (inner circle) EIN HER EI GELO EIN DOEP; (inner field) THO MVNSTER 1534. Reverse inscription: (rim) SO MACH HE GADES RIKE NICHT SCHEI; (inner field) DAT WORT IS FLEIS GWORDE VN WA VN VNS. The rim legend (starting on the obverse and continuing on the reverse) gives a Low German rendition of Luther's translation of John 3:3 ("Es sei denn, daß jemand von neuem geboren werde, so kann er Gottes Reich nicht sehen"/"Unless someone is born anew, he cannot see God's kingdom"). The inner circular legend on the obverse says "One Lord, one faith, one baptism." The inner field of the obverse gives the place and date of minting ("In Münster, 1534"), while the reverse field gives a version of John 1:14 (in place of the traditional "The word became flesh and dwelt in us," the tenses on the coin give the phrase more immediacy: "The word has become flesh and resides in us.") (Westfälisches Landesmuseum für Kunst und Kulturgeschichte, Münster, Germany)

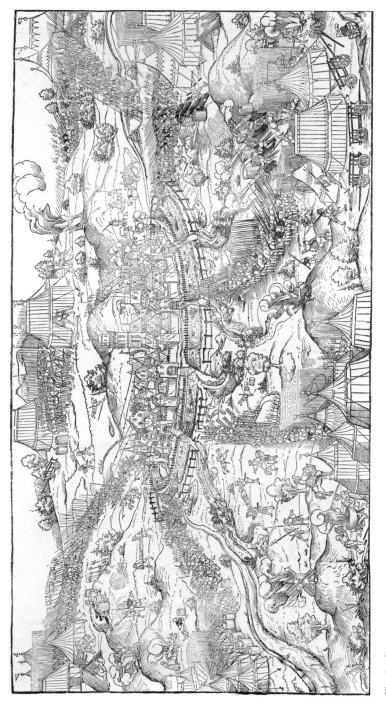

Fig. 6. Contemporary woodcut of the siege of Münster by the Nuremberg artist Erhard Schoen. Although Schoen was not an eyewitness, and the rolling countryside seems to indicate that Schoen was not personally familiar with the location, a number of details in this schematic overview of the siege (e.g. the burning of windmills and the executions being carried out in the cathedral square) show that he had detailed knowledge of events that took place during the siege. In this regard it is perhaps noteworthy that the portrayal of the besieging forces and the activities outside of the town is far more detailed than the rather cursory representation of the town. (Stadt- Museum, Münster, Germany; photo: Tomasz Samek)

Fig. 7. This scene of artillery being fired at the city comes from a series of woodcuts produced in 1535 by the Nuremberg artist Erhard Schoen. Note the wickerwork mantelets used to shield the besiegers. (Westfälisches Landesmuseum für Kunst und Kulturgeschichte, Münster, Germany)

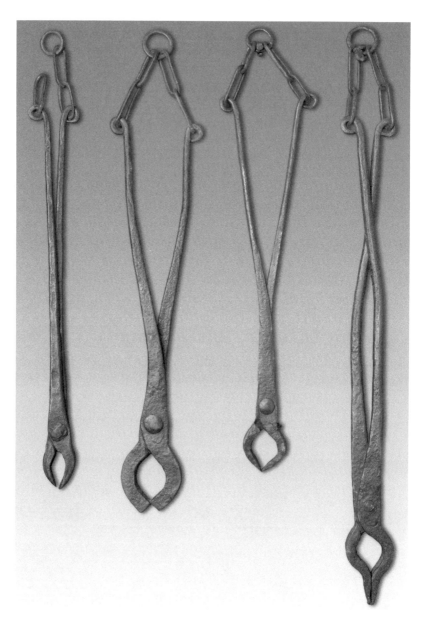

Fig. 8. Kerssenbrock reports (629D) that the tongs used to torture John of Leiden, Knipperdolling and Krechting were preserved on columns of the city hall. Later written reports also mention them, but there is no drawing preserved of them before about 1800. There is no reason to think that the instruments in this photograph are not the actual ones used in 1536. The gruesome practice of tearing the flesh of the condemned with blacksmith's tongs that had been heated to the point of glowing in a brazier was a common element in early modern executions (the number of tears was actually specified in the verdict of condemnation). (Stadt- Museum, Münster, Germany; photo: Tomasz Samek)

Fig. 9. These replicas of the cages which were hung from the tower of the Church of St. Lambert in 1536 to expose the bodies of John of Leiden, Knipperdolling and Krech- ting (see 629D) were made privately in 1888 on the basis of the originals, which by that point were falling apart as a result of long exposure to the elements. While it was a not uncommon practice to expose the bodies of the executed, it was unheard-of to keep the bodies permanently displayed and to leave the cages of exposure as a permanent memorial to the infamy of the executed even after the bodies had disappeared. Other replicas of the cages were made in 1898 to replace the decayed originals, and these can still be seen hanging from St. Lambert's. (Stadt- Museum, Münster, Germany; photo: Tomasz Samek)

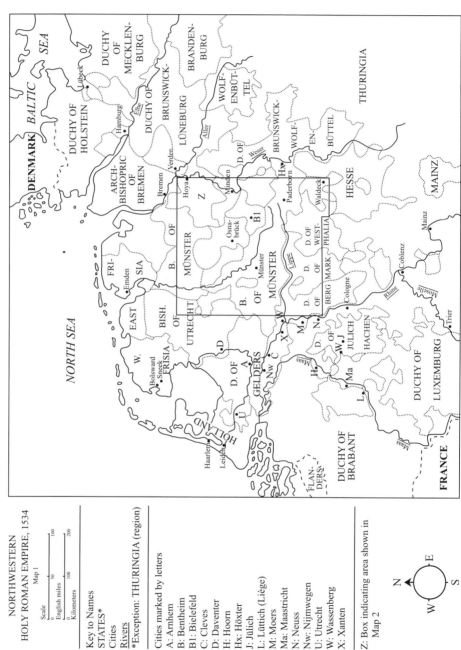

NORTHWESTERN
HOLY ROMAN EMPIRE, 1534

Map 1

Scale

0   50   100
English miles

0   100   200
Kilometers

Key to Names
STATES*
Cities
Rivers
*Exception: THURINGIA (region)

Cities marked by letters
A: Arnhem
B: Bentheim
B1: Bielefeld
C: Cleves
D: Daventer
H: Hoorn
Hx: Höxter
J: Jülich
L: Lüttich (Liège)
M: Moers
Ma: Maastricht
N: Neuss
Nw: Nijmwegen
U: Utrecht
W: Wassenberg
X: Xanten

Z: Box indicating area shown in
Map 2

LOWER
BISHOPRIC
OF MÜNSTER

BISHOPRIC

LORDSHIP
OF WILDES-
HAUSEN

DUCHY OF
OLDEN-
BURG

Wildes-
haus-
en

•Cloppenburg

COUNTY

OF HOYA

Coervorden

Vechta•

•Meppen

EMSLAND

COUNTY OF
DIEPHOLT

COUNTY OF

LOWER
COUNTY OF

BENTHEIM

LINGEN

•Fürstenau

Ems

BISHOPRIC OF

BISHOPRIC

OF UTRECHT

Bentheim

UPPER
COUNTY
OF
LINGEN

COUNTY

OSNABRÜCK

OF MINDEN

Weser

•Gildehaus

•Rheine
Bevergern•

OF

•Osnabrück

•Lübbecke

Minden

Ems

TECKLENBURG

UPPER

COUNTY
Burgsteinfurt
OF

Nordwalde•Greven

•Iburg

Herford•

COUNTY OF
RAVENSBERG

Ahaus•

Schöppingen•

BISHOPRIC

Horstmar•

STEIN-
FURT

Altenberge•

Schöneflieth•

Telgte•

Lemgo•

Stadtlohn

•Büren

Billerbeck•

Havixbeck•

Aa

Sassenberg•

Bielefeld•

PRINCIPALITY

Coesfeld

Darup

Münster•

Warendorf•

Ems

OF LIPPE

OF MÜNSTER

Hiltrup•

•Wolbeck

LORDSHIP
OF
RHEDA

COUNTY
OF
RIETBERG

•Borken

•Dülmen

Senden

Sendenhorst•

Ems

• Raesfeld

Werse

UCHY

Lippe

VEST

Drensteinfurt•

Ahlen•

•Beckum

•Paderborn

Lippe

OF

RECKLINGHAUSEN

Werne•

Hamm

Lippe

BISHOPRIC

LEVES

•Bottrup

IMP
FREE
CITY
DORTMUND

Soest•

OF PADERBORN

Dortmund•

•Büderich

COUNTY OF

Ruhr

DUCHY

Ruhr

MARK

COUNTY
OF
LIMBERG

Arnsburg•

DUCHY

OF

PRINCIPALITY

OF BERG

WESTPHALIA

OF WALDECK

Waldeck•

Map 2

Historical Narrative of the
Anabaptist Madness,

which overturned Münster, the famous Metropolis of Westphalia

by Herman of Kerssenbrock,
master of arts and laws, schoolmaster of the Church of St. Paul

Master Herman of Kerssenbrock to the Reader:
The baneful wars of the grim rebaptized
  I once composed as a boy in a boy's poem;
Now these and also their cause in prose
  I relate more broadly, but still with rude art.
The king of Westphalia and the savage wars in true
  Order I sing with Westphalian honesty.
The sad narrative crawls on the ground, but the true
  deeds of the madness it describes with the historian's good faith.
1564 A.D.

The King of the Anabaptists on himself
when hanging in an iron cage by the tower of St. Lambert's

I once bore the loft sceptre of the rebaptized.
   Now a bitter tower holds me aloft.
Having refused to nourish my subjects with blackbread,
   Now with my own flesh I nourish the wild birds.
With murder I seized the throne and with sexual acts unspeakable,
   I was not a *basileus* but a *basilisk*.
Omnipotent Father, please forgive my sins,
   Lest the Infernal Beast devour me!
Forgive my sin and remove my heinous crimes,
   Lest your creature should reach the threshold of Hell.

Herman of Kerssenbrock, Master of the Arts and of the Laws, Knight,   3
greets the honest readers at whose instigation this narrative has been
undertaken.

Very learned men have completed careful and accurate accounts, both
in prose and in poetry and in Latin and in German, of the Anabaptist
madness that befell Münster, the famous chief city of all of ancient
Saxony (that is, Westphalia) and afflicted it with a most grievous disaster.
Nonetheless, since these writers omitted very many facts relevant to
the origin and development of this madness, either because they were
unaware of the events that had happened or considered them old wives'
tales, I thought that if I narrated in chronological order many events
not yet published that relate to this uprising, I would perform for you
a service that you would appreciate, since you have encouraged me to
write of this. While for the most part I saw these crimes committed in
the city during my boyhood, I received some information from writings published here and there, and I received other information from
participants of whose account I harbored no suspicions. My purpose
is not the arrogant pursuit of vain repute and splendid acclaim, since I
have never been desirous of a little piece of fleeting glory, | and even   4
if this were my greatest wish, I do not have the means of acquiring
it. No, I have many purposes, the first being to serve my homeland
and posterity by preventing future generations from completely forgetting the most glorious deeds of the most reverend prince and lord,
Lord Francis, the true head of the Church in Münster, the scion of
the ancient and high-born family of the counts of Waldeck, when he
suppressed and eradicated the very foul and cruel heresy that threw
not only Westphalia but virtually the entire Holy Roman Empire into
turmoil. (As a boy I wrote a boyish poem on the topic of this same
history, imperfectly told, in praise of this excellent prince.) It is also
my purpose that once the savagery and turpitude of the Anabaptist
madness is revealed and made public, all good men will reject and
shun it—we avoid an evil only when we know it as such—and that
both civil and ecclesiastical governments will gaze upon the wretched
face of these Anabaptist affairs and evaluate accurately what sort of
disaster the commonweal suffers as a result of their neglect of duty. For
after learning from the example of this distasteful uprising they will be
able to move more expeditiously against future outbreaks, so that they
may either completely scatter or stamp out and extinguish the embers
of any evil at its birth. This will make sure that the embers will not

be revived through the addition of kindling and result in the destruction of all good men, and eventually blaze up into a horrible fire that
even the entire Empire could not put out. My final purpose is to offer
more learned men the opportunity to compose works on these events
to greater profit and in a more polished style.

Many things written by me would seem to a more prudent posterity
to be groundless, contrived and fictional, not a serious tale but a comedy
performed by costumed actors on a stage as is the custom in the public
performances of comedies and tragedies, were it not the case that in
our age there still live very many witnesses to these events who had
both seen them and been present, to their great detriment. | It is right
for very great authority and trust to be granted to their testimonies,
which agree with each other in every regard. The witnesses are good
citizens and natives of the city of Münster, who preferred to suffer
exile, some voluntarily, some by force, with the loss of all their goods
rather than involve themselves in the Anabaptist madness. In addition,
the truth of my account is attested to by the city's new fortifications,
by the sacking of the churches, by the pulling down of the spires onto
the churches, by the plundering of all goods, public and private, by the
various monuments to the Anabaptist madness scattered throughout
the city, and by the well-grounded traces of it that can still be visited
today. From all this information it is easy to grasp the savagery of the
madness and the great extent of the chaos. Accordingly, whoever reads
this account of mine should do so with the conviction that whatever
seems made up, groundless, clumsy, stupid, ridiculous and implausible
is nonetheless totally true. For it is not possible to think up anything
too horrible, too impious and too laughable for that lecherous actor
king not to have dared to try it.

Finally, this madness of the Anabaptists and the concomitant overthrow of the city of Münster cannot be described accurately by passing
over and suppressing the names of those responsible, since by doing so
the reliability of the events would not merely be rendered suspect in the
eyes of many but would even be weakened and undermined. Accordingly, if, in order for the narrative to acquire greater credibility, the faults
of certain individuals who deviated from the virtue of their ancestors
are described by name, the pious reader should know that it is hardly
the purpose of these details to insult the entire family. For what is said
of the bad people does not harm the good ones unless they implicate
themselves with the bad by defending their evil deeds. Furthermore,

there is virtually no family line in which no faulty individuals are found. For just as a tree or vine that is otherwise good nonetheless sometimes generates, through the fault of a root or branch, useless and excessive sprouts and twigs that are regularly cut off to prevent them from over-whelming the better-born branches, | so too are certain people who 6 abandon the integrity of their stock through degeneracy sometimes cut off. Therefore, it is not right to ascribe the latter to the family, just as it is not right to ascribe the former to the tree. Accordingly, good men should not grow angry at me if mention is made in this historical narrative of abortive and faulty branches of their family.

To learn the method of my undertaking, the well-disposed reader should know that I will first, in a few introductory chapters, write of the disturbances[1] preceding the rebaptism from which the flames of Anabaptism and the overthrow of the city of Münster emerged as if from the Trojan horse; next, the dissensions that blazed up in the city after the acceptance of the re-baptizing, the cruelty with which the good people were expelled from the city by the rebaptized, the way in which the city was besieged, stormed, captured and plundered, and the deeds of the Anabaptists in the city in the interim; and finally the way in which the privileges that had been lost through criminal acts were restored. It is certainly not with a splendid panoply of words thought up to rouse and captivate the reader's emotions that I will describe all these matters, but with a lowly style that slithers along the ground. For it is appropriate (to use the words of Polybius)[2] for a writer of history not to stir up human emotions or strive after a method designed for this purpose, but to report the words and deeds of men on a reliable basis. Hence, histories should be read not so much for the purity of their Latin diction as for the importance of the events and the vicissitudes of empires, and the reasons for this. For anyone who would listen to the mass for the sake of the noise created by the priest's words and neglect their sense would be acting back-to-front. The reader would likewise be

---

[1] I.e., the efforts to set up a Lutheran reform in Münster, which is here conceived of as being responsible for allowing the Anabaptist takeover. Note that in his use of the image of the Lutheran reform movement as a Trojan horse, K. implicitly suggests that the complicity of the Lutheran faction in later events was conscious.

[2] Greek historian of the second century B.C. He was famous for his theoretical dis-cussions of proper historiographical method, and criticized predecessors who strayed from the truth for emotive purposes (see Polybius, 2.56).

stupid, and the writer very stupid, if he paid so much attention to the words that he neglected the true understanding of the events.

Farewell, honest readers, and think that I have to some extent satisfied your importunate requests.

CHAPTER ONE

STATES ARE OVERTHROWN BY GOD BECAUSE
OF THEIR SINS

In order for the pious reader to understand the nature and greatness of the state that was first undermined by religious discord and other monstrous crimes, and then altogether destroyed by the surreptitious entry of the Anabaptist plague, I thought it worth my while to point out first how the city started, and then how it came to flourish more than the other cities of Westphalia. For a comparison of its greatness and superiority with the lowly start of the disaster will easily show that it was not by human planning but by the action of God on account of crimes and outrageous sins that so outstanding a city was overturned. For just as God protects and saves states that are excellently established in terms of religion, justice and the other virtues, so too does He on the other hand scatter and overturn those that are tainted with impiety, arrogance, ambition, riotous living, greed, and other crimes. This is how Greece, when she began a fight to the death about views concerning religion, fell first into horrible errors, then into impiety, and finally into loathsome suicide when she turned her weapons (to use the words of Justin) from foreign guts to her own.[1] This is how the face of the Roman state was changed by the lechery of Sextus Tarquinius alone.[2] This is how this same city was ruined amidst its glory by the arrogance, ambition and riotous living of its other leaders and nobles.[3] This is how

---

[1] An author of the Roman Imperial period, Justin wrote a historical summary. The passage cited (3.2.1) comes from a section on the period of ancient Greek history leading up to the Peloponnesian War. The conception there derives from Thucydides' famous analysis of the division of the cities states of the Greek world in the mid fifth century B.C. between the two hegemonic powers of Sparta (leading the oligarchic states) and Athens (leading the democratic ones). The chronological position here (before the discussion of the establishment of the Roman Republic, which is traditionally dated to 509 B.C.) suggests that this period is what K. has in mind, but what this has to do with a dispute about religion (*fides* or "faith" in the Latin) is by no means clear.

[2] The Roman historical tradition held that the ancient kingdom had been overthrown and replaced with the Republic as the result of a noblemen's conspiracy that was formed after Sex. Tarquinius, son of the last king, raped the wife of Collatinus.

[3] This refers to the fall of the Roman Republic. The sense here seems reminiscent of the presentation of the city council's role in the downfall of Münster.

Carthage, the most splendid city of Africa, brought destruction upon itself through arrogance, ambition and the zealous pursuit of rivalry.[4] This is how the inhabitants of Sodom and Gomorrah provoked God's outrage through their riotous living and lechery and were burned up by Him with flames of pitch and sulfur. This is how Troy, how Babylon, how Nineveh and other such magnificent states cast themselves headlong into ruination through their crimes. It is quite clear from these events that no great and flourishing state (like the city of Münster) is thrown into chaos and overturned by God without cause. Hence, a presentation is necessary of how this city of ours started and flourished for some time, since on this basis it will be easy to perceive the grievous nature of its downfall.

---

[4] Carthage was destroyed by the Romans in 146 B.C. at the end of a prolonged struggle.

CHAPTER TWO

BEGINNINGS OF THE CITY OF MÜNSTER

Münster, like most everything, started from a crude and small beginning, but gradually grew into a flourishing city and state. The story starts in the year A.D. 568, when Justin II, the nephew of Justinian by his sister, ruled the Roman Empire. The Winili, who later were called Langobards in a Latinized German name, either because of their jutting thick beards or rather because of their long axes, were neighbors of the Saxons, and grew to be so numerous within the confines of their own territory that there was not enough land to provide sustenance for such a large population. Accordingly, when necessity suggested the appropriateness of seeking a larger and more fertile land, they first prepared everything for an expedition and invited a large band of the ancient Saxons (that is, Westphalians) along to increase the strength of their army, and then under the leadership of Albwin they invaded that part of Italy which lies between the Alps and the Apennines. By their habit as barbarians hostile to the true faith, they profaned all shrines, plundered what they had profaned, and seized the profaned property as if they had acquired it by fully legal title, expelling some of the real owners and killing others. They abolished the worship of God, and in place of it substituted foul idolatry, ordering that divine honors be made to a goat's head that they set up. Many Italians were moved by love of the present life to supplicate it with tilted heads facedown as they passed by, wishing to avoid being killed by the Langobards if they despised the newly established religion. About four hundred people, however, preferred death to tainting the purity of their faith by such foul idolatry, being fearfully tortured and then executed by the Langobards for this reason. The Langobards exercised their insufferable tyranny in Italy for some years. They seized Treviso, Vicenza and Verona by storm, and among other famous cities which they razed to the ground was Milan, where they killed about 30,000 inhabitants. | Thus, the   9 Langobards subdued virtually all of Transpadane Gaul, which is even now named Lombardy (from Langobardy) after them. They afflicted Italy with various misfortunes for a period of 204 years from the time of their first king, Albwin, until that of Desiderius, the last king, and his unconditional surrender. But in A.D. 776 the renowned Charlemagne smashed and crushed their tyranny and violent savagery.

In the year 568, as I said, the Saxons followed the Langobards' army, serving for fourteen years. After successfully performing such deeds during these years, they returned home from this war richer. Now they were no longer Saxons, but in order to distinguish themselves from the Langobards, they changed their name to that of the race living across the Weser, preferring to be called Westphalians, partly from the quarter of the land where the sun sets,[1] and partly from their symbols. For as their symbol the whole race sports a young white horse, which in their ancestral tongue they call *"ein fall"* ("a foal"). We used to see an image of it wrought of white stone placed long ago for some special reason on a column supporting the choir vault from the outside (the Anabaptists knocked it down). Up to the present day, the archbishops of Cologne keep this foal among their insignia along with the title of "Duke of Westphalia" (if the fates should consent, I will follow up this matter more fully in a description of Westphalia).[2] After that, the whole

10 population | between the Rhine and the Weser kept the designation "Westphalia," being fond of the new name.

Two years after the return of the Saxons from Italy, the leaders and nobles of the race began in the year 584 to build a new town in the area between the Rhine and the Weser, calling it Mediolanum (Milan) after the name of the Italian city conquered by them so that they might thereby hand down to posterity the memory of their brave achievements in Italy.[3] The nobler races of Westphalia inhabited the city, and they fortified it with a surrounding wall and ditch for protection against the assault of brigands and plunderers. For while other crimes had stiff penalties and were very severely punished among this race even before the adoption of Christianity, no one was faulted for plundering. It brought no disgrace so long as it was practiced outside of one's own

---

[1] This explanation interprets *"Westfalen"* (The German form of "Westphalia") as meaning "fall (of the sun) in the West."

[2] There is no indication that K. ever did write such a work.

[3] The erroneous notion that Münster was named "Mediolanum" back in 584 can be attributed to the chronographer Valentine Müntzer, whom K. cites as his source about the foundation of the city in his later *Catalogue of the Bishops of Münster* (the story is also found in the cartographer Sebastian Münster).

territory, and for this reason it lacked any penalty or punishment; they allowed this either to train the youth or to thwart sloth.[4]

The town kept this name for some years, but in the end it gave up the old name and came to be called Mimimgardford, a word I find written for the first time in the year 696 in Chapter 15 of St. Marcellinus[5] in the time of Willibrord, the merciful first archbishop of Utrecht. | I have not yet discovered the reason for the change, but if one may resort to guessing, it appears that this designation consists of three elements. "Milan" is the name of Mediolanum in the Italian vernacular, "gard" the Vandal and Langobard name for "fortress," and "ford" is the German term for "crossing," so Mimimgardford is the crossing at the Milanese fortress, since the river Aa flows by on one side (the west), and over this river there was a crossing to the town (fortress). When a city was in some way taking shape as a result of the scattering of inhabitants around it, Milan ceased to be designated as a town and began to be called the Milanese fortress. No one should be surprised that in the first element the letter "l" was changed to "m" and "a" to "i," and that in place of "Milan" the barbarous country folk, being ignorant of the Italian language, pronounced it "Mimim, since we perceive that countless words have been, over the course of time, corrupted in this way or in an even more monstrous one. The final, native elements, on the other hand, were maintained uncorrupted.

Next, in the year 772, when Charlemagne received a public decree at the assembly of leading men at Worms to force the Westphalians and Saxons to embrace Christianity, Mimimgardford too was conquered and began to obey his rule. In order to strengthen the religion, which had first been introduced by St. Swibert, he erected in this town a famous monastery of regulars and canons and an episcopal see, which he endowed with various privileges and immunities. He put St. Ludger, a man of outstanding piety and a monk of the order of St. Benedict (as Witte attests,[6] all his successors down to Herman I adhered to this rule), in charge of it. Ludger was appointed on the understanding that by preaching the Gospel he would soften this people who were

11

---

[4] This sentence is a modified version of Caesar, *Gallic War* 6.23.6, which likewise explains why brigandry was permitted among the ancient Gauls.

[5] I.e., in Marcellinus' *Life of St. Swibert.*

[6] A Benedictine monk of Liesborn, Bernhard Witte (ca. 1465–ca. 1533) wrote a work on Westphalian history entitled *Historia antiquae occidentalis Saxoniae seu Westphaliae* ("History of ancient western Saxony or Westphalia"), which was published in Münster in 1778.

still uncivilized and their stone hearts which were not yet converted,
12   and win over many as a profit for Christ. | This holy man, who was
the first bishop, was not remiss in his efforts but performed the task
assigned to him with great profit. As the Christian faith and the zeal for
piety grew, so too did the honor, and especially the reverence, shown
to God's servants, and so too did their wealth. For whether at the urging of simplicity or of religion and piety, the inhabitants of that town
voluntarily dedicated to God not just all their own buildings in town
but also all their pastures, fields and manors outside the town when
they died without children, or at the request of the servants of God
they sold these to them at a tolerable price (it was considered sinful for
anything to be denied to the servants of God), or consecrated themselves
and their property to the Order. Thus, in a short time control over the
entire town and over all the surrounding properties was placed under
the legal power and discretion of the canons.

Since the vows to this monastery and its resources were growing,
many people were induced both by the piety of the canons and by
the advantages of the town to move their residence there, having first,
however, received permission to build on the Lords'[7] land. Hence, the
houses of many citizens are bound by servitude down to the present
day.[8] For every year the citizens purchase the right to dwell by paying
to the lord canons a certain fixed land rental called "*wordtgelt*" ("ground
money"), thereby attesting that the land (plot) for their buildings belongs
by right of ownership and possession to the canons.[9] Many people
thronged into the city, and being scattered around it and placing their
residences outside it, they made a fairly splendid suburban area. Eventually, after the number of inhabitants had increased and they acquired
the right of being burghers, this area was surrounded by a wall and
other fortifications. Accordingly, the fame of the monastery, which was
adorned with pious men (canons), endowed with various gifts, privileges and resources, and made lustrous through the great sanctity of
13   its prior, soon established the prosperity of the town and state. | This
is the reason why this famous monastery gradually overshadowed the

---

[7] This is K.'s term for the canons (see 95D).
[8] "Servitude" is a term of Roman law (though traditional Germanic law is meant
here), signifying that a piece of land had certain permanent obligations attached it
that the landowner owed to someone else.
[9] K.'s interpretation of this payment (quitrent) as betokening the canons' control of
the city was one of the points which drew upon K. the city council's ire and which he
was eventually forced to retract (see General Introduction 3b).

name "Mimimgardford," and both cities (the one in the center and the surrounding one) came to be called Monasterium (Münster), the specifying appellation turning into the proper name. Therefore, the name was given to this city not (as some believe) from the convent of noble nuns situated across the river[10] but from the convent of noblemen that is a monastery of pious men, since the monastery was superior in rank, splendor and age, which is the usual grounds for giving a name. For we read that the monastery was founded by Charlemagne, the most Christian emperor, whose feast day is still celebrated in the basilica on July 27, while the convent was founded by Herman I, the fourteenth bishop of the Church in Münster. Furthermore, the list of bishops refers to St. Ludger, the first bishop of this Church, and all his successors down to the tenth (Dodo) as bishops of Mimimgardford, and then for a while it calls the next successors the bishops of Mimimgardford or of Münster without distinction, and for this reason it can be established without dispute that this city was not named after the convent of nuns, which was established by the fourteenth bishop. Therefore, the remaining conclusion is, as I too would believe, that the city took its name from the principal and more noble monastery of men. It would not, however, be my wish in stating this to lessen the authority of others, and I leave the matter undecided for each person's consideration and opinion.

This is what I thought should be said about the town's humble beginning.

---

[10] I.e., the Convent Across-the-River (see 48–57D).

CHAPTER THREE

14   LOCATION OF THE CITY AND NATURE OF THE PEOPLE

If one examines the surface of the earth, the Saxon Milan or Mimimgardford (now Münster) was built in just about the center of Old
Saxony, which is now Westphalia, between the Rhine and Weser and
not far from the Aa, in a place that is level all around and green with
very pleasant pastures. For this reason it is properly considered the
leading city of Westphalia. Outside the city there are also very pleasant gardens planted with various kinds of shrubs and plants, and the
citizens go out to these gardens and enjoy themselves there, washing
away every sort of mental distress and grief with good wine and beer.
In these gardens, there also grows such a plentiful supply of cabbages,
turnips, roots and other such produce that you would think that the
inhabitants would live on this alone if the great number of pigs did
not consume a large part of it.

 If we take a look at the face of the sky, the city is placed in the
temperate zone mixed of heat and cold, between the tropic of cancer
and the arctic circle, or, to speak more expansively and exactly, between
the last star to the south in the tail of Ursa Major (called Bononatz by
the Arabs)[1] and the middle star to the north in the same constellation.
Its zenith (to use astronomical terminology) or vertical point is the
rather dim little star that forms a triangle with those more noticeable
or brighter stars. Every day, this star traverses the vertical point of the
city, but on April 19 at the eleventh hour of the night, when the last
decury of Sagittarius encompasses the horizon in the east, as Gemini is
setting and Aries holds the corner of the earth, it looks directly down
on the city in a perpendicular manner. For this reason it is justly called
the city's zenith or vertical star. The latitude (elevation of the pole) is
measured at 52 degrees, 14 minutes, and from this it is easy to agree
under what part of the sky the city is located.

 It is not difficult, if we learn the nature of the sky and of the heavenly bodies to which the city is subject, to determine the nature of the

---

[1] The normal form in Western languages of the Arabic name for this star (techni-
cally, star eta of Ursa Major) is Benetnash.

location and of the people living in it. For by their motion, light and influence, the sky and the stars act upon our composite bodies, as the natural philosophers[2] insist, | in some way impelling them, with the   15
secret powers that they produce, to produce similar works. It is not, therefore, ridiculous that as even Ptolemy[3] attests, the nature of men should be especially dependent upon the various aspects of the sky and the qualities of locations. For it is impossible for behavior not to follow the temperament and mixture in bodies.[4] We have no doubt that Cyrus, the king of the Persians, also noted this. After the Persians had decided to abandon their mountainous, rough and unpleasant region and to move to a softer and more pleasing one, Cyrus did not allow this, saying that the habits and traits of plants and men also resemble their location.[5] In this way you would find regions that provide their inhabitants and visitors with inducements not merely to virtues but also to many faults. For this is how the delights of Campania broke Hannibal, who was undefeated in battle, and gave the Romans the opportunity to defeat him.[6] Hence, it is clear that the qualities of locations have a great force and energy, and when these are poured into bodies that use them, they affect them in the same way. The legal commentator Baldus[7] also claims, on *Digest* chapter "On the aedilician

---

[2] "Natural philosophy" is the aspect of ancient and medieval philosophy that examined the natural world. Gradually separating from philosophy during the sixteenth and seventeenth centuries, this study would eventually turn into the discipline that we know as "science."

[3] Ptolemy of Alexandria was a second-century Greek astronomer whose *Almagest* (to give it the Arabic title by which it was later known) was the standard treatise on astronomy during the Late Middle Ages.

[4] Late medieval medical thought held that the body consisted of a mixture (temperament) based on the relative amounts of the four basic elements (earth, air, fire, water), and according to astrological theory, the different heavenly bodies exerted varying influences (which literally "flowed down") upon these elements, and thus upon the temperament.

[5] This story comes from a climactic anecdote in Herodotus' *History* (9.122) in which Cyrus states that soft lands breed soft men, and that the same land cannot produce both pleasant crops and hard men.

[6] The Carthaginian general Hannibal inflicted a number of crushing defeats on the Romans during the Second Punic War (218–202 B.C.). After his victory at Cannae in 216, the Romans refused to meet him in open battle in Italy, where he remained for more than a decade. Campania was the rich area to the south of Rome, and some in antiquity attributed his failure to achieve another great victory after Cannae to the enervating influence of his long stay in Campania.

[7] Petrus Baldus de Ubaldis (1327–1406), an influential Italian jurist who among other works wrote a commentary on the *Digest* (a massive ancient collection of excerpts from the works of Roman jurists).

edict," law *"Quod si nolit,"* section *"Qui mancipia,"* that people's traits are improved or worsened as a result of the disposition of the air or of the location.[8] Accordingly, since this city of ours is subject to the constellation Aquarius and to Saturn as its lord, and since it has been built not in the middle of the temperate zone but virtually at its end near the arctic circle, it by no means enjoys a uniform moderating of heat and cold in either direction, and is more affected by the cold of the nearby arctic circle and the influence of those stars.[9] Therefore, the inhabitants of this location, living as they do under a colder part of the sky, are mostly tall in stature, and have wild and uncouth habits. Hence it is that in many a place they call a crude person who deviates step-by-step from civilized behavior a Westphalian, as if the influence of the stars and the nature of the location have impressed

16 upon this race of men a certain crudeness which they cannot escape. | They are more sensible than stupid (though they despise the liberal arts),[10] and are strong and fit for enduring any hard work you please. They are, however, bad at tolerating thirst and hunger and are more ravening than other races, though they are content with a simple fare that is by no means extravagant. They have a pale complexion and hair that is not curly but long and flowing. They are not clever or tricky, but straightforward, serious, and steadfast. Once they have adopted an opinion, they would not rashly change it were it not for Saturn's working of greed, suspicion, deception, faithlessness, obstinacy, envy, and strife in them. All these characteristics are not suddenly increased by Saturn. Rather, because of his fairly slow movement he increases them gradually by dripping them down from above. Eventually, their minds are inflamed on both sides, and if not a resort to arms, then certainly manifest divisiveness, and after that strife among the nobles and the heads of the state, bursts forth. By this the commons too are tainted, and become involved in the same evil, and in the end it is only with difficulty that this contention can be lulled, to the great detriment of the inhabitants and commons. We find by experience that this evil has been instilled in the location by nature. For history attests that from

---

[8] The relevant passage in the *Digest* (21.1.31.21) discusses the seller's obligation to reveal a slave's ethnic origin.

[9] Here "arctic" is not used of the extreme north, as in modern usage, but signifies the northern regions in general (from "actos," the Greek for bear, which is also the name in Latin for the Big and Little Dippers or *ursa major* and *minor*).

[10] Presumably, this statement reflects the attitude of a disgruntled educator.

the very beginning of the city right down to the present day there have never been eighteen continuous years of steady peace without it being disturbed or cut short by new disturbances.

From these qualities there flow many others which I find it more appropriate to shift to the general description of Westphalia.[11] Do not, however, imagine that the people of Münster are so imbued with and constantly devoted to these habits that they cannot adopt others.[12] The nature of the location does offer up these and other characteristics to them, but | this "disposition"[13] of nature is sometimes changed. This is why you could see some who are short, some dark-complexioned, some weak and unwarlike, some calm and hostile to unpolished crudeness, some clever, some fickle and unreliable, some extravagant in their dinner service. These people changed their residence and moved here from elsewhere, or intermingled with foreign stocks through marriage, or shed their in-born crudeness through living with other races for a long time, or, after bringing here what they learned while abroad, imitate these customs like apes and pass them on to their children. Hence, the townsmen have been so transformed and made so soft and effeminate through following a more dainty way of life that there seems to be just about nothing in the state that savors of and reflects the renowned humbleness and crude simplicity of the ancient days. Sometimes, however, there is a return to native character. Small wonder, too. You can drive off nature with a stick, but it always rushes back.[14]

Hence, the people of Münster use partly their own customs and partly those of other, foreign races, and this dissimilarity in habits has begotten a disparity in attire. For some follow the Spanish, some the Italians, some the Turks, some the Mongols, some the Poles, some the English, some the Brabantines, some the Brunswickers, who are always responsible for novel clothing in Germany. Few people now reflect in the humbleness of their attire the renowned simplicity of the ancient days. What is the cause? We despise our own things and exalt those

17

---

[11] I.e., to his envisioned work on the subject (see 9D).

[12] In this paragraph, K. shifts away from the immediately preceding discussion of astrology and returns to the earlier notion of geographical determination of character. Here, K. seems to imagine that the pristine simplicity of honesty of the locals was negatively affected through the corrupting influence of foreigners, but according to him the native goodness of Westphalians will reassert itself (presumably as indicated through the reestablishment of traditional Catholic religious practice in Münster).

[13] The Greek term διάφεσις is used.

[14] A slight modification of Horace, *Epistles* 1.10.24.

of others. While local things stink, exotic and foreign things have a delightful smell. While we cast off things produced here, we hanker after imported ones. While we shun old things, we embrace new ones. Things that are now new in our eyes readily become dated. Hence it is that we always pant after new things without ever being content with what we have. In fact, if God, who favors all men equally and wishes none to perish, had not now in His great mercy sent to us from elsewhere learned, eminent and well-spoken gentlemen who are steadfast in the business of the faith, in order that they should restrain those eager for novelty and protect the ancestral religion through the aid of God, a period of five or even two years would hardly pass without horrible strife and new disturbance.[15] For through such men as His tools, God

18   Almighty | preserves states in the recognition of the truth and in the best condition. It is these men by whom this people, with its inclination to certain faults and thirst for new disturbances, is attracted to the loving pursuit of virtue and tranquility. It is they who teach men to avoid what is base and to copy what is respectable. It is they who retain the citizens in their duty. It is they who change or avert the influences of the stars. It is they, finally, who rule the stars. Accordingly, press on industriously with your calling, you most honorable gentlemen, and toil without shirking or flagging in the vineyard of the Lord! Upon you the state rests as on columns. It is so strengthened by your teaching and examples that it will never be shaken by new disturbances here in the world, but will stand firm like the Marpesian cliff[16] against all the waves of heretics.[17]

Let these statements about the location of our city and habits of the inhabitants suffice.

---

[15] It is not clear who exactly these pious foreigners are. Perhaps K. has in mind the efforts of the Jesuits to bolster the Catholic establishment and to encourage the attempt to restore Protestant areas to allegiance to Rome.

[16] A reference to *Aeneid* 6.471.

[17] Now how in this paragraph K. begins with a specific complaint about the adoption of foreign attire (with a parochial swipe at the Brunswickers), generalizes this into a disparagement of preferring novelty to tradition, and finally converts the topic to the adoption of foreign religious practice (i.e., Protestant reforms) in place of Catholic tradition. Implicitly, the Protestant religious developments were in K.'s view of no more significance than the wearing of flashy fashions from abroad (and should be cast off as quickly).

CHAPTER FOUR

FORTIFICATIONS OF THE CITY

If cities deserve praise by virtue of their outer fortification, then this
city will be pre-eminent and distinguished not only among those in
Westphalia but also among those in many regions.[1] For it is heavily
fortified with gates, ditches, ramparts, walls, towers, and other bulwarks
made both of stone and earth and of wood. It would certainly have
a circular shape if could extend to the north-northwest. Its diameter
is 1610 short paces (steps), that is, 4002 1/2 feet. From this it is easy,
since the periphery or circumference of any circle is three times the
diameter plus one seventh of it, to calculate that the circuit of the
walls measures 5031 5/7 feet.[2] It has ten gates named after the saints
to whom most of the churches are dedicated. Hence, it can be inferred
without obscurity | that the churches are much older than the gates.   19
Accordingly, I would imagine that since they gave their names to the
gates, most churches were already built before the city was surrounded
with walls and gates.[3] We enter through these gates not in a straight line
but in a diagonal path with much to-ing and fro-ing, and the example
of many other cities shows that this was brought about through careful planning in order to prevent frequent blows made by artillery from
opening up a straight path into the city for the enemy. Instead, the
great momentum of the shots was to be slackened when they smashed
into the obstruction furnished by rampart or wall.

In the direction of sunrise on the equinox, the direction from which
the constellations first begin to shine, and the winds from the south-
southeast and east stirred up torpor in the air with their gusts, there
is a gate that it is called Maurice's since it faces the prominent college

---

[1] This entire chapter was the initial cause of the city council's disquiet about K.'s
work, and it continued to take a prominent place among the passages to which the
council took exception. The council objected to K.'s detailed description of the city's
defenses that even included measurements, and given the importance of the walls to
the city's safety, it is easy to see how those who were anxious about such matters would
have taken this account amiss (see General Introduction 3b).

[2] The schoolmaster cannot resist adding in an edifying lesson in arithmetic!

[3] Logically, this circumstance demonstrates only that the *names* of the gates were
more recent than the dedications of the churches.

dedicated to St. Maurice that is located outside the city. From this gate there goes a road that is higher than the public one and is paved at the expense of the college. Protected on one side by garden walls and shaded on the other by leafy willows, it extends all the way to St. Maurice's cemetery. With a wondrous sort of delight it receives travelers already worn out and directs them to the city after making them forget their weariness. This entrance to the city has two bulwarks raised up out of earth on the right side. While the lower bulwark protects the ditch and rampart extending to the Horst Gate, the neighboring one, because of its height, protects not only the gate itself and the other fortifications to the city's left but also the fields all around. Within the stockade on the right side is the chapel dedicated to St. Antony, where a certain number of paupers are fed. Full provision is also made for their heavenly nourishment, and on every holy day the mass is celebrated for them by the priests. The parish of St. Maurice is responsible for the administration of the sacraments. For we read that by the authority and at the expense of Louis, the thirty-fifth bishop of Münster, the chapter of St. Maurice built and founded this chapel along with the cemetery and alms-house in their parish in the year 1368, on the understanding
20   that the city council had the right | to appoint the parish priest for the chapel and that the men of St. Maurice's would authorize such appointments.[4]

In the direction of sunrise in winter, at the time when the southeast wind also blows, there is a very great bulwark that juts out in a circular shape. Starting with a stone foundation at its root, it rises up to a height of almost ten feet above the water, and on top of it is placed a tall mound of earth that has low bastions attached to it on both sides, rather like breasts. The construction of these bastions, which are situated back from the water, is such that to a great distance on both sides they can protect the ramparts and ditches against enemy assault with projectiles. Through the middle of this mound there is a path to the gate that is named Servatius' after St. Servatius, whose church is near the wall. Outside this gate is a mill that grinds grain by being driven by the gusting of the wind and for this reason they call it a windmill.[5]

---

[4] In 1531–1532, there would be much wrangling about the prince's desire to have the radical preacher Bernard Rothman removed from the position of preacher at St. Maurice's.

[5] The point of this circumlocution is that Classical Latin had no word for "windmill" (such mills were a medieval invention).

There is a fairly long interval from this gate to Ludger's Gate, and in just about the middle of this distance can be seen a bend or jutting corner in the course of the rampart and ditch. For this reason, a certain underground fortification has been built there in the palisade, so that it can protect the ditches in both directions (towards both Ludger's Gate and Servatius' Gate).

Ludger's Gate, named after the nearby church of St. Ludger, is exposed to the south and has a very broad and strong fortification. Its base and foundations are quite large and made of the hardest stones, while its upper part above the circuit is rather narrow, being built in a circular shape out of bricks and filled with earth on the inside. Under the cover of this vast work there is a road by which the city is reached. | 21 Between the city's ramparts and ditches is the house of the archers, in which they feast after their practice sessions and celebrate holidays. To the left of this gate there is a rather low bastion raised up out of stones that can protect most of the rampart and ditch with arrows and catapults in the direction of Giles' Gate. Outside of this gate can be seen two windmills and a fairly large field in which the citizens keep their timbers for construction. From the Horst Gate to this one the ground level of the city is pretty much flat, but from here on it can be perceived that it gradually becomes lower and more inclined. For this reason, the ditch between Ludger's Gate and this one is blocked with a stone barrier that separates the upper water from the lower, preventing them from flowing together. Otherwise, no water would stay in the upper part of the ditch, since it would all flow downhill by the force of nature.

Giles' Gate faces south-southeast, and it takes its name from the church dedicated to St. Giles, as does a whole lane. On the right side of this gate there is a bastion raised up out of earth, and outside of the gate there are seven mills driven by wind.

Before the siege there was also a gate towards the winter sunset in the southwest, which was named Bischoping Gate after an ancient line of noblemen. It is now torn down and in its place has been erected a massive, strongly fortified structure, so that the enemy could secure no access to the city from this direction even if the townsmen were all asleep. At its base the wall protects its defenders by extending too far for any gunshot to reach them. From here a few barriers are built across the ditches. For at this point the ground level of the city rises up and becomes more sloping.

22   In the direction of the sunset on the equinox, the gate named after the church of the Holy Virgin Mary receives the gentle west wind. This gate is surrounded by a huge mass of earth placed on a stone foundation, and a road passes through the middle of it to the gate. This fortification is so tall that if necessary it could also easily protect the other palisades and ditches in either direction against any shots. Here there are, to the left above the water in the ditches, fortifications made of strong timber and resting on beams, being full of loopholes on all sides. They call these fortifications "swallow cages," and from them the surfaces of the ditches can be protected by the efforts of a few townsmen from being attacked or assaulted by the enemy. In this same ditch there is a barrier (obstacle) that blocks the downward flow of the water and hinders its loss.

In the direction of the sunset in summer, the Jewish Gate faces the northwest wind. It is named after the Jews' Field, a place that they once occupied in which they placed their abodes. This is demonstrated well enough even now by the heads of Jews made of Badenberg marble that are placed there. The Jews were bleeding the Christians dry with their greedy usury, as they cleverly cheated them with their business deals, carried off everything for themselves, and in their customary way they left no stone unturned in their destruction of the Christians, their only aim being to pile up their own possessions.[6] For this reason, they were driven into exile, and both their synagogue and their houses were pulled down. Their tombs and stone inscriptions were relocated to the New Bridge Gate, where they are placed both in the wall on the right hand side and on the other side within the city, in the place above the water where there is a privy for public use; they can still be seen on stones jutting out from the wall. This gate has stone towers attached to it like sores on either side for the defense and protection of the ramparts and ditches. The gate also has other very strong barricades on whose stone bases are placed massive structures of earth. In this place the roughness of the ground means that there is no need

---

[6] The vehemence of this unmotivated tirade against the Jews shows that K. shared the virulently anti-Semitic views that were common in late medieval and early modern Germany, and the nonchalance with which he expresses himself indicates that K. expected his assertions to be uncontroversial in the opinion of his anticipated audience. The sharpness of these comments, which is out of keeping with the normally restrained tone adopted by K., seem to reflect a hostility that is even stronger than the antipathy which he felt about the Anabaptists.

for obstacles to hold back the water in the higher sections. From this tower can be seen four mills for grinding grain.

The Cross Gate, which is struck by the snowy gust of the northwest 23 wind, looks at a strong bastion on its right. On the stone base of this bastion is placed a great mound of earth, to which a fort of unexpected design is attached. Here there are also some water barriers across the ends of the ditch. If the force of the water along the gate were not checked to an amazing height, we would see some sloping ditches completely bereft of water. This gate retains to this day the name "Cross" that was bestowed on it in ancient times. For the following custom concerning a large wooden cross on top of the church had been received by our ancestors, and was handed down to posterity. This cross was a gift from Frederick, the twenty-second bishop, and onto it was fixed a bronze image of the crucified Christ that was covered with silver plates and supported by the relics of saints on the inside. The cross was kept hanging by an iron chain above the intervening space that separates the choir from the rest of the church (this area is commonly called the "Apostles' crossing"). The custom was that on the feast of Pentecost, the cross would be attended by two chanters, and carried through the individual houses of the citizens. Neighbors would take it in exultation from neighbors, as if they shared in the sufferings represented by the cross, and readily and joyfully desired their neighbors to be relieved of every affliction. This was certainly a great incitement and spur to mutual affection. When this was finished, the cross was put back on the Friday directly preceding the feast of the Nativity of John. For on that day it was handed over to the butchers, who would bring it with some specific songs to the Cross Gate at about the third hour of the night after the celebration of a mass in the Church of the Holy Virgin. Having brought it there, they put it on a cart, making use of the services of the beadles. Then it was passed on from one peasant's cart to another at fixed intervals, being transported for a few miles. In certain places, a sermon was given for the benefit of the accompanying crowd. In the end, after it had been carried around in this way, they return it to the Cross Gate, where in the customary way they washed off with wine the dust that had stuck to the Cross during the journey, and gave it back to the butchers, who brought it to the church, singing in dissonant, confused voices. | There the cleric received it and put 24 it back in its place. If the chain by which it would be dragged back up creaked several times, it was superstitiously thought to foretell that there would be fertility.

In the direction of the northern pole, where the north wind assails the walls with shivering from the cold, there is a gate that takes its name from the New Bridge that was first built there. It now has bastions to the right of the butchers. Here the Aa, which flows through the town and takes off every sort of filth, departs under the bridge. In this place, the river grazes the walls, which are protected by a piled up rampart, for a distance of some feet outside the city. The river departs from the walls by the citadel, which is exceedingly strongly fortified by the thickness of the walls and is located outside all the walls of the city. This citadel is thought to protect not only the gate but also the part of the city that extends to the Horst Gate.

In the direction of the north wind is the Horst Gate, named after the word "*horst*," which in our language means an "inclined field suitable for pasturage or sowing." The gate has on the left a very large forecourt that is surrounded from top to bottom with a stone wall and stuffed with earth on the inside. To the left of this court is the lower citadel, from which an enemy can be warded off in the direction of Maurice's Gate. Outside of this gate there were two windmills before the siege, but now there is only one.

The whole city is surrounded by twin ditches, which are fairly broad and deep. While the first ditch abuts on the open fields and gardens, the second one, which is dug out on the other side of a rampart, is equipped in various locations with assorted barriers, barricades, defensive works, and swallows' cages, so that it would allow no enemy, however violent, to pass. In between the two ditches there is a rampart made of earth dug up from both ditches. This rampart is fairly thick and steep and 25 has a sheer face. | It encloses the second (inner) ditch with a continuous circuit, and is crowned on its ridge and high point with a wooden stockade that has teeth on top. A little bit lower down, not very far from the water, a thicket of dense, bristling briers and intertwined brambles goes around, and not only can this not be penetrated but it is not even possible to see through it. These two defenses will easily check the ascent of those who have already crossed the ditch. The rampart also has within it very many shelters, hidden passageways and concealed tunnels from which the enemy can be attacked on all sides with guns and pikes, but it is better to pass over these matters in silence than to make them public knowledge.

Next there is a double wall whose circuit is broken only at the gates. These walls surround another rampart, which is set between and supported by them on either side. One wall is close to the second ditch.

Being exceedingly strong and tall and distinguished by its bastions and loopholes, in which the night watches are kept, this is the real wall of the city. Since there is a very long interval between Servatius' Gate and Ludger's, two towers are added to the wall between those gates. One tower is named after Nitzing, a nearby convent of nuns, and it terrifies prisoners with just its name.[7] The other, which lacks its own name, is made famous by the residence of the hangman. There are also two towers between the Cross Gate and the New Bridge Gate. One is called the "Bogey Man's Tower" because of spectres seen there at night and the fear of ghosts. It is said that the other used to be the gate of the count of Tecklenburg, and that through it he had access to the city at his own discretion. They say that he sold this right to the city council during a banquet. In this interval there is also a little tower in which gunpowder is ground.

The other wall is lower and encloses a sloping rampart that is surrounded by a fairly roomy open area throughout the city. I pass over many things in this account: the secret hidden passageways out of the city through | the ramparts and ditches; the multiple doors at each   26 gate that are equipped with a zigzagging course; the swinging doors at the first doorway, which we call gateways; the supply of every kind of armor and weapon, which is so plentiful that not only are there enough for all the defensive works of the city but in their placement along the entire circuit of the rampart hardly one foot's space is unoccupied (and in addition, you could see larger guns mounted on wheels placed, if need be, across the marketplace and certain lanes). I also pass over the very pleasing and delightful aspect of the area between the ramparts and ditches, which virtually surpasses Thessalian Tempe.[8]

So much for our terse glance at the circuit and fortifications of the city. Now we will enter the city to describe the churches.

---

[7] I.e., as is often the case with medieval and early modern towns in Germany, the prison for detaining suspects was located in one of the towers in the city walls.

[8] A rural area of Greece much celebrated in ancient poetry for its idyllic beauty.

CHAPTER FIVE

DESCRIPTIONS OF THE CITY'S CHURCHES

In just about the center of the city there is a gentle hill with a roomy flat surface. In the past, after the Saxons returned from the Italian Milan, they surrounded this flat area with a few fortifications and filled the inner area with private buildings. This area took on the shape of a city and it was first called Mediolanum (Milan) and then Mimimgardford, and finally it, along with the surrounding urban area, took the name Monasterium (Münster), as was stated in Chapter Two. The diameter of its surface area amounts to 390 steps (shorter paces), and its circumference to almost 1226. When a violent dispute arose between Count Derek of Winzenburg, who was the eighteenth bishop of the Church of Münster, and the Lord's Lords, the latter conspired unanimously against the bishop with the nobles of the diocese, who are called vassals, and with the citizens of the outlying city. The Lords claimed that the bishop was not in charge of them, and expelled him from the diocese. As the leader of the just cause and in reliance on his friends, the bishop took refuge with Duke Lothar | of Saxony across the Weser, who was later distinguished with the imperial crown.[1] Being aided both by the power of this prince and of the counts of Winzenburg and by the protection of arms, he attacked Münster with an armed force on May 7, 1097, and plundered everything. He burned both private and public buildings as well as the churches (apart from the chapel dedicated to St. Ludger across the water), hurling into the city burning arrows and javelins that gave off fire, and he razed to the ground the walls that surrounded this open area, which is now called the Lords' Field. But the noble lords and the citizens, who now became suppliants, he restored to favor, forgetting all indignities done to him, and he returned the privileges which he had taken away, and added new ones to boot. Lothar, however, took off with him those responsible for the insurrection, and eventually released them after fining them heavily.

27

---

[1] Lothar was Holy Roman Emperor in 1125–1137.

After being thrown down in this way, these walls were restored by Borchard of Holte, the nineteenth bishop. He raised them higher, so that they would be safer against the attacks of the count of Arnsberg and the lords of Meinhoevel, who were constant enemies of the Church of Münster, and kept on attacking it. He also repaired the burnt down church and the city gates through which there is access to this field at the cardinal points of the compass. At the eastern gate he placed a church to the Archangel Michael and at the western one a chapel dedicated to St. George (its tower is now named after a mirror[2]). Above the northern gate, the pastor of the church of St. Nicholas lives in a dwelling that was built there, and to the south there is an exit over an arch girded with stones on both sides. All these gates are now open without ever being closed. For the inhabitants | of this field are satisfied if they are surrounded by the fortifications of the outlying city and are protected by the common watches of the citizens, and for this reason they allow their walls to collapse and decay over the passage of time though intentional neglect.

28

Along the inner side of these walls, the prince built a very large palace, which is distinguished with his insignia, and the Lord's Lords built magnificent halls and residences that are very appropriate for their duties. There were very pleasant gardens sown with various trees and very nice smelling vines and plants, and these they enclosed by raising up a different set of walls from the earlier ones in a continuous circuit. They shared out the dwellings among themselves, so that each had his own home, but the separate dwellings were divided up with a priority given to age. They each had their own gate, on which they hung the heads and feet of beasts taken by hunting or shooting, and the common people measured their splendor on this basis.

Living in a circle, they trespassed on the open area at the edge of the town, and abandoned in every direction the wide, open area in the center. In this open area can be seen the splendor of a most august and illustrious church. It was truly a basilica, being built in the shape of a double cross out of smoothed stones and extending to a length of 360 feet and a width of 103. The arms of the cross spread out to a fair distance, and are roofed with lead plates from which the rainwater is taken by gutters and drained off. Above the choir there rises up from the roof a tall and graceful spire held up by columns. It is so tall that

---

[2] "*Spiegelturm.*"

it gives a vista in all directions and displays a bell hanging in it that marks off the hours with hammer blows. This tower is, like the others, distinguished by a gilded globe, a cross, and a weathercock.

29 Attached to this basilica on the southern side towards the choir is an edifice consisting of a very magnificent and very tall column, the right side of which is decorated with an image of St. Walpurgis and the left with one of St. Gertrude that is awe-inspiring. Above them are placed images that are wondrously sculpted of Badenberg marble and painted in a lifelike way with various colors, showing the angelic annunciation, the nativity of the Lord, the offering of the Magi, and the passion and burial of Christ. At the top there used to be a stone statue that was knocked down by the Anabaptists. Now it has been restored in bronze and portrays Christ in his triumphal resurrection. Weighing 106 pounds apart from the iron by which it is attached, it gives no little increase to the church's majesty, and in its hand there is a rotating symbol made of iron that is gilded and shows the direction of the wind. On the outside there are also very tall columns and various arches and pinnacles around the church. On these there used to be various monuments, but the Anabaptists knocked them down, and these have not yet been repaired. Among the ones on top of the choir were a likeness of St. Walpurgis, the image of a white foal (the symbol of Westphalia), and countless statues of Solomon, Sampson and other pious men.

In the same direction (the west) there is also a building attached to the church not far from the towers. The common people call it "Paradise," and it is famous for the noise of legal cases. Above its threshold can be seen statues of the First Parents[3] that portray the violation of God's command under the tree of life, and they are represented with such skill and accuracy in local marble that you would think them alive.

30 On the columns of this building statues | of St. Ludger, the Archangel Michael, St. George, and Charlemagne were arrayed at intervals.

To the west are two stone towers of pretty much the same height. These were built by Herman of Katzenellenbogen, the twenty-fifth bishop of the Church of Münster, and on them were placed two lofty, lead-covered steeples that used to adorn the city before the Anabaptist uproar. One resounds high up with a multitude of bells by which it summons the priests and congregation to divine services both by night

---

[3] I.e., Adam and Eve.

and by day, while the other one, which lacks bells, provides a home for jackdaws and crows on its roof. At the bottom, the vaulting sometimes resounds with the ringing of a large number of coins, since this is the location of the common treasury for the whole diocese. In between the towers there is a place, enclosed partly with walls and partly with doors and wooden fences, where the prince restores military benefices to the nobles after interposing an oath. This place has been described by Master Henry Rupe, the procurator of the bishop's consistory, who stands out for erudition and judgment among all the procurators of this court, in a learned and elegant poem that he published[4] in praise of the election and installation of Lord William as the bishop of the Church of Münster:

> There is a place, where the sun descends to the western axis,
>   And where the two towers stand like masses of stone.
> In the midst of these a new wooden frame with iron
>   Is clad, where the double door opens a path.
> This structure has five wooden columns
>   And new stones provide new flooring.
> Here a straight seat, worthy of your rule of the place,
>   Is set, adorned with its decoration.
> Here the assembly of nobles, famed for its old-time ways,
>   Is kept with customary rites that are theirs.

31

To the north, a square-shaped colonnade enclosed with a colored balustrade surrounds a path paved with stone. From here there is a little garden sown with fragrant plants and shrubs. It is very pleasant and is surrounded by a wooden fence and then a green thicket of brambles. In these locations (both on the path and in the colonnade), the Lord's Lords have their burials with glorious epitaphs. Here, in addition to many other monuments of famous men, there remains that of Rudolph Langen, who was a very important and learned man in the eyes of all the learned, and brought this college a great addition to its prestige.[5]

> Famous, while Langen lived in our world, as
>   Protector of the learned and salvation of the poor,
> Then, when the envious fates took such a jewel away,
>   He brought grief to the learned and hunger to the poor.

---

[4] The poem was published in 1555 for the installation of William II of Ketteler.
[5] Langen died in 1519.

There also remains the epitaph to the deacon Roger Smising, who
had such influence with everyone because of his learning, experience
and authority that they did not hesitate to call him the father of his
homeland,[6] on the grounds that by his sage advice he put out part
of the blaze of Anabaptism.[7] At his funeral not only did the people
of the whole diocese seem to grieve but so did the domestic animals,
churches and paving stones. Here I pass over other memorials to pious
men, since it would take a long time to describe them all. The vicars
have mostly taken over for their burials the inside of the little garden,
which is completely surrounded with thickets and brambles.

    In the colonnade towards the east there are three chapels, each
32 equipped with one altar and fairly substantial revenues. | The largest
and most elegant of these was dedicated in the past to St. Clement
and now to the Holy Virgin, and in it the choristers celebrate the mass
for the dead starting from the hour of six in the morning. The second
(middle-sized) chapel is dedicated to St. Anne, the mother of Mary,
while the third (smallest) one, which also lacks windows, is dedicated to
St. Elizabeth. In the middle of the colonnade an image inscribed on
white stone portrays Christ on the Cross with the thieves hanging on
either side of him, and admonishes the passers-by to piety.

    Lest I should seem to have passed over the origin of the Old Church,
I have decided that a few words need to be said about this. Most people
ascribe its foundation to Charlemagne, but those people are suffering
from the gravest delusions. For in the year 696, when Frisia, Holland,
and the surrounding areas had abandoned idolatry, learned of Christ,
and become quite strong in the true faith, Swibert, the joint bishop
or suffragan of St. Willibrord, the first bishop of Utrecht, took some
learned and pious men (Williric, Gerard, Derek, and Boso) and set
off for ancient Saxony (modern Westphalia) to preach Christ to those
33 crude men whose hearts were worse than stone-like. Here and there |
in that land, he began to spread the Gospel successfully with his eloquence and miracles, and then, at the approach of winter, he came
to Mimimgardford (modern Münster), where he very bitterly and to
the point of astonishment inveighed against the idols among savage
men because they despised the true creator and worshipped empty
creations. He softened the hearts of the people to such an extent that

---

[6] *Pater patriae*, an honorific born by Roman emperors.
[7] Smising died in 1548.

they abandoned their obstinacy, and competed with one another in uniting around the words of life, which they earnestly embraced. He also confirmed his doctrine by performing a few miracles. For a certain wealthy woman whose name is not recorded was severely toiling from convulsions and the paralysis of her limbs. She succumbed to such an extent that none of her limbs could perform their functions, so she spent a great deal of money on doctors and surgeons—in vain. Perceiving no help from them and hearing of the presence of such a pious man, who was preaching of an unusual god, she was now confident of relief and asked to be taken to meet and see Swibert in person. There this holy man immediately restored her to her prior health and to the use of her limbs before an assembly of the entire people, using not the drugs of doctors or the plasters of surgeons but only the saving name of the crucified Jesus Christ and the sign of the Cross. In returning home, she was aided by assistance not of porters but of Jesus Christ, and she glorified God. Being a wealthy woman, she wished to gratify her doctor, and upon Swibert's advice she built at her own expense beside her house a church in which the glory of Jesus Christ, in whose name she had regained her bodily health, should be propagated among the pagan nations and the newly-converted Christians would invoke His holy name and receive the sacraments. This church was not unreasonably dedicated to St. Paul, since it was on the day of Paul's conversion[8] that this noble patroness felt the benefit to her body and soul when she was at the same time converted to the faith and received salvation. Such reasoning would lead me to believe that the old Lord's Church was built by a noble patroness and dedicated to St. Paul before Charlemagne's expedition against Saxony, and that after the conquest of Westphalia it rested upon pious men who had been convened in a single monastery and college to support the new religion like firm columns. Since piety was increasing there greatly through the succession of good men, the church seemed too meagre | 34 to suffice for the great multitude that was rushing to join the Christian faith every day, and therefore they hurriedly finished the structure for a new church, eagerly tearing down the incomplete old one. We read that Dodo, the tenth bishop of Münster, incurred some expense and difficulty in transferring the canons of the Old Church along with their properties and revenues. After the Frisians in particular had brought

---

[8] January 25.

very rich gifts, and the other races in the surrounding area had been
kindled with love for the new religion, the canons became so wealthy
that they could barely understand the nature of the change which they
had undergone and the abundance of their suddenly piled up riches.
In those days piety begat wealth, but in the present day, now that this
wealth has grown up, it is trampling upon its mother.

Since they were awash in opulent resources, the church that had been
dedicated by Dodo, burned by Derek of Winzenburg, and repaired by
Borchard of Holte, was to a large extent torn down and then rebuilt
in grander fashion at great expense, as can now be seen, because large
numbers of people visited it on a regular basis from the surrounding
population.[9] Accordingly, Count Derek of Isenburg, the seventeenth
bishop of Münster, summoned workmen and a very knowledgeable
architect, transported stone blocks and bought lime, timber and the
other things necessary for construction, and in the year A.D. 1225 set
35   down the first stone while reciting the words of a fixed formula, | and
ordained that that day should be celebrated as a festival. Approximately
thirty-six years intervened from that day until the consecration,[10] which
was performed by Gerard of Mark, the thirty-first bishop, who himself
presented to the new church two large bells dedicated by him.

After Dodo effected this transfer of the brothers (canons), the old
church was so stripped of divine worship, so divested of its revenues
and income through their transfer, and so denuded of its decorations,
that nothing seemed to be left apart from the walls. This abandonment and desolation lasted until the time of Borchard, the nineteenth
bishop, who thought that the worship of God should not be lessened
but increased, and therefore this good prince restored twelve prebends[11]
to the old church. One of them was to provide for the canons present,
and is called "Bishop Borchard's prebend." His main intent was that
since the prebends of the brothers, who performed most of the work
and lacked any other support or maintenance, were meagre, they should
at least get more recompense and consolation in connection with their
work. This act of Borchard was confirmed with sealed letters not only

---

[9] Actually, Borchard preceded Derek as bishop, and the cathedral was burned three
times, in 1071, 1121 and 1197.

[10] Here K. follows the *Chronicle of the Bishops of Münster*, whose dating implies a
dedication in 1261, but documentary evidence shows that it took place in 1265.

[11] A prebend was the portion of the cathedral's income that was given to each
member of its chapter.

by his immediate successors but also by Herman I, the twenty-fifth bishop, in 1184, as well as by Derek, | the twenty-seventh. At that time (Borchard's), there first began to be two colleges, which differed in function and location. One was that of the Old Church, the other that of the New Church, and they have lasted down to our days in a continuous succession of pious men, though with much differentiation. For the one allows only men of a military order or of undiluted nobility into its assembly, and for a while they were also called the Brothers of St. Walpurgis. For it is said that this church is dedicated not only to St. Paul but also to St. Walpurgis as if under the protection of a co-patron saint, as is reasonably well indicated by the statue to her that used to stand towards the east on the roof at the top of the choir but was thrown down by the Anabaptists. The other college, however, admits anyone, provided they are freeborn, and as a distinction most people called them the Brothers of St. Paul. The former college grew not only in wealth and power but also in the number of noble canons, while the latter one seems to have seen no great increase in either numbers or wealth, though they do have sufficient resources for a respectable life in comparison with their duties. The canons of the Old Church have a deacon (and the second-rank clergy a chaplain) who is chosen from their own college, and they also have a provost, who is always chosen from the college of the New Church and receives a large part of the income.

But no one should imagine that the church which is now called the Old Church is the one that the famous matron built at her own expense at the suggestion of St. Swibert! For that church was in the location where the colonnade and cemetery of the canons now are. Consequently, between the ancient church and the New Church there was a small area for the burial of priests, and since this area seemed insufficiently large for all the dead bodies, since the Old Church blocks the windows of the larger one, and since the excessive closeness made the Lords disturb each other when singing rather loudly, especially on festival days, it was thought a good idea to have the Old Church relocated. Hence, by Florentius, the thirty-eighth bishop, they were granted ownership of the Bishop's Chapel with the consent of Harting, its rector, and to it they transferred everything once the Old Church was demolished, attending to their pious duties there to the present day. They shifted the Bishop's Altar (and its revenues), which is dedicated to St. Andrew, from there to the north side of the cathedral. To facilitate the move, the chapter of the cathedral also added to the

36

37

Old Church an open area with some buildings located alongside the Bishop's Chapel (this area was in the past owned through inheritance by Gertrud of Stoyfener).

Hence, with the removal of the oldest church, the greater basilica began to be more illustrious and the cemetery of the priests to be larger, and from then on the extreme closeness of the churches no longer caused the singing to become confused. That time was also the first to see the construction of a very splendid colonnade. It was in the year 1377 that the bishop's authorization and endowment were conceded and that the two colleges entered into their contractual agreement. Apart from the highest altar and the one in the chapel, there are now five altars in this church and ten vicars who tend to them.

38   There is an organ that plays many notes at once, and it is praised with the following verses, which are inscribed on the wall:

> This work wrought in sweetly beaming finery—
>   How it sounds when played by a learned hand!
> Not the dying swan, nor the nightingale with its chirp,
>   Pours so varied a song from its sweet mouth!

The canons of the Old Church do not have their own bells, it being sufficient for them if they are summoned for their duties by the same bells as the priests in the cathedral are. Every Sunday they take part in what are called the solemn processions of the canons of the greater church. On the feast of the nine chaplains and the other widely frequented holy days, they enter the cathedral and take the seats of the Lord's Lords, and just like them they are assigned to singing in the choir and receive along with them the sums of money that are called "presences." Each college (both old and new) has one school master and one cantor, who presents to the assemblies of each college candidates for induction as canons, and attests to their worthiness to join (the induction of novices does not normally take place without such presentation by the cantors). But no one has ever been allowed to hold ecclesiastical benefices in both colleges. When the canons of the Old Church are ill, they take the sacraments in the cathedral. On this basis, some people validate the assertion that there are not two churches but in legal terms only one, even if there is disagreement as to the number and location. There are also other decorations all over the outside of the cathedral, but in circumspection I pass over them.

Now I will enter the cathedral to describe its inner adornment. The first thing to strike one's attention is the floor, which is paved with cut and polished stones with plumb-line accuracy, and gives the viewer's eye the impression of being perfectly level and smooth. On the floor are placed the tombs of three bishops, namely, Henry of Schwarzen-berg, Conrad of Rietberg, and Duke Eric of Saxony, and on Eric's sarcophagus, which is made not of domestic but foreign black marble, are carved the insignia of the great-hearted prince. | In addition to the 39 walls, a double row of columns down the middle holds up the vaults, which rest upon them on both sides, and keeps them from collaps-ing. This row creates a triple series of painted vaults (the ones in the center are higher and the flanking ones are lower). Next, the function of providing light is performed by four rows of windows. In the past there were stained-glass windows that gave the appearance of gems because of the many colors put into the glass when it was formed by heating. These windows were made by the princes at great expense and presented by them as gifts, but have now been knocked out by the Anabaptists. Twenty-three altars dedicated to various saints can be seen, and these are endowed with large annual incomes and adorned with excellent painted screens and sculptures. In addition, there is the one in the chapel, as well as another that is under the other tower in the chapel dedicated to St. Catherine, where aspirants to church functions are examined. This is awe-inspiring, since St. Catherine was considered the patron of the liberal arts by the ancients.[12]

On the other side there is a heated chamber to which in winter the priests retire in turns to dispel the cold. There they sit around a movable iron brazier that gleams with hot coals and engage in various conversations, now about sacred matters, now about secular ones, now about matters of no consequence. | There is also a second hearth, 40 larger than the first, which is kept alight in winter by the beadle, who throws on coals, for the benefit of the indigents clothed in rags.

The place in between the two towers and over which the altar is set is virtually enclosed on both sides with wooden benches. They call this the old choir because this is the place where the choir of the Lords was in the ancient church of Dodo. This is the site of the baptismal font to which, by ancient right maintained since its consecration, the first-born son of every parish throughout the city is brought for baptism and

---

[12] The fourth-century martyr Catherine of Alexandria was reputed to be a philosopher, and for this reason was considered the patron saint of students and philosophers.

serves no other use. From this it is obvious that this church possesses a loftier status compared to the others.

Though the expanse of the church is great, a dais made of local marble was raised up next to a column and covered with a wooden roof carved with great skill, so that when the priest gives forth his voice, it is not immediately received by the vaults to be diffused and dissipated there, but is bent downwards to strike the ears of the listeners directly.

In front of the choir there are two paintings, one portraying the mother of God and the other St. John the Baptist, who points to the Lamb of God. These were painted by Brother Franco of Zütphen with such skill that they compelled astonishment in all the best painters. During the siege these paintings had holes cut in them by the Anabaptists | to make toilets. Two organs with divergent but harmonious sound were built at great expense, but they were destroyed at the time of the Anabaptist madness and only one has been rebuilt. Around the wall of the choir, the prophesies of the Sibyls along with pictures of them were arranged with wondrous skill one after the other at fixed intervals. In sum, the whole church was full of sculptures arranged here and there on the walls and columns, but these are nowhere to be seen, having been broken and smashed to pieces by the Anabaptist madness.[13]

The chapter house, to which the Lords customarily retire to deliberate on more important affairs, faces north. Its inner walls are covered with cut and planed timber, on which can be seen skillful engravings of insignia of nobility and arms that were passed down to the Lords by their ancestors. In obedience to you its backdoor yields in whichever direction you choose to turn.[14]

The library on the upper floor to the right is not very well stocked, since it only has a few authors through the gift of Master Herman of Busch, a man of noble birth, who is undoubtedly very learned, a poet laureate and deacon of Lord Roger Smising. The old, very well stocked library | was destroyed by fire on September 7, 1527. It surpassed all the libraries of Westphalia in the nobility of its authors and the age of its books, and was an irrecoverable treasure. It is said that in it were

41

42

---

[13] For the destruction of the decorations of the cathedral, see 522–523D.

[14] The sense of this is not clear to me. Perhaps he means that the door opens both inwards and outwards.

preserved manuscripts of many authors written by themselves in books made of bark.[15]

I think that I should not pass over the clock that was carefully built with great invention, and in the time before the Anabaptist madness brought no little increase in the majesty of the church and its college. We discover that with no less skill has it been repaired through the diligent efforts of the astronomers Master Derek Zwifel (a burgher) and Doctor John of Aachen (a monk) as well as Nicholas Windemaker (a blacksmith). On the clock there is not merely a hand that moves so as to divide the hours into their minutes. Not only is the very swift motion of the *primum mobile*[16] portrayed driving the lower spheres, but so are the particular motions of the individual planets through the signs of the zodiac and their own gradients, the rising and setting of the sun through the zodiac, and the waxing and waning of the moon, and various other things that I circumspectly pass over for the sake of brevity. Above the hand, images of the three Magi come out. Attended by their servants, they offer gifts to the Newborn King as the star leads the way high above, and the boy, who is held in the arms of His mother, Mary, receives the gifts with a sort of good-natured nod. This is accompanied by clinging bells that play a hymn. All of this is driven by the skillful construction of the clock. Lower down, a little wheel goes around slowly on which the inscribed names of all the months, days and feast days can be read through a grating. In the center of this is fixed a picture of St. Paul that always points to the present day. On the other | side are two statues, one of a woman and the other of a man. The man puts a horn to his mouth and blows into it. Once he has done so, he sticks it in front of the woman's face as if in jest, but as if irked at the joke, she raises a hammer that she holds in her left hand and makes ready to strike the horn in front of her face with an energetic blow. But when the man pulls the horn back as she strikes at it, she is thwarted by him and hits the bell that hangs in the middle instead of the horn. In this way the hours are counted by repeats strikes. At the same moment, a bronze rope pulls the heavy hammer of the upper bell and causes it to

43

---

[15] In the primitive days before the invention of paper, bark served as a cheap material to write on (parchment was expensive and papyrus was unavailable for most of the Middle Ages).

[16] The *primum mobile* ("first movable thing") was the outer sphere that drove the spheres of the planets below (and in the medieval Christian conception of astronomy it was God who moved the *primum mobile*).

give a rather loud ring. So that the excellence of skill will not escape men in their ignorance, this clock is at present under the careful and accurate control of Master John Wilkinghof, an excellent astronomer and most diligent professor of the liberal arts.

To the east, one rises up to the choir from the general floor level over a few steps between the columns, and the choir is separated from the rest of the church on all sides by a stone railing and some twisted and polished little columns. A noteworthy structure made with keen ingenuity between two columns of the church faces west and is held up by columns and arches. Lower down, it reveals two entrances to the choir, while higher up, above the vaults, it is paved with smoothed stone and is surrounded on both sides with a barrier fence, so that it can contain a fair number of people without any fear of them falling. On just about the upper rim of this structure by the church, images of the twelve Apostles carefully made of local marble by a craftsman's ready hand on a delicate lathe detain the eyes of beholders for some 44   time. | For this reason it is commonly called the Apostles' crossing. In the middle of it is suspended an image of the crucifix. The other side by the choir is supported and decorated with many figures that are carved with equal skill and have little columns interspersed. Two spirals are attached to this structure on either side along the columns of the church, and the covering over these spirals, which surround the steps, is made of the same marble, being circular like a crown. Consummate skill polished this covering and adorned it with little towers and pinnacles, so that it seems, if not to surpass, then at least to equal the workmanship of any goldsmith. In short, the splendor and elegance of this structure are such that by its artistry any artisan would be compelled to dumbfounded astonishment. The priest customarily recites the Gospel on the top of this structure.

In this choir, the ordering of the singing clerics in three ranks is most suitably marked off with benches and pulpits. The top row is decorated here and there with hanging tapestries, and in it the Lord's Lords have their place, each at a level corresponding to his dignity. The next row contains the vicars, and among them the choirmaster conducts the singers by waving a knotted stick. The lowest row holds the twenty-four singers (who are called chamber men) and boys summoned from the school to sing. In the four corners of the choir, statues of the Evangelists holding books of the Gospel in their hands seem to hold up the columns. Then there are two other columns holding up the vaults of the choir, and St. Paul on the right-hand column and St. Peter on the left-hand one trample Simon Magus under foot to give warning that no blemish of simony should be let into this assembly of Lords.[17] On the other side of the choir there juts out a container for the Lord's body,[18] which is carved with various pinnacles like a little tower.

From the choir of singing priests there is an ascent over a few steps to the high altar, which before the re-baptizing was outstandingly adorned with gold, silver and gems. | Around it can be seen images raised a little   45 from the floor level that portray certain Fathers of the Old Testament making sacrifice. Abel offers a lamb with the words:

> From the flock may this rich gift of first fruits
> Be carried high up to You from the altar by the sacred flame.

Cain offers stalks with the words:

> A handful cut down from the field with a scythe
> I bring forward, and I will not donate to the altar rich ears of grain.

Melchizedek offers bread and wine, and Aaron incense:

> We sacrifice mystical things: bread, wine and pious incense.

A bit higher up above these statues along the outside of the high altar, images decked out with gold, silver and other colors stand at fixed intervals, and these portray the choir of angels and carry in their hands wax candles placed on candelabra. On the vault of the choir a picture of the Trinity and representations of other saints and the shapes of stars gleam forth in an impressive way across a blue background. Here I pass over the countless lamps around both choir and altar; the great brightness of the candelabra; the large size of the crosses; the strong fragrance of the censors; the purity of white vestments; the brilliant shining of the gold and silver vessels; and the other decorations of various kinds that greatly inflame the congregation with love of the awesome mysteries. I also pass over the very fetching delightfulness of the Lords' Field, which easily surpasses all other locations in the city. For this field is made very pleasing not only by the magnificent edifice of the basilica but also by the outstanding palaces of the Lords, which have been raised up on all sides at great expense.

---

[17] Simon Magus was well-known in the Middle Ages for being a magician, but here he symbolizes "simony," the (theoretically) illegal practice of buying ecclesiastical benefices.

[18] I.e., the eucharist host.

I pass over the flourishing lindens and oaks; the very expansive vista; the grass that grows everywhere; the frequent visits of people taking strolls and engaging in conversations, and the large variety of sights. All these things greatly increase the delightfulness of the field. But if I were inclined to describe all these things, I would certainly make the reader sick and tired.

46   In addition to the cathedral, there are three churches located in that field which I cannot pass over. One of them is in sight of the Paradise. It is built with great skill out of local marble, and has a splendid spire. This is a parish church dedicated to St. James. Since it is for the benefit of the servants of the Lords, who live all around in the field, it lacks a baptismal font. (There would be no use for it, since everyone leads a life of celibacy in that place, and no married couples or any childbirths are allowed there.) There are two cemeteries, one receiving the funerals of the servants of the Lords, and the other the burials of the cathedral singers.

On the lane to the south, we enter the other chapel, which Odinga, a noble lady of the Büren family, once dedicated to St. Margaret at her own expense in a garden that she cultivated by hereditary right, and endowed with revenue. At her death, she transferred her ownership to the chapter as a mark of piety, with the restriction that the income of the church benefices founded by her should always remain in the possession of the inhabitant of the house.

The third church is to the north and is dedicated to St. Nicholas. It rests on smoothed columns, and apart from the stone spire that rises from the roof, it is adorned with a few altars, marble statues and stained-glass windows.

47   Next, there is a building nearby that is 126 feet in length. That its cellar was once a repository for wine, beer and other kinds of drink, and that on the next floor there was a feasting hall for the Lords, in which they enjoyed a common meal at a common table, is reasonably well demonstrated both by the name "refectory" and by records of the distant past. This building has now been converted to three uses. The basement and first floor are occupied by the public schools for youth. The middle floor is occupied by the cathedral singers and is divided into rooms which they call chambers, and for this reason the singers are called "chamber priests" (*Camerpapen* in the vernacular). The top floor underneath the roof serves as the Lords' granary. Since the small size of this house does not allow it to contain all the singers, they also inhabit a neighboring house (directly next door, in fact).

The singers number twenty-four in total and have their own college. They have their own deacon, their own laws and regulations on how to live, their own cook and butler (they call him "provider"), and their own steward, who also sells beer to the public, earning a profit for himself and his colleagues. They share a common table and heated room. When about to enter the choir, they wear an attire that practically reaches their ankles, clad sometimes in linen stoles and sometimes in woolen hoods hanging down in the back, and follow the practice of other priests. It is their duty to devote themselves to chanting hymns both by night and by day, and for this reason they receive as a reward the daily necessities apart from drink. Neglect of the prayers at matins is punished by loss of breakfast. Only those who excel in both voice and knowledge of singing and who make a vow of celibacy are admitted to this college. If any of them becomes a father, he is fined with the cost of one banquet, though he has the privilege of sending to the pregnant woman the first steinful of the penal beer. With this expense he redeems his good name and absolves himself of every blemish of the prior sin, unless he taints himself with lawful marriage | contrary to the custom   48 of the college, in which case such people exclude themselves from the college. The older members receive preference in seating and in dignity. For their education, the younger members are turned over to the study of literature in the public school, and for this reason the schoolmaster is paid twelve gold pieces every year for tuition. They are bound by no specific religious vow from which they cannot release themselves if so inclined. For when they lay down their office, they also lay down the obligation to keep the oath, and once freed of it, they are restored to their original liberty and can get married (age permitting).

But to make sure that I do not, in the midst of my efforts to be brief, exceed the plan which I have undertaken, and incur the readers' disgust with an unrefined mass of dull words, I will laconically complete the description that I have decided to write about the churches.

After the Lords' Church, we first come upon a magnificent church with a convent of noble nuns. This church, which is dedicated to the Virgin Mother of God, surpasses the rest by dating back to ancient days, having been built across the river Aa by Herman I, the fourteenth bishop of Münster. In the past, when the faith was first growing, it was called the Marienthal, since it was dedicated to the Virgin Mary and is located in a rather sloping region of the city (a valley). After the bishop had finished the construction of the church and convent at his own expense and endowed it with many fine manors for the support of the nuns, he finally adorned the buildings by establishing a convent of nuns from the higher nobility, appointing his own sister as the abbess.

Then on December 29, A.D. 1041, in the presence of the reigning emperor, Henry III, the high altar was dedicated in honor of the Holy Cross and the Virgin Mary by Archbishop Herman of Cologne, with the assistance of Archbishop Alebrand of Bremen and Bishop Bruno of Minden. | The southern altar was dedicated to St. John the Baptist and All Saints by Archbishop Bardo of Mainz in the presence of Switger of Bamberg, who was later elected pope,[19] and of Bishop Detmar of Hildesheim. Bishop Hunfried of Magdeburg, with the assistance of Carro and of Alveric, the bishops respectively of Zeitz and of Osnabrück, dedicated the northern altar to St. John the Evangelist. The western altar was consecrated under the auspices of Sts. Peter and Paul by Bishop Herman of Münster, the founder and builder of this convent, in the presence and with the assistance of Nithard and Rudolph, the bishops respectively of Lüttich and of Schleswig. Amid this well-attended dedication in the presence of the bishops, Emperor Henry, who was himself present, was moved by pious zeal to grant a wealthy manor to the nuns for their upkeep.

After the completion of these arrangements, the convent remained intact for some while following the dedication, and the nuns spent thirty years in devotion to the worship of God and to the singing of hymns. At the end of this period, in the year 1071, an interruption of the successful course of the vows which they had undertaken led to a temporary obstruction and suspension, when the outbreak of a fire in April reduced the entire structure of the convent and church to nothing but a mass of stones. But within fourteen years virtually everything had been repaired with greater elegance, so that on January 11 of the year 1085, when Henry IV was ruling the Holy Roman Empire, the western part of the convent was re-dedicated by Erpo, the bishop of the diocese. On March 25 of the same year, the altar in | the chapel called Jerusalem, which had been ruined by fire, was also dedicated by this same Erpo.

I could imagine that this chapel preceded the Lords' Church in age. For we read that before the time of Charlemagne, St. Swibert along with certain pious men who were priests not only taught here in Münster and in neighboring areas but also with his eloquence and the

49

50

---

[19] As Clement II in 1046.

performing of miracles converted many people, so that they embraced the faith, and that he consecrated a certain number of churches (as things went back then), in which the Christians gathered in their zeal to strengthen their piety. Accordingly, I have no doubt that this chapel too was built before Charlemagne's campaign against Westphalia. It was also dedicated by St. Ludger, the founding bishop of Münster, who was brought here from Bilderbeck after his death, and rested for thirty days in the chapel without smell, with blood pouring from his nose at the arrival of his brother Hildegrin.[20] Hence, this chapel, which also used to be adorned with many relics, has been called not Jerusalem but St. Ludger's chapel down to the present day. The church itself and the altars were reconsecrated in the year 1086 on December 29, while the chapels were graciously consecrated by Erpo in the year 1087, the southern one on January 24, the northern one in the year 1088 on February 1, as was the choir of the nuns on August 16 of the same year. | A few years later, this building was burned to ashes along with   51 the other churches and private buildings, when Derek of Winzenburg, the eighteenth bishop, threw torches into the city. Borchard of Holte, the nineteenth bishop, was busily engaged in repairing the burned houses of this convent but did not finish the job. Cut short by death, he left the completion to his successor, Egbert. After Egbert had finished everything sumptuously, he recalled the nuns, who, in the time since the fire, had been wandering here and there among their friends and relatives, but since they had for some time learned to pursue a rather licentious and dissolute life among their own people, many greatly resisted the bishop's summons. Having grown used to freedom, they shrank from imprisonment. Nonetheless, when he fulminated against the rebels with the dire threat of ecclesiastical sanctions, he eventually achieved his desire, though with great difficulty. He therefore constrained those who had returned with a tighter form of custody.

In the year 1340, during the days of Louis of Hesse, the thirty-fifth bishop, the church and its tower were rebuilt in a much grander and more magnificent manner than before, at the expense of the entire diocese, which had by now increased in population and wealth. The church and altars adopted a new appearance, which they have retained to the present day. The nuns of this convent are no less noble than

---

[20] Absence of physical corruption of the remains was a frequent feature in the medieval conception of sainthood.

are the Lord's Lords of the cathedral. Those who belong to the lower
nobility are refused entry, and accordingly the daughters of the burghers
and patricians of the city are never allowed into this order. They make
a vow of perpetual virginity to God, and devote themselves to singing

52   hymns of praise in honor of God. | They have the right to choose their
abbess, but in the past they had chosen her not from the noblewomen
of their own order but from elsewhere (the more prestigious bloodline
of counts). At that time, the nuns did not share a common fare, as they
do now, but lived privately in their own cells on meals brought from
the mistress' (the abbess') kitchen. Since this circumstance in some way
provided the opportunity to live in too licentious a way, John of Bavaria,
the forty-fourth bishop, resolved to change it and to impose a stricter
rule for living. Accordingly, in the year 1460, he did not confirm as
abbess the daughter of the count of Werthen, who had been chosen by
free election in the traditional way, and refused to lend his authorization to the election. In her place, Richmoda of Horst, who had been
summoned from the Convent of the Maccabees[21] in Cologne and was
brought over at great expense to the nuns of the Convent Across-the-
River, was appointed as a substitute by the authority and command
of the bishop. At that time, the looseness of the earlier way of living
was to some extent changed through the imposition of tighter reins
and thereby restrained, the practice of eating at a single table being
introduced. Upon the death of this abbess in the year 1461, they chose
from within their own convent (as had not been the normal procedure
previously) Ida of Hoevel, and John of Bavaria granted his episcopal
authorization to this election. But when she too had breathed her last,
the nuns clung to their old ways and were driven by the ardent wish to
recover their old liberty, relapsing into their ancient custom of choosing
the abbess from the bloodline of counts. Their aim in their persistence
was to shake off and remove the yoke of reformation and the restraint
of a stricter way of life.[22] Not long after the election, however, she too
died, and in the meanwhile the resignation[23] of John of Bavaria, who
preferred the archbishopric of Magdeburg to the Church of Münster,
had resulted in administration of the diocese devolving upon interim

53   officials called "commissioners," who | are normally kept in charge until

---

[21] A Benedictine foundation that already existed in the late twelfth century.
[22] Here "reformation" obviously has the narrow sense of internal reform (which in
the medieval context usually signifies the restoration of stricter monastic discipline).
[23] In 1466.

the new election (or postulation)[24] and its confirmation by the pope. These commissioners were then authorized by the elected nobleman, Prince Henry of Schwarzenberg, who was no less eager for the reformation of the nuns than John of Bavaria had been, to summon an abbess from the Convent of St. Giles and install her against the wishes of the nuns of the Convent Across-the-River. At the same time, they decided by their own authority that while any nuns who refused the yoke of the more restricted way of life and preferred to leave should receive twenty florins every year by way of support, those who wished to remain could try out the regimen of the life which they had now undertaken for an entire year after the fashion of novices, and if, at the end of that year, they judged themselves to be too weak to embrace that kind of life and to persevere in it, they were free to leave without any blemish of disgrace. But after this matter had dragged on for some years in no clear direction, it was finally decided to put a definitive end to it. So in the year 1483, they were, on the day of St. Boniface,[25] reformed, enclosed, and forced to make a profession of the Rule of St. Benedict by Henry of Schwarzenberg, the forty-fifth bishop of the Church of Münster. Thus, this good prince completed what others had several times attempted in vain. This mode of living in the Convent Across-the-River would have lasted down to the present day through the continuous succession of moral and chaste abbesses, had not the intervention of the Anabaptist madness briefly interrupted it.

Although the majesty of the church had often been greatly reduced through damage caused by frequent fires, nonetheless, as if cleansed by the new misfortune of fire, the old church rose up again to be more impressive. In the end, it was built in its present form, which is not only remarkable but magnificent, both inside and out. | It is roofed with   54 lead tiles, and its painted vaults are supported by very tall columns. Both the choir of nuns on the west and that of Lords on the east are resonant and are decorated with the images of various saints. The organ, which plays with a multi-note harmony of sounds, marks off the singing of the nuns with such a sweet intervention that you would assert with Pythagoras that you were hearing the concordant symphony not of humans and instruments made by human ingenuity but of the

---

[24] A "postulation" was a request to recognize the election of someone not eligible for the position (for instance, because he was underage or already in possession of another bishopric).

[25] June 5 (but the bishop's document is dated to St. Dorothy's day, i.e., February 6).

heavenly spheres.[26] There is a very tall tower that is built with polished stone both inside and out, its one room being closed with fairly strong wooden doors. On both sides, spirals extend from the lowest foundation to the top of the base, where the edge is protected by very many pinnacles and little towers built with learned skill, so that people who go around it are protected from accidentally falling. Next, a lead-covered steeple of amazing height seemed to pierce the very clouds. In the past, before it was torn down by the Anabaptist madness, this steeple would, to a distance of eight Westphalian miles (which are quite long),[27] cause viewers' eyes to wonder at it, even though it is placed in a valley. For there is no taller, more splendid or sturdier tower in the whole city.

To this convent is attached the parish of the neighbors who live around it on all sides, which has gradually increased to its present large size and population. Not only the people contained within the city's walls but also a very large number of peasants living here and there on the outside within the territory of the abbess belong to this parish. The abbess's authority is so great that she has her own rights and privileges not only outside of the city but also within it.[28] | For she has an asylum (place of immunity) confirmed by imperial charter and long usage: whoever seeks refuge at it, even if guilty of a capital crime, cannot be taken away from there against his will by a member of the government, but for a year and a day, if he has not run off in the interim, he is by custom fed with meals from the convent. In the early period of the convent's foundation, its right was easily acquired from the emperor, who was living at Dortmund, to show favor to the burghers and to increase the city's size. This arrangement was entrenched by many instances of its use and has been brought down from the days of our ancestors to our own. To preside over the Word of God she has the archdeacon of the parish (called the dean) along with two chaplains, who are fed with meals provided by her at her own expense. Before the Anabaptist madness, she also had her own tribunal, which had been built at the convent's expense alongside the

55

[26] The "music of the spheres" refers to the idea that the distances between the heavenly spheres were governed by "perfect" ratios equivalent to those thought to underlie harmonic music (a notion that can be traced back to Plato, who attributes it to the numerology of the Pythagoreans).
[27] A "common German mile" was much larger than the corresponding English unit, equaling 4.6 of the latter (and 7.42 kilometers).
[28] This assertion of the abbess's rights was one of the passages in K.'s work to which the city council took exception.

church cemetery to the east, and on account of it the abbess receives nine gold pieces every year from the city council down to the present day. In this court, the same judge as presides in the public forum would handle on Mondays and Fridays the cases, both criminal and civil, of the inhabitants of this parish alone, and no one was allowed to take any of the parishioners to any other tribunal against his will. Those who were arrested there for capital crimes could not be held in any prison but that of this parish. For they would be taken to the Gate of the Holy Virgin or to the Jewish Gate, and there they would be subjected to questioning under torture,[29] and then would suffer the public censure of this court in the presence of the councilmen, who would stand all around. The place of execution for those sentenced to death was the Tuckesburg, | a prominent open area outside of the   56 Gate of the Blessed Virgin. Shaped like a circle, this area is covered all over with willows and is very pleasant in the center, where grass and flowers grow. Those condemned to execution by the gibbet or to some other variety of death pay the penalty for the crime which they have committed, not far from the brick kiln.

This parish also had its own market on the other side of the cemetery to the west, and there, apart from merchandise of every kind, the pledges taken as surety by the authority of this court are also smashed[30] in the same way as in the public court. This is also the location of the stake of disgrace, to which those who are besmirched with lesser crimes are attached and thereby marked with infamy.[31] The parish also has the privilege that it allows no funeral, however large, even that of the prince himself, to be taken elsewhere if it pertains to the parish, and instead the funeral is brought to either the church, if permission has been granted, or to the common cemetery. Hence, when not only the Brothers of the Fountain but also the superintendent of the alms-house of St. Mary Magdalene, which is located in the parish between the two bridges, demanded to be allowed to inter their dead within their own burial ground and to have their own church, there arose between them and the abbess of the Convent Across-the-River very bitter disputes, which were eventually appealed to the Roman

---

[29] This was the normal mode of criminal investigation at the time.

[30] I.e., if forfeited.

[31] "Infamy" is a technical term for someone whose reputation is officially stained and is thereby barred from various public activities (like giving testimony).

curia by legal quibblers who were well fattened by both sides.[32] After the case had dragged on there without any sure outcome and was draining the treasury of each party with its vast expenses, the Brothers of the Fountain finally emerged victorious through the decision of the
57   pope. When news of this victory was brought more quickly | to the abbess than to the brothers, the nuns employed the clever stratagem of sending good men who intervened to bring about peace and arranged the permanent settlement of the dispute, which the brothers believed to be still pending in a case of doubtful outcome, on the condition that in return for the right of private burial and their own church they would offer the abbess a gift every year. The superintendent of the alms-house, on the other hand, refused to give in, hoping that he would achieve his desire through cleverness, and so in the name of the alms-house he sent a supplication to Pope Gregory in the very midst of the case. The pope, being a circumspect man, issued a rescript to Ludolph, the twenty-eighth bishop of Münster, in the following words. "Bishop Gregory, servant of the servants of God, sends greetings and apostolic blessings to our venerable brother, Bishop Ludolph of Münster. Our beloved sons, the master and brothers of the hospital of St. Mary Magdalene, have requested of us in humble supplication that for the work of the brothers and the guests living in the hospital, we should deign to grant them permission to have their own chaplain in a chapel of their own, who is to present them with the sacraments of the Church, as well as their own cemetery. It therefore being our wish to delegate this matter to you, who are the diocesan of the area, by apostolic letter, we order you, our brother, to grant their requests if you think it appropriate, without prejudice to anyone else's rights." Seeing that these requests could not be granted without harming someone else's rights, the bishop was fearful on behalf of the alms-house, and so he intervened in the case along with the cathedral chapter and the city council. They intervened to bring about peace and arranged that the alms-house should receive both its own administration of the sacraments and a private burial for their dead in the year 1240 under
58   Innocent V. | There was also once a dispute about property between

---

[32] It would seem that the original dispute between the convent and the alms-house of Mary Magdalene was settled in 1241, whereas the brothers were established in the city only in 1400. The brothers then entered into a second dispute with the convent regarding the alms-house.

this alms-house and the Convent of St. Giles at the time when Uda held the reins of that convent.

By whom this alms-house was founded and who was primarily responsible for this is not entirely clear, but it would be my belief that it is more ancient than the Convent Across-the-River, since in the period before Herman I, who founded the convent, Siegfried, the thirteenth bishop, bestowed certain properties on the alms-house in the year 1022, though I have no doubt that the chapel of the alms-house was built much later. There was once both an alms-house for foreigners and an infirmary, that is, a place in which sick foreign paupers were fed. Now, on the other hand, there is an alms-house for old folks, that is, a shelter in which the indigent old people of both sexes who are burghers are looked after and fed (these days no one is accepted in it who is not a poor person who has held burgher rights for some years). This alms-house has seen a very great increase in its wealth and privileges through the munificence and favor of both nobles and commoners on the one hand and successive bishops on the other. For (to pass over the other bishops) in the year 1186 Herman II, the twenty-second bishop of Münster, in addition to endowing it with other manors, made all its properties located between the two stone bridges free from any burdens or exactions imposed by the city. He ordained that all those who died in the alms-house could not give away their possessions by will but should leave them there to increase its revenues, and also issued a prohibition | 59 stating that no one, whether he be superintendent, inhabitant of a monastery or monk in general, or else a cleric, should keep a concubine, lest what ought to serve as a solace for necessity should turn into the licentiousness of impermissible pleasure. From this it is clearly shown that the bishops used to have jurisdiction over this alms-house, which had already been turned over to the city council by 1330, on the understanding that it would now be called the hospital of the city of Münster and that the council alone would possess the power both to accept the indigent and to appoint and remove the pastor and the superintendent (manager). They call the two members of the council who are in charge of this the "providers."[33] It is their role to examine how the manager has carried out his duties every year, and to ensure on behalf of the indigent that everything is run respectably in a way giving glory to God and relief to the poor, and that the house itself

---

[33] For further discussion of these "providers," see 107D.

suffers no harm. In the year 1330, the city council decreed that no more than ten individuals be accepted into this alms-house unless this should represent a useful situation from which some benefit could accrue to the house. Providers from the city council were given to this alms-house after 1305, while prior to this time it received overseers from among the burghers. Hence, the title was changed along with the status of the appointee.

There are also three male monasteries, and these I will describe briefly, not because they surpass the other churches in age but because they too are included within the boundary of this parish. For I think that I will act more rightly if I proceed with them one after the other in a fixed order than if I ignore any order and mix them all up, randomly wandering back and forth. Chief among them in dignity is the one that is dedicated to St. George and contains men of knightly rank. These men are called Teutonic Lords, either because they prefer the German language to all others or because they are chief among the German knighthood | and protect the Christian faith in Germany.[34] Because they themselves do not know or do not wish to know their origin in this city, I have toiled in vain in the attempt to track this down. In any case, their order was founded in 1216 under Gregory IX. It is not without reason that they go forth in a white cloak with a black cross on it, being endowed with very great wealth. For when the religion suffers a lapse and the Cross of Christ is overwhelmed and blackened with the stain of heretics, they are rightly obligated to bring it immediate assistance in arms and to defend it against, and deliver it from the onslaught of heretics. Among them there are also priests of lesser rank, who struggle against the enemies of Christ not as knights with external weapons but with constant prayers. These priests, who are assigned to the divine offices, are left at home. The purpose of this arrangement is that when the Church is in danger, the Teutonic order may succour it with both sets of weapons. The Knights occupy a very large and pleasant spot, residing along both banks of the river Aa. They possess splendid buildings, and retain the right to fish in that river for a great distance from the city. On the two banks, they have two mills (one for grain, one for oil), which constrict the river in such a way as to allow

60

---

[34] The order of the "Teutonic Knights of St. Mary's Hospital of Jerusalem" was originally founded in 1198 for the protection of the Holy Land, but soon turned to the conquest and forcible conversion of the Slavs in the Baltic area.

them to operate. For it is only from the day of St. Michael[35] to the feast day of Easter that they have the right to use the mills, it being taken away from them during the summertime for the public good, to avoid the retention of water behind the mill dams, | which would harm the   61 pastures outside the city. They have a fairly large church, which has moderate decorations both inside and out, possessing various other images in addition to a statue of St. George the dragon slayer.

Nearby, there is another area of immunity, which is called the Bischopinghof.[36] Whoever inhabits this place is free of all burdens imposed by the city. For the Bischoping family and its successors do not allow the jurisdiction of the city council to extend to it. The widow of John Kerckering, a matron descended from the Bischopings (the family after which the place is thought to have been named), now possesses jurisdiction over this place by hereditary right.

The second monastery in this parish is that of the Brothers of the Fountain. It was founded under Pope Martin V by the venerable Lord Henry of Ahaus, who was vicar of the Lords' Church. | Being very   62 devoted to piety and honorable pursuits, he readily attracted similar men with his singular saintliness and grave demeanor. Those whom he had attracted he invited in a friendly way to share a common life, and in the end arranged things so that they would frugally enjoy the property which they had contributed to a common fund, and would instead devote themselves to divine service at their appointed time. To forestall any wicked idleness, time not spent in pious functions is used in gaining the necessities through the practice of physical labor. Furthermore, since they are bound by no personal vow, they are very much distinguished from the brothers who profess the Third Rule of St. Francis.[37] Accordingly, they prefer to be called canons rather than monks. At first, they lived in a small house in the Chicken's Field (*"Bei den Honekampe"*), but they quickly became richer, and in a more spacious

---

[35] September 29.

[36] K.'s discussion of this immunity was another point on which the city council thought that K. had impugned its authority (see General Introduction 3b).

[37] In founding his new order, Francis of Assisi divided it into three suborders. The first consisted of religious under monastic vows (the *fratres minores*), the second of consecrated maidens (called *clarissae* or "Poor Clares" after St. Clair, a follower of St. Francis who asked to be allowed to adopt his practices and persuaded other women to join her), and the third of members of the laity ("tertiaries"), who bound themselves to various forms of devotion without the strict obligations of proper monks. For this last category, Francis composed a "third rule" to govern their behavior and duties in 1221.

location near the open ground behind the walls they placed a very large house and a splendid church (on its altars can be seen painted screens that surpass the hand of Apelles).[38] They moved here after giving up the earlier location. They have a very well stocked library, but before the Anabaptist madness it was even better stocked.

This order is subdivided by offices. The man who runs the whole college in both temporal and spiritual matters is called "father" as a mark of honor and respect. They have the right to appoint him by election, and, after the appointment, to remove him from office if he does not satisfactorily fulfill the office he has taken up. The man who manages the necessities for the kitchen and for the whole house they call the "manager," and the man who is in charge of work duties they call the "record keeper." This man distributes the jobs to individuals, and to the college's profit he receives from employers the fees paid for the jobs. In particular, services are sold to those who devote themselves to writing or to the preparation and thinning of animal skins suitable for writing on or for use as book covers (such skins are called parchment) or to bookbinding.[39]

63   Soon after Ahaus founded his college, he noted the lack of papal authorization, and realized that as a result of its absence the college would not long remain intact and at peace. Accordingly, he went to Rome to ask for privileges from Eugenius IV, who was at that time in charge of the Papal See.[40] But the mendicant orders of the Franciscans and Dominicans intervened, thinking it detrimental to the Christian faith to approve just any little assemblies that had been rashly formed and to introduce into the Church of God new and unheard-of ways of living. Gerson, however, earnestly took up the cause of the brothers with the pope and gained not only his desire but even more.[41] The founder therefore returned to his people in joy, and filled out the years of his righteous old age in tranquility. Thus, the house which was begun in this way, finished in this way, and finally endowed with privileges in

---

[38] A Greek painter who worked in the later fourth century B.C. He was reputed to be the best painter of antiquity in Classical literature, and K. was no doubt familiar with him from his readings in Latin.

[39] These very activities would represent a notable element in the complaints lodged against the spirituality during the early (Lutheran) period of religious unrest in Münster in the 1520s.

[40] Ahaus did not in fact go personally to Rome.

[41] John Gerson (1363–1429) was a famous French theologian who was very influential in ecclesiastical politics.

this way, has remained unharmed down to the present day, contrary to the expectation of many.

The third monastery in this parish is that of the Knights of St. John. Located along the open ground behind the city walls, it has not only a very large orchard of various fruit trees and a very well equipped garden of fragrant plants, but also well-watered pastures, fish ponds, and bowers that have been erected to improve the delightfulness of the location with human skill aiding nature, and that always remain green in summer. In these bowers, | while birds of every variety chirp away 63 with a varied harmony and bees flit among the flowers in search of honeydew, adding in the low rumbles of their very charming buzzing, the eyes and ears of men receive a great deal of pleasure. If the place were surrounded by a sloping grove that broke the gusts of the winds and with their green boughs held back the cold or if it enjoyed the presence of beautiful Eve and the tree of life, through whose favor the blush of youth would be maintained in man without any harm from old age, then you would certainly say that here was the city's Tempe or Paradise. They reside in a splendid house, and their church, which is dedicated to St. John and is fairly impressive, holds up on its roof a spire notable for its two bells.

We read that their order was founded in the year 1308 in order that they should attack the enemies of Christ's Cross and name, and strengthen the fortifications entrusted to them with such defenses that the Turk, that most savage and dangerous enemy of Christendom, should be kept from their borders. It is thus not without reason that they wear white crosses on their black cloaks. Rather, they are to be reminded of the task undertaken by them, which is the reason for the wealth in which they abound. We gather that they have always fought stoutly, apart from their inflicting the blemish of disgrace on Christians when they were overwhelmed by the disaster at Rhodes. But they did expiate the disgrace committed through the surrender at Rhodes with the famous defense of Malta, which was more than heroic and cost them dearly. This very grand victory redeemed all their previous dishonor.[42]

---

[42] This history of the Order of St. John is rather misleading. Its tenth-century origins go back to men dedicated to a Benedictine hospice in Jerusalem, but the proper origin is dated to 1113, when Pope Paschal II took the order under his protection because of its good services to the crusaders now in possession of the Holy Land (for this reason, members were also known as "Hospitalers"). Upon the loss of the last Christian foothold there in 1291, the order first migrated to Cyprus, but in about 1308 they occupied the island of Rhodes off the coast of Asia Minor. What is uncharitably referred to here as

In the olden days, this monastery was called "*Up den Berge*"[43] after the rise on which the chapel is built, and this is how the whole Mountain Lane[44] got its name. | To prevent any ignorance of the monastery's origin, a few words should be said about its foundation. Within the walls of the city of Münster, the college of the Knights of St. John in Steinfurt[45] owned, by the open ground behind the walls, a spot that is naturally very pleasant but swampy on one side, as well as some little houses or huts that were built in a row and covered over with a single, continuous roof, and when the brothers were laying the foundations of a new chapel in 1311, they supplicated Louis, the scion of the very noble house of Hesse and the thirty-fifth bishop of Münster, with the request that they be allowed to build a chapel in that place. This magnificent prince and pious descendant of St. Elizabeth not only agreed to such a holy wish, but immediately added many privileges of his own accord in order to enhance the worship of God. His urging also encouraged many rich men to complete the construction with their munificence. The church was thus built, and some priests were summoned from Steinfurt and established in this place to perform the worship of God, a house, at first humble enough, being set up for their residence. After such a felicitous start, this undertaking also had a successful development through the protection of good men, but the intervention of a seven-year war delayed a happy outcome for a time. For although the chapter, which alone had the right to choose the prince, had chosen Walram of Moers in the year 1450, the burghers and their adherents wished Eric of Hoya to be bishop, and so the whole diocese was wrenched apart, everything being thrown into chaos and set ablaze with factionalism, discord, plunder, flames, theft, and murder. The disastrous misfortunes with which the Knights of St. John in Steinfurt were afflicted by the burghers of Münster during this uproar were incredibly great even though they were not involved. For

---

a "disgrace" is the knights' forcible eviction from that island in 1522, when the Ottoman sultan Suleiman the Magnificent undertook a massive assault on the island, and the knights put up such a stout defense that he allowed them to withdraw under terms rather than wiping them out. In 1530, the Holy Roman Emperor Charles V gave the knights the island of Malta, where they successfully withstood an even greater attack at the hands of Suleiman in 1565.

[43] "On the Hill."

[44] I.e., *Bergstrasse*.

[45] The county of Steinfurt was located to the north-northwest of Münster and was completely surrounded by the territory of the bishopric. Its capital city was Burgsteinfurt.

without making any distinctions, the burghers threw torches on their roofs, devastated their fields, sacked their manors, | drove off their herds, stripped their oaks, and plundered everything after the fashion of invaders. Hence, Lord Bernard Schedelich, the bailiff of the Order of St. John throughout Westphalia and the commander of the house in Steinfurt, was greatly angered, and in the name of the entire order he brought suit against the city because of the losses inflicted on it. But some men of knightly rank intervened to bring about peace, and in the year 1471, on the Vigil of St. Margaret the Virgin,[46] the case, which had been dragging on for some years through the greed of the ravening legal quibblers contending on either side, was settled, and the previous goodwill was restored, through the agreement that the College of St. John On-the-Hill that was located within the walls of Münster, as well as some adjoining huts, would, by the authority of the city council and of all the guilds in the city, be forever free from burdens and taxes imposed by the city, and that in addition two neighboring houses with gardens on this side of the open ground behind the walls would be bought at the council's expense and added to the Knights' property. Finally, according to the terms of the agreement, they also received 60,000 bricks for the fortification of the new building. For this reason, the old structure immediately gave way to a new one. Then, in 1472, this same Lord Bernard Schedelich noticed that the college was making the small sum of a few marks from the fact that some prostitutes were earning a profit in those huts by indecently giving anyone access to their bodies, and he drove them out, denying access to their immodesty. He turned the brothel into a women's alms-house, and made good the loss of a few marks' income with his own money in order to avoid the objections of his colleagues. He thereby immortalized his own name with the glory of eternal remembrance among posterity.

Since the Christian population was growing, the churches, too, began to increase in number, being endowed through the munificent generosity of pious people. At the expense of the peasants, a chapel dedicated to St. Lambert was erected for the faith of the monks who were living here and there, | but a few years later it was made much grander at the expense of the patricians and other burghers, the first structure being torn down. The peasants, however, reserved the nicer parts of the church for themselves as the founders of the first church and have

[46] July 19.

handed it down to their descendants through continuous possession, so that even today they seem to own it. This church, which is located in just about the center of the city between the public marketplace and the fish market, is now very splendid, gleaming with such fine adornment, both inside and out, that the craftsmanship is said to surpass the materials for the most part. We read that the first stone of the enlarged choir was laid in the year 1375 on the day of Mary Magdalene.[47] The tower had originally been raised to a moderate height by the parishioners, but Cornelius N.,[48] the undertaker of the parish, is said to have increased it to its present height at his own expense. This tower does not have a steeple made of wood like the other towers, but on top of the stone base has been placed a circular structure made of wood in the shape of a basket or hamper and covered in lead, so that on all sides it provides a broad edge and roomy circuit for the city's watchmen as they go on their rounds. A double row of iron rods that surrounds the perimeter provides the guards with additional protection against falling. On this tower, watches are kept at the council's expense both day and night. When horsemen approach from a distance during daylight, the guards receive them with the blowing of a horn to advise the guards at the gate to be more alert in their protection of the city. Every hour they play a song on a flute into the city in every direction, so that it can be surmised that they are on duty. They also not only mark off the hours of the night by blowing their horn, but also report nighttime commotions and fires with the fearsome ringing

68   of a bell | that was cast with singular care, so that when it is struck, it instills the entire city with terrified trembling, and makes all the males rush to the alarm and the women wail at home. At the sound of the bell, it is found that men of all classes and guilds immediately attend to the duty to which they have been appointed. Some are assigned to the marketplace, where the two chief members of the government also reside, for putting out fires. Some rush in arms to the ramparts, some to the fortifications, some to the gates. Each person keeps watch at his duty station, whether the disturbance is caused by the enemy or by a sudden conflagration. At the sound of the bell, even the clergy hurriedly occupy the Lords' Field in arms, and they stand ready for whichever

---

[47] July 22.
[48] Apparently, Cornelius' last name was unknown to K. ("*N.*" for *Nomen* is the abbreviation used in sample Latin documents for a name that was to be filled in.)

part of the city a civilian magistrate may summon them to defend or for whatever job he orders them to undertake. The same bell in that tower is wrung by city servants to give warning that wrongdoers are being produced in the criminal court. The bell summons the council-men to their chamber for deliberations, and the night watchmen to the keeping of their turn at guard duty, forbidding to others the use of the public lanes at night unless they sport a flame on their brim. The protection of the fire makes it safer for them to walk at night through the wards of the city, and the chief of the watchmen, whom they call the "master of force" ("*Gewaltherr*"), arrests those found without such fire, either putting them in jail or asking them the reason for their strolling about at night.

The two colleges of canons and their churches (one dedicated to St. Ludger, the founding bishop of Münster, and the other to St. Martin the bishop of Tours) were originally founded by Herman, the scion of the ancient and noble Katzenellenbogen family who was the twenty-fifth bishop of the Church of Münster. He strengthened them with his own wealth, | and put in charge canons who were also outstanding   69 in their piety and learning and who were able in their days to acquire wealth with less toil than the present canons can maintain the wealth which they have inherited. Like most everything, each college started from a small beginning to reach its very grand honors and resources. Each has its provost (chosen from the main clergy) and each has its deacon and schoolmaster, which they call the "*scholaster*." Each has prebends that vary in revenue, but the daily stipends, which they call "presences," they distribute in equal portions among those present. In each college, the priests of lower rank and dignity are content with their income and devote themselves to church functions. These priests are called "vicars," and they share not so much the revenues as the burdens with the canons. We gather that in the one college there were twelve positions as canon from the start, while in the other there were five. The number of the latter, however, grew through the munificence of successive bishops and of other pious men, so that now the larger prebends number not five but seventeen, to which two lesser ones called "*Kinderproven*"[49] have been added, the bishop claiming their revenues for his own benefit. Whenever those possessing one of the greater positions as canon die in an ordinary month, the lesser ones are promoted to the

---

[49] "Child prebends."

greater ones, and the prince always substitutes replacements in their places. The former college has always been superior in age, and the latter in the importance of its canons. The fabric of each church is fairly magnificent both inside and out, the choir for the chanting clergy being separated from the congregation of the laity by a stone barricade. The shape of their towers is not the same. For the tower of St. Ludger's | greatly deviates from the common shape, being crowned on top with many pinnacles made of highly worked stone, and its roof, which is made out of copper plates, is hemmed in fairly low down within its base by surrounding walls, so that it escapes our notice. Nonetheless, the rainwater is received from the roof in gutters on all sides, and pours out as if from the center of the tower. The tower of St. Martin's, on the other hand, is no different from the usual shape of other towers, and has on top of a square stone base a very tall steeple sheathed in copper. In the year 1217, when by the authority of Otto I, the son of the Bentheim family who was the twenty-sixth bishop, the two churches were increased and confirmed by episcopal sanction, parishes of burghers were added to each, and the deacons of each college administer the parishes just as the parish priests do.

In this parish of St. Martin, along the banks of the Aa, there stands a very grand monastery of the Minorites, which is equipped with a complex of palaces. It also has a splendid church decorated through the munificence of the pious, in which men distinguished both for learning and piety devote themselves both day and night to the chanting of hymns of praise for the glory of God Almighty, and spend just as much energy on instructing the congregation. It is said that nuns lived in this place many years ago, and I would believe this to be true, since there still exist certain traces of this circumstance that are not, I think, misleading. Since the manors, fields, pastures and the other sources of income that these nuns lived on were in Coesfeld, while the Minorites within the walls of that town cultivated nothing apart from their poverty, it was decided that they would exchange the locations of their residence, to the benefit of both sides of the transaction. | For being close to their manors was useful for the wealthy little nuns, and the large number of wealthy people in the very populous city was useful for the indigent monks. Therefore, the nuns moved from Münster to Coesfeld, and the monks from Coesfeld to Münster. The Franciscans, therefore, have an entire convent of monks here. As for the other orders of monks that are called "mendicant" because they support themselves through begging, such as the Augustinians, the Carmelites and the Dominicans (Preaching Brothers), these orders lodge individual monks in private dwellings in various locations in the city (such monks are called "terminaries").

The parish church dedicated to St. Giles the Abbot has provided for its pastor out of its own income since its foundation, but when a convent of the order of St. Benedict consisting partly of noble and partly of low-born nuns experienced a great increase in its wealth and was added to the parish, the abbess transferred to herself the income for the pastor and the governance of the whole parish, so that she would look after both, and turned the pastor into her own provost. The nuns of this convent, who had run loose for some time in a loose way of life, were restrained with stricter controls in 1468, when their confessor was changed from the one in Marienfeld to the one in Liesborn. The church is quite fine given its size, and its spire, which is attached next to the choir, rises to a moderate height.

Towards the sunrise in winter, the direction from which the east   72
wind also blows, there is a parish church with a spire near the open ground behind the walls. Dedicated to St. Servatius (once the bishop of Tongeren), it is certainly small in comparison with the others, but fairly large given the number of parishes.

Nearby there is a convent of nuns who take the vow of St. Augustine. It was in 1401 that these nuns first began to reside in the parish of St. Ludger in a certain house called "*Nitzing*", and in 1404 some nuns adhering to the same monastic vow were added from the convent in the city of Schuttorp. About fifteen years later, they moved from their earlier residence to the one they now hold in the Parish of St. Servatius, taking along with them the name of the earlier place. Now having increased resources, they built a church that is resplendent on the inside with such carefully executed lustre and refinement that you could hardly find another church more refined in the whole city, and it would cause anyone to marvel at it. The daughters of both noble and common families are admitted to this convent. I gather that the first abbess, whom they call "mother," was Adelheid of Keppell.

Since mention is made of it several times in connection with the   73
Anabaptist madness, I should also not pass over in silence the college of St. Maurice, which, though outside the city, is within sight of it, being only about 93 paces away. It was founded in a very pleasant location by Frederick, the brother of the marquis of Meissen and sixteenth bishop of the city of Münster, who dedicated it to St. Maurice, the very brave general in the service of Christ. He endowed it with no small amount

of wealth, and placed in charge of it men, both noble and low-born, who were devoted to the pursuit of piety and true religion (they are called "canons"), his sole aim in this being to expedite the business of the faith. He ordained that for the protection of his college there should always be a provost chosen from among the main clergy, who would keep two-thirds of certain revenues for himself, and leave the other third to be divided evenly among the others. Houses for both the vicars and canons were built very conveniently around the church and
74 cemetery, and they are protected by a surrounding ditch, | which is not very deep but full of fish. On the west, the church's magnificent main building ends with a lofty tower that resounds with many bronze bells, and with its massive structure protects the church from being harmed by the weather. The choir, on the other hand, is surrounded on both sides by two rather low little towers that lack bells. We read that Borchard, the nineteenth bishop of the Church of Münster, built the colonnade and the palace for the provost. The parish of the peasants who live in scattered settlements around it has been given to this college.

75   I have gone on with this description of the churches, which, while certainly meagre, is nonetheless accurate, in order for the fair reader to learn that the madness of a few months destroyed the very costly labors of a great many years.

CHAPTER SIX

PUBLIC AND PRIVATE PLACES AND BUILDINGS OF THE CITY, ITS AMENITIES, AND A FEW OF ITS CUSTOMS

In order for posterity to understand that in this city of ours we have a plentiful supply of everything that pertains either to obligatory needs or to a well-adorned and delightful way of life, I have decided to add this chapter to the preceding ones, partly treating the things that are necessities in a civil society and partly those that are not necessities but from which the majesty and grandness of our state can be surmised.

To begin with, in the city there are four marketplaces, that is, public places for buying and selling.[1] The common and general marketplace, in which merchandise of every variety is set out for sale, is located between the cemetery of St. Lambert to the north and the steps of disgrace to the south,[2] and is enclosed on both the west and east sides by very large buildings. On it towards the east is the council hall (or burghers' house), located in a row with other houses on both sides. | 76 Held up by smoothed columns, it is prominent because of its various statues of saints, and rises to a summit of uncommon height. On top of its pinnacles can be seen images of winged angels hewn of local marble. In the basement, the council's wines are sold. This hall contains various rooms for the council members, the foremost among them being the one in which the entire council normally convenes for public business on Mondays and Fridays (they call it the council chamber).[3] The building also has differing underground prison cells that vary according to the rank of the criminals. On the north side is the weighing hall ("hall of the scale" or *Waagehaus*), in which everything can be weighed as a benefit for the city. An alley intervenes to provide access to the council's stable and its registry (called the *Scriverei* in German), and separate cells for defendants are also concealed under this registry. At

---

[1] The seemingly pointless explanation is necessitated by the ambiguity of *forum* (translated here as "marketplace"), which could also be taken to mean "court."

[2] These steps of disgrace are presumably to be identified with the location for exhibiting criminals mentioned at the end of this paragraph.

[3] The council's meeting room is famous as the site for the signing of the Treaty of Westphalia, which brought an end to the Thirty Years' War in 1648.

one end of the marketplace to the south, there is a house that juts out in front of the rest of the row, and is conspicuous for its solitary little tower, and while those who are to be marked for some crime which they have committed are kept in the lowest room of this house, there is a place higher up where scoundrels condemned to lashing or branding are first restrained by the hangman in iron shackles and presented for public viewing before being punished with flogging or the cutting off of an ear or being marked with a sign burned onto them with a cautering iron.

77 On the other side of the cemetery of St. Lambert, the grain market lies to the west and the fish market to the north. | In the latter is the common hall of all the city's guilds, in which according to the circumstances sometimes everyone and sometimes only the aldermen and the guilds masters meet to deliberate for the common good. Here the views of the common people are so firmly stitched together with hempen ropes that the council cannot unravel them, and for this reason this hall is justly but ominously called the "*schowhaus*," which means "sewing hall," or the "viewing hall" from the word for "look at" ("*schauen*"), because the low-born burghers are wont to hold meetings here to carry out public affairs, and when they depart from there in a long row after ending their deliberations, they are looked at by the throng that rushes up.[4] It may be called the council hall of the workers. This synagogue of Satan was more or less always annoying to the city council.[5] For it gave rise to every civil disturbance, first introducing various novelties in religion, and finally begetting the monstrosity of Anabaptism, which it reared for the destruction of all good men. In addition to this common hall, each of the prominent guilds has a hall of its own which they acquired for deliberating and for feasting.

The fourth marketplace is in the Parish Across-the-River, and in the past offered goods of every kind for sale just like the common marketplace. In addition, there are two meat markets that during their times of operation are supplied with various cuts of fresh meat. One is in the general marketplace, and in its cellar both domestic and imported

---

[4] The building was called *schohus* in Low German, a word of uncertain derivation. K.'s short (negative) assessment here of the guilds' role in contributing to the Anabaptist takeover led the guilds to object to K.'s work (see General Introduction 3b).

[5] "Synagogue of Satan" was a term for "conventicles," that is, illegal gatherings of heretics, which Satan himself was thought to preside over in the orthodox conception.

beer was provided at the council's expense for its own benefit, but now a very splendid hall has been built by the council for this purpose at great expense. | The other meat market is in the grain market, and its upper floor is used by the city council as a granary to see to the needs of the public.   78

The more populous parishes have their own infirmaries to which those infected with the plague or some other contagious disease are brought. Their infirmaries are administered by men chosen for this purpose, since it has been found in practice that in the midst of such dregs of humanity it is an excellent and wholesome procedure for those who are infected to be removed from contact with the healthy. This prevents the spread of the illness through contagion, and prevents the poorer people, who are bereft of the aid of friends, from being altogether abandoned and fading away through thirst and hunger as a result of lack of human assistance. There are also two lime kilns along the walls in different parts of the city, one having been built for the use of the city council alone and the other for that of the burghers.

The alms-houses number fifteen, some for men, some for women, some for both. There is one strangers' alms-house, which, as the story has it, was built on Horst Lane by the council and accepts both male and female foreigners who are bereft of help and means. There are two alms-houses for men, one in St. Ludger's parish and the other in the Parish Across-the-River, both named after their capacity of twelve inhabitants. One provides for the assistants of the Lord's Lords who are decrepit with old age or disease, and the other does so for their serfs in the countryside who are reduced to penury. There are eight alms-houses for women. Of these, four are in the Parish of St. Martin: Wessede's, generously founded by the widow of Meinburg of Wessede in the year 1302; Busch's, by William of Busch; Wieck's, by Gertrud of Wieck; Ae's, by the brothers John and Henry tor Ae, who were tanners. In the Parish Across-the-River there are two: the Pruessen house donated by the widow of John Pruessen, | and the house along the cemetery of St. John, which once was a public brothel but was converted for the very respectable benefit of poor womenfolk by Bernard Schedelich, the commander of the house at Steinfurt. Finally, there are two in the Parish of St. Ludger, one built by the widow Swenthoevel and the other by the widow of Eberhard Bischoping. There are four alms-houses for both men and women. Three of these are in the Parish Across-the-River. The first was built by the noble Wieck family, and the second one, which is located by the open area behind the walls near   79 the tower named after ghosts (the "*Buddenturm*"), was built and endowed at the expense of a respectable citizen of Büderich[6] in the year 1542 for the benefit of twelve men and twelve women who are struggling under an old age of poverty, and it is now maintained by the abbess of the Convent Across-the-River and the servants of the Jews' Field Parish. The third one, which is between the bridges, and the fourth one, which is by the Gate of St. Maurice, were mentioned above in the description of the city. In addition to all these, there is a shelter for lepers outside the city, which has a very well endowed position as pastor that is in the council's gift.

In addition to the weekly market days every Wednesday and Saturday, there are six markets days. Three of these are visited by throngs of people outside the city by the Gates of St. Ludger and the Jews' Field on the feast days of St. George, St. Laurence, and St. Clement,[7] and three within the city in the Lords' Field and the public marketplace. The latter take place at the time of the two synods, that is, on the Monday in spring after the Sunday "*Laetare*,"[8] the Monday in fall after the feast of Gereon,[9] and on the feast of Sts. Peter and Paul,[10] and since ancient times these market days have been so endowed with 80 privileges, liberties | and immunities, and so accepted in practice, that everyone is granted full and inviolate permission to come here to engage in buying and selling. Whoever breaks the public peace at this time and in wounding someone sheds the least amount of blood is punished with execution. The dedication of the cathedral, which is celebrated on the day of St. Jerome,[11] enjoys the same privileges. These liberties are posted on a public sign attached to one of the cathedral's towers so that no one may excuse his transgression on the grounds of ignorance.

What is the point of describing at length the greatness of the cleanliness and beauty of the public lanes and private houses when Münster leads all the cities of Westphalia in both these and other adornments?

---

[6] The phrase is *civis Butepagiis*, which seems to imply a Latinized town name *Butepagus*. The first element is clearly Germanic, but the Latin *pagus* means "country district," which is seemingly a translation of some German element. No town (with a name like Butenfeld) readily lends itself, but perhaps Büderich to the southwest of Münster is meant.

[7] April 23, August 10, November 23.

[8] The fourth Sunday in Lent.

[9] October 10.

[10] June 29.

[11] September 30 (for the dedication, see 34D).

All the buildings abut one another, and are drawn up in rows so that none protrude in front of the others. Some are magnificent because of the resources of their inhabitants, and are carefully constructed with great skill, gleaming just like churches, both inside and out, with various statues and outlines carved from Badenberg marble. There is a quarry on Mount Badenberg, two miles from the city, and blocks of the noblest stone are carved out of it.[12] When smoothed by plane, this stone takes on any shape, needing no more effort in the working than does real marble, and once it has taken a shape, it keeps it. For experience shows that it suffers no damage from the weather, and for this reason most buildings in the city endure. Some humbler buildings are constructed out of wood on account of the lesser resources of their owners, and are enclosed with walls formed of clay or brick (such houses are mostly seen outside the circuit of the walls). All the buildings, however, are roofed with bricks or terra cotta tiles, either mortar or bundles of straw being inserted between them to keep out the depredations of rainwater.

The city also receives no little adornment from the impressive unbroken row of houses that extends along the marketplace, and surrounds just about half of the Lords' Field. | Resting upon vaults and   81
columns spaced at the right intervals, it is held up in such a way that a public path is left underneath it at times. Those who live in these vaulted houses are mostly merchants, and their wives and daughters are commonly called "vault matrons" and "vault maidens" after those vaults, as if they are thought to surpass other women in beauty and good character, since they have their residence in their market, at the heart of the city.

The river Aa is enlarged from various gurgling springs, and enters the city walls from the south through heavily re-enforced gratings. The river flows through the downhill section of the city, and with a regular rubbing action, it scrapes at its banks, which are adorned on either side, at one point with pastures, at another with orchards, at yet another

---

[12] This variety of stone is now known as "Baumberg sandstone," and is quarried in the Baumberge to the west of Münster in the vicinity of Havixbeck and Nottuln. Presumably, K. has "German miles" in mind (one German mile equals 4.6 English miles or 7.42 kilometers), and Badenberg must be an older name for Baumberg. This stone, which is geologically different from marble (a form of limestone that has undergone metamorphosis), was commonly used as the material for prestigious building projects throughout northwestern Germany and the Low Countries since the later Middle Ages.

with buildings. This river drives not only the mills of the Knights of St. George, where it first enters the city, but also the mills of some nobles of the Wieck family in approximately the center of the city. Here it is separated into two branches, and as these are reunited downriver, it seems to form a kind of island, though this is joined to the mainland by bridges. Above this river, some privies have been installed and are maintained at public expense to increase the cleanliness of the city. In short, the river takes virtually all the filth of the entire city, which flows in from either side, and carries it off as it exits from the city to the north with its peaceful current. As for what is left in piles in the lanes, this is taken away in wagons belonging to the city council to increase the size of the ramparts. The right to fish in the city between the mills of the Knights of St. George and of the Wieck family is held by the venerable Lord Geoffrey of Raesfeld, deacon of the Lords' church and provost of St. Maurice's through the prince's gift (this military benefice is always in his gift by feudal right).

82   All the lanes in the city are covered with paving stone in plumb-line accuracy, so that water from rain or any other source that pours off the houses on either side with washed-away filth flows by the force of nature down the sloping gutters made in the center of the lanes and eventually swells the waters of the Aa. Whatever filth is collected here and there in the sewers also gushes into the river when it is pushed there by sudden downpours. At a time of sudden disturbance, all the lanes are also defended with iron chains that are dragged across them and pulled taut, a form of defense that is very effective against cavalry.

Now I will say a few words about some customs and habits handed down since ancient days.[13]

On January 1, they make an auspicious start to the year by inviting each other to feasts, singing festive songs and exchanging gifts, with German music added in, and when they meet, they wish each other a happy outcome to the year, being fully convinced that the end of the year will resemble its beginning. At the same time, the matrons knead

---

[13] In the following sections, K. gives vent to a curmudgeonly exasperation at certain raucous customs that did not meet with his favor. Unfortunately for K., in its anger at K. for the trouble he was causing with his historical work, the city council decided to take offense at some of these criticisms on the grounds that they brought the city into disrepute among its neighbors (see General Introduction 3b). Some of these objections (such as those about his discussion of the New Year's cakes) are frivolous, and K. can hardly have been alone in his dislike of the more extravagant customs such as the Carnival revelry.

a sort of dough made of flour mixed with honey or mead or clear, tasteless water, as their means allow, adding pepper and other spices. From this they pull out as many portions as there are individuals in the family, and after first assigning God and the Blessed Mary their own portions, which are later used for the benefit of the poor, they finally share out the portions among the members of the family in a certain peculiar ceremony, reciting a fixed formula. Making a fist with their right hand, they strike the individuals on the chest one after the other, adding the words, "Small portion, good fortune! The kindness is better than the cake!" ("*Klein stuck, groiß glucke! Besser ist der gunst dan der kuche*"). That is:

> We give little presents, may the luck be greater than these!
> The intent is better: take it as a gift!

Then they eagerly tear the cakes up, though they put in charge of this business one of the stouter members, who keeps for himself the last piece of everyone else's cakes for his efforts. As each one surreptitiously snatches cakes from another, he wins himself no little praise for his hard work from the others. Meanwhile, | they engage in hard drinking and spend a large part of the night in these pursuits. They banquet as much on the feast of the Three Magi[14] and give themselves over to the cakes. Apart from these activities, they also appoint a "king" by lot, who assigns duties to the whole family after the fashion of kings, and by his royal authority penalizes those who neglect their duties. In addition, on these days as well as on the Nativity of the Lord, individual houses are purified and expiated by the male heads of the household with incense and holy water, and as he sings hymns, the whole family follows after him with lit torches. On the feast of the Purification of Mary,[15] tapers are consecrated in churches the way that palm fronds are on Palm Sunday, and with these they fortify themselves against lightning and the stabbing of demons.

    They celebrate carnival with such lechery and licentiousness that they think that at this time there is no foolishness that is forbidden them. Egged on by a sort of voluntary craziness, both males and females transform themselves with horrible masks and weird attire, and with lit torches in their hands, they rush through the wards of the city,

83

---

[14] I.e., Epiphany (January 6).
[15] February 2.

accompanied by the crashing of drums and the plucking of stringed instruments. The men wear women's clothing, and the women men's. Many people also deceptively adopt the garb of foreign races and of other religious beliefs and at times even that of the black Evil Spirit,[16] and in their anonymity they commit crimes worthy of him. By vote they choose a chief dicer who is to be in charge of throwing the dice, the profits and losses from this belonging to everyone. While he presides over gambling, the rest give themselves over to dances. Invited to drink by their host's generosity, they guzzle without removing their masks. Instead, they put into the cup a tube that is made of silver or pewter and hangs from their neck, and suck out the liquid.[17] When this tube is removed, the part of the drink left in it pours back into the cup in a thoroughly disgusting manner. Since everyone shares the same Westphalian origin and stupidity, such crudeness in manners is noticed by no one, but is concealed by ancestral custom.

84   The apprentices in the individual guilds appoint one of their number who is not only outstanding for his physical strength and height but also more splendidly attired than the others, and to him they entrust the task of bearing the guild standard, half of them preceding him and half following. Just about one standard bearer can be seen for every guild. Marching through the city ward by ward, from the members of their own guild or from those who have at some time made use of their services they beg for money, meat and sausages, and from what they get they deck out feasts and banquets of great immoderation and excess. If perchance some members absent themselves from these feasts, as despisers of the fellows they are placed on ladders in a shameful and humiliating way and brought by force. In this way, they guzzle liquor, they get drunk, they devour food, almost as if they had been born for the purpose of squandering everything. What they do not use up they ruin, as if it were considered a sin to keep something back for obligatory uses, having no concern for the morrow. In excess of Westphalian practice, there are just about as many cups as there are individuals at the banquet. In challenges, they force each other to drink the same amount in one gulp, even at the risk of their own lives, and by this they inflict disaster on their bodies and their purses.

---

[16] I.e., the Devil (*der böse Geist* is a frequent term for him in Early Modern German).
[17] K. could find no word in Latin for "straw"!

For some days and nights, the whole city resounds with the din of the drums and the spontaneous madness of crazy people.

The butchers are also driven on by madness at the dictate of a similar custom. At nightfall, one of the masters of this guild carries the standard on horseback, and the other is led on foot by not just any maiden but the eldest daughter of a butcher in the whole guild, while the sons of meat sellers ride on horses, decked out extravagantly in gold and silver, and baby boys still wrapped in swaddling clothes are carried on horseback by certain other servants. By riding a horse in this way, they acquire for themselves the right to a butcher's table in the meat market, the parents running it until the children reach adulthood, since no one is entitled to this right except for the legitimate male son of a butcher who has been carried around on a horse in this procession. Behind them, all the male heads of households from the whole guild follow the maiden in a row two-by-two. Here and there, strong men are mixed | into this arrangement carrying on their shoulders large torches   85 composed of oakum, flax, fat, pitch and resin to light the way. On the other shoulder they place a heavy club as a form of protection. A large number of such men follow this procession at the end of the column. At the head, public flute players ride on fairly gentle horses, playing songs through the lanes with their varied harmony. Specially hired foot-men lead these horses by the bridle to keep them from grazing, since the flute players cannot hold the reins with their hands occupied with playing. Finally, a large throng of youthful servants closes the column. These people hold circles of oakum in their right hand, and by stick-ing their other hand in someone else's circle they are joined together like a chain. Their leader wrenches the connected row of servants in gyrations from one side to the other, so that the people at the other end, who are almost always separated from the rest by a great distance, are dashed to the ground in a great heap, which easily raises a laugh among the spectators. This procession is led to the individual houses of the meat sellers, where as much wine as they want is shoved in front of the heads of households and the other more respectable characters who are responsible for these theatrics, while it is beer for the rest. Finally, after a song has been sung in the marketplace (and no longer understood by anyone), they go their own ways. That same night, in the Lords' Field they set up rather long poles encased in straw, and after a fire has been lit at the top of them, they burn downwards as the flame gradually spreads. They also place in the market and some lanes pitched barrels on which some residue of the pitch remains, and set fire to them, or instead of this they raise up green yews, placing candelabra on top, and the young men and girls dance around them, at times to the loss of their chastity.

How much license is granted to stupidity can also be understood from the fact that a certain number of the richer young men sometimes form a sort of society for themselves, calling it a "tavernship" (that is, a college of drinking companions) and establishing it on a firm footing with certain regulations—for the purpose of upholding the association's respectability, as they claim. | The members hold banquets very frequently, reveling and guzzling liquor, often throughout the night, then sleeping during the day. These are the kind of people who turn night into day and day into night; who squander their own funds and increase others'; who promote not their own interests but that of others. For in getting drunk and feasting, they use up their own means, and in the meanwhile they carelessly ignore their own affairs, and enrich the innkeepers. Sometimes on horseback and sometimes on foot, they make a public spectacle of their own stupidity, when they wear masks or foreign clothing bought for this purpose. On the Thursday that directly precedes the Sunday of Pentecost, a few young men belonging to this college put on masks or falsely adopt the attire appropriate for jesters or some other position, and dash quickly through the lanes in a chariot prepared for this, carrying hidden with them in the chariot a clown manikin sewn out of rags and stuffed with straw. On horseback, many members of the society precede the chariot wearing masks, and many follow it. After leaving the city, some wear out even heartier horses by rushing through the open countryside, while others work out amidst this horse racing by jumping through iron circles held up by pine spears. Then, having returned to the city, they show off the fabricated clown in joyful triumph, as if it were a prince brought from elsewhere to whom they were giving a magnificent welcome. After escorting him with a liveried horse guard consisting of the entire college through some lanes of the city and three times around the marketplace to make sure that the potentate's presence escapes no one's notice, they receive him with the greatest honor in a hall well supplied with drunkards, and there, for days and nights, they guzzle, they gobble and they bring virtually no end to the drinking. Nonetheless, they have certain regulations for the preservation of their respectability, and these are particularly beneficial to young men, who, being otherwise licentious and unbridled by nature,[18] are excellently kept to their duty by them. For they allow no one who has transgressed against the regulations to get off scot-free. The college is laudable on this account in particular, since it is considered to be a school for unbridled youth. | Anyway, once the potentate is   87 brought in, an unbelievable amount of stupidity (sorry, I meant jollity) is committed not only in this hall but also in various places throughout the city. For everyone thinks that he is granted immunity in countless varieties of idiocy as if in the presence of a patron[19] of stupidity. This potentate also strives to extend his sway as far as possible, and for this reason towards nightfall masked members of his retinue are often sent forth armed with lit torches and accompanied by the din of drums and strings. They act with such confidence that they break in on nighttime feasts, and with their playing of dice and skill at drinking and danc- ing they entice people of both sexes to similar insanity, increasing the kingdom of stupidity with this stratagem. These efforts at extending the kingdom of revelry last until the Thursday before the Sunday "*Invocavit*,"[20] at which point his retinue, noticing that they have worn themselves out with excessive drunkenness and altogether emptied the bottom of their purse, lay aside this voluntary craziness of theirs, and they come to their senses and think that the person responsible for such misfortune deserves the supreme punishment. Accordingly, they seize the clown as the instigator of their previous madness, and carry him around again ward by ward, but this time not in a triumphal chariot as before but in a lugubrious wagon accompanied by guards and a priest for confession. A very large number of horsemen are present to act as guards in order to prevent the least possibility of flight opening up for him anywhere and to prevent him from being rescued by his people and escaping the execution he deserves. At this point, after they have given the random crowd its fill with this spectacle on horseback, the wagon is driven three times around the marketplace and then the king of stupidity is snatched out of it and brought before a capital trial constructed in the general market out of theater masks. Here he is accused of many crimes: being a drunkard and wino who can never get enough beer;

---

[18] Presumably, the schoolmaster is speaking from experience.
[19] I.e., patron saint.
[20] The first Sunday in Lent.

a greedy glutton and a gambler who squanders all his goods; a liar; a thief; a harborer of felons; a corruptor of youth; a whoremonger; the inventor of every kind of inconsequential stupidity; a disturber of the peace and instigator of many stabbings and murders; a raper of virgins who is befouled with the crime of incest; and a despiser of all God's commandments. Since he has been caught red-handed committing these crimes in public, he cannot deny the charges and does not dare to, lest he increasingly call down upon himself the indignation of God, and worsen his punishment. Therefore, he excuses the charges with silence and atones for them with tears, as it seems, awaiting with trembling a sentence worthy of his deeds from the judges. Since this

88 pile of crimes seems by right to demand a more severe penalty, | it is properly judged in the public decision that he should be consigned to the flames to be burned up. Immediately, the poor wretch is cast by the theatrical executioners onto a pyre that has been hurriedly piled up there, and is reduced to ashes. When these ashes are carried up by the flames, the wind takes them and scatters them throughout virtually the entire city, putting an end to the licentious stupidity. In this way, the voluntary madness gradually dissipates. When, in the year 1565, the very prudent city council was inspired by God to stamp out all these kinds of insanity as the causes of many misdeeds, to the applause of all good men these were quickly suppressed and halted through the fear of the punishment, so that almost no trace of them remains to be seen.

After the burning of the clown, they composed themselves so earnestly for praying and fasting that they passed through the entire period of Lent without the sustenance of dairy products. They would keep the fasts of the four seasons[21] on bread and warm water, and celebrate all the festivals instituted in ancient days by the Catholic Church as well as the associated ceremonies, which rouse the people to piety. The regular, customary prayers would be offered, and in addition to these, extraordinary ones would be decreed by the prince as necessary. After the introduction of the new religion, however, not only would they eat butter, milk, and eggs, but the chickens, cows, and fatted calves themselves had to fear for their lives. For at that time no distinction was made between the foods for various days. The holy days along with virtually all their ceremonies were abolished, the images were cast

---

[21] I.e., Ember days, which were four periods of fasting that more or less corresponded to the start of the four seasons (hence, the name in Latin).

from the churches, and prayers began to be called superstitions and fun was made of good works. All these things were restored for us and brought back from exile, as it were, after the end of the Anabaptist madness and the siege.

On the feast of St. John the Baptist, girls would, here and there, hang wreaths and crowns from a rope drawn across the lane, and offer a cup to passers-by, inviting them coaxingly to drink. On this pretext, they ambushed certain people's purses and emptied them of money. With the proceeds, | a feast was prepared, to which they invited young   89
men. These young men took part in the feast and danced. Since this practice often provided many girls with an opportunity to sully their chastity, it has now been forbidden with very good reason by the civil authorities, and is considered abolished.

The feasts of St. James and St. Martin[22] are the ones most celebrated by the Lord's Lords with their own presence. For the received custom of the one feast ordains that the year's grain should be divided in equal shares among the Lords who are present, while on the other the same procedure is used for the income in cash.

On the Monday before the feast of St. Margaret the Virgin,[23] a solemn purification of the city takes place. The eucharist is carried around accompanied by the entire clergy and city council. Public attendants carrying white clubs surround them, and push back the commoners who press upon them on either side. A sizeable portion of the burghers and matrons participate in this supplication with great humility and piety. Very many people also follow bare-footed and in white linen clothing, which often brings tears to many spectators.

The young men of the school of St. Paul sometimes relieve with licentiousness the discontent which they feel as a result of their constant pursuit of learning. Every year, all the youths are led out three times on expeditions, without weapons of course. The first one takes place on the Tuesday directly before Pentecost, and on that day they are drawn up in order (arranged by instructional class) and leave the city. They immediately head for bowers that have been erected the day before, and there they gobble food and guzzle with such immoderation that they almost seem to have gone insane. They do everything with such licentiousness that on that day the masters who are present | can do   90

---

[22] July 25 and November 11.
[23] July 13.

nothing to restrain them. They are driven with such madness that they shake off the advice of the more cautious and seldom or never leave that place without sheer bedlam. Finally, they are persuaded with great difficulty, partly through threats, partly through beatings, partly through entreaties, and they have a hard time entering the city as they carry boughs in their hands and sing songs. When they reach the colonnade of the cathedral, they disperse. You might say that the teachers would prefer to thresh grain all day rather than be worn out with such worrisome cares. (The vicars of the cathedral also celebrate their own frond holiday, including well provisioned feasts to which they invite not only the leading men of the city but also the more respectable matrons and maidens.) The second school expedition takes place at the public recitation of the school's poem, which they have learned in school with great loss and detriment to public reading and with severe annoyance for the masters. The final expedition is undertaken on the vigil before the feast of St. Nicholas.[24] On this occasion, a bishop chosen from among the pupils is solemnly escorted to the Lords' Field by the whole company of the youth with lit torches, and when the dregs of humanity who have nothing to do with this associate themselves with the pupils, assorted disturbances are stirred up. After a few poems have been recited there, they immediately disperse in order to hold a feast.

The only reason why these school expeditions were originally instituted was so that the students, who have done violence to themselves through immoderate study, should find enjoyment in these means of recreation, and after regaining new strength, so to speak, in this way, return the more eagerly to their interrupted lessons. Now, however, since the expeditions delay their studies and, as it were, distract the students, and they moreover make the youth insolent and in some way estrange them from their learning, they have been justly abolished, and the students retain only the right to hold the ceremony of the fronds, with which Herman, the fourteenth bishop of the Church of Münster, who died in the year 1042, is said to have endowed the pupils of St.

91 Paul's school from what was then his own manor, | as can be seen in the catalogue of the bishops.[25] To prevent this same right from being lost or falling into abeyance, it has been established that every year each

---

[24] December 5.
[25] This right is not attested in surviving documents.

student should pay one farthing (since then changed to a half-penny), and from this money the chanters who are called chamber men should buy themselves wax tapers to use in a proper mass for the dead in memory of this same Bishop Herman in the Church Across-the-River, which was founded and consecrated by him.

CHAPTER SEVEN

DUAL JURISDICTION IN THE CITY

There is a dual jurisdiction in the city: ecclesiastical and secular. Only the bishop holds the ecclesiastical jurisdiction, and not only are the disputes of the ecclesiastics dealt with there but so are those of laymen, particularly in order for debtors to be struck with the ecclesiastical fulminations let loose by the judge and thus forced to repay their creditors. As for these fulminations, although they inflict no wounds on the body or cause blood to be shed, they terrify debtors to an incredible degree, and with good reason. For they lessen the debtors' fortune and undercut their spirit. It is not permissible to strike a citizen of Münster with these weapons against his will in connection with a case that is both civil and secular. This court, which they also call a curia or consistory, has several different officers. The first is the judge, who is appointed by the bishop and receives his authority from him. They call him the "official of the court of Münster," not, as Calepinus thinks,[1] from the verb "*officere*," that is, "to harm," but from the "office" over which he 92 presides. | At present, Lord Derek of Hamm, a man famed for his knowledge of the law, attends to this duty in a praiseworthy manner. Next comes the seal impresser, or rather clerk, who makes the decisions of the court official by affixing the court's seal into green wax. They call him the "chancellor," and sometimes he also carries out the function of sitting as an assessor. To him the prince assigns a special house to live in on the Lords' Field. This house is commonly called the "chancery," and every year ecclesiastical fulminations and censures bring large sums of money into it, to the prince's profit. Lord Jacob Voss, a deacon of the Old Church who possesses great erudition in the laws, is the present chancellor. Next come the three scribes who draw up documents, who are called "notaries." Either because they were found to be rather careless or because the three were by no means enough to write down all the cases, Bernard, the fifty-second bishop of the diocese,

---

[1] The Latin dictionary (*dictionarium latinum*) of the Italian Augustinian Ambrosius Calepinus (ca. 1440–1510) was first published in 1502, and provided the basis for many subsequent (often multi-lingual) dictionaries.

added a fourth, Arnold Isfording, a man who, while being talented in his skill, pays very much attention to his own interests. These scribes write down a reliable summary of the arguments put forward on either side by the contending parties, and then they take their summaries and stitch them together in verbose formulas filled with such contemptible redundancies and pointless blatherings that they cause nauseated disgust in the judge who reads them and sometimes lead him astray from the straight path into a trackless morass, thinking it the greatest sin and infamous heresy if someone deviates from the traditional phraseology. For the purpose of this sly grasping, they support at home a swarm of amanuenses, earning from this a splendid profit for themselves and their employees. Such faith is placed in the documents they draw up that these cannot be doubted. There are also other harpies—buzzards or swallows of paradise—who defend cases, thereby making no small gain for themselves as they drain the insides of purses, and those of them who are assisted by their tongue are so puffed up with haughtiness that when a poor man speaks, they turn to the side not just their face but their entire head, looking at him not directly but at an angle. This is the origin of the solicitors, who on behalf of their party remind the lawyers, who are involved in a plethora of cases, of the dispute. These solicitors often intercept with clever arguments of persuasion what the lawyers would otherwise get, and they snatch, as it were, the mouthful from the lawyers' jaws. From this group, then, arises the great mob of vulgar scribes called "benchers" (*bancales*) who devote themselves to writing up less significant orders. | Next, there are the letter bearers, who, 93 through their own peculiar assistants, distribute among all the parishes of the diocese the judicial decisions that have been certified with the court's seal. Finally, there are others who are given the task of carrying out sentence in connection with the seizure of sureties. These men are commonly called "expeditors" or "expanders" in the vernacular. Many years ago, their job was in the hands of the letter bearers, but it has now been made a separate office in order to expedite the legal process and bring cases to an end. This single court not only provides a small income to all these officials along with their wives and a fairly large body of attendants, but fattens them with sumptuous feasts and bestows magnificent palaces on them. They send appeals from here to the court of the archbishop of Cologne.

Some years ago it was the traditional practice that because of one person's fault the worship of God would be suspended in the churches if someone accursed (struck by the thunderbolt of fulmination), that is, excommunicated (ordered, as a form of censure because of his obstinacy, to withdraw from taking communion with his fellow man), was found there. But since it is unfair to punish the blameless for someone else's crime and to deprive them of the sacraments and the Word of God, William, the fifty-first bishop, for excellent reasons completely abolished the practice of interdicting divine services and changed this to the invocation of the secular arm.[2] Thus, while it had previously been at the judge's discretion whether he should achieve his end through the secular arm or through an interdict, once the latter course was abolished, the use of the secular arm was made obligatory. They call the location of this court "Paradise,"[3] and when it is in session, there is in it such screeching and thronging of strangers, such squabbling to the point of hoarseness among the pettifoggers who compete within the court's enclosure, that you would think that these sober men were drunk and that you were passing by an inn full of drinking buddies.

The secular court is always held in the area of the public marketplace that is fenced in with barricades, under the vaults of the council hall. In addition to civil cases, criminals are also tried there whenever
94 the situation so dictates. The judge | is presented and offered to the council by the prince, who entrusts the management of the matter to him after exacting an oath.[4] Unless there is an impediment for some just cause, the council accepts the appointee with the appropriate reverence and assigns to him two assessors from the ranks of the council. When, many years ago, the bishops claimed for themselves not only the rights over this entire court but also the revenues, returns and income (what is called "*grute*"), the result after 1277 was that Eberhard of Deist, the thirty-seventh bishop, took up arms against the city in defense of his Church, and at the urging of certain men who hated peace, he put the city under close siege. But the nobility and the leading clergy refused him assistance against the city, either because they thought that the reason for the siege was too trivial to merit such disturbances, and that it was imprudent of him to resort to arms, or because the war that

---

[2] "Secular arm" (*bracchium saeculare*) is the medieval term for the use of the powers of the secular authority to impose temporal sanctions upon those convicted of ecclesiastical offenses (particularly, the burning alive of those whom the Church had condemned as heretics, since such activities were considered incompatible with the sanctity of the servants of God).

[3] See 29D.

[4] The city council took exception to K.'s account of the relative claims made by the prince and by the city to jurisdiction over this court (see General Introduction 3b).

had been begun could be brought to an end only with great loss to the subjects and with bloodshed if there was to be a full-scale conflict with enraged spirits on both sides, or because they would call upon themselves the city's undying enmity, and accordingly the bishop, who was not equal to achieving his end by himself, despaired of taking the city. Bereft of assistance, he not only moved his camp and abandoned the undertaking of the siege, but under compulsion bought peace at the cost of half the secular jurisdiction and the loss of all the revenues and returns of the *grute*. Having acquired these rights in this way, the council has kept them for itself down to the present day, though certain people have tried to violate them.

This court makes use of one scribe, and the services of this man 95 alone are more than sufficient for all the court cases that are drawn up in documents. Six attendants undertake the task of protecting all the cases. Appeals from this court are lodged with the council, certainly not by a general right but by a peculiar one that has been confirmed by long custom.[5] The judge alone claims the profits from the act of applying the seal; as for the other revenues (income) from the court, he first keeps half for himself in the bishop's name and then leaves the rest to be distributed in equal portions between the assessors and the council.

Apart from these statements, many more things could be said about each court, but for the sake of brevity I think that they should be passed over.

---

[5] Once again, the city council objected to this conception of the appeals process, though K.'s description seems to be phrased neutrally without prejudicing the issue in the prince's favor.

CHAPTER EIGHT

DIVISION OF THE CITY'S INHABITANTS INTO ESTATES

The whole city comprises two categories of people, one consisting of the religious (ecclesiastics) and the other of the profane (laymen). Since the religious fall to God's lot, they adopt the designation "clerics."[1] The totality of the religious is called the "clergy," being divided into the main and the lower clergy on the basis of dignity in rank. The higher clergy consists of the forty canons of the cathedral, whom the commons call the Lord's Lords.[2] Admission to this order is granted to no one of blemished birth, and instead only those who possess the full and complete grandeur of knighthood in their ancestors, particularly in their four great-grandfathers on both sides and are outstanding in
96 the integrity of their character and in their learning. | In the intervals between bishops, the administration of the diocese falls to these men alone as if by hereditary right, and they also have the sole right to choose the prince. Accordingly, this order of the clergy is justly called "main." A careful investigation is made into the grandeur of their birth. In this they do not simply trust a title to nobility but summon men of venerable ancient lineage whose reputation and nobility are unsullied, putting faith in their attestations in this regard when these are confirmed by oath. In addition, no one is admitted to this renowned group who has not first, as ecclesiastic regulation dictates, spent some hundreds of crowns to study at a famous university across the Alps.

Hence it happens that most members of this order surpass the others in learning, culture and personal integrity. The Emperor Frederick I,[3] who had at that time selected Dortmund as his capital, graciously granted the chapter the right to choose the bishop. To be sure, it was easy for the chapter to get whatever it wanted from the emperor, since peaceable relations between emperor and pope were uncommon, and their rivalry severe. It had not been the case that the bishops were chosen

---

[1] The term "cleric," borrowed ultimately from Greek, is a derivative of the word for "lot" (*kleros*).
[2] *Herrenherren*, i.e., the lords who serve the Lord.
[3] Frederick Barbarossa, Holy Roman Emperor 1152–1190.

through election by the chapter but instead the emperors appointed those whom they had learned to be outstanding for their piety and unusual virtue. Accordingly, Count Otto | of Bentheim was the first 97 bishop (the twenty-sixth overall) to be appointed by the free election of the chapter, being confirmed by Pope Honorius. From that time down to the present day, the unrestricted election of the prince has remained in the hands of the chapter, although other arrangements for the diocese have at times intervened, to the great detriment of the diocese and the commonwealth.

The main order has over the years witnessed such an increase in its power, dignity and wealth that it hardly has its equal. So great is its influence that it keeps in subordination to it not only the entire nobility and knighthood through ties of kinship, but the prince himself through the constraint of an oath. For without the authorization of the main clergy, the prince can hardly make a decision that will remain valid in trivial matters, much less in troublesome ones that pertain to the well-being of the diocese.

This order is very fittingly divided up by offices. The provost surpasses the others in dignity, and the dean does so in the authority of his office. The former is the archdeacon of all the parishes in the city (apart from the Parish Across-the-River) and censor of their morals, but involves himself in the chapter's business only when asked to. After the prince, the latter is, even against his will, the head of not just the main clergy but also of all the ecclesiastics belonging to the lower clergy, and sets the standard for them in their way of living, receiving respect and reverence as a father and a teacher. He has the power to establish regulations for the clergy's way of living and to punish transgressors with either the deprivation of their income or imprisonment. For the Lords have their own prison, and the fearsome terror it instills in the clergy keeps them to their duty, with the result that the prison today can be seen covered with dirt and cobwebs as a result of long neglect, | 98 there hardly being any use for it nowadays. Even today, the dean displays the attire of canons (regulars) by wearing a black garment with a white stole wrapped over it.

The schoolmaster not only defends the rights of the public school and takes care of the youth, but he also restrains the novice canons with his hand and rules. Letting them graduate at the appropriate time, he releases them from his rules and subordinates them to the chapter's, and from this procedure derives the very beautiful graduation ceremony. The sacristan guards the gold and silver vessels and the

other adornments and treasures of the cathedral through the efforts of
the beadles and other attendants appointed by him, and for this reason
they call him the guard of the Lords' Church. The steward has some
hundreds of manors under his control, and from them he collects some
thousands of gold coins every year for the use of the Lords, providing
for them at fixed dates with the transportation of wood and with wines,
candles, meals, cakes and other such things. The bursar is named after
the leather purse[4] from which he makes daily distributions of sums of
money among those who are present in the choir and dutifully engaged
in the worship of God (these distributions are called "presences," since
they given only to those who are present). This procedure is excellent
for preserving the ecclesiastical order and keeping them to their duty.

Here I pass over the cantor, who is the overseer of the cantors and of
the chamber men; the archdeacons, who are the eyes of the bishop and
inspect the parishes of the entire diocese, assessing their behavior; the
superintendents of buildings, whom they call the building master,[5] who
is in charge of the workmen and necessary construction in the basilica;
and the sick attendant, whom they call the rector of the ill, who keeps
hog heads preserved in brine, so that when any of the Lords are sick
with an inescapable illness, he will, after the supreme unction, offer them
these heads along with bread, beer and a burning taper for three solid
days, if they survive that long. There are many possible reasons why
this custom has been established. Perhaps the reason is in order that
since the Lords originally shared a common meal and did not provide
anyone with separate sustenance at home, they should, when they give
solace to the sick man with their presence, themselves be nourished
from this act, or that this should be a final act of charity (for these
meals are brought to the city's alms-houses and distributed among the
poor), or that by offering these thing to the dead they might propitiate
Death and forestall their own fate, or that they should understand from
this custom that they never lack anything either in life or in death, and
should, as they are about to die, give thanks for this gift of God's, | or
that they should recall that throughout the course of their lives they have

99

---

[4] Lat. *bursa*.

[5] The description is necessary to indicate the sense of the Latin *aedilis* (rendered
here as "superintendent of buildings"). In Republican Rome, the aediles had a number of duties involving the regular commercial and public life of the city, including
oversight of the marketplace and of public buildings. The last duty is presumably why
the term is chosen to translate the German *Kämmerer* (see further reference to them
on 98D, 106D).

been wrapped up like muddy pigs in the filthy dirty pleasures and were drowning in them, but should now cast such things from their minds and bewail the life which they have led, and then, under the admonition of the burning candles, seek refuge in Christ, the establisher of eternal light, and seek forgiveness for their sins in supplication. Finally, I also pass over the lower offices of the other canons.

When not engaged in the practices of piety, the men of this order devote themselves to hunting, fowling and other delights after the fashion of noblemen, considering this a grand and elegant way of life. They go forth in public escorted by a great retinue of attendants, and they are impressive in stride, reverend in speech, splendid in gestures that are excellently suited to their words, and ready for arms if the safety of the commonwealth dictates. If they have to go a longer distance, they ride on the spirited horses that they maintain at home or on wagons. When engaged in the worship of God, they wear linen stoles that are particularly thin, fine and diaphanous. The clothing they put on is woven of quite pure wool or silk and faced with the soft furs of wild animals, flowing down almost to their ankles. Their necks are encircled by golden necklaces twisted into many coils, and their fingers by gem-encrusted rings decorated with the insignia of their forebears. The younger ones wear tunics curled or frilled around the neck like garden or romaine lettuce. When about to make a public appearance, most cover their heads with silk hats, a form of attire that distinguishes them from the commons. Instead of shoes, the elder canons wear cloth-covered slippers, and avail themselves of other luxuries. They do not, however, think that they have been so exalted and enriched only for their own sake or in order that they alone should devour everything, since their particular aim is that the poor should not be neglected. For apart from the daily alms that they distribute everyday to the students of St. Paul's, they give alms in common. This alms-giving was instituted in the past by Lord Lubbert of Rodenberg, a noble canon, and the revenues for it | have been gradually increased, so that the man in charge, who is   100 always appointed by the chapter, contributes some thousands of marks in local money every year for the benefit of the poor.

In the lower clergy are placed the canons (and their vicars) of all colleges of both the city and the entire diocese; all the parish priests and chaplains, apart from the one who is in charge of the Church of St. James as the officiant; and the abbots and priors of all the monasteries, and the men and women who devote themselves to the chanting of hymns and engage in the worship of God both day and night. (The monks and nuns do intermingle other exercises during the day, but divide up their time in such a way that virtually no hour passes without them being occupied with certain pursuits. This is why people who are devoted to respectable activities cast off and shun base free-time, which is the cause of many crimes.)

Apart from the cathedral college, there are four others: those of Old St. Paul's, St. Ludger's, St. Maurice's Outside-the-Walls, and St. Martin's. Apart from the one that we have said to be in the Lords' Field, there are six parishes: the Parish Across-the-River, St. Lambert's, St. Ludger's, St. Martin's, St. Giles', and St. Servatius'. There are four male convents: the Brothers of St. George, the Hospitalers, the Brothers of the Fountain, and the Minorites; and seven of nuns: the Sisters Across-the-River, St. Giles', Nitzing's, the Roseum (named Rosenthal after a valley of roses; when its nuns willingly made themselves subject to the Rule of St. Augustine, only | Adelheid Helleberndes resisted, though in vain), the Ring's, Hofrugging's (named after a certain nobleman called Hofrugging, who bestowed his house on his two sisters for use as a convent, and after summoning certain other girls to it, these sisters were the first nuns there), and the Reinanum (in German, Reine) founded by Ermingard and Matilda, who were sisters from the noble Büren family, in the year 1344 on the day of St. Vincent the Martyr.[6] The individual monasteries also have their own churches, apart from Hofrugging's and Rosenthal, whose nuns enter the common church of the Parish Across-the-River when they are going to engage in worship. St. Martin's takes the nuns from Reine's, and St. Ludger's, those of Ring's. These convents do, however, have their own chapels with altars at which they sometimes tire themselves with private prayers, and, when necessary, hear the solemnities of the mass in private rites.

Thus, the body of the entire clergy and all its members is divided into the two orders that have been described. The members are free of all civil burdens, unless they change their old residences which have been exempted from burdens since ancient days and inhabit the houses of burghers, in which case they bear the civil impositions on account of these houses. In all assemblies of burghers, both public and private, they receive preference on account of their religious vows and assume the leading role. The laymen treat them with such honor and reverence that you would think them not mortals but gods on earth. They all

101

---

[6] January 22.

lead a life of celibacy, and they prominently exhibit a certain gravity in their behavior, gait and splendid clothing.

This ecclesiastical order is restrained from the many varieties of sin 102 and is kept to its duty by two synods, one in the fall and one in the spring. In them, the clergy, in the presence of the bishop (or at least his suffragan) and of the heads of the main clergy, are deterred from sin with Latin sermons, so that they are struck with the fear of both God's vengeance and the penalty, and dare not commit any act that contradicts what is right and honorable and is in conformity with the behavior of the main clergy. The rule for living and teaching is laid down in these synods, so that everything should savor of the doctrine of Christ. The faults of the parish priests are also done away with through the censure of the archdeacons. In this way, everything throughout the entire diocese is kept in order.

Below this order, that is, midway between clergy and laity, we properly place the masters of the public schools, who teach the youth with wholesome maxims and instruct them in the mores of a liberal education. To be sure, we do not do this on the basis of their prestige and authority, since they are considered lower than the lowest, as Mimimgardford bears witness in her lament[7]:

> The crude lackey and the breaker of horses is worth more,
>   And the cheap guide of dogs receives more honor,
> The hunter, and the clever bird catcher are worth more,
>   The whore selling her crotch is more valued,
> The crowd of camp followers, useless in war, is worth more
>   Than those who teach the crude youth character!

| Because of this order's benefit to the public, we have assigned them 103 this place (directly after the clergy). For when the body of each commonwealth[8] is broken down with old age, they renew it with fresh, healthy members, and once the body is thus renewed, they foster its daily increase in strength, by cherishing and encouraging it. It is upon them, therefore, that we will bestow the highest repute in the city. For we are going to have the kind of priests and burghers that they will rear.

There are public schools in three colleges of canons: St. Ludger's and St. Martin's teach boys the rudiments of the Latin language, while

---

[7] The reference is to K.'s earlier work *Mymingardevordae lugentis querimonia* "Grieving Mimimgardford's Complaint" (see General Introduction 3c).
[8] That is, ecclesiastical and secular.

the school of St. Paul's, which has always been more renowned and noble in its age and the number of its students, is superior in language instruction through public and private exercises. For the young men are carefully trained with instruction not only in Latin but also in Greek and Hebrew, and with public demonstrations of their talents in the form of disputations and recitations. The principle aim is that the youths should not bob on the surface and run riot with a very shallow verbosity, but should instead acquire both a familiarity with the principles and an understanding of the subject matter. The students of this school who are burdened by poverty are supported with the receipt of loaves of bread through the remarkable generosity on the part of certain Lords.

104   In addition to these public institutions, there are also in almost every ward little at-home tutors who teach private lessons, which results in the downfall of the public schools. This matter begets such confusion, such variation in behavior among the youth, such wrangling about the most monstrous opinions that they throw into chaos not only the public school system but also a large part of the citizenry. Accordingly, parents would look after their children's interests more correctly if they preferred the light of day to the darkness of shadows, and sent their children to public schools, where, as one urges the other on and a very splendid rivalry prevails among the pupils, they would make great progress. In such a situation they would, from their first years, become used to not shunning their fellow men, those among whom they are going to live in the public sphere. As for the other situation, to an incredible extent the boys' talents waste away in a lonely room, which they find wearisome and which they also shun like a prison cell, preferring to spend their time in daylight, that is, in the midst of many fellow students. If they were moved by the example of the Athenians and Spartans, the members of the government would justly consider that they in particular had the responsibility to care for the youth and their instruction, since the safety of the state particularly depends upon the public schools being equipped and supported with privileges and subsidies, so that the gentlemen who emerge from them will be fit to run the state. But if this can hardly be achieved, it can at least be granted without, I think, any public harm that the private schools should be abolished, and the public ones administered in such a way that the instructors and lecturers in them will not be indigent through the fault of the government. All the schoolteachers are virtually dependent upon the wealth and number of their pupils, since none of them is looked

after with a public salary.[9] As for the school of St. Paul's, it is only the generosity of certain Lords of the cathedral that maintains it, and the city council's authority lends it support in place of a salary.

The laity (profane people not initiated in sacral matters) differ from the clergy in their way of life, customs, and clothing. I divide them into two orders: the patricians and the commoners. For the members of the knighthood do not | submit to the jurisdiction of the burghers   105 or the city's statutes, regulations or laws (though some of them own splendid mansions in the city). Instead, being scattered outside the city, they individually defend their privileges in their castles or strongholds and constitute a fourth status within the diocese that is separate from the other three, living on the income of their manors and by their own farming. Accordingly, the laity (the profane inhabitants of the city) have been divided by me into two groups. Out of these groups arises a third. From both groups, older men who are by comparison wealthy, outstanding for their probity, and experienced through long engagement in affairs are elected, even if they are unlearned, to run the government. These men comprise the third group, namely the order of city councilors, and to them is entrusted the civil administration of the entire city. There are twenty-four men in this order, and they are appointed by ten electors, who are confined within the council chamber, now on the Tuesday after the feast of St. Antony,[10] but previously on the first Monday of Lent. In the past, it was only the workers[11] who selected these electors, but now the entire body of burghers does so on a ward-by-ward basis. Since the aged councilmen are esteemed for the venerable excellence of their grey-haired wisdom, we call them "senators," inasmuch as they see to the needs of the public interest with weighty votes in the council hall.[12] On the other hand, inasmuch as they represent individual voting districts ("*leyschoppe*",[13] as they call them), they are called judges ("*scabini*") and when disputes arise among

---

[9] It would now seem that K.'s objections to private education are not entirely based on pedagogical considerations!

[10] January 17.

[11] I.e., guild members.

[12] The Latin word *senator* is related to the word for "old man" (*senex*). It is not clear whether "we" refers to the author specifically or to all those who use Latin to speak of the city's institutions, but in any case the explanation indicates why this particular Latin translation is used of the city councilors, whose duties were much broader than those of the Roman senator. (Whereas the Roman senate's traditional role was advisory, the city council of a German city had executive and judicial functions.)

[13] Literally "laities" (German *Leienschaften*).

the burghers of the district, especially as a result of construction, these judges investigate the disputes, try them after the investigation, and settle them after the trial. The purpose of this arrangement is to avoid having the entire council afflicted with such annoyances when it is occupied with more important matters. If, however, this procedure would not be helpful, the matter is remitted to the council's judgment.

106   The city is divided into six voting districts, that is, geographical areas: St. Martin's, St. Lambert's, St. Ludger's, St. Giles', | St. Mary's,[14] and the Jew's Field. Each of the first four appoints two electors but the last two only one (to reach a total of ten instead of twelve), and by vote these electors choose the members of city council from among both the commons and the patricians. If those elected shirk the honor of serving, they are penalized as haters of the public good not only with a fine but also with banishment for an entire year and the hatred of the burghers. The order of councilmen is divided by duties into several categories, and it is not the electors but the elected councilmen who distribute these duties among themselves for the well-being and advantage of the public.[15]

The heads of the burghers and of the council are the two senior members of the government,[16] who surpass the others in judgment, diligence, reliability, watchfulness, authority, wisdom, influence, and experience. Two superintendents of wine[17] administer the council's wine outlet and its wine. The two assessors[18] sit beside the civil judge on his tribunal and aid him with their advice in the trials of cases and the passing of sentences. Two superintendents of buildings oversee the public works and fortifications.[19] Two financial officials who receive the city's revenues are called the superintendents of the "*scormorrium*" tax ("*gruethern*").[20] They used to collect the tax on myrtle beer, which

---

[14] I.e., the Parish Across-the-River, whose parish church was dedicated to St. Mary.

[15] The city council objected to this fairly innocuous description of the electoral process and to the subsequent discussion of the offices exercised by members of the council on the grounds that K. had thereby revealed the council's secrets (see General Introduction 3b). It is hard to see how this account could have been much of a revelation, since such procedures would seem to have been common knowledge.

[16] Burgher masters (the term to be used in the text henceforth).

[17] *Weinherren* ("wine lords").

[18] *Richtherren* ("judge lords").

[19] *Kämmerer* (also mentioned on 98D).

[20] "Lords of the myrtle (beer)." *Scormorrium* was a neologism in Latin for the distinctive myrtle beer of Münster.

was once the principal beverage in the city and is referred to with the neologism "*scormorrium*," and the name given them for that reason has lasted until the present day. | There are also two assessors[21] of the secret   107 Westphalian court that is set up to punish evil-doing. This court is called the "assize" ("*vriegraf's*")[22] and its tribunal in a lonely location outside the city is surrounded by leafy oaks on all sides. It is not, however, the oaks that expiate the acts of wrongdoing, as was the case in the past, but gold.[23] There are two beer masters,[24] who are entrusted with the care of beer, both domestic and imported, to make sure that the price does not exceed the value. Two superintendents of alms receive their title from clothing the poor[25] and are in charge of all the "providers" of the entire city (overseers of the public alms that are distributed in each parish).[26] Two officials each superintend the hospice for foreigners between the bridges, the leper shelter outside the city, St. Anthony's alms-house for old folks, and the brick yard.

The whole order of the council used to consist only of patricians. Then, as commoners were gradually admitted, a mixing of the two orders began to take place, on the understanding that one of the two burgher masters would always be elected from the commons and the other tasks would be administered partly by commoners and partly by patricians, each with equal authority. This set-up, after having been preserved for so long, lasted until the patricians, in the eager pursuit of knightly status, withdrew from civic functions | and shunned the rights   108 of the city. For this reason, few patricians now belong to the order of the council, and even they do so against their will.[27]

---

[21] *Stuhlherren*.

[22] High German *Freigraf*.

[23] I.e., offenders are fined rather than hanged. The implicit condemnation of the practice of fining malefactors was one of the charges laid against K. by the city council (see General Introduction 3b), and in the later "Apology" in which he defended himself against the city's councils attacks against his work (see General Introduction 3c), K. noted that whereas many criminals had been hanged by the court in the past, during his twenty-five-year tenure as rector of the cathedral school, no one was hanged by this court's sentence (he notes two men who were fined in it for adultery and were executed only later by other authorities—the bailiff of Senden and the city council—for repeat offenses). Clearly, K. was a firm believer in the exemplary effect of execution and lamented the leniency of this court.

[24] *Bierherren*.

[25] *Kleiderherren* ("lords of clothing").

[26] See also 59D.

[27] The patricians objected to this characterization of them (and to the comments in the paragraph after next), which in their mind seemed to detract from their claims to belong to the nobility (see General Introduction 3b).

This order has great authority in the city. It has the power to establish and disestablish, to pass laws and revoke those that have been passed, to command and forbid, to punish or absolve the accused, to mint copper coinage (though this is used only locally), to bestow the ecclesiastical benefices in the council's gift not only on learned adults but even on boys or virtually speechless babes (though ones from whom there is the expectation of good fruits or whose parents have increased the public good with some skill).[28] In short, this order's writ extends not only to the city's lanes, but also to its walls and towers, not only to the lowliest commoners but also to the most exalted patricians. The council also has a spokesman, hired at great expense, who is called a "syndic"; an amanuensis, who is called the secretary; a guard for the doors to the council chamber, and four mounted escorts, six attendants and a certain number of messengers, who wear the silver insignia of the city (their right arms are encircled by a circle of silver-leaf roundels attached to their cloaks); a master of force,[29] to whom is entrusted oversight of the night watch and of uproars at night; and finally, to terrify criminals, a hangman who is distinguished from the other servants by his green attire.

Then there are the patricians. These are the highborn burghers, who represent the remains of ancient bloodlines and the posterity of ancient families. The commons call them "Erffmans"[30] as if the indigenous successors by hereditary right of their ancestors, who, having received their images from their ancestors, pass them on intact to the descendants,[31] so that they accept no commoner, however wealthy, into their order unless | he is begotten of parents possessing the same ancestry.[32] This is the reason why for so long now this status has retained

---

[28] K.'s complaint about giving benefices to minors was one of the accusations lodged against K. by the council, but it is to be noted that the parenthesis at the end of this sentence was meant to obviate a negative interpretation by indicating that those who were granted such positions at an admittedly young age nonetheless came from families that would lead one to expect satisfactory results from the incumbents in adulthood (i.e., the respectable well-to-do). Whatever the truth of the matter, K. was clearly trying to soften his criticism.

[29] *Gewaltmeister.*

[30] "*Erbmänner*" ("men of heritage").

[31] The allusion to "images" refers to the ancient Roman practice whereby death masks (*imagines* or "images") were made of the heads of prominent families. These images were set up in the forecourt of the house and taken down for display in funeral processions, being tokens of the antiquity and splendor of the family's lineage.

[32] This last clause is not clearly expressed, since anyone of the same ancestry (presumably as the patricians) by definition is not a commoner. Seemingly, what is

its significance in contradiction to that of the commons. Content with their revenues and farming, they imitate the knighthood. We have not, however, excluded them from the category of burghers, since the burghers consist of patricians on the one hand and commoners on the other, both groups being bound by the city's laws. I also include in this category those who have been ennobled through appointment to offices on account of their learning, such as the doctors and licentiates of various professions, even if they are of common origin.[33]

The order of the commons encompasses the undifferentiated mob of the whole city apart from the councilmen and patricians, including freemen and serfs. The serfs live randomly among the freemen, and the freemen are partly common burghers and partly cerocensuals.[34] The cerocensuals are those who are under the control of the sacristan or the superintendent of the fabric of the Lords' Church[35] and recognize them as their defenders and patrons. They are named "*wastinsich*"[36] after the words for "wax" (*cera*) and "tax" (*census*) and are also called the "freemen of St. Paul" ("*Sanct Pouwels frien*"),[37] purchasing the freedom of their goods with a payment of two pennies every year and one florin as a death duty.[38] This category was introduced to make sure that no one among the commoners in the entire diocese should lack a "head" (as they themselves say), that is, a defender and patron. (The burghers have the city council, and the serfs have a lord.) Whenever anyone of common status (always with the exception of the knights) breathes his last who is not a burgher, cerocensual or serf, the prince becomes their heir, | excluding any children and seizing the property as if in escheat, though it is not in escheat when there is a lawful heir   110

---

meant is that only those of patrician ancestry are accepted, which therefore excludes commoners.

[33] This refers to the grants of nobility given to those appointed to senior governmental positions (the "nobility of the robe," to use a later expression). Such offices normally required a university degree and thus offered a route to noble status for commoners of intellectual ability. Here "doctors" refers to the possessors of doctorates in any disciple, while "licentiates" signifies advanced doctoral students who already possess a master's degree and have been given official permission ("license") to give lectures at the university (the high expenses involved in receiving the doctorate often resulted in those qualified as licentiates not bothering to get the degree itself).

[34] "Payers of the wax tax."

[35] Chamberlain.

[36] High German *Wachszinsig*.

[37] High German *Sankt Pauls freien*.

[38] This group consisted of erstwhile serfs of the church, who used to purchase their freedom with a payment in wax, which was later commuted to cash.

to it. It seems harsh and savage that we should cast away the lawful heirs and devour the sweat of someone else's brow, plundering what another person has properly and justly acquired without any effort or trouble on our part, and that after stripping the children of their goods and reducing them to abject poverty, we should drive them into exile, producing an excuse for acting wickedly and increasing our own possessions through robbing someone else in a way that is contrary to nature and extremely grievous. Let those in whose interest it is to do so defend this practice.

Just as the commons comprises several different groups, so too do they seek their livelihood through differing pursuits and practices. This includes all those craftsmen and workers who practice a trade for profit, working with both their mind and their hands. Some of these have guilds endowed with certain privileges, while others enter certain associations (called "*broderschop*")[39] that are distinguished by professional pursuits. Yet others are not attached to a specific guild or association, each man engaging individually in the private practices from which he earns a living.

The guilds number sixteen. Three are beholden to the city council by oath, since they depend upon a decree of the council: the butchers (who are divided into two sub-guilds, one for the old market and one for the new), the wool workers, and the bakers. The remaining guilds operate by their own rules and regulations: the garment cutters, ped- dlers, blacksmiths, tanners, | tailors, shoemakers, furriers, goldsmiths, tawers, stone masons, coopers, and pewtersmiths; while the painters, saddlemakers and glaziers share a single guild.

Each guild has two superintendents or masters, whom they call "*Gildemeisters*" or "*Meisterlude*," apart from the butchers, who have four since they have a double guild. The guilds also have their own servants, who wear multi-colored clothing when they go forth in public. These servants are employed for the swift execution of the guilds' business affairs, and for this reason they are called the "messengers" of the guild to which they belong.

There were once separate guilds for the wooden shoemakers, the fish mongers and the cobblers, who fix worn out shoes by attaching soles, but now the wooden shoe makers, the carpenters, the cabinet makers, the cloth shearers, and weavers are distinguished from the guilds by

111

---

[39] High German *Brüderschaft* ("brotherhoods").

having associations. Those who practice other professions do not have collective organizations in the form of guilds or associations, but engage in the pursuit of profit individually: scribes, barbers (who also act as surgeons), dyers, belt makers, purse makers, yoke makers, lathe workers, millers, brewers, merchants of various goods, booksellers, linen workers, druggists, perfume sellers, wine merchants, and butter merchants.

The peasants rent their pastures and fields from the clergy or noblemen or patricians, since these groups own the majority of the land around the city. They either sow this land with grain stuffs or use them as pasturage for thin cattle brought down from Denmark, | which they   112
fatten up and then drive to market in Cologne, where they earn a good profit by selling them retail. A few, however, do sow their own land.

Finally, there are two tribunes of the plebs in imitation of the Roman constitution. These they call either "*allermans*" because as representatives of all inhabitants they are the heads and presidents of the commons or "aldermen" after the word for "old age," since it is presumed that the experience in which they ought to be outstanding is found in old age.[40] In conjunction with the guild masters, the aldermen's authority is so great that they can even rescind decrees of the city council if they so wish. Accordingly, in difficult matters that pertain to the well-being of the entire city, the council generally makes no decision without their participation in the deliberations.

The youth are occupied with various pursuits. Some are turned over to school for learning, some to commerce, some to the profit-making trades of workers. The activities of women and girls mostly concern linen weaving, which is their principal business. In women there is an astonishing haughtiness that in its ambition surpasses general human nature, and this is particularly true among low-born women, who, in their zeal to make themselves the equal of richer women, are arrogant to the point of scornfulness and often forgo necessities for the sake of adornment so that they can parade around with greater refinement and beauty. In the inhabitants of both sexes can be seen a remarkable combination of friendliness, affability, wit, culture, and civility, and it therefore seems amazing that in the middle of Westphalia, which is girded all around with remarkable crudeness, such a splendid sort of character has arisen, since even the nature of the location resists this.

---

[40] The German *Allerman* does in fact mean "man, or representative, of everyone." The alternate derivation from *Alter* ("old age") is false.

Before the Anabaptist uproar, there had been such a connection of friendship and closeness between clergy and laity, such a tight bond of mutual concord among all the orders of society, that this bond could not be broken by any contrivance. The clergy lived among the laymen with such distinction in their chastity and their modest self-restraint that you would have said either that angels had assumed the shape of humans or that humans had adopted the character of angels. Hence, the clergy were greatly enriched through the munificence of pious men and respectable matrons. As for the laity, their lives used to

113   be resplendent with such impeccable piety | that they strove not only to equal but even to surpass the clergy, and such saintliness had suppressed the wantonness of the flesh, which rebels against the spirit, that it was a sin for them to have tasted diary products on Fridays. There had been such love and veneration for the worship of God that those who had not attended mass every day and poured forth their prayers to God thought that they would not outlive that day, or would at least meet with extraordinary misfortune. As a result of this pursuit of piety and loving concord among the orders, this commonwealth gradually grew in wealth and power to an incredible degree. The city remained unharmed and prospered amidst this prosperity for as long as every single person kept himself within the limits of his own calling. Once those boundaries and restraints were broken, however, when in the licentiousness of their meetings the workers burst through the barriers marking off the ecclesiastics, and in their transformation into soldiers and merchants with their trafficking, the ecclesiastics burst through those of the workmen, with the property of the churches, which had been dedicated to God by pious people, being turned into the salaries of soldiers, informers, hunters, gluttons and pimps, everything began to be turned topsy-turvy. Each result was caused by an excessive abundance of material things. For among the clergy this abundance begat dissipation, dissipation begat drowsiness, drowsiness begat carelessness or neglect, and once this was let in, Satan could sow his seeds in greater security as the clergy snoozed. Among the laity, on the other hand, this abundance begat ambition (which is the companion of prosperity), ambition begat haughty arrogance, arrogance begat extravagance, extravagance begat poverty, poverty begat defiance of the government (the hungering commons know not how to fear, as the poet attests),[41] defiance begat

---

[41] Lucan, *Civil War* 3.58.

impunity in committing any act at all, which finally suggested the endeavor to snatch other people's property and the eagerness to dump out the contents of other people's strong boxes. They had not called this rapine (the etymology of the world would display its wrongfulness),[42] but with a milder term had designated it as a "sharing of property," which they would justify with the excuse of rebaptism.

Accordingly, when the earlier situation, which was excellent in both regards and was maintained with the greatest concord, could no longer be tolerated by Satan, the enemy of the human race and hater of all peace, who instigates and expands discord, | he waylaid the prying,   114 mutinous hearts of men, and through the clever use of these hearts he first introduced dissension and disagreement about the worship of God, as a result of which a very great conflict in religious affairs arose between the clergy and commons. For as each man strove not only to defend to his own view tenaciously but also to propagate it as far as possible, they became entangled in mutual animosity and hatred. Thus, since a single religion had enjoyed the greatest prosperity in this commonwealth without dissent in any regard, it was contrary to everyone's expectation when a faction crept in consisting of those who gave themselves the false title of evangelicals, condemning the good works and all the ancient and traditional ceremonies and enactments of the Catholic Church. The uproars which such innovation caused not just in this commonwealth but in very many surrounding ones, to their great misfortune, were of an incredible magnitude. Examples of what was done need not be cited from far off. For if you will carefully examine the neighboring towns of Westphalia (I pass over those of other regions), you will see that it was only with a horrible uproar that they first adopted the dogma of the evangelicals, and that from this dogma the greatest wantonness[43] flowed forth, as if from the start of a looser way of living.

---

[42] Derived from the Latin verb *rapio, rapere* (to "snatch," or "steal"), which K. used of "snatching" other's property in the preceding sentence.

[43] I.e., the Anabaptist regime.

CHAPTER NINE

OMENS AND PRODIGIES THAT FORETOLD UPROARS IN WESTPHALIA AND THE DESTRUCTION OF THE CITY OF MÜNSTER

We learn through the reading of history that virtually no commonwealth was ever afflicted with some notable disaster because of crimes without God having first, in His gracious omnipotence, terrified it with horrible omens and prodigies in order that He might thereby make manifest the offense that He feels and give advance warning of the destruction to come, in case the astonishment caused by these portents might cause people to lay down their impiety and really come to their senses. It would not be difficult for me to demonstrate this with countless examples from very many cities if it were not the case that with such verbosity I would cause nauseated disgust in my readers, who are in a hurry to reach the actual subject matter.[1] Indeed, I do not think that anyone with even a moderate familiarity with literature would have any doubts about this proposition, since the writings of both the Greeks and Romans on the one hand and the Jews on the other are filled with such omens 115 and prodigies, incontrovertibly sent by God, which | foretold devastation and inevitable destruction to the latter and miserable death and a change in their affairs (as the outcome demonstrated) to the former. Let us, therefore, omit prodigies that once foretold the overturning of other cities and look at our local prodigies, which in fact are so many and so manifest that it would hardly be thought that I should neglect them as I am about to describe the transformation of the polity of Westphalia and of Münster in particular.

We find that since the days of Charlemagne, that most Christian prince and the apostle of all Saxony, who waged very wholesome wars on Westphalia and first successfully beat down that very recalcitrant and fierce race by arms and then softened them by teaching them the saving Word of Jesus Christ, there were no notable religious uproars in

---

[1] The conceit comes from the preface of Livy's Roman history, in which he imagines that the reader wishes to ignore the salubrious lessons to be learned from Rome's early history in order to hurry to the racier material concerning the fall of the Republic.

this province. But in the year 1517 there were many omens: on January 12 at about 3 o'clock in the afternoon three suns pierced with bloody swords were seen in the sky in certain places in Germany, and on January 13, a sun of fearsome appearance could be seen surrounded by certain half-circles of various colors; next, on January 10 and March 17 three moons appeared. These omens indisputably foretold that the clarity of the one sun and faith was to be buffeted with hazy opinions and torn to pieces and that the leaders of states, which the study of history has shown to be what suns signify, would disagree among themselves, and after that year there arose many sects in certain provinces of Germany that gradually tainted almost all of Westphalia as if by contagion, not only stirring up many commonwealths but imposing horrible innovations on them.

The very outcome indicated what was foretold by that terrifying omen seen in the sky by many people four hours before sunrise on October 11, 1527, being particularly visible to the north. | What they saw was the shape of a bent arm extending from the clouds, and in its hand could be seen a double-edged sword with a rather obscure star on either side and another star that was larger and brighter than the rest on the blade. On the sides could be seen bloody daggers with human heads intermixed, which struck the viewers with such terror that it almost made them faint. What was the presage of that fatal outbreak of the sweating disease called "English," which broke out all over Germany with sudden and vast mortality in the year 1529, and within twenty-four hours of infecting people either caused them to choke to death or restored them to their former health at no cost to life?[2] This outbreak terrified people so much that as they walked around, the living who still enjoyed their health proclaimed that they were dying. As this disease was going about in its depredations, randomly seizing very many victims and laying them low, the priests who administered the sacraments to the bed-ridden, being so few in number, were necessarily held in such honor and veneration that you would have thought them gods on earth. Certainly, the only thing which this universal malady of Germany and

116

---

[2] The "sweating sickness" (*morbus anglicus*) signifies a disease that was first attested in England in 1485, and apart from the outbreak mentioned here never spread to the continent (hence the adjective "English"). The onset of this highly infectious disease was swift, and frequently its high fever and profuse sweating (hence the name) soon resulted in death. After several recurrences in the first half of the sixteenth century (Henry VIII was terrified of it), this dreaded disease swiftly disappeared in the second half, and its exact identification is unclear.

the affliction of its inhabitants foretold was the magnitude of a greater misfortune: the overthrow of the ancestral religion. This unusual and sudden veneration that was shown to the priests contrary to habit presaged nothing but the fact that there would be a metamorphosis in the business of religion that would result in the priests being held in the highest contempt. For the situation now reached the stage where the priests would hardly be compared even to lackeys and the lowliest dregs of humanity or indeed be considered worthy of the designation "human."[3] Instead, they were called wolves who lead men astray, though Christ had no hesitation in calling them the light of the world and the salt of the earth.[4] In fact, these are those times in which Christ foretold that if the salt became foolish, it would be trampled under foot by men.[5] Therefore, just as that outbreak of the deadly sweating disease swept Germany like a plummeting lightning bolt from the southeast to the northwest, terrifying all the country districts and cities with its carnage, so too did the new religion, which, with its condemnation of the ancient ceremonies and good works, had been recently intro-

117   duced, | to the commons' applause, by certain vagrant Paphian priests who were cowl-wearing oath breakers,[6] first crashed with thunder into the cities of the southeast and then finally swept across these cities of ours in Westphalia with a deadly momentum.

When some articles were brought to Münster by certain merchants, the rabble stirred themselves up and threw off the tranquility of the ancient religion, rising up not only against the clergy but also against the leading men of the city.

Seizing the city of Soest, this doctrine begat a destructive uproar among the citizens, and when the government tried to cure this, the two burgher masters and five council members, who were important, wealthy men, were arrested by the commons in 1531 and put in jail.

---

[3] A rather forced interpretation of the supposed omen.

[4] Matt. 5: 13–14.

[5] This would seem to suggest that in K.'s opinion the ecclesiastical hierarchy had itself to blame for the indignities it suffered at the hands of the reformers.

[6] This is a reference to the propagation of Protestant views by monks who had given up their vows (the *cucullus* or cowl was a form of headgear peculiar to monks) and by priests who showed their denial of the validity of the Church to establish practices not justified biblically by rejecting celibacy and taking wives (the mandatory imposition of celibacy on all the clergy was an innovation of the eleventh century). The reference to the latter is a rather obscure piece of Classical erudition. Paphus was an ancient city on the island of Cyprus, which was associated with goddess Venus. Thus, "Paphian" means "associated with the goddess of love."

The prince of Jülich, to whose jurisdiction Soest had submitted when it seceded from the diocese of Cologne in 1444, wished to calm the rebellion, and in 1532, on the Saturday after the conversion of St. Paul,[7] he convened in Wickede an assembly of his nobles and cities to deliberate on the matter. There, it was decided that the people of Soest should be warned in a friendly way to give up their factious plotting. Accordingly, a delegation with official authority was sent several times at the prince's expense to reconcile the commons with the council, but not only could the rebellious commons not be dissuaded with any reasoning from the course which they had undertaken, but being further enraged against the government, the commons seized control of the city after the peaceable men had been removed from the council by the factious.

Also in 1531, the religious innovation in the city of Lippstadt led to the public roads around the city being occupied to cut off access to the city under the authority of the bishops of Cologne, Münster, Paderborn and Osnabrück as well as that of the prince of Jülich and the count of Lippe.

In 1532, the city of Paderborn was greatly disturbed by religious innovation. The factious had elected themselves twelve apostles, and under their leadership they cleverly set a trap to seize the goods of the clergy and of other rich men (before the plundering, they secretly divided up the residences and possessions of the main clergy among themselves), but on October 9, the very day of his installation, Herman of Wied, the archbishop of Cologne and the administrator of the Church in Paderborn, subdued this disturbance with an amazingly sensible course of action, and it faded away. (I can attest to this as an eye-witness.)

Around the same time, the new religion undermined the tranquility of Minden, Osnabrück, Herford, Lemgo and other surrounding towns.

In the year 1533, the towns of Warendorf and Ahlen got involved with a similar faction. When their pastor, Lord John Harmen, | a man of ancient nobility and piety, was engaged in the worship of God, the men of Ahlen disturbed him with their German hymns, and in violation of custom, they interrupted him in church with their shouting. It is said that he then got some noblemen to drive away all the cattle of the troublemakers in a very thick fog on the Friday after the feast

118

119

---

[7] January 30.

of St. Matthew.[8] The herds that were suddenly taken away in this way disappeared without the men of Ahlen ever setting eyes on them again, and the cows went off without even a calf coming back. As for Warendorf, it was besieged by the bishop himself, and after the town eventually surrendered, it paid the price for its rashness.

The rebellions in these cities were foretold not only by the portents narrated above along with the sweating disease, but also by other omens in the sky. To pass over the more distant eclipses that took place on September 10, 1526 and October 16, 1529, an investigation of the historical record of the more immediate period shows well enough that in the following years, three eclipses of the sun, three of the moon, and three terrifying comets appeared in the sky in the three successive years as sure tokens of coming disaster. It is not a single generation but the agreement of many centuries that attests that eclipses of heavenly bodies as well as comets have always been omens of destruction, and accordingly it would not be rash to pay attention to them as heavenly warnings, since they urge us as we drown in sin to beg for God's mercy and to correct our previous way of life. For even though eclipses of the heavenly bodies foretell very many disasters, nonetheless, God has often been placated by the supplications of pious men, so that He averted them. Therefore, whenever we see such events, let us be advised to make God propitious to us, knowing that otherwise nature will be left to take its course and very many misfortunes will descend upon us.

These uproars in the cities of Westphalia, then, and this bloody war in Münster, which disturbed not only the surrounding towns but almost the entire Holy Roman Empire, were directly preceded by three complete eclipses of the moon. The first was seen on October 6, 1530, lasting from 10 pm until 1 am of the next day. The moon began failing in the twenty-fourth degree of Aries, which indicated a result specifically affecting us. | For whenever eclipses of the heavenly bodies take place in Aquarius, Virgo or Aries, astronomers have noted that we are threatened by famine, rebellions of the base and low-born commons, wars, and civil uproars.

120

The second was on August 4, 1533, when the entire moon was concealed by the earth's shadow, beginning to fade at 31 degrees, 30 minutes in Aquarius. This eclipse began before 9 pm and lasted until 1 am.

---

[8] September 30.

Next, the third eclipse, which took place on January 30, 1534, starting at 10 am at 20 degrees in Aquarius, foretold misfortunes to us in
particular (we showed in Chapter 3 that Westphalia is subject to the
sign of Aquarius).

The shining of the sun was also removed from our sight through the
interposition of the moon's sphere three times before the Westphalian
disaster. The first time was on March 29, 1530 from 4 am to 7 am at
18 degrees in Aries, which is ascribed to Mars, the second on August
30, 1532 from 11 am to almost 1 pm at 16 degrees in Virgo. The third
time was not long before this calamitous war, on January 14, 1534. This
time, the sun suffered a terrible eclipse from 12:30 pm until 2:30 at
3 degrees 38 minutes in Aquarius, the constellation of Westphalia. We
also think it noteworthy that an eclipse of both heavenly bodies (the
sun and moon) took place in the same month and the same sign of
the zodiac. The learned bear witness that this event has always been
followed by remarkable misery and sweeping changes unless God averts
these events in light of His own, specific goodness.

Furthermore, just as God foreshadows unpleasantness by means
of eclipses, He also does so by means of comets, which in everyone's
judgment have portended wars, great changes in affairs, the devastation of powerful states, and bloody slaughter, as well as other disasters
of this kind. In 1531, then, a fearsome comet blazed forth in the sky
around August 6. For a few days, it appeared before sunrise, | then
it followed the sun and was visible after sunset for about three weeks
until September 3. Its path was through the third of the zodiac that
encompasses Cancer, Leo, Virgo and Libra, and it disappeared in the
last sign. This comet brought destruction to all of Germany, stirred up
the Swiss War, killed Zwingli, the priest of Zürich, along with thousands of men, and made many cities in Germany rebel against their
governments and prices to rise.[9]

In 1532, a comet was again seen two hours before sunrise for a few
weeks in September. It started in the bright star located in the chest
of Leo, which they call the Basilisk,[10] then progressed through Virgo
to Libra. Leo, which is the sign opposite our region, stirs up many

121

---

[9] Zwingli died leading troops in a battle against the forces of five Catholic cantons.
[10] Old name for the star now known as Regulus. Note that K. calls John of Leiden
a basilisk (a poisonous lizard) in the opening poem ostensibly giving John's regretful
retrospective interpretation of his actions.

upheavals, and when a comet first becomes visible under the Basilisk, it usually foretells that some foreign king coming from elsewhere will stir up wars for the sake of his ambition. This is amply proven to have happened to the people of Münster. Finally, in the year 1533, a comet that blazed with a much larger and brighter flame came fairly close to the place of the star directly above us as a more sure and closer harbinger of our disaster. For this reason, it never set on us, but wheeled around in a circle with the northern stars. In the morning, it seemed to hang suspended at the vertical point or zenith of our city, emitting a flame of wondrous length like a staff or long sword in the direction of the spot where the sun's nadir (the point opposite its zenith) was found, this always being the direction in which comets extend their tail. (The circumstance that their movement is sometimes faster and sometimes slower brings it about that they do not always direct their tail toward the same area of the sky, since that area changes along with the zenith of the sun.) While this comet was also looking upon the provinces of Lower Germany[11] with a specific omen, for a while it directed its tail at our city in particular like a fearsome sword. It first appeared under the constellation The Goat, which astronomers conceive of as a poor man carrying a goat on his shoulders, and moved to the constellation Cassiopeia through the drawn sword of the armed hero Perseus, who

122 holds in one hand a sword and | in the other the head of petrifying Medusa. For a while it also appeared with a flame of unusual size and brightness in the Milky Way. Furthermore, it could be seen to retrogress from west to east in a backwards motion.[12] All these phenomena were harbingers of an unusual uproar in affairs and of sudden innovation and terrible change. For what other operation was caused by the influence of this smelly, lecherous goat, carried by a poor man and always lusting after sex, its eyes looking sideways, to use Isidore's words,[13] because of its burning desire, emptying its bladder in the water it is about to drink

---

[11] I.e., the area of the lower Rhine.

[12] "Retrogression" is the apparent backwards motion of a heavenly body (usually a planet) that is caused by the forward motion of the earth in its orbit relative to that of the body. This phenomenon was inexplicable in the ancient and medieval conception that the planets revolved around an immobile earth, and to fix this theoretical problem Ptolemy came up with the idea that the planets were not exactly fixed to the orbs that carried them around but actually spun around in little circles as they swung around the earth in their orbits. The motion of comets was even more problematical for the traditional Aristotelian/Ptolemaic theory.

[13] Isidore of Seville, *Etymologies* 12.14.

along with the rest of the herd, rearing up, as the bold mate of many she-goats, against anyone—what other operation was caused by him than that the lowest dregs of humanity were going to choose a leader[14] of the people who would be salacious like a he-goat, befouling his entire herd with his doctrines, stirring up many new uproars, raising himself against many men, mating with and raping many women? What other result was divinely pointed out by the Milky Way, which is called the Royal Way, and by armed Perseus than that some royal majesty would for a while rage against his subjects, then collapse by arms? What else did petrifying Medusa foretell than that many men would be turned in some way to stone by rebaptism, it being impossible to soften them with any wholesome advice and to drag them back from this? What did the retrograde motion of the comet portend but the repeal of ancient laws and the substitution of contrary ones? What of Cassiopeia? She certainly signified nothing but unheard-of danger to the female sex and the deaths of many virgins because of rape.

Furthermore, I do not think it obscure what was portended when a prodigious dead fish[15] 68 feet long and 30 feet wide and with a gape 13 feet wide was beached in August, 1531 not far from Haarlem, a town in Holland. For John Matthisson of Haarlem put to shore[16] in Münster and was considered a marvelous prophet there, though at the beginning of the siege he was run through by the enemy in front of Ludger's Gate before he could manage any crime worthy of note, and no province of Germany begat more Anabaptist monstrosities than did Holland. | In fact, the chorus master, head and king of all monstrosi-   123 ties, John Bockelson of Leiden, came from there.

In order that God could produce surer signs of the coming disaster and show clearly that this disaster was hanging over our heads right now, in case the signs that frequently appear and are open to varying interpretation did not move us sufficiently, He used more unusual and more manifest portents, seen and heard partly above the city in the air and partly within the walls, with extreme terror. As a very merciful father, His ultimate wish was to frighten the minds of the inhabitants away from the indecent way of life with these omens, which directly preceded the downfall and overthrow of the city of Münster. First,

---

[14] I.e., John of Leiden.
[15] Presumably a whale.
[16] Metaphorically, since Münster is located inland.

many torches, sudden flames, and unusual gleamings were seen con-
tending with each other over the city for some time, in the end either
falling down or licking the tops of the spires, though without harming
them. The sky seemed to gape open, splitting into long cracks from
which terrifying fires flickered out. Peasants who were either staying in
neighboring manors and country districts or watching over horses or
other herd animals at night often saw the city as if ablaze, and when
they rushed up to investigate, they found that the flames had not only
been harmless to the city but had disappeared altogether. Sometimes,
the watchmen reported that the city was covered with fiery clouds
that directly threatened to create a conflagration by suddenly falling
down. Monstrous progeny of both farm animals and humans were
born. A rabbit—the sort of animal that otherwise shuns contact with
men—was caught entering the city. Chickens unnaturally crowed in
imitation of the males, while effeminate roosters clucked. Three suns
were seen on Feb. 9, 1534 at 1 pm, foretelling the threefold religious
division into Catholics, Lutherans and Anabaptists, just as the three
124   suns seen after the death of Julius Caesar foretold the triumvirate.[17] |
Certain people were seized with the madness of prophesying, being
filled with the Anabaptist spirit. Rushing through all the wards of the
city, they terrified the people with their fearsome bellowing, and called
upon anyone they met to repent, shouting that the great day of the
Lord was at hand.

   The daughter of George tom Berg the tailor, a sixteen-year-old
girl as far as I could tell from the appearance of her body, was filled
with the wondrous and terrifying inspiration of God on the afternoon
of February 8, 1534 in the house of Bernard Swerthen.[18] In a high
location in the house, she sat under a vault with a large throng of
people standing around, and gave a sermon to the point of astonishment, now on the punishment of the sinners, now on the exaltation
and rewarding of the pious, now on the destruction of the city and of
the whole world that would happen three days later, frequently mixing
in the words, "Woe, woe to the inhabitants of Münster! Woe, woe to
the impious!" She spent several hours chattering away in this aimless

---

[17] Julius Obsequens (who wrote a late-antique collection of prodigies derived from
Livy) 128 and Pliny, *Natural History* 2.99. The triumvirate was a dictatorship of three
men that was established after the assassination of Julius Caesar and marked the demise
of the Roman Republic.
[18] This event is also related on 484D.

manner like a magpie. As we stood by and listened, this event instilled in us not so much astonishment as the greatest horror and a foreboding of coming disaster.

Also, women who were tricked with the devil's deception demonstrated with their linen dresses that it had rained blood on February 9 of that year.[19] Some people adamantly insisted that on that day, various spirits and horrifying spectres appeared in the air. Around the same time, a man was seen aloft wearing a jewel-encrusted crown of gold, seeming to grasp a sword in his right hand and a rod in his left. The image of another man was seen squeezing both of his blood-covered hands, and they saw blood drip from them. Many people also saw in a clear sky an armed cavalryman with a threatening expression on his face brandishing a sword in his right hand. The night watchmen were terrified when the bolts to the city gates jumped by themselves without any human moving them. Toddlers and boys armed with clubs carried military standards made of paper or linen through the lanes, and often engaged in play fights, imitating the sound of drums and gunfire with their mouths. | I pass over the shouts of the soldiers, the crashing of   125
weapons, the thronging together of infantrymen and cavalrymen, the neighing of horses, the crying of babies, the keening of women, the melancholy howling of dogs and hooting of owls, the sad groaning in tombs and cemeteries, the various gasping sobs in churches, the sounding of guns, drums and trumpets that were heard at night in the open areas behind the walls and in the out-of-the-way recesses of the city.[20] Finally, I pass over the fact that sometimes during daylight the sound of military pipes and drums went through the air in a long procession, attracting the attention of many people. The people of Münster would have easily sensed both by hand and by foot that all these phenomena were not meaningless events but instead foretold manifest and fast-approaching disaster, had they not been misled by the foolish interpretations of their prophets, convincing themselves that these events did not at all relate to them. Therefore, since they did not allow themselves to be warned by any prodigies and omens, however terrifying, and no hope of a better way of life remained, it would be

---

[19] For this and the following omens, see 500–502D.
[20] The last item sounds like a reflection of folk beliefs about the "wild hunt" or "raging army" (*der wilde Jagd, das wütende Heer*), in which marauding armies of dead souls were thought to roam about at night battling other such armies and wreaking havoc; see Behringer (1998) 72–81.

unjust to ascribe to God the cause of the overthrow. Instead, this should be ascribed to the rashness of theirs by which they voluntarily flung themselves headlong to their death.

What now remains to be said is how they rushed from crime to crime until their eventual extermination.

THE EVENTS OF 1524–1525

Through the whole doctrine and saintly way of life of the ecclesiastics, the wisdom and authority of the city council and the obedience and pious imitation of the best burghers, Münster carried on with the religion that St. Swibert first taught and Charlemagne strengthened without admitting any novelty since that time. But in 1517 the doctrine of certain men who condemned good works by their doctrine and rejected the Church's ceremonies began to break out like a disease throughout Germany and to spread to almost all cities, and later around 1524, when Frederick of Wied was bishop (he was appointed by free election on November 6, 1522 after the death of Eric of Lowenburg), Eberwin Droste and John Boland were burgher masters, Derek Münsterman, Henry Travelman, John Droste, John Osnabrugge the younger, John Herding, Wilbrand Plonies, Eberwin Stevening, Bernard Kerckering, John Oesen the elder, Richwin Meinershagen, Bernard Paell, Henry Drolshagen, Bernard Grolle, John Bischoping, John Schencking, Henry Mesman, Anthony Jonas, Gerard Oeken, Henry Moderson, Gerard Averhagen, Adolph Niehus and Herman Bisping were on the city council, and Ludger tom Brincke, and Henry Rotgers the furrier were the aldermen, preachers of this stripe surreptitiously crept into four parishes of this city, contrary to the expectation of good men. | Courting the public's fickle acclaim and slandering the priests to the commons, these preachers fanned the flames that had first been lit by certain merchants, and these flames, which spread further when no one put them out, quickly set fire to many men of the lowest sort. Although John Tant of St. Lambert's, Lubbert Kansen of St. Martin's, Frederick Reining of the Parish Across-the-River and John Vinck of St. Ludger's had sown the word of God for some years without criticism, in this year they began to puke out words that roused the commons against the clergy and civic officials. Their zeal was increased by certain lecturers in the schools and most of all by the schoolmasters at St. Martin's and St. Ludger's, the latter of whom (Adolf Clarenbach) paid the penalty for sinning at Cologne as a violator of the Sacraments.[1] They would

---

[1] He was burned at the stake at Cologne on September 28, 1529.

never have been able to raise a faction with their own learning, most being completely lacking in education, if they had not condemned good works and done away with the reward for them, if they had not granted to the people the extravagant evangelical freedom, which easily erupts into licentiousness, if they had not raged with a fair amount of license against the clergy, as a result of which the rabble, who had already squandered their own possessions, seized the opportunity and reached such a pitch of madness that they not only despised the clergy but also thought that they were allowed to do anything against anyone.

First, the rasher members of this faction and those for whom noth-ing was more pleasant than idleness would sometimes enter the mon-asteries in bands to get a meal, | some asking that morsels of food be given to them, others demanding this as if by right. Thunderstruck by this unheard-of novelty, the monks complied to avoid greater violence and uproar. Emboldened and made more daring by their impunity in committing this deed, they prepared more unpleasant plans against the clergy and richer burghers.

Towards dusk on May 22, 1525, three men were sent by the factious to the cemetery of St. Servatius, which is located along the city walls away from any large numbers of people. Their purpose in gathering there was to attack the wealthy Nitzing convent, which is nearby, if the opportunity arose. Then they would open it for robbing, the rest of the troublemakers and their own wives standing nearby on the rampart with sacks, baskets and other containers and ready for looting. To avoid losing the opportunity for plunder, they sent a boy to let the others know immediately that the assault had been made. At this time, the abbess of the nuns at Dülman, who had by chance come to Münster to visit friends and been entertained by them with a meal, was coming, as nightfall threatened, with a servant girl to the Nitzing convent to spend the night, and the men followed her, plotting to launch their attack. When they were asked who they were and what exactly the reason was for their having come here towards nightfall, they intentionally gave false names to avoid being recognized. The first said he was Derek Hloschen, the second Piepenkenneken and the third Rudolf Potteken. But the abbess's servant recognized and then betrayed them, giving Derek Hloschen as the name of the first, John Grever the maker of glass cups as that of the second and Rudolf Schomaker as that of the third. Hearing this, they realized that the ploy was revealed, grieving greatly at this. For this reason, they undertook no hard against the nuns, fearing for their own safety. When the lookout boy reported this to the harpies

standing on the rampart, the group broke up, each person going his own way. | Nonetheless, the nuns, who were terrified by this unusual   129
turn of events, entertained the three men in the convent's hospice with more respect than was reasonable given their status. The nuns did this to avoid provoking the troublemakers, who were upset at the failure of their enterprise, into hostility against them and to soften them instead with kindness. They eventually left, being stuffed to the point of sickness with beer and wine. When this matter was reported by the servants to the burgher masters in the early evening, they realized that manifest rebellion would ensue if it was not countered with a swift response and punishment. When the council was convened to deliberate on this matter the next day, those responsible for the preceding day's uproar were summoned by attendants. These men were directly followed by almost all the guilds, who thronged together in their zeal to protect the men. The guildsmen created a terrible uproar in the marketplace and council hall with their confused bellowing, and their ringleaders were mostly Reiner Stell the glassmaker and Lubbert Lenting.

Meanwhile, as the councilmen in their chamber heard the uproar, they trembled, they made all sort of proposals and looked for opportunities to escape and ways to calm the raging commons. Finally, it was decided to send a delegation of four councilmen whose influence and authority among the commons were great. Relying most of all on God's protection but also on the civility of certain men, the four men exposed themselves to the danger of undertaking the delegation. When they inquired after the reason for the uproar and what they wished to be done by the council, a fearsome shouting suddenly erupted, with men bellowing all at once to the point of hoarseness. The clergy, they said, were free of any tax and burden from civil obligations and were protected by the burghers' fortifications and watches, but they caused the destruction of the burghers by engaging in money-making crafts and secular business deals, they took from their burghers their livelihood, taking possession of everything for their own profit, contrary to their status and calling. They said that what they therefore wanted was that the account books of the nuns of the Nitzing convent and the Monks of the Fountain should be taken from them and that stewards should be appointed to dispense to them as much as was needed for life's necessities, but the rest should be used for the benefit of the poor. (They did not dare to irritate the other monasteries, which contained nobles, | to avoid calling down the anger of more powerful men upon themselves.) Next, they said that since God's soldiers ought to be completely   130 removed from the business affairs of the world, the equipment with which they weave linen and fit leather onto paper sheets[2] should either be broken up or taken away from them so that the profits hitherto purloined through the clergy's malfeasance should be restored to the burghers. If the council did not hurry up and remedy these losses to the citizens by repressing the greed of the papists, the guildsmen said that they would view the council and the papists as equivalents and consider them both as tyrannical oppressors of the burghers. It made little difference, they said, if swords were drawn against such people even without public authorization, and once they were gotten rid of, good men who would look after the burghers' interests were put in their place. These sentiments and very many others they expressed not simply with words but also by making faces and gesturing. When this was reported to the council, they decided, as the situation dictated, to pretend to forgo the penalty that ought rightly to have been inflicted on those responsible for the strife rather than forget it, and to deal with the present emergency they promised the commons that they would take into their own custody the account books and work equipment from those two monasteries and would to the best of their abilities implement all measures that seemed to contribute in any way to public tranquility and the benefit of the burghers. With these pacifying promises from the council, the ferocity of the troublemakers was broken, and being appeased it subsided. Accordingly, they dispersed in exultation at the successful completion of the prologue to the play, in the meanwhile giving thought to the start of the main action. For at the suggestion of certain priests and with their assistance, they were hammering out for presentation to the council some articles and theses about the burghers' burdens.

The council wished to be obliging to the commons in order to avoid provoking them again by any long delay in fulfilling the promise and to do away with any cause for further uproar, and on May 26 appointed
131   two delegations | that were to be undertaken at the same time by different men. In the council's name, these delegations were to ask for the account books and work tools from the Brothers of the Fountain and the nuns of the Nitzing convent, not, as the raging commons imagined, to confiscate them but to protect them by saving them from the commons' raging. The members of one delegation were the councilmen John

---

[2] Seemingly a circumlocution for bookbinding.

Droste and John Osnabrugge and the commoners Bernard Gruter, Henry Swedarth, Herman Ramers,[3] and John Langerman. The reason for choosing these men was not that they favored the trouble-making faction of commoners but that they could the more easily settle the commotion, since they had great influence with the commons. The members of the other were the guildsmen and councilmen Derek Münsterman and John Herding and the commoners John Oesen the younger, Henry Bureck, Roger Tos, and John Baggel. While the first delegation completed its mission with the Brothers of the Fountain without any uproar and quickly too, the other one encountered difficulty with the nuns of Nitzing, partly because of the recent uproar, on account of which they had made the commons hostile to them, and partly because of problems in taking apart the looms. For the dismantling and removal of the looms they employed the carpenter Derek Trutling, who would rightly have been very beholden to the nuns because of their services to him, if goodwill had been changed along with fortune. Nicholas Munth, who had a big mouth and was exceedingly long-winded, also greatly increased the madness of the commons, falsely claiming before the council and the entire populace that the nuns of Nitzing had one hundred looms to the great detriment of the commons, but when only eleven were found, he was publicly accused of lying by Münsterman and withdrew in shame, complaining that he had been deceived by the talk of certain men. While the looms were being dismantled inside by Trutling, the rabble formed crowds of incredible size outside as they took up position for looting and prepared an assault, and the members of the delegation barely succeeded in restraining the rabble by virtue of their authority. A certain troublemaker called John Groeten was also heard to say from the middle of the crowd | that it was good   132
enough for the rich if they owned no more than 2000 gold coins. The only thing he seemed to mean by this was that after looting the good ecclesiastics they would dump out the moneyboxes of the richer burghers too and make all property common. So, the account books and the machines, which were snatched off with the warp and weaving still attached and placed on wagons, were hurriedly transported to

---

[3] Ramers would give lodging to John of Leiden during his visit to the city in 1533 (see 372, 523K), and the following year he would defect to the bishop and reveal to him a scheme to assassinate him (see 506–507K).

the council hall, where they were protected in custody until the Feast of the Birth of Mary.[4]

While these actions were being taken by the delegations from the council in the two monasteries, the leaders of the troublemakers by no means calmed down. Instead, on the same day (May 26), they unexpectedly rushed around in bands and mobs, seemingly throughout the wards, either egging on everyone they met to similar madness with cajoling words or rebuking them with rasher ones. They asked why they did not join in and why they were acting so remissly. Were they unaware that what was at stake was the burghers' liberty, to which everyone was rushing by natural inclination? Did they not know that the evangelical light had dispelled the shadows of errors and was dawning over the world, though the power of the arrogant, greedy papists had up till then suppressed it? Now their frauds had been uncovered, now the heavy yoke of good deeds had been removed, now the evangelical freedom had removed the servile status that everyone in his right mind rejected. The discordant voices of the rioters were thrown into a jumble with such immoderation that they could not understand each other. Many blackguards were privy to the factious plan and many were enticed by the novelty and unusual aspect of these events, but a few rushed up to calm the uproar. The more intelligent people, however, saw the folly of the mob and stayed in their own houses. This outbreak of madness greatly surpassed the earlier one, and if you compared the first with the second you would call it mere child's play. Their eyes were flashing, their teeth gnashing, their lips frothing, their feet prancing on the ground, as they pounded their fists in threats against both clergy and magistrates, bellowing inarticulately, and some struck their heads to heighten their anger, muttering and mumbling to themselves. With 133 equal zeal | they rushed to the council hall and stuck certain articles in the faces of the aldermen for them to show to the council. The council was to extort from the various estates within the diocese the ratification of these articles under seal; otherwise, they said, there was no hope for peace. The diocese is divided into four estates or orders, the first consisting of the bishop, second of the main clergy, third of the nobility, and fourth of the cities, and whatever decision is reached through the unanimous authorization of the four estates is considered to be a official enactment of all the members of the diocese. Accordingly,

---

[4] September 8, 1525. The fate of the property of the monks is not known.

it was not without reason that they demanded the estate's authorization of their theses. The text of these runs as follows.

"1. Since by right of inheritance the main clergy always takes possession of the goods of the bishops after their deaths, it seems to be very fair that they should also pay off the dead bishops' debts, so that the members of the other orders in the diocese should not be burdened on account of the debts.

"2. Upon the death of the bishop, the main clergy will not only take   134
possession of the strongholds in all the diocese and administer them at their own discretion, but they will also admit one man each of knightly and councilor rank (or a respectable burgher in place of the councilor) to each stronghold for the common administration, until such time as a new prince will be appointed by unanimous vote.

"3. When Eric, the bishop of Münster, took the stronghold at Lingen from Count Nicholas of Tecklenburg in the year 1518, many burghers of Münster were robbed of money and others of merchandise during the uproar, and the main clergy should make good their losses and expenses from the possessions of the dead prince.

"4. No member of the clergy will oppress a burgher with pontifical (ecclesiastical) fulminations and commands, but if he is to take just action against a burgher, he should put his claim to the test in a secular court.

"5. No ecclesiastics (e.g., those in holy orders, priests, monks, nuns, the concubines of clergymen) will engage in any form of secular business or put oxen to pasture or make any profit from linen or its weaving and working or from baking or any other thing, whatever its designation. For this reason, they will voluntarily sell at retail all the equipment acquired for such purposes, whether it be in monasteries or in the houses of canons or priests. Otherwise, they will be deprived of them by us.

"6. No ecclesiastics will henceforth be free of the public burdens imposed by the city.

"7. Both secular and ecclesiastical officials will restrain their subjects in the country districts outside the city walls from practicing any professional skills within two miles of the city or from acting in any way | as retailers, brewers or bakers, which would result in lessening the   135
burghers' profits.

"8. Two councilmen, two guild masters and two burghers without official position will be appointed, and after taking custody of the account books of the Brothers of the Fountain will receive their annual income and distribute to the monks of that monastery as much as will be needed, for the necessities at any rate. No one will be substituted in place of monks who die, and each one will be granted permission to leave, change his habit and take with him only the possessions that he had brought, without any stigma of infamy.

"9. These six appointees who are elected by the commons as stewards will sell back to the burghers the pastures and fields of the brothers at the original purchase price. Whatever will be left over after purchasing the necessities they will spend on poor burghers in order that provision should be made for them too.

"10. The Nitzing Convent will also be under the control of six stewards, who will, by the council's authority, fix the number of nuns to be maintained there. No one will be admitted there for the sake of wealth or any other benefit or advantage or because of high birth, but only for the sake of God. It will, however, be lawful for them to bring their adornments bestowed on them by their relatives and to make use of them.

"11. Both the cathedral college and others in the city will also be subjected to correction by us after the dissemination of the reformation instituted in Cologne, which we expect any day now.

"12. All those inhabitants of monasteries, whatever their sex or order, who pollute themselves with monstrous secular crimes will without distinction or privileged treatment be punished in the normal way on account of the crimes they have committed.

"13. No "outlying" or "stationed" monks (e.g., Carmelites, Augustinians and Dominicans) are to be tolerated in the city, and the pigs of St. Anthony[5] and St. Hubert are not to be fattened in the lanes.

136   "14. No one among the burghers of whatever sex will leave legacies to people of ecclesiastical status in their wills or fund memorials, exequies, funeral rites or confraternities. For all these ceremonies are abolished as pointless and vain and will in no way be celebrated.

"15. The pastors of all the parishes of the city will neither install nor remove chaplains or preachers without the agreement of the "*scabini*,"[6] providers,[7] burgher masters and all the parishioners.

---

[5] Patron saint of swineherds.
[6] See 105D.
[7] See 59D, 107D.

"16. No foreign ecclesiastics (e.g., monks) of whatever order or variety will be allowed to preach.

"17. There is no time when it is not permissible to celebrate a Christian marriage, and for this reason the laws prohibiting the celebration of weddings at certain times are to be repealed.

"18. All harlots and priest's concubines are to be distinguished from respectable women with certain marks, in order that due honor should be given to honesty and due disgrace should attend lewdness.

"19. No one should graze oxen and instead they should graze only cows in the meadows near the city that are normally fertilized with dung transported from the city.

"20. Fields enclosed within the last fifty years to which herds from the city are driven should be re-opened, the fencing being cut down.

"21. No one among the burghers who has rented fields from the clergy will rent them out to someone else for a higher cost than what he himself rented them for or possessed them in ancient days.

"22. No one, whether ecclesiastic or layman, will presume to extract annual income from the burghers by force unless he either bought it or inherited it or produces a title that is authenticated with seals in such a way that it cannot be contradicted.

"23. To prevent the cases of burgher litigants from dragging on for many years | at great expense, they will be settled by the judge's decision within six weeks.   137

"24. The butter sellers who are burghers and sell their produce in the public marketplace should not be forced to pay an annual rent for their location.

"25. No burgher who is prepared to offer surety will be imprisoned by a magistrate unless the issue is a criminal case.

"26. The merchants who bring wines to this city should be able to take them out of their wagons without paying a tax, as used to be the custom in ancient days.

"27. Burghers should be allowed to sell all varieties of local beer at retail, as has always been the case.

"28. Anyone should be allowed to sell wine at whatever price they can get if they pay the usual tax to the council.

"29. No one but a burgher may be a baker or brewer.

"30. Ecclesiastical benefices in the city's gift will be granted to none but the children of burghers, who will be deprived of them unless they occupy them themselves.[8]

"31. Children of burghers who enter an ecclesiastical order will not transfer property that they inherit to another member of their order, that is, to an ecclesiastic, either by will or by gift or by any other means.

"32. Burghers will not pay any toll or tax for crossing at the two bridges across the Ems River at Gelmer and Schöneflieth, but will be altogether immune from this burden.

138 "33. The payment of quitrent owing for certain fields outside the city | and of the ground rent owing for the Lord's land (that is, of the Old Lords' Church) in the case of certain houses in the city will no longer be made by the burghers.

"34. The memory of the victory at Varlar will no longer be celebrated with the festive ringing of bells, but will be erased for the sake of the general peace."

(The victory at Varlar resulted from a dispute about an election. Once, when the main clergy, in whose hand rests the right to elect the prince, had chosen Walraf of Moers, but the city interfered with the election, preferring Eric of Hoya, things reached the stage of open fighting. In the year 1454, on the Feast of St. Arnulph,[9] near the Varlar monastery both sides fought a fierce battle with the troops they had hired. When the burghers' force was defeated, Duke Frederick of Lüneburg and Count Ernest of Schauenburg were captured, and after slaughtering many burghers Walraf and his supporters triumphantly carried back from that battle not only a remarkable victory but also monarchic rule over the diocese. In memory of this victory, the clergy used to celebrate the Feast of Arnulph with joy, while the burghers would receive it with lamentation in the monastery of the Minorites, to which the bodies of the slaughtered burghers had been transported.)

If someone judges these articles by the standard of natural law that preserves human society, that is, by the rule that nature does not allow anyone to increase his own resources at the expense of someone else, he will see that the tendency of many of them is such that they are completely inimical to Christian love, and for this reason we have no

---

[8] The last clause aims at preventing the practice whereby the holder of an endowed benefice hired someone else to carry out the attendant ecclesiastical duties for a sum less than the annual income and pocketed the difference.
[9] July 18.

doubt that they were stitched together by trouble-makers in violation of all divine justice and of fairness. Nonetheless, they stuck them in the face of the council with impudent shamelessness, demanding their ratification. After the councilmen had been shown the articles in their chamber by the aldermen and they read them, they were stricken with a great terror that made them blanch, especially when they noticed that the commons had come in swarms to the council hall with the intention of insisting vigorously on the ratification of the articles, even to the point of bloodshed. | At this critical moment the council   139 promised that they would, to the best of their abilities, plead the case of the city's liberty before the other estates of the diocese when the opportunity arose. The commoners, on the other hand, shouted out that agreement could easily be wrenched, even against their will, from the main clergy, who were present, still being enclosed within the city's walls, and that once this had been gotten, it would not be hard to get the votes of the other estates, especially since they had no doubt that the cities were following their lead. Without delay, then, they said, the matter should be put to the main clergy. To avoid calling down upon themselves the onslaught of the raging commons, the council promised to do everything the commons wanted. Satisfied with this promise, the commoners dispersed.

After the gates had been closed to satisfy the commons' expectations, on the Friday after the Feast of the Lord's Ascension in 1526,[10] the burgher masters and aldermen, accompanied by a small escort, set upon the main clergy, who with more boldness than wisdom were present and gave them the articles for reading and ratification. When the Lords had read them and examined them more carefully, they realized that these articles related not so much to themselves as to other groups in the diocese. Hence, they gave the response that they would submit the articles for the deliberation of all groups to avoid giving the impression of having forged the authorization of those who were most affected by the ratification. To this the burgher masters replied that they did not see how they could calm the commons' angered frame of mind or protect the Lords of the chapter against attack by the commons if the articles were not ratified and sealed by them. From these words of the burgher masters it was obvious what dangers the Lords should expect in the closed city, and so they gave in to necessity and put their

---

[10] June 26.

seal to some of the articles in order to satisfy the violent demand in some regards, promising that they would put the remainder before the assembly of the Lords who were absent and give them deeper consideration. But on the Thursday after the Sunday *"Exaudi"*[11] they sent a

140 letter of complaint to Bishop Frederick, | informing him of the whole affair just as it had happened. They told him that since those articles represented the overthrow of not only their own liberty but also that of other estates, he should give deep thought to them. For their own part, now that the uproar was to some extent calmed, the Lords chose to go into voluntary exile, realizing that they were involved in a potentially fatal situation and could no longer remain in the city without bringing about the downfall of the church's liberty. They therefore left that prison barracks, each returning to his relatives, apart from Reiner of Velen, the provost of the Old Lords' Church, whose departure was prevented by a serious illness.

Scattering across the earth with much complaining, they brought upon the townsmen the hatred not only of their blood relations and friends but also of foreign princes. The lower clergy, on the other hand, stayed in the city since they could not maintain themselves abroad in the way that they could at home, and for this reason brought upon themselves no little hatred and resentment on the part of the main clergy. Nonetheless, the presence of the lower clergy in the city was very helpful. For the terrible flames that had broken out in the business of the faith upon the main clergy's withdrawal into exile would have spread to all the best burghers had not the quick thinking and vigilance of the lower clergy put it out. The college of St. Martin's, in which we learn that there have always been very weighty men of the greatest learning, relieved its priest, Lubbert Kansen, a man who did not refrain from participation in the troublemaking, of his duties with the council's consent. Completely forgetting all shame, this man had attempted to seduce the young maiden daughter of an important family with love letters that were filled with sentiments taken from the Holy Scriptures and distorted to give a lewd meaning, though he had given his word that he would marry the daughter of a good burgher with whom had previously fornicated, and these were read out in a full session of the council. For innovating, John Tant too was cast down

141 by Timan Kemner, the priest of St. Lambert's | and the very vigilant

---

[11] Fifth Sunday after Pentecost (hence the date is June 1).

principal of St. Paul's high school, when the parishioners (especially the merchants in the vaulted houses) resisted and greatly objected. Godfrey Reining was deprived of the office of preaching by John tor Mollen, a great expert in law who was also the dean of the Parish Across-the-River, though he thereby brought upon himself the ill will of certain parishioners. John Vinck, the priest of St. Ludger's, for a while at any rate defended in his sermons the introduction of innovation in religion, to the applause of the parishioners, but after his mouth was plugged up with a rich benefice on the advice of good men, he forgot the innovating and was unable even to mutter against the Catholics.

Though during the exile of the main clergy the lower clergy and pastors brought it about that trouble-making chaplains were relieved of the duties, the rioters went on with their business in a more relaxed and leisurely way. They were just like that fire that lurks still living among the hot coals when the firewood has been removed. In the beginning it had been the case that the commons would be stirred up against the leading men by trouble-making preachers and go around rioting in amazing ways, but with the removal of these chaplains the commons ceased to run riot. This was just like the situation when a spark is lit onto green, unseasoned wood. At first, when it is kindled through blowing, the fire crackles on the bark and chars it, but if the blowing stops, the fire dies down and eventually burns itself out.

This departure of the main clergy was unwelcome not so much to the council as to the more insightful burghers, who had an inkling that it would bring misfortune to the city. Even many workers complained that their livelihoods were being harmed, and merchants sat idly at home, their business activities being halted to their detriment, but they did not dare to leave the city through fear that they might fall into the hands of the exiles and suffer a kind of shipwreck on land involving their life as well as their merchandise. Various mutterings, therefore, could be heard among the mob within the city walls. Hence, the lower clergy were worried about a new uproar and began to fear for themselves in case they should have to pay the price in the end if further extension of the exile resulted in harm to the public wellbeing. For this reason, they sent a delegation to the dean and elders of the main clergy to plead for a pardon for the rioters | and to invite the main clergy to return.   142 They urged the dean and elders to recognize that it was not they alone who were involved in this fate, to forgive a misfortune common to all Germany, and to allow themselves to be assuaged. They asked them to return to their homes and to the worship of God that had been long disturbed and interrupted through the excesses of certain people and to consider that God had been the avenger of insult and the protector of innocence. The lower clergy likewise pressed for the recall of the main clergy before the prince, pleading that since they feared a new disturbance and extreme measures against themselves, he should in his mercy grant amnesty to the burghers for any insult given and crimes committed, since the council and good men had never acquiesced in these acts but had resisted them at risk to themselves. They argued that he should not let the good men, who still constituted the majority in the town, be punished as if guilty on account of the rioters and should instead advance the cause of general tranquility, connive at certain crimes as necessity dictated, and tolerate the trouble-makers for the time being, lest violence be done to the grain when the weeds are pulled up.[12] He should spare the evil men in the interim for the sake of the good so that the innocent would not be overwhelmed at the same time. The delegates said that they were leaving everything to the prince's wisdom and inborn mercy for deeper consideration, having no doubt at all about his favor and kindness towards peacemakers.

The prince gave the following response. It was not just the liberty of the clergy and knighthood, which he had sworn an oath to defend, but also his own jurisdiction and esteem that had been abused by force, and all this would lead to nothing being safe against the use of force and no one's liberty, rights and jurisdiction remaining intact. Accordingly, he ought not to turn a blind eye to those acts if he wished to adhere to his oath.

For this reason, the violence and insult inflicted on the clergy by the townsmen lodged deeper in the heart of Bishop Frederick than the burgher masters imagined. For he had no doubt that this withdrawal of the clergy would give rise to greater misfortune among his subjects, and for this reason, he warned the council on June 7 in the following 143   words. | The councilmen had forcibly extracted from the main clergy their approval of certain articles that would subvert the liberty not only of the ecclesiastics but also of the knighthood and of the entire diocese, and had violently taken over from certain monasteries sealed records of their income and other things, doing so without any just cause sanctioned by law, but acting by their authority contrary to the standard of reasonability and fairness and to the decrees of emperors

---

[12] A reference to the parable of the weeds (Matthew 13:24–29).

and popes. He said he would hardly have expected this of them, since it was his business to punish the clergy with lawful reformation and deserved penalties when they commit errors or crimes. Accordingly, he advised them to refrain from such unheard of behavior in future and to restore what they had extracted by force and unjustly made off with. If, on the other hand, they had anything to say against the main chapter, he told them to laid this out in the diocesan synod. He, along with the other orders, would do what reason, fairness and the law of the homeland demanded.

On June 16, the council replied as follows. The commons of their own and of other cities in the diocese were complaining that their daily bread was being purloined from them without ancient precedent by bakers, brewers and other workers practicing trades at various locations in the country districts, and that certain members of the clergy and inhabitants of monasteries of both sexes were engaging in professional skills to the detriment of the towns and their burghers, even keeping workshops specially equipped for such purposes. For this reason an uproar was caused in Münster by the commons, and during this uproar certain articles were drawn up and presented to the council. If there was to be any hope of calming the stirred up commons, a matter in which the councilmen undertook no little effort and danger, the council had been forced to accept these articles. | The council had therefore 144 laid these articles in a courteous, friendly way before the main clergy in order to assuage the angered commons and asked for a meeting to deliberate more broadly about this matter. The main clergy, meanwhile, had hurriedly withdrawn from the city, absconding from the cathedral and from their duties (with what intent they did this, the council did not know). Furthermore, it was not clear to the council that they had even offended consecrated places and persons contrary to the standard of reasonability and fairness, much less that they had done violence to them. As for having asked for and received for safe-keeping sealed records of income from the Brothers of the Fountain and the nuns dedicated to God in Münster, this was not done violently or without just cause, and the council would give an accounting of this to anyone who asked this of them. Nor was there any hint of rebellion in this action, which was undertaken and implemented for the safety of the burghers and for the benefit of the common good.

The prince responded to this on July 10, as follows. The only thing that he could see was that the action of the inhabitants of Münster and their articles had been thought up, written down and made public

contrary to all reason and fairness for the purpose of bringing the prince
into disgrace and contempt, of repealing and destroying his jurisdiction and sovereign rights, and of harming and ruining the knighthood
and the entire diocese. Accordingly, it was his earnest demand that the
council should give back the sealed copies of these articles that had
been extracted from the main clergy and restore to the monasteries the
records of their revenues that had been made off with, and that the
council, by whose talent these articles had been thought up and through
whose authority they had been implemented, should immediately allow
them to fall into abeyance and die away, keeping within the confines
of received tradition and of the homeland's privileges and remaining
content with those privileges. The council should be satisfied with this
and keep quiet. Instead they should thus plead with him regarding
the violation of his episcopal jurisdiction through their disobedience.
Once this was done, then if they thought they had anything that they
were within their rights to say against the main chapter or the other
ecclesiastics of this diocese, both those residing within the city walls
and those without, they should entrust this for decision to the judgment
145 of the prince and of the diocese. | As it was, the council should write
back to say whether they were willing to acquiesce in the decision of
the prince and knighthood.

To this the council replied on July 27, as follows. The council could
tolerate the abolition and repeal of the unjust articles and they would
restore the documents to the Brothers of the Fountain and to the Nitzing
nuns as a favor to the prince. As for the professional tools with which
the livelihoods of the burghers were being pilfered and purloined, the
burghers thought it most just that these should not be returned. Since
it had done nothing tantamount to disobedience and had not violated
the episcopal jurisdiction, they thought that the council should not be
punished on account of disobedience or the violation of the jurisdiction
and therefore there was no need to plead with the bishop. As judges
of their actions they would accept the prince with his councilors, the
knighthood and any other members of this diocese whom the council
did not hold in suspicion.

146 To this Bishop Frederick replied on August 26, as follows. Since the
council was contriving to whitewash their own unfair undertaking and
the violence committed by their own authority, so that it was impossible
to tell for sure what their intention was, he accordingly warned the
burgher masters by the obligation imposed on them by their oath that
they should immediately allow all the articles without exception to fall

into abeyance, return whatever they had taken, seized or extracted by force from the clergy, and give a guarantee to the Lords of the chapter about a safe-conduct for them to return to the city and stay there. When this was done and the council claimed to have a privilege against them, the bishop would, with the assistance of the knighthood's advice, do what consideration of the diocese's rights and privileges demanded.

To this the council responded on September 23, as follows. The council said that they had hardly expected that the prince would condemn it without hearing the legal arguments. Be that as it may, the council would, as a favor to the prince, allow the articles to fall into abeyance and the possessions that had been taken from the Brothers of the Fountain and the Nitzing nuns for safe-keeping to be restored to them. By written documents they were giving guarantees to the Lords, whom they had not banished, about their safe return, and the prince could himself consider how disadvantageous this was for the council. The council could also allow those men to return to their own city and to leave it at their own discretion, just as had always been the case. The council would, however, invoke the homeland's privilege to protect its position against any harm.

To this the prince responded on October 16, as follows. He said that he was astonished that the burgher masters were invoking the privilege of the diocese to protect themselves when they themselves had violated it, treating the prince with remarkable contumely. It was, however, appropriate that he should leave everything for the future, it being his preference that they should set off down a fairer path to avoid running into a great misfortune, one for which they will have no one to blame but themselves.

Next, the prince decided to send a embassy to his brother, the Most Reverend Herman of Wied, the archbishop of Cologne, in his capacity as metropolitan and to the Most Illustrious Duke John of Cleves, who was bound to the people of Münster by virtue of proximity. The members of this embassy were Nicholas of Münchhausen and Master Eberhard Aelius, his secretary.

The sense of the embassy to the most reverend archbishop was as follows. The prince of Münster had no doubt | that news had long since reached the most reverend archbishop that the burgher masters and the council and common rabble of the city of Münster had set upon the dean and chapter of that city during a riot and forcibly compelled them alone to authorize with their seals certain articles, though this act actually belonged to all the estates in equal measure, and that

147

they terrified the chapter to such an extent that in fear of threats to
their lives and property they withdrew from the city and have been
afraid of returning to the present day. Next, turning their violence
to other places and persons consecrated to God, they seized account
books and other property belonging to monasteries, and then, without
any prosecution or trial by law, they also thought up, stitched together,
wrote down and desired to make operative a large number of articles
to the severe contumely, disgrace, loss and detriment of the prince,
the knighthood, the entire region and all its inhabitants. Therefore,
since these acts are all contrary to both secular and ecclesiastical law
and they cannot be deterred from their undertaking by any warnings,
however friendly, from the bishop, being instead rendered rasher as if
they had the right to do whatever they wanted, the prince, on whose
behalf the envoys were performing their mission, asked that the most
reverend archbishop not fail him in his plans, and, in order for the
people of Münster to be restored to obedience, begged the archbishop
to revoke the safe conduct of the residents of the city and not to allow
any property belonging to them to be transported through his territory.
The result of this would be that they would come to terms with their
prince and the lords whom just fear had driven out.

    To this the most reverend archbishop responded as follows. If for
this reason he were to revoke and take away from the burghers of
Münster the privilege of safe passage through his territory, this would
give rise not to peace and tranquility but to greater disaffection and
dispute and would greatly obstruct the cause of public concord. For as
148   a result of this the burghers | would become increasingly angry at the
prince and the chapter. The envoys should therefore report back to his
brother the prince that he should ponder the matter more deeply and
chose a milder path for himself, giving up the harsh one.

    Given this response from the most reverend archbishop, the undertak-
ing to continue the embassy before the Duke of Cleves was abandoned.

THE EVENTS OF 1526

A few weeks later it was decided to send another embassy to the most reverend archbishop. The two parties having previously reached an agreement by letter as to the time and place for carrying out this meeting, on January 8, 1526, the bishop's embassy was sent to Brühl. There the same information was conveyed to the most reverend archbishop and the request was made that as metropolitan he should plan to punish this insulting use of force and to avenge the demeaning insult inflicted on his brother, lest impunity in their prior deed should embolden the inhabitants of Münster to greater rebellion. The most reverend archbishop was of the view that this matter deserved further deliberation. Much later, on February 25, 1526, he asked his brother to inform him of what had been done in connection with the dispute concerning the inhabitants of Münster. The bishop answered that nothing had been done and matters | were still at the same stage as they had been several months before, adding that he was even now awaiting his brother's advice, as they had agreed. To this the archbishop replied on March 2 that he would long since have sent an embassy to Münster, but had not been able to because of the hindrance of very great affairs in his own diocese. He said that he would nonetheless do so as soon as an improvement in the weather permitted.

149

Some days later he sent this peace-making embassy to Münster, and on it were the brother of both bishops, the high-born and noble Count John of Wied, lord of Runchell and Isenburg; Bernard of Hagen from Geseke, a doctor of laws and chief notary; and Derek of Heyden, an orator from Mühlhelm. Finally, on March 27, after these men had for some days considered the dispute between the chapter and the council from both perspectives, with the agreement of both sides the following "recess" (record of the proceedings) was drawn up.

"As a favor to the archbishop, the council will restore the sealed copies of certain articles that were extracted from the chapter, and all the articles conceived and written by the burghers will collapse as if dead and be repealed. Upon these acts, the lords of the chapter will return at their own discretion to their ecclesiastical functions, dwellings and property in the city of Münster without any obstruction on the part of the burgher masters, council, burghers or any of the inhabitants,

150 | and as in the ancient days they will come and go and reside in the city freely, without fear or danger to their lives and property. If anyone, either within the city or without, will on his own authority wrongfully undertake and presume any act of violence against them or any one of them (it being hoped that this will not happen), the burgher masters and the council will, to the best of their abilities, protect them and curb those responsible by inflicting due penalties. Both sides accepted these terms and gave their word that they would abide by them without any violation. As a token of perfect concord, three identical copies of the proceedings were drawn up and validated with the seals of the most reverend archbishop of Cologne and of the chapter and council of Münster on behalf of both itself and the entire community of burghers, the advisers of the most reverend archbishop who were assigned to the proceedings keeping one copy for themselves, and one of the other two being handed over to each of the parties. Issued on the Tuesday after Palm Sunday in the year A.D. 1526."

Next, certain other, very severe disputes and controversies were stirred up by the people of Münster against the prince and knighthood, and in the synod convened at Dülmen on May 28 these were altogether disposed of by the same envoys of the archbishop and by the high-born nobleman Count Eberwin of Bentheim and Steinfurt, Gerard of Recke, a knight, Roger of Diepenbrock from Bocholt, Henry of Merfelt, the bailiff of Dülmen, and Arnold of Raesfeld. All these men were nobles of the diocese who had been sent as representatives in order to reestablish peace and who had been detained for four days

151 with great effort and at great expense to our prince. | The quarrel that had been festering between the estates of the diocese was turned into a harmonious agreement that was confirmed with sealed records by all the estates in order that it should remain unbroken.

After these matters were transacted in this way, the clergy were sure of their ancient safety and did not hesitate to return from exile to their homes without fear. As they came back, the joyous celebration with which the burghers received them was greater than the contemptuous hatred with which they had sent them on their way. Thus, after the main clergy returned and the trouble-making preachers who had not ceased to stir up the commons against the clergy and councilmen were driven away by the lower clergy during the exile, everything seemed to have returned to the previous harmonious situation, but the commons, who always strain after novelty and cannot tolerate either concord or poverty, could not keep themselves within the limits set out for them by those responsible for the peace.

THE EVENTS OF 1527

For when the bishop's ordinary judge (called the "official"), Justin Brandenburg, a man reputed for his knowledge of the law, was deciding cases in the customary way from his tribunal, Anthony Cruse, along with some trouble-makers, made an interruption. With his face contorted and his right hand threateningly placed on the hilt of his sword, he vigorously abused the judge with every offensive insult imaginable, stirring up such a commotion that he terrified all the judge's attendants with this unheard of turn of events. I have no doubt that this commotion gave rise to many evils. For as a result, the authority of both | government-ments[1] came to become diminished in esteem and the commons began to assure themselves of immunity in doing anything imaginable. These two developments usually cause the overthrow of the political order and of all rights. The judge thought that this remarkable insolence, which had not been inflicted so much on himself as on the prince, ought not to be ignored, lest the authority of the Church's jurisdiction in the city become diminished in esteem, and he accordingly informed the prince of the affair, just as it had happened. When the prince learned of it, he took great umbrage (as was reasonable) and immediately sent a written command to the council ordering that since not only the city's laws but decrees of emperors that had been renewed in almost all Imperial Diets indicated that he should be punished, the council should arrest him and impose on him the appropriate penalty. The council, however, perhaps because it was afraid to offend the parties in this affair and create an uproar, changed sides, claiming as their excuse that the man responsible for the crime had taken refuge in the sacred place of the Monastery of St. George as an asylum, from which it was not permissible for them to remove him. To this the prince responded that the man should be taken away from there to prison by his authority and permission, since no one could enjoy the protection of a place that he had himself had the effrontery to violate. He said that public crimes should not be ignored or left unpunished, so that evil men should not be given a greater opportunity to commit crimes and overwhelm the good men and the prince should not call down upon himself great

---

[1] I.e., secular and ecclesiastical.

outrage on the part of the Imperial government. Disturbed by this letter, the council ordered Anthony to be arrested at the monastery of St. George and taken to the prison at the Gate of the Virgin, where he was to be kept under close guard. The arrest of Cruse first upset his father and his brother, Conrad Cruse, then all his blood relations, who in turn stirred up Bernard Knipperdolling, the chorus leader of the whole faction, and the whole gang of trouble-makers, inspiring them to plead insistently and endlessly for his release before the council. By very persistently urging this course upon the council with warnings, requests and supplications, the members of the faction won the hope of release, though this was to be delayed. They refused to accept any delay, and their threats and unbridled thronging caused the council to conceive such a fear for its own safety that it allowed Cruse to be snatched away

153 without any bail. | With a drum leading the way, the whole mob of the faction followed him to a wine shop as an insult to the magistrates and demonstration of their boldness. There they washed away all the filth of prison and his sadness of heart with a plentiful supply of wine. While drinking among themselves they conversed on various topics, as happens, but far into the night they mostly spoke rather immoderately about crushing popery and spreading their own beliefs.

This violent impertinence in language seemed to be tolerated by the council, but when the opportunity to exact punishment arose, the councilmen summoned the aldermen and the guild masters to a deliberation on this wanton behavior. The councilors set out the following viewpoint to them. Since the council knew that it was bound by oath of office to foster the public good, there were several measures that they could fail to take only at risk of breaking their oath. First, they had to avert, as far as they could, the disaster that was assailing the commonwealth, and attempt to restore with the help and assistance of God and good men the concord that was in no small way shattered by the impertinence of criminals. Then, once concord was restored, they had to protect it with strong defenses against attack by the troublemakers. Since the right to do this was not theirs alone, the council would, in striving to bring this matter to a safer conclusion, avail itself of the advice of the aldermen and guild masters in particular, since ancestral custom had made use of their advice in very troublesome situations and the council knew they had a responsibility towards the city that was virtually the same as the council's. The council had no doubts about their complete reliability in using their acts and advice to aid the oppressed city, knowing that they were more vigilant in saving the city than those human dregs were

in destroying it. For the aldermen and guild masters held their own wives and children and all good men dearer than they did the rash trouble-makers, and the council knew that they had not squandered their own property and were not hatching unjust plots against other people's property, preferring the preservation of their homeland to its devastation, security to danger, peace and tranquility to bloodshed and plunder, and the glory of immortal fame to disgrace. This being the case, the council was accordingly asking the leaders of the commons to set aside all emotional upset, be present with their uncorrupted reason and examine the present uproar in the city, which caused both the divine and human justice and both the ecclesiastical and the secular polity to fear for themselves. This Cruse fellow had assaulted a public personage in the form of a judge of the prince, and amidst a large gathering of people public justice | had been violated by a private   154
burgher in a sacred place before the tribunal, by which the prince and the other estates of the diocese were greatly offended. It was possible that a very small spark could be ignited into a vast conflagration that would consume and destroy the city. The leaders of the commons should consider this for themselves: if Cruse and his followers in this madness, who had not stopped harassing the council, emerged unpunished, all the laws dictating obedience would be annulled, all the bonds of concord would be snapped, and no official would be safe. Instead the officials would be nothing but hollow names and the example of this impunity would open the window wide for similar madness. The council would gladly hear what advice for the public good the leaders of the commons would give under these circumstances.

After the council finished speaking, the leaders of the commons dispersed to take counsel. Putting their heads together, they disputed among themselves with various wishes and views, but without any contradiction they agreed that in order to make sure that the state not be harmed,[2] it was necessary to suppress those who plotted domestic ruin, to put out the internal fire, and to protect the city against the criminal activity of the trouble-makers. As to the kind of penalty, there was no agreement. The judgment of some was that those who undermined the tranquility of the state deserved to be executed, and that the punish-

---

[2] The phraseology of this last clause was modeled on the so-called "final decree of the senate," a sort of declaration of martial law that was passed only during the most severe rioting in Late Republican Rome.

ment inflicted on a few would benefit the many. The counsel of some
was that they should be fined, of others, that they should be banished,
and of yet others, that the whole thing should be ignored and that the
highest dangers should be sedated with the least uproar. In this way,
the deliberation dragged on for some time without any definitive resolution. Since there was no agreement as to the penalty, their answer
was that the troublemakers should not be tolerated with impunity in
the city, but they left the method of punishment to the council's decision. Partly from the long deliberation conducted by the aldermen and
their delay in responding and partly from the response itself, the senate
readily understood that there was a difference of opinion among the
deliberators and that Cruse had not lost popular favor. For the commons
perhaps considered him worthy of favor on the grounds that compared
to the others he was raging more openly and boldly against the clergy,
who had gotten such a bad reputation that they were almost spoken of
badly even among the Catholics. Accordingly, the council was afraid
that if it passed an overly rash decree against the faction members, they
would stir up a new uproar in the city, but if they passed an overly
slack and lenient decree, they would anger the prince. It was therefore
decided to banish them temporarily, this decision being made known
to the aldermen. Thus, the troublemakers were cast out of the walls,
155 | though not without the hope of eventually returning. The prince
relented, and after being propitiated by a delegation from the burgher
masters, he renewed the terms agreed to the preceding year at Dülmen
and pardoned the city for its misdeed. This act greatly undermined the
confidence of the criminals and revived the hopes of the good.

It could have been hoped that the tranquility that had been returned
to the city would have lasted longer, had not Bernard Knipperdolling
been possessed by such immoderate impulses and gone so far in his
madness that in disparagement of the prince's honor and esteem he
called him a spindle turner, because as a youth he had, after the manner of noblemen, learned the craft of using a lathe to avoid ignoble
idleness. A burgher always eager for novelty, this Knipperdolling was
driven by his poverty and hatred of the clergy to throw the state into
chaos, relying on the throng of blackguards whom he easily enticed to
himself through the hope of plunder. One day he was about to travel
to Bremen on horseback and, as an insult to the prince, was wearing
on his hat spindles with a little wheel made of wood, fearing no evil
and without any worry. In the city of Vechta he was arrested by order
of the prince, because of not so much the insult as the trouble he had

caused in the city, | having been primarily responsible for the release   156
of Cruse, who had violated the bishop's tribunal. When the commons,
who relied very much on his authority, found out that Knipperdolling
had been arrested, they compelled the main clergy and the council,
partly through requests and partly through threats, to dispatch a letter
of supplication and delegates of the greatest authority to seek his release,
and these delegates pleaded earnestly on his behalf before the prince.
They say that when the delegates would not bring their pleading to
an end, the prince spoke as follows. He graciously consented to their
wishes but expressed his surprise that at the cost of so much trouble
and expense to themselves they were pleading so earnestly in order to
secure the release of someone who had not ceased to stir up disturbances in the city, who had placed the clergy in the greatest danger,
and who had always been rebellious towards the council and loud in
his complaints against it. The bishop said that he had no doubt that
the man would overturn the city and the entire diocese. (And the good
prince was proven right in this prophecy.) Accordingly, after providing
sureties and swearing an oath not to avenge his arrest, Knipperdolling
was released from jail, which would cause the complete destruction
of all good men. For after returning to the followers in his faction, he
felt no shame at ignoring his oath and saying repeatedly in public that
to settle accounts for his arrest he would turn everything topsy-turvy,
confusing top and bottom, sacred and profane,[3] so that the diocese
would atone through the pointless spending of thousands of gold coins
equal in number to the pennies that he had lost because of the arrest.
The eventual outcome, when the diocese spent vast sums on the very
difficult siege, proved the truth of this.

    Not only Knipperdolling himself but no member of the faction was
able to curb his tongue and keep it from uttering witticisms and con-
demnations against the Catholics. | Some workmen were casting lead   157
tiles during the process of strengthening the roofing of the "Paradise"
(the seat of the episcopal court), and on September 7 their negligence
in not watching their fire with sufficient care happened to cause the
roof to catch fire at night. This destroyed not only the roof itself but
also the library, that astonishing treasure of all Westphalia. In addition

---

[3] This phraseology of turning everything upside down and of confusing the sacred
and the divine was standard terminology in the Late Roman Republic to describe
those who were thought to threaten the social order by stirring up the lower orders
against their betters.

to codices made of bark, this fire also reduced to ashes many copies of works written in the hand of their learned authors and other remarkable records preserved of Charlemagne himself. Though this loss almost moved good men, and especially those of learning, to shed tears, the members of the faction chortled with glee and rejoiced, shouting that the fire had been sent by God, that His outrage against the papists could readily be understood from it, and that Cruse's innocence was now revealed by God. Now, they said, the axe had been put to the tree,[4] now the harvest of the Lord was at hand, now papist chaff would be burned up as tares.[5] They bellowed here in various places that the house and chapel of Satan had been destroyed by the flames of God, the roof of papist justice had been melted away, and this fire was no vain harbinger of papist downfall. In all their meetings and feasts, they uttered disjointed, mouthy screechings like these, so that they could not understand one another and resembled madmen.

Although this verbal attack was very severe, it nonetheless neither frightened the clergy from their duty nor lessened the authority of the council. To the contrary, like the Marpesian[6] cliff both of them stayed at their posts on the walls, keeping such careful watch against the commons' madness that nothing worth noting in a work of history happened from this point until the year 1531. The grim visage of the sweating sickness that swept across Europe in 1529 and the calamity of a huge outbreak of the plague in the following year that laid low a large section of the population so terrified the survivors that since being stricken now with fear, they had no thoughts of innovation in the faith and its ceremonies. In addition, the Emperor Charles V was afraid that this city might be infected with the contagion in neighboring cities and increase the number of the rebels by defecting from the 158   ancestral religion, | and in his desire to warn the city and frighten it away from the prohibited Lutheran sect, he issued the following letter at Augsburg on August 9, 1530.

"We, Charles, by the grace of God the ever august emperor of the Romans, wish grace and all good things for the burgher masters and council of the city of Münster. It is not without the greatest anguish that we learn that the inhabitants and subjects of certain cities and

---

[4] Matthew 2:10.
[5] Reference to Matthew 13:24–29.
[6] Reference to *Aeneid* 6.471.

communities around Westphalia have, in violation of our Imperial decree against the Lutheran faction that was issued and made public at the Diet of Worms, embraced that sect and gone into rebellion against their government. We hear with pleasure that you and your subjects have obeyed our Imperial decrees until the present day. Whereas, however, it is to be feared in these perilous times that the contagion of this sect might creep forth from your neighbors and sneak into your state at the instigation of certain people, infecting your burghers in such a way that they would burst through the bulwarks of obedience and stir up in your state a rebellion that would bring with it the immediate destruction of all good laws, accordingly, we, in our great desire to assure your subjects' salvation and our wish to remove any detrimental thoughts from their minds, in order that a violent sect like this, which begets turbulent rebellion, should be suppressed and that the boon of political order, concord and tranquility be preserved in your state, do earnestly prescribe by our Imperial authority that you should keep strict watch on those who are violators of the Imperial edict and roam about as troublemakers, and that if they are found to be rebelliously causing insurrection or are suspected of doing so through manifest indications,[7] they should be imprisoned and speedily subjected to the appropriate penalties to make amends to the Imperial edict. Do what you will think needful for the preservation of good government, peace and tranquility, and do not be remiss or careless in this matter if you wish to avoid outrage and punishment from us and the Empire. It is our further wish by this Imperial authorization, that such rebellious and trouble-making disturbers of the public peace should not gain immunity, security or safe passage anywhere, and if they receive any of these things from anyone in violation of our edict, we prescribe that the act is to be void and to lack any import or significance."

This letter from the emperor provided the state of Münster with   159 almost one year's respite from innovations.

---

[7] "Indication" (*Anzeigung*) is a technical term from criminal law that signifies circumstantial evidence of guilt.

THE EVENTS OF 1531

In 1525, the council had, at the commons' insistence, prescribed by edict that no one was to drive oxen to the meadows near the city that could be manured with dung from the city, the clever purpose being that the clergy, whom it by no means befits to practice agriculture, should transfer their fields to the burghers through leasing. The nuns of the Convent Across-the-River, however, did not obey the decree, and in a meadow of theirs near Gievenbeck that was within sight of the city they put to pasture six oxen for use in their own kitchen. For this reason, the commons complained to the burgher masters that the decree was not doing them much good and was instead being haughtily despised by the clergy. Hence, they said, their request that the burgher masters reassert their authority and force the nuns who were enclosed within the city's walls to obey its laws. The burgher masters answered that they could not take away from anyone what was his without violating the obligations of natural and civil law. This, they said, was especially true of the very ancient Convent Across-the-River, which had been endowed with many privileges by both emperors and bishops and with its generous alms supported the children of burghers reduced to penury, in addition to many other advantages that accrued to the burghers from the convent. The commons, however, were by no means satisfied by these words and pled their case much more insistently. The burghers' liberty should not only be defended, they said, but also be increased in every way. The greed of the clergy and their annual revenues were, they said, in some way draining the wretched burghers and reducing them to extreme penury by exhausting their resources.

In order, then, to indulge the importunate commons and keep them from engaging in some new uproar with a sop, the council sent Ludger tom Brincke to the abbess, requesting that she obey the decrees issued in previous years and remove her oxen from the pastures near the city in order to prevent the commons from using that as an excuse to cause more trouble. Through her dean and steward, the Lord William Staell, 160 she gave the following answer. | She was keeping her oxen, bought at her own expense, on her own pastures and not common ones or ones belonging to others, she was encroaching on no one else's rights, and she was merely exercising her own. Therefore, the burgher masters should allow her to make use of her rights without harming anyone else as she saw fit. If, on the other hand, her oxen were seized or driven off, she at least would have to put up with this, but she would entrust the harm inflicted on her to God, endurance and the passage of time. As it turned out, the oxen were fattened in those pastures for the use of the nuns without any interference.

In this same year there emerged a certain Bernard, who by some arrangement of fate had the last name Rothman as if a "factious man."[1] For he was responsible for almost all the factionalism and religious dissension in the city of Münster, so that the poet was very right to say: "The names for things often suit them."[2] This man's homeland was Stadtlohn and his father was some blacksmith named Henry. (Stadtlohn is a little town in the diocese of Münster; the river Berkel, which touches it on the north side, drives a few grain mills and then, after passing the ruins of the old stronghold there, flows downstream to Vreden.) His ancestors and parents, who were accused of witchcraft,[3] were generally considered to be of bad reputation. It is said that when Cardinal Raymond[4] brought papal indulgences from Rome to Germany, Rothman's grandfather, who was doing penance for witchcraft, carried around a butter churn at Deventer | and in this way received forgiveness for the crime he had committed through the protection of indulgences. (A "butter churn" is what they call the container in which whey is made to solidify and congeal into butter through constant motion.[5]) This Bernard, then, being a boy of very fickle and clownish temperament, was reared in various schools through the efforts of his parents, learning the rudiments of letters. However, since his parents were too poor to bear all the expenses of schooling, he was, through the assistance of Lord Herman Sibing, a relative who was also the vicar of the college of St. Maurice's, enrolled among the chanters (choir singers) in the Church of St. Maurice, where he applied

161

---

[1] K. associates the name, which ought to mean "Red man," with the German word *Rotte* ("gang" or "mob").

[2] This aphorism is attributed to the late medieval poet Ricardus da Vesona.

[3] *Veneficium* could also signify simply poisoning.

[4] Raymond Perault (Raymundus Peraudi, 1435–1505). A high-ranking papal functionary (made cardinal in 1492), from 1476 on he engaged in a number of campaigns to sell indulgences in the Empire (and other countries) and eventually became embroiled in the increasing hostility to the practice in Germany.

[5] This definition is made for the benefit of those who might not understand the obscure neologism used here for "butter churn."

himself to singing and gained a livelihood. After living there for some years and insinuating himself into familiarity with many people through his affability and very ready capacity for compliance, he won for himself no little favor in many quarters. When he matured, however, and his voice became harsh instead of high-pitched, so that he no longer seemed suitable for performing this function, he undertook to run the school at Warendorf and taught the youth there for a while, at the same time making some progress in the liberal arts. Then, at Sibing's urging, he set off for Mainz to pursue the studies that he had begun, and there, with the monetary support of the Westphalians who were residing there for education, he achieved the master's degree in, I think, 1524. Having returned from there, he received not simply a position as chaplain but also an ecclesiastical benefice from Sibing in the Church of St. Maurice's Outside-the-Walls in the year 1529. After entering holy orders, he was given permission to preach, | and in this capacity he at first taught Catholic doctrine, even receiving the approval of the Lords. But gradually he began to mix into his sermons doctrines that seemed to be inimical to Catholic dogma, and as he began to incite the commons to anger against the clergy, he attracted to himself some among the burghers who were eager for novelty. The clergy of St. Maurice's thought it better to send him off at their expense to some Catholic teaching institution rather than implicate themselves in the protection of novel views, hoping that he would either not come back at all or at least do so with more acceptable views. Accordingly, the canons of this college decided to give him support for his studies on the condition that he should go to Cologne and devote himself entirely to theology. From the vicars he also got twenty florins, though he bound himself by a signed contract to repay them. Perhaps he will do so after Plato's long year![6] In any case, he feigned one thing and kept another hidden in his heart, promising that he would set off for whatever destination the lords had in mind. Following the advice of certain evangelical merchants, who also secretly contributed money for his travel expenses, he went to Wittenberg. Meanwhile, Sibing acted in his place. It is said

162

---

[6] An example of jocular erudition. The "long (or great) year" refers to the period of time necessary for the seven ancient planets (the five planets visible to the naked eye plus the sun and moon) to proceed through their various motions from a given configuration compared to one another until they recreate the same configuration. The notion goes back to Plato (*Timaeus* 39A), who does not state the length of time required. The term used by K. (*annus magnus*) derives from Cicero (*Nature of the Gods* 2.20), who relates that this period consisted of 12,954 solar years.

that after becoming familiar with his natural character, Melanchthon[7] remarked that Rothman would be either remarkably good or remarkably bad. | From there Rothman wandered through the cities of Southern   163 Germany to learn the novel rites. This is demonstrated fairly clearly in the following letter, which he dispatched from Speyer.

"To the honorable and virtuous Gerard Reining, who lives on the marketplace at Münster, his excellent friend and supporter, or in Reining's absence to the wise and reputed John Langerman, member of the council, greetings!

I offer to you in particular, my very beloved friend, the grace of Christ and the declaration that I owe regarding my duty. I have always suffered anguish because you were absent when I left Münster, and for this reason now that a messenger is available I cannot refrain from sending my letter to you so that you may know where I am and how I am doing. Be advised that I am now at Speyer and thanks to God I am enjoying good health. Having written this letter, however, I have suddenly resolved to leave here for Strasburg, since I perceive that Strasburg is the crown among all Christian cities and churches and wins first prize. I will restrict myself to a fourteen-day visit there for the sake of my desire to inquire into everything. I do, however, fear that because of the high price of food in these parts I will be stripped of my travel money and forced to abandon my plan to go there, so on account of both our friendship and the salvation that (I hope) will accrue not only to us but also through God's grace to many others because of this journey of mine, I beg you to meet my supporters and friends on my behalf, asking them to contribute twenty gold florins for my maintenance. First ask Bernard of Beckum, a burgher of the town of Warendorf to whom I am also writing—I have no doubt that he will immediately and readily give you five florins—then Havichhorst, who lives on the fish market, John Langerman (my main supporter), Caspar Schrodercken, | and all the others who you know support me   164 to give help as soon as they can. By a reliable messenger send the money contributed by the good men to the inn with the sign[8] of green boughs here in Speyer. For its keeper, being a man very much devoted to the Gospel[9] (like most other burghers in Worms, Speyer and the

---

[7] Luther's learned collaborator and right-hand man.

[8] An early modern inn described by the distinctive symbol on its sign.

[9] The phrase "devoted to the Gospel" (*evangelio addictus*) implies that he is "evangelical" (i.e., Lutheran).

other towns of southern Germany), will keep a reliable watch on the money being sent until I ask him for it. I was unwilling to reveal to the bearer of this letter my intention to depart, and I ask you to do the same. (I convinced him that I was pressing forward with a lawsuit in the court of the Imperial Chamber.[10]) I am quite confident that you will not fail me in this matter, and the sooner the better. Make a careful list of how much each of my supporters contributes, for if God keeps me safe, I will in good faith return everything. At the present time I cannot write about other matters, but on my behalf please greet all the brothers and sisters in God in the most dutiful possible. By this letter I commend you to the Lord God. Dispatched at Speyer on the Vigil before the Lord's Ascension,[11] 1531.

Bernard Rothman

"Necessity dictates that my requests need to be fulfilled within one month of the writing of this letter. Otherwise, the money will arrive here too late and in vain. For in that case I will no longer keep myself in southern Germany but will hasten my return to you. God be with you! Please make sure that this letter is attached to yours when you send it to the addressees, and I beseech you to write back at the first possible moment."

After his return from southern Germany in July, 1531, Rothman cleverly refrained for a while from any sudden innovation when he gave sermons at St. Maurice's. Gradually, however, he reproduced in an ape-like imitation all the ecclesiastical innovations and evangelical rites that he had learned at both Wittenberg and Strasburg, spewing forth from jaws now full all the venom that he had sucked in during the past years. | After all the ceremonies of the Catholic Church were annulled and rejected as human fabrications, the new ones thought up by the spirit of the Lutherans were substituted. While good works were condemned, the extravagant evangelical freedom, which was turned to licentiousness, promised impunity for committing sins, and with it Rothman attracted to himself through the hope of seizing other people's property a large number of people reduced to abject penury. In short, to make a name for himself, Rothman's doctrines smacked of all sorts

165

---

[10] The *Reichskammergericht* had been recently instituted in an attempt to provide a general court of appeal for the whole Empire.

[11] May 17.

of uproar and faction, undermined the general peace in the Church, enraged the commons against the clergy and the burghers' government, did violence to the Catholic religion, and did away with all the Church's enactments and rites. For the sake of this insane innovation nature begot Rothman, his will trained him, and his fortune preserved him.

Many people, especially those weighed down by debt, revered him like some godhead, hung from his every word, and were convinced that he was driven in his actions by the Spirit of God. Despite official orders to the contrary, they followed him in crowds from the city on account of their eagerness to hear him speak, their desire to do so being so great that they considered that there were no preachers but him and despised, condemned, and cursed the others along with the entire clergy. Many people had no doubt that certain councilors of the bishop were patrons and advocates of his doctrine, since on January 25, 1532 Leonard Maess, the prince's secretary, had Henry Wichman, an employee in the chancery, inform Rothman that he should have no fears for his own safety. For if the bishop made any sort of rash decision against him at the urging of certain spiteful people, Rothman would learn of it soon enough through secret intermediaries from the chancery. This is what Wichmann informed Rothman by letter. But after the main clergy and the city council had notified the prince about the innovation in religion and the troublemaking stirred up among the burghers by Rothman, | the authority of weighty men was more influential with him than were the urgings of certain light-weight, oath-breaking courtiers, and for this reason the bishop immediately banned Rothman from the office of preaching. Hence, Rothman, who had not feared any such thing, was terrified and approached the bishop with the following letter of supplication, which was dispatched on November 1.

"To the excellent and most splendid prince and lord, Lord Frederick, elected and confirmed as bishop of the Church of Münster, his most merciful lord and prince, grace and peace from God through Christ!

"With groans and in supplication, I cast myself at your knees, O most glorious bishop and famous prince! I do so not with the external adoration of the body that I owe your lordship according to God, but in the way that I can, namely by lovingly and humbly laying my wishes before the eyes of your loftiness through this letter. Do not turn away your eyes, I beg you, most merciful prince, but look at my tears! If only it were possible to paint a picture of them as true as the great sadness that causes them to pour forth in large numbers from the eyes of me, your abject little client! And why should I not say "little client," when

166

I have so often named and styled you both judge and patron? Still, it is with great distress to my conscience that I obey the command of your loftiness that I should not publicly preach Christ, not look after the salvation of the souls entrusted to me, not light up the glory of the name of God, not advance the cause of piety and uproot impiety (for I cannot further the progress of all these tasks with my customary zeal if I cannot preach). It is not my wish at this point to emphasize the burden on my mind. For on the one hand it is overwhelmed by terror at the judgment of God, in that it might seem that I cannot cast off all fear and confess Christ as his own, and on the other it is taunted, harassed and vilified by the tearful complaints of the pious and the biting rebukes of the impious and their insulting criticisms of my having abandoned my duty. The only thing that I say is this, most merci-

167   ful prince: If only you would see | the tears and lamentations of the pious people all over the place here, as they bewail not so much my lot as theirs and the insult to Christ! For your lordship has been so influenced by the lying accusation lodged by the impious that you have thrown me out of my office, deprived them of hearing the Gospel, and even surrendered the Gospel of Christ to the scoffing of evil men. For when these men lambaste my doctrine, which has always been no less in agreement with the Gospel than is the very Gospel itself, and accuse it of falseness, they insult Christ Himself. I beg you, excellent prince, to imagine what sighs, what sobs this situation wrenches from the pious when they consider it. You would swear that the Israelites lamented no more at their misfortune when they were oppressed in Egypt than the pious people here lament that I am being wrongly weighed down by the defamatory accusations of my enemies and that they are being deprived of hearing the word of God, as far as I am concerned. I say this not because I think that I am the only prophet on this earth but because all those who have ever heard me are agreed that I engaged in the business of the Gospel with equal measures of faith, zeal and diligence. Therefore, they grieve the more greatly that a man whom they have not found to be guilty at any time or in any place, a form of praise that the envy of evil people will never be able to take away, is now being thrown out as a peddler of the eloquence of God to the disgrace of the Gospels, this without him receiving a hearing or any charge being made. Accordingly, since it is impossible for me to keep quiet and neglect the office of preaching any longer without distressing my conscience, aggrieving the pious and disgracing the Gospel of Christ, I earnestly beseech you in the name of your salvation, most

pious prince: grant me the favor of being allowed to preach Christ freely among Christians, take pity on the lamentations of the pious and do not allow impious men, of whom I have no doubt that they used contrived calumnies to wrench from you an order like this against me, to profane the sanctuary of God with impunity. Your lordship's order was a temporary prohibition, lasting until such time as some other decision could be made on the basis of a more exact investigation. Look, most civilized prince: it has now been more than three weeks that I have been in these difficulties, hearing the tearful keening of the pious and the criticism of the impious. | Take heed finally and have   168 pity on your supplicant, who both constantly pleads for your clemency under the compulsion of necessity and likewise rejects no form of trial or judgment. So please lessen the sternness of your order, fairest of princes, and command me, as I await judgment and desire to receive a hearing, to act beneficially, that is, to teach the word of God, to care for the souls entrusted to me, and to console the oppressed consciences of the pious. If I look after this duty in a manner too remiss, I would certainly be worthy of harsher penalty. As it is, you will help rather than hinder me, excellent prince, as I bustle with zealous activity and make an earnest attempt at this very thing. I am confident that as this is a righteous and pious act, your lordship will not perform it grudgingly. Indeed, if those cheating accusers of mine will not allow this, but will lay charges too serious for you to think that this indulgence should be granted to me, please grant me this much, which I think has never been denied to anyone, that if someone makes an accusation I will be allowed to plead my case. It is an old practice deeply ingrained in the natural customs of all nations that no one should be convicted without being given a hearing to plead his case. Everyone receives a trial and has sentence passed on him. Certainly, I am in fact so far from lacking confidence in my case, that if given the opportunity to plead my case, I will have won. This I boldly state, that I will refuse no form of punishment if I am truly convicted of any crime such as the many ones that are probably being lodged with your lordship. If, on the other hand, a struggle will have been fought with main force, it is up to your lordship for the most part to determine what will become of me. For if your lordship will be my defender, the situation is safe, but if you will forsake me, there will be danger in it. Nonetheless, I will not despair, relying on my good conscience. I at least have placed my hopes in the Lord, and He will rescue me, lest my enemies should, like a lion, ever tear away my soul, while there is no one to deliver or rescue me.[12] For I know: Many dogs have compassed me and the assembly of evildoers has besieged me.[13] Rather, God will turn aside the evils inflicted on me by my enemies and in His truth will destroy them.[14] There is no doubt but that Christ, who looks upon everything, is directing His vengeful eyes toward this misfortune of mine, in which I am being so overwhelmed with defamatory lies because of my free and pure confession of His name, that my very fair and pious lord's mind has been rendered less propitious to me. But what wonder is there that what should have commended me in the eyes of the good has

169   caused offense in the eyes of the wicked? If, then, you have, | most excellent and illustrious prince, been worn down by the obstinate wickedness of the false accusations made by those men (whoever they may be) who keep lodging denunciations against me with your lordship in this hateful way, and have for this reason heeded them and forbidden me from my duty, you ought not to give in to them any further without my having been first convicted by your judgment of the accusation slung at me. I am so sure that you will do this that I am stopping worrying about myself any more. I turn my entire self over to the discretion of your loftiness, so that you may in this matter reach a decision that is just and pious, since you are a prince whose innate character is such that by disposition you are no less observant of justice than of piety. Hence, the case itself would cause you to protect me in this situation and to grant in your great mercy the request that I am making, even if I did not do so myself. In addition, I am urgently requesting an answer from your lordship in the most humble terms possible, so that I may understand where I should turn now that I am placed in such difficulties. May Christ the Savior preserve your lordship for as long as possible through His grace and in His mercy lead you to the Kingdom that He obtained for us. To Him be the glory along with the Father and the Holy Spirit. Amen! Dispatched from my study at the Fields of St. Maurice, November 1, 1531.

> "Your lordship's most abject little client,
> Bernard Rothman,
> Servant of Christ's Church in Münster
> at St. Maurice's"

---

[12] Paraphrase of Psalm 7:1–2.
[13] Paraphrase of Psalm 22:16.
[14] Paraphrase of Psalm 54:7.

The prince sent back notice through his councilors that for the time being Rothman should abandon his seat and leave the homeland, postponing his return until the decision of the future diet (assembly).

Having received permission from the councilors to consider his answer, Rothman responded the following day as follows.[15]   170

"Yesterday, you excellent and magnificent gentlemen, who are also most reverend and splendid lords and very wise councilors of our prince, explained the situation for me at the prince's command, telling me that for the time being I should leave the homeland and depart from here until the completion of the future diet (assembly). With due carefulness I have weighed the matter in my mind, considering what needs to be done to the extent that I could discern this by my painstaking efforts. I ask that given your courteous nature you deign to listen with goodwill to my reply, which I will strive to set out briefly.

"I wish and am justly obliged to give my ready assent not only to our most merciful prince's requests but also to his commands, even if they cannot be carried out without physical harm. For it is written: It is necessary to obey one's superiors, even bad-tempered ones.[16] Thus, even if this departure of mine cannot be undertaken without great harm to my body and property—for I have such modest means that I cannot maintain myself in exile for even the smallest period of time, and also the resources, such as they are, with which I now eke out my existence will be taken away by my chapter if I set off without their agreement, and in this way I will become bereft of both homeland and livelihood at the same time; and furthermore, given the malice of certain people, I would not be rash in fearing the possibility of a greater danger—yet, if such will be the prince's absolute wish, then despite

---

[15] Many events about the bishop's dispute with Rothman are omitted here, and the undated letter that immediately follows is clearly out of its proper chronological place. On November 14, 1531, the provost and dean of St. Martin's complained to the bishop that Rothman was continuing to preach despite the prohibitions of the bishop, and on December 17 the bishop issued another prohibition and also wrote to the city to forbid attendance at seditious sermons. On December 24, the chapter of the cathedral wrote to the bishop to complain about Rothman's continued disobedience, and on January 5, 1532, the bishop revoked Rothman's safe conduct. Rothman's response to the revocation appears in a letter dated January 16, which K. reproduces at the start of the events of 1532. Since the present letter refers to Rothman's confession of faith, which is dated January 23, 1532, and is addressed to the bishop's councilors, who did not enter the city until January 27, it belongs later in the account and is not a direct response to the actions taken by the bishop directly after the letter of November 1.

[16] 1 Peter 2:18.

these considerations and without any delay I would quite readily accept
these physical losses and withdraw in obedience to the prince's will. But
since this cannot be carried out without permanently | blemishing my
171 conscience with the affront, offending my people and incurring the anger
of God, I have absolutely no expectation that our very merciful prince
will, after giving this matter closer consideration, burden me with such
immediate danger to body and spirit. For many people have received
the doctrine of the Truth from me through the grace of Christ. But
if I leave in this way, abandoning the Word, which I have taught, they
would certainly be right to consider me faithless minister of the Word
and a perfidious[17] apostate and to accuse me as such. There are also
many others who have not yet grown deep roots in the doctrine of the
Truth, and if I left without bidding farewell to the host, as the saying
goes, as if I had committed some rather criminal act, they would certainly be scandalized. For the impious slanderers, who do not cease in
other ways to tarnish, slander and blaspheme my doctrine with their
deceitful carping, would in that case certainly spit upon it and trample
it under foot, defaming me as a very base and fickle wretch. Also, I
have offered a summary of my doctrine to my beloved brothers in
Christ, my spiritual collaborators, asking for their assessment, but if I
forestall their decision by leaving at this point, it is easy to guess what
their conclusion and pronouncement is going to be about me and my
doctrine, which I ought to defend, even at the risk of my life. If I save
my skin as if fleeing, I would, because of the scandal caused to many
people, incur these injuries without a doubt and perhaps other, harsher
ones as well, to the eternal damnation of my soul. It is written: If
anyone offends against these little ones who believe in me, it would be
better for him if he were dropped into the depths of the sea with a
mill-stone hung around his neck.[18] Accordingly, if I will be thrown out
altogether by force, if I will be forced into exile because of the slanders
of impious men who decline to make an accusation in person, then since
I have a clean conscience, I thought that I should follow the example
of Christ, my contest master,[19] and of His soldiers and overcome my

---

[17] In the ecclesiastical context, this adjective signifies someone who has broken the
Christian faith.

[18] Matthew 18:6.

[19] *Agonothetes*, a Greek word that literally signifies one who sets a contest. Though
the word properly refers to a pagan magistrate who is in charge of putting on games,

fortune by enduring it. For in that case, whatever danger or scandal ensues will redound to the detriment not of me, who am being forced to shake the dust from my feet in testimony about them,[20] but of those people, who are responsible for my flight. Far be it from me, indeed may it be a sin for me, to have any such suspicion about our prince, | who is endowed with both innate mildness and the honesty that is   172 inherent to Christian piety. I am so far from thinking that I will in any way offend him with this steadfast position of mine, that I am instead confident that my hesitation to give up rashly the office handed over to me by God will be greatly welcome to his lordship. For just as it is base for a soldier to abandon the position assigned to him by his leader, so too will it be dangerous and disgraceful in equal measure if I rashly abandon the activity entrusted to me by our leader Christ. Yet, if it is the prince's absolute wish to prohibit me from teaching doctrine to the congregation entrusted to me and governing it, then since the command is the bishop's, I will ask Christ not to hold *me* responsible and I will readily obey to the extent that the fear of God and my conscience allow. If this is not permissible, then (to speak honestly what I feel) it is preferable in my mind to fall into the hands of the enemy than to incur the judgment of God, which is a source of terror in human plans. In any case, as for the fear that uproar and rioting will ensue on my account, while this fear has hitherto proven groundless and has perhaps been feigned by the impious, for whom there is never any peace, if any evidence of such a connection, however obscure or hypothetical, comes to light, I will yield to whatever chastisement or fine the prince will, in his great mercy, wish to inflict on me for it. I have constantly striven with the greatest zeal to uphold the state's tranquility, as I could with no difficulty at all demonstrate with many proofs, and I expect that I will always strive after this. Accordingly, since my presence will be a nuisance to no good man and my absence will be a minor offence to many, I would ask in the most strenuous terms possible that our most reverend and illustrious prince deign to grant, if nothing else, then at least the permission to remain safely in the homeland in which I have

---

in the Christian context the word "contest" often refers to the martyrdom, since the Romans executed Christians as part of their public games.

[20] A reference to Mark 6:11.

never committed any but a respectable act or one for which I am not prepared to give an accounting. Just as I expect that his lordship will do this ungrudgingly, so too will I await his merciful answer with the most ardent vows.

Bernard Rothman

THE EVENTS OF 1532

The councilors promised that would take this answer of Rothman's to the prince. But the prince, who was still not mollified by it and instead was further angered against him by Derek of Merfelt, the bailiff of Wolbeck, summoned Rothman to the city and revoked his safe conduct, as it is called (that is, he removed his right to reside and live in the Parish of St. Martin in safety). Rothman, however, secretly enjoyed the liberty of the city by restricting himself to the company of the followers of his faction, and thinking that this abrogation of his safe conduct harmed him as he fervently toiled in the business of the Gospel, he begged rather vigorously for the prince's forgiveness in the following letter of supplication that was written on January 16.

"Grace and peace in Christ! Although your reverend piety seems to show itself to be rather harsh and not very well disposed towards me, most excellent bishop, I cannot in any way bring myself to believe that it has now become so hardened and that the bowels of all your compassion toward me have become so stiffened that I can no longer find any opportunity to defend my innocence before your reverend lordship. I confess, lying calumnies even have their own divinity, Pitho the goddess of persuasion, who sometimes fools wise and good men with deceit, and we not infrequently see that more liberty is granted to lying than to truth, and to calumny rather than to innocence. Nonetheless, it is characteristic of a spirit that is unfair and less than civil to accept the defamatory denunciations of accusers (or rather revilers) and to deny the innocent man's defense. | I consider it sinful even to harbor such a suspicion about your lordship's civility, and for this reason I do not think that the hateful calumnies spoken against me by tricksters have led you to conceive such a sense of outrage against me that you will not in your mercy allow me to respond and submit myself. For you have had and do have such a reputation in my eyes for innate piety and fairness that if someone offers a defense of his innocence before you, he would be readily granted the grace of your piety and fairness against all accusations, however defamatory. Furthermore, if, as I hardly expect, your lordship had, as a result of being persuaded by the lying calumnies of my enemies, unshakably conceived some altogether implacable sense of outrage against me, nonetheless, you will, I have

no doubt, willingly undertake and strenuously uphold the cause of truth
and justice. For your most saintly piety and the inborn fairness of your
truly heroic spirit will not tolerate allowing the offence of a single man
of private station to endanger truth and justice and to cause a minor
offence to many people at the same time. If these considerations will
be maintained through your protection, then whatever will become of
me in this case will be easy, even if will also be very bitter. Accordingly,
most glorious prince, a few days ago your bailiff in Wolbeck, the honorable Derek of Merfelt, came to your city of Münster and summoned
me to him from my house in the suburban countryside of St. Maurice's.
I readily complied, as I ought to, I went and he met me. Oh, what
misfortune! Completely unexpectedly since I had a clean conscience,
he informed me of your lordship's rescinding of my safe conduct. At
this statement, my sweetest lord, I was, I confess, dumbstruck! My hair
stood on end and my voice stuck in my throat (if I might be allowed
to express my astonishment with Virgilian poetry).[1] For why should I
not have been struck dumb at such unexpected news? Since I have
always offered myself to your jurisdiction and judgment and in particular to trial by your princeliness, readily recognizing you as the
appropriate judge for me, and to all the other ones to which I think I
ought to, there is nothing that I could have expected less than that I
should, when seeking the verdict of justice, be stripped of official protection without being tried or convicted. For my part, I grieve most
heavily at this fate of mine, and along with me almost all pious men
grieve and lament. For we see that it is to the detriment of many souls
175   and the disgrace of the Gospel that this happens. | Hence, in the name
of your salvation I pray and beseech you, most courteous lord: let heed
be taken for the salvation of souls and the glory of the Gospel before
I am forced into exile from the homeland in which I have never committed any criminal act for which I am not prepared to give an accounting. Since the glory of the Gospel and the salvation of souls will be
upheld through your protection, then whatever will become of me will
be easy, even if it will also be very harsh. This will happen if your
princeliness will order my accusers to make a public accusation before
your lordship, so that I will have an opportunity to defend myself. If I
am found guilty under such circumstances, I will incur shame and
punishment. In that case, the Gospel will gain its glory and the souls

---

[1] He quotes *Aeneid* 2.774.

their salvation. If, on the other hand, I am outlawed without trial, some of these souls will think that I have been unjustly cast down along with my doctrine, and others that I despise the Gospel, being offended at the scandal caused by my being cast out. If it were a brigand or parricide seeking permission to speak his case before being forced to hear the sentence of conviction, there is probably no race so barbarous as to think that this should be denied. For everyone is granted a trial. As for me, since I am innocent or at any rate have not yet been condemned as guilty, I hope that your lordship will in your mercy grant this to me too, especially since I am requesting asylum only until such time as I should make good my claim of innocence or undergo the penalty for conviction of guilt. Look, then, most merciful prince, in reliance on the gentleness of your Christian mind's benevolence towards the afflicted, I fling myself at your clemency's knees and once again, as so often in the past, offer my entire self to the judgment, trial and decision of your clemency, ready to take a stand against my accusers. Lest anyone be able in any way to accuse me justly as someone who causes delays or declines a hearing of his case, I did the same thing before the venerable chapter and the city council of Münster. In offering myself I am prepared not only to give an accounting of my doctrine but also to undergo an examination of my life and character and of all my actions. For although I confess myself to be a sinner before God, nonetheless I know that I owe nothing to the sword of secular justice. Let my defamatory denouncers oppose me, accuse me, revile me as much as they want: they will make no charge stick apart from my having preached the name of Christ too freely, which perhaps is the greatest charge in their eyes. Oh, if only I could plead this case before you as judge, particularly since I ought to endure or have no one but you as my judge! | If in that case someone proved me guilty of any crime subject to penalty, I would certainly not refuse any punishment. For my request is not that any form of pardon be given in this case. I ask to be judged with the utmost severity. What more should I do? If your civility will be unwilling to accept this abject surrender on my part, if the calumnies of evil men have stuffed up the ears of your piety to such an extent that you cannot hear the requests of an innocent man, if, in short, I abandon my duty and leave my beloved homeland when merely accused, then since I know that all of this is happening to me for the sake of Christ's name, I also turn over this case to Him. Just as He looks upon everything, so too will He in the future turn His vengeful eyes to this calamity. Yet, I am so firmly and unshakably convinced

176

of your piety and fairness that even though your clemency seems to display a stern visage, nonetheless I do not cease to cherish the highest expectations of you as if of a very well-disposed father. Therefore, excellent prince, take heed, I ask you, of the exigency of this case, take heed of your reputation and the very high esteem in which you are held not simply by me but by everyone, and grant that by your protection I may live with security in this homeland of mine for a little while until I am proven guilty of some crime by my accusers or at any rate until the confession of my doctrine, which I will produce any day now in order that its nature can be determined by the public judgment of everyone, will, after examination, be approved or condemned at my risk. Since considerations of fairness demand this, I ought not to doubt that your lordship will act with clemency. On this basis, I commend myself to you, having confident expectations of your most illustrious lordship! May the Lord Jesus Christ preserve and exalt you for us to the eternal glory of the Gospel! Amen! In supplication I ask for your lordship's merciful response. Dispatched on the Vigil of St. Antony.[2]

> In abject submission to your lord.ship,
> Bernard Rothman
> Priest of St. Maurice's"

The confession of Rothman's doctrine alluded to in the letter had been sent by him to the pastors and presbyters of the churches, although in a form quite different from what he had often taught orally.

To this letter John Langerman added a preface written in the vernacular, which I have rendered literally as follows.[3]

177   "John Langerman sends greetings to the reader!

"The grace and peace of God through Jesus Christ, pious and honest reader! For the benefit of you who cannot read Latin I have now translated into German the confession of his doctrine which Lord Bernard Rothman published, having composed it in Latin and divided it into articles. My purpose is that after seeing and reading it, you may judge whether his doctrine that he has up until now professed and is now setting before the eyes of everyone, is in conformity with the Holy Scripture and the Gospel. For although you do not know Latin,

---

[2] January 16.
[3] Langerman, who was a councilor, not only added a vernacular preface but also translated the entire confession into German and published it.

it is nonetheless your task and duty to distinguish in a sure manner which spirits are from God, since Christ appears to have spoken to no specific kind of person. Protect yourselves against false prophets,[4] but also protect everyone in general who does not wish to be led astray. Everyday you hear that this Lord Bernard is reviled and taunted by certain slanderous people as if his doctrine smacked of heresy and were foreign to the Word of God, but now that he is bringing his doctrine into the light of day and setting it before the judgment of everyone, his false accusers cannot fault or blame it. It can easily be seen from this in whose hands the truth is presumed to be. It is said by Christ: "He who does evil hates the light and shuns it, lest his works be reproved."[5] Hence, honest reader, to make sure that you are not moved by the calumnies of impious, crazed men—for the truth can never be safe against the calumnies of the malevolent—weigh this confession carefully and use the Holy Scripture on it as the touchstone by which all doctrines should be tested. If you find this doctrine to be in conformity with Holy Scripture, if it attributes to Christ alone the remission (absolution) of sins and all salvation (as | the Scripture too does), do not be thrown   178 into confusion or upset by what human enactments to the contrary and ancient custom, which would justly yield to the truth, think up, decide and ordain. For if we wish to be the sheep and disciples of Christ, it is also necessary for us to listen carefully to the voice of our shepherd and master and not to let ourselves be led astray by others. May God bestow on us His grace for the steadfast fulfillment of this matter. Dated, 1532."

"Summary of the confession of the doctrine
of Bernard Rothman of Stadtlohn, priest of St. Maurice's
"To the venerable gentlemen and lord servants of Christ, the lord deans, pastors and presbyters of the city of Münster and of the college of St. Maurice's Outside-the-Walls Bernard Rothman sends greetings!
"Grace from God the Father and sincere judgment through the Holy Spirit of Christ! Certain impious men do not cease to blaspheme and spit upon the Gospel of Christ Jesus that I have up until now propounded with equal measures of faith and zeal, and this now compels

---

[4] Matthew 7:15.
[5] John 3:20.

me, my brothers, to undertake to publish in a written composition
what I have up until now propagated faithfully by tongue and voice
in public to the extent allowed by my modest share of grace. Since
the matter bandied about in this way by the calumnies of evil men
has led to my being forced to refrain from the office of preaching in
public, I thought that it was necessary to use pen in place of tongue,
and in writing I will attempt, as far as my humbleness allows, to carry
out what I am forbidden to do by tongue: demonstrate the truth of
the Gospel propounded by me. I think that it is necessary to oppose
by all means these impious blasphemies by which I know that evil men
most outrageously revile not my but Christ's doctrine as hare-brained,
crazy, erroneous and heretical. If I am willing to turn a blind eye to
this insult to Christ and blasphemy against the Gospel or to pass it over
with indifference, I will be faithless both to Christ, Whose Gospel it is
that I have propounded, and to myself and my brothers, who achieve
salvation through the Gospel. Accordingly, as I am duty-bound to
zealously advance the glory of God and the salvation of the congregation entrusted to me, I thought it worthwhile to set against the lying
calumnies of the impious a true confession of my doctrine as a kind
of counter-argument. | For I am inspired by the fair hope that as soon
as a true confession of my doctrine is made public, the refrains of the
impious by which they hold the uneducated mob, the ignorant commons in thrall and scare them away from truly learning the Gospel's
truth, will either be completely uprooted or at least reduced in their
harmful effects. Just as the man who walks in the light stumbles less,[6]
so too will the defamatory tricks by which the impious strive to cast the
truth into shadows be less likely to trip up the minds of the simple folk
if the clear light of the truth is set beside them. And so, my brothers,
this is the reason, this, I say, is the explanation of why I have been
forced to reduce to articles and to confess in public the main points of
my doctrine, against which certain aged and virtually atheist men rage
with such fury. Although these articles are of limited scope, nonetheless
I think that they satisfy someone who has a moderate amount of wise
experience with the Holy Scriptures and the knowledge of Christ, these
being the sources from which whatever I have taught has flowed as if

179

---

[6] John 11:9.

from a spring.[7] Hence, such a reader will not lack much for the purpose of assessing and judging my doctrine. To the extent that I could recall the essence and order of my doctrine, I have omitted nothing that he would not find reliably written here in the same form as it was preached. I readily submit this confession of my doctrine, my brothers, to the judgment of the whole Church, which makes its decision in accordance with Holy Scripture through the inspiration of the Holy Spirit, but I do so to your judgment in particular, not only for some other reasons but most of all because you, who have been entrusted with the same function as I have, ought, like me, to undertake to defend the cause of the Gospel's truth and of the people's salvation against the baneful calumnies of informers, even if no one warned you to. You will clearly do your duty if you assess this doctrine of mine against the standard of Holy Scriptures and do not refuse either to approve or disapprove it. However this is done is fair in my eyes so long as the light of the Gospel and the salvation of the people are upheld. For my own part, I have a clear conscience and know that I have never taught anything outside of the canon of Scripture, the only thing to which the faith conforms, as Augustine taught. Yet, by Paul's example,[8] as if making a contribution, I am readily submitting to your assessment what I have propounded, in order that the Gospel should be the safer through your support. | I beseech you in the name of your salvation, my brothers,   180 that just as I am honestly and readily submitting to review through your assessment, you in turn should likewise be willing to read and judge this confession of my doctrine with equal honesty. If you can provide a truer doctrine, like an obedient son I am not going to spurn the doctrine of my fathers. Farewell! Münster, January 23, 1532.

"On Holy Scriptures
"It is only to Holy Scriptures that we yield and adhere without dispute.
    "Holy Scriptures are those writings that can render us knowledgeable for the purpose of salvation, which is through faith in Christ Jesus, in

---

[7] This is a reference to the theme very common in the Reformation (and made popular by Erasmus) that the original sources (that is, the books of the New Testament and, in the minds of some, ancient patristic writings) are comparable to springs giving forth pure water, while the doctrines of the medieval church are castigated as dirty ditch water.
[8] Romans 15:26?

order that God's man should be whole, being ready for every good work.

"On the Word of God

"Christ Jesus is God's true and natural Word, in which and through which everything was created and has been restored.

"Scriptures which promise the remission of sins and salvation in anything other than Christ are both vain and impious. Those, on the other hand, which make this promise in Christ are properly called the Word of God. It is necessary to give firm agreement to this Word of God in all matters, and this Word of God must not be invalidated by any reasoning or by human doctrines. Every word is possible with God.[9]

"On God

"According to the exposition of Holy Scriptures and both the Nicene and Athanasian Creeds, God alone and by Himself is by nature good, true, omnipotent, just, wise, the creator and overseer of all things visible and invisible. He is the Father, Son and Holy Spirit: three persons to be sure, but they have a simple, uniform essence.

"On the Incarnation

"In a true manner only the Son assumed on our behalf and out of the immaculate and perpetual Virgin Mary the flesh and the entirety of human nature or rather the entire man consisting of body and soul 181 and became a man. | This man Christ Jesus was subsumed into the unity of the hypostasis (person) of the Son of God while at the same time being a single inseparable and indivisible person.

"Also, those statements made by Holy Scriptures and the Creed of the Faith about the single nature of God and the trinity of persons are correct.

"On Man

"God, Who from eternity for ever looks upon everything with a single, simple view, created man, who in the beginning was simple and honest, though He foresaw that man would later fall through disobedience. He likewise decided from eternity to clad His Son in human nature in order that He should repair the fall. By this means, God's goodness has been

---

[9] Cf. Matthew 19:26; Mark 10:27; Luke 18:27.

made manifest in every regard. Man, therefore, being by nature good, was made evil through disobedience. The contagion of this evil spread to all of human nature, making it so faulty[10] that all men begotten by nature are born with the sin as sons of wrath.[11] This general fault of nature truly is sin, damning all those who are not reborn by discovering Christ, that is, through baptism and the Holy Spirit. Thus, all men, being the linear descendants of Adam by nature, are shut up under sin as servants of sin.[12]

"On the Law

"Through the Law we recognize this servitude to sin, the curse of human nature and the anger of God. Accordingly, the Law has been given as a cause not of righteousness but of mortification.[13] It causes mortification when by recognizing our sins through it we both realize the inability of our nature to do good and are forced to despair of our own strength. Those subject to sin are condemned to eternal damnation.[14] No one can be freed from being a captive to sin by the pursuits of human reasoning and by works. Human nature can by itself do nothing but sin. According to the right belonging to sin, He alone can give freedom Who is without sin. Satisfaction for sins can be carried out only by Him Who does not know sin. Christ Jesus alone did not make a sin, but was made a sin on our behalf, in order that we may live for righteousness. Righteousness, that is, the remission of sins, falls to the lot only of those who | believe in Christ through the   182

---

[10] The image in the Latin is hard to render in English. The noun *vitium* literally signifies a crack in a piece of pottery and is used metaphorically of a "flaw" or "fault." In the ecclesiastical context, it refers to a "vice" (the form of the English borrowing) and the derived verb *vitiare* (literally, to "render faulty") refers to making someone "vicious." Unfortunately, all of the English borrowings have developed noticeably different meanings in regular discourse and are not normally thought of as being related to each other. To remedy this, I have chosen to translate the words literally (though perhaps with some loss of the implication that the "faults" in question are the sins that ruin human nature).

[11] Ephesians 2:3: "We were by nature sons of wrath like the others."

[12] Ephesians 3:22: "But Scripture has shut up all things under sin"; Romans 6:17, 20: "Servants of sin."

[13] Here there is another Latin play on words that cannot be readily transferred to English. The Latin adjective *justus* signifies not simply "just" in the secular sense (as the English derivative does) but also "righteous" in the ecclesiastical sense. Thus, "justification" signifies "making righteous" (a sense normally lacking in modern English) and is opposed to "mortification," which literally means "making dead" (again a sense lacking in the English derivative).

[14] Cf. Mark 3:29?

promise of the Gospel. When their sins are remitted, men are then truly made righteous.

"On Faith

"Only through faith in Christ are sins graciously forgiven by God. This grace is made manifest to the elect through the Gospel and is perceived through faith. Just as nothing but faith gives righteousness, so too is there no sin but lack of belief. Faith, furthermore, does not give salvation because it believes but because God promised salvation to the believer. Faith means the firm conviction and steadfast awareness, through the Holy Spirit, of righteousness and salvation, which is acquired through no good works at all but only through the grace of merciful God as a result of hearing His Word. The greatest happiness in this faith is knowing that you are the heir of eternal goods. Just as no one can please God without faith, so too is it impossible for faith to exist without many constant great works. Faith that does not work through charity is not faith but dead opinion.[15] Without the fruits or enjoyment of faith, which alone works wondrous mortifications in men, no one is saved. By faith one tastes how sweet the Lord is, and with the discovery of this most precious pearl, the notion of becoming righteous through works is considered rubbish.

"On Good Works

"There is no merit of human work by which grace can be received. Good works are the fruits of faith, evil works those of lack of belief. Works contribute to salvation to the extent that fruits contribute to the essence of the tree. Man produces the fruit of good works to the extent that he has put down roots in Christ. It is not faith or righteousness that come from works but works that come from faith and righteousness. Every work that does not derive from faith is sin.[16] A good work sometimes is done through the opinion of seeking righteousness and salvation through it. Such opinion is complete impiety, unhappiness and idolatry and sins against the faith, the promise of God's truth and the entire first tablet.[17] Only those works approved by Holy Scripture

---

[15] Cf. James 2:26 (also 17, 20).
[16] Romans 14:23.
[17] Presumably a reference to commandments one through four, which concern God (as opposed to five through ten, which deal with human relations, and are

are good and only those disapproved by it are evil. According to the goodness or badness of our works, we will be adjudged to eternal blessedness or damnation, because works are testimonials to our piety or to impiety.

"On Human Enactments   183

"Works connected with human enactments are either pointless or impious. Those who publicly promise the remission of sin, righteousness and salvation on the basis of works connected with human enactments are the most impudent deceivers. Those who fight on behalf of human enactments as being necessary for salvation are unworthy of the designation "Christian Church," since the Church is nourished and governed not by human decisions but by the revelations of God.

"On the Church

"The Christian Church is the congregation of the saintly. The saintly are those believers who are marked out by the spirit of sanctification, which belongs to Christ. The spirit of sanctification falls to one's lot as the result of the preaching of the faith (the Gospel). Faith comes only from the Word of God. The Church does not invalidate the Word of God. Similarly, the Church does not have the power to draw up any article of the faith. It never has done this and never will forever. He alone has the power to make articles of the faith who has the ability to make promises and grants. The Church of God ordains and arranges all faith, customs and actions by the standard of the Word of God. Hence, those human enactments which conflict with the Gospel of Christ must not be obeyed. It is not the agreement of men, received tradition, the authority of the Doctors,[18] or the devotion of the mind, as they say, that make a work good, but the testimony of Scripture alone. It is not because of ceremonies that believers are called the "Holy Catholic Church" in the common expression but because of the fact that they hold the one God, the same Word of the Gospel, the same spirit and the same head, which is Christ.

---

conceived of as occupying the first of the two tablets on which Moses inscribed the commandments.

[18] Literally, "teachers," the technical term for the writers recognized as orthodox and authoritative by the medieval Church.

"On Ceremonies

"The Church of God has the power to ordain ceremonies, provided, however, that these ceremonies do not conflict with the articles of the faith or the prescriptions of works, that they are possible and in the Church's power, and that they do not disturb or oblige the conscience. Ceremonies are the rites that have been enacted by the agreement of the Church, so that ministering the Word, the administration of the sacraments and the other observances of piety may be performed in the ordained manner. These are considered to be indifferent according to the assessment of the practice.[19] Just as those ceremonies that are performed in a superstitious manner should be considered both useless

184   and impious, being contrary to the faith and the Word of God, | so too should only those that are performed in accordance with the faith and in conformity with the Word for the edification of the Church be considered useful.

"On the Ministers of the Church

"There is only one true master of the Church, namely Christ, Who, for the purpose of salvation, gives internal instruction through the Spirit in the faith of the Word. The reason why He has given external bishops, pastors and deacons to teach and guide the Church with the external Word is to assure that everything is done in the ordained way. All Christians are priests, because they all ought to offer their bodies as a holy sacrifice. They are not all ministers of the Church, however. The true servants of the Church and spirituals are specifically those who, having been enlightened through the Holy Spirit, are in charge of teaching the doctrine of the Gospel, administering the sacraments and serving the poor. Through the Gospel three things are presented to the Church: the doctrine of the faith and of works and the tokens of the promises.

---

[19] The term "adiaphoron" derives ultimately from Stoic philosophy, in which it signified matters that are not morally obligatory and are thus matters of indifference to the sage: the term literally means "that which is indifferent." This term was picked up by certain reformers, especially Melanchthon, to designate doctrinal and ritual matters that are considered to be neither directly enjoined by the New Testament nor contradictory to it. Such matters thus do not "matter" and can be adopted or rejected at will. A liberal attitude in defining the practices that fall into this category would allow a certain amount of the ritual and dogma of the medieval Church to survive, while a stricter interpretation would lead to much more thoroughgoing changes. Luther clearly leaned in the former direction.

"On the Sacraments

"The tokens are neither righteousness nor the fruits of righteousness but the things by which we are reminded of the promise and made sure of God's grace. There are two tokens of the New Testament, that is, of the promise of grace: baptism and sharing in the Lord's Supper.

"On Baptism

"Baptism is a sure token by which it is betokened that we pass through death to life. Just as the people of Israel considered the crossing of the Red Sea to be a sure testimony to God's grace, so too is being baptized with water in the name of the Father, Son and Holy Spirit an indisputable pledge for us of God's favor. Our being baptized in the name of the Father, Son and Holy Spirit betokens for us that our sins are remitted by this same Father, Son and Holy Spirit. If salvation is the purpose of grasping this promise, a process that takes place through faith, then it is worthwhile that it should be announced to the listeners in open language.

"On the Eucharist

"Sharing in the Lord's Supper is a token that reminds us of the grace that is given through Christ. The sole and true purpose of this sacrament is to make the heart's faith certain through Him. Just as Gideon was made certain of a successful outcome through receiving the fleece,[20] | so too are we made certain of the grace given through   185
the Gospel by eating the body of the Lord and drinking His blood. In accordance with what Scripture attests and Christ instituted, we are all obliged to take communion in both kinds, as the saying goes.[21]

"On the Mass

"The Mass, as they call it, is not a sacrifice but the token of true sacrifice. Just as Gideon offered nothing in receiving the fleece, so too do we offer nothing when sharing in the Lord's Supper. Among Christians there is no more sacrifice on account of sin. For with His unique offering, Christ has rendered ever perfect those who are made saintly. Just as Christ no longer dies, so too is He not offered. Masses

---

[20] Judges 6:37–40.
[21] In traditional Catholic practice, the communicants receive only the wafer, the wine being reserved for the officiant. Protestant practice gave the communicant both "kinds."

that are celebrated on behalf of others (and this for sake of money) are completely impious and blasphemous, so far from being of any benefit. Just as each individual is baptized in his own name, so too does each individual participate in the Lord's Supper in his own name. The only use of the Mass (the meal of the Lord, which they call the Mass) is to remind us of the death of Christ and to make us certain in our hearts of the promises made by the grace and will of God. Through the Word meaningfully uttered, the use and fruit of this sacrament is made known. This Word should be uttered openly in understandable speech. Masses and rites for the dead intended to secure their release from Purgatory are of course tricks with which to snare other people's money. Apparitions of the spirits of the dead are either dreams or illustrations of the Devil. It is sinful to ask the truth from the dead, and an abomination in the eyes of God.

"On Purgatory

"Also, Purgatory, which is thought to expiate the sins of the dead, is nothing but an impious fabrication. The opinion about Purgatory conflicts with all Holy Scripture. For if Purgatory and its accoutrements are able to wipe away the filth of sins, then God's promises are pointless lies. For it is only through Christ that He promises the remission of sins and grants it to believers. The believers fit for this promise are in truth those who are led everyday by their repentance for their sins to crucify their flesh along with their lusts. Such is the true cleansing of our ancient sin.

186

"On Repentance

"Repentance is the mortification of our ancient sin and spiritual renewal. Such mortification takes place through the Law, when it shows sin. Vivification,[22] on the other hand, takes place when the remission of sins is bestowed. In showing sin, the Law scares and kills it. In proclaiming that sins have been pardoned because of Christ, the Gospel consoles, encourages and vivifies. Repentance leads us to confess our sins and to yearn for absolution. Without repentance, confession is pointless.

---

[22] The granting of (eternal) life.

"On Confession

"Repentance does not consist of five 'Our Father's,' a fast or any bodily observance but of the earnest hatred of sin through the Holy Spirit. They truly confess who recognize their sins and in giving themselves up for lost remand themselves along with their hatred of sin to Christ. They truly remand themselves to Christ who vigorously strive both to become and to be in conformity with His image.

"On the Works of Charity

"Christ dedicated all His efforts to helping and saving His brothers. Thus, those who wish to be Christians ought to have the same urge when training themselves in the works of charity. In their works, Christians look not towards some merit but towards the will of God and the benefit of their neighbor. Just as the limbs of the body do not serve their own interests, such is the case with Christians. Loving one's neighbor is the perfection of the Law and works no evil. The reason why Christians constantly train themselves with a view to piety by praying, fasting and holding vigils and so on is to chastise their body and subordinate it to the service of love.

"On Prayer

"Prayer is the ardent spirit sighing within us to God the Father in order to receive some necessity or anything at all with faith through Christ. In this way, the pious strive towards God with a certain constant perseverance, and for this reason Christ says: "It is necessary to pray all the time."[23] True prayer does not need a voice or words unless it will be appropriate to strengthen it with the common agreement of the Church. Nonetheless, we do not reject spoken prayers that come from the heart. Yet, the muttering of words and the chattering of lips, | chants and the other supposed prayers that are produced without   187 paying attention and faith are abominable. The prayers of the pious believers are common to all. No one may, with money or a reward, usurp a Christian's praying for himself alone or for anyone he wants to. As for those who peddle their prayers for profit for any reason at all, their praying turns into a sin.

---

[23] Luke 18:1.

"On the Intercessor

"Just as there is a single God, so too is the prayer of Christians, like everything else, welcome to God through a single intercessor, the God and man, Christ Jesus. The means through which the Heavenly Father is prevailed upon to accede to prayers belongs to Christ alone.

"On Invocation

"Those who invoke dead saints as guardian deities deny the faith. For faith, being fixed in the promise of God, patiently awaits the promised help which it ardently asks for and is certainly granted. It was not in the name of the saints that any promise of salvation was made but in the name of Christ. Dead saints should not be honored with any religious worship but through the imitation of their faith and good works. Since all the saints love God with all their heart, with all their soul, and with all their strength, no loyalty is more welcome to them than that we should love God most ardently just as they did. From the beginning of the world down to its culmination, it is only through Christ that all the saints have secure access to God. As for the person who heads towards God from some other direction and not through this opening, he is a thief and a brigand.[24]

"On Statues

"Whoever places the name of some saint on a statue and in time of need invokes it under the guise of religion is an impious idolater. Images that are set out like harlots for worship are not to be tolerated by Christians since they are in diametrical conflict with the Word of God. As for those that are not set out for worship, we are so far from condemning them that we recognize both the painted and sculpted portrait of God as gifts.

"On Pilgrimages

"Visiting statues and carrying them around for the sake of religion is an impious superstition. Whoever vows such pilgrimages commits sin through this very vow, because he makes a vow in violation of the faith.

---

[24] Cf. John 10:1.

"On Vows

"Just as a woman has no right to make a vow without her husband's consent even in connection with permissible acts, so too should Christians make no vow contrary to the will of Christ, their bridegroom. Just as anyone who makes a vow contrary to Scripture truly sins, so too does anyone who makes a vow of something that is not within his power slip the noose of death around his own neck. An unlawful vow can be lawfully disregarded.

"On Exorcisms

"Exorcisms performed on animals, statues, water, candles, plants, church bells and other such things are of no avail. Every creation of God is good, being sanctified through the Word. They cannot be improved with our exorcism; they are good or bad for us according to whether we use them properly or otherwise. All things are clean for the clean.[25] Lack of faith and misuse are evils in connection with all things.

"On the Higher Power

"For misuse to be corrected or done away with in connection with all things, a two-fold form of governance is necessary: spiritual and bodily.

"On the Ecclesiastical Government

"Spiritual government is the government in which consciences are taught the Word of God and are ruled. This government is administered through the ministers of the Word, as is proven by Christ (Matthew 16,[26] 1 Corinthians 4[27]). In giving some injunction by the Word of God, the administrators of this government should be listened to just like Christ. If, on the other hand, their decision stands in contradiction to the Word, it is necessary to watch out against false prophets and to obey God rather than men.[28] The bodily government is civil administration by which the body is restrained, property is divided and force is prohibited.

---

[25] Titus 1:15.
[26] Perhaps Rothman has in mind Verse 16, in which Christ gives Peter the keys to the Kingdom of Heaven.
[27] Verse 1: "Let man consider us as ministers of Christ and dispensers of the mysteries of God."
[28] Cf. Matthew 7:5 and Acts 5:29.

"On Secular Government

"This government is administered through the official who is called secular. The secular official is the one to whom God has entrusted the right to use the sword to punish the evil and praise the good.[29] Christ gives His approval to such an official (John 10[30] and Romans 13[31]). Honor and obedience are owed to him on account not simply of wrath but also | of conscience. If the official gives a command in accordance with the will of God, he should be obeyed like God. If he gives a tyrannical command, in this case too he should be tolerated for the sake of charity. If, however, he gives a command contrary to God, he should not in any way be obeyed. Any act that is contrary to the Word of God and the approved laws should be punished without regard for anyone's status by the official, who is the minister of God's punishment. Whatever evil act the official permits freely or with impunity, of this he is himself guilty. The official who wishes both to be and to be considered a Christian one ought to punish pseudo-prophets too. The official not only is compelled, like any private individual, to avoid those who lead astray but may not even tolerate them in the state without endangering his own salvation. Just as God causes a hypocrite to rule because of the people's sins,[32] in order for the sin to be punished and the people scattered, so too is there a gushing away of the public salvation if an impious official is in command. Above all else it is worthwhile to pray on behalf of those in power that they should rule in the fear of God, in order that salvation and peace should remain intact for everyone forever. Amen!

"Here then, my brothers, is the abridgment of my doctrine, which I firmly believe, teach and defend just as has been set out. So long as I am allowed to breathe, on the basis of my duty I neither can nor ought to do otherwise. For it has been brought forth not from the workshop of my mind or from the gutters of human enactments but from the archives of God's revelations, from which only the doctrine of salutary knowledge is imbibed. For all that, we have performed the task in a crude and succinct way because of the shortness of time, the annoying distraction of other affairs and a meagreness of talent and grace. If only

189 (margin)

---

[29] 1 Peter 2:14.
[30] Presumably Rothman has in mind the statement that shepherds should give up their lives for their flock (Verses 11–14).
[31] Verses 1–3.
[32] Job 34:30.

we had been able to expound everything more deeply and more richly! But because the occasion does not allow this, we remain content with these statements, though if necessary we will go over individual points more broadly in the future. We think that the words that we have set down here and have taught up until now are such that someone could easily scoff at them (and what can be safe against reproaches in the present day?) but no one can uproot them. But if some one wishes to try his luck, he will certainly recognize and perceive that the truth is by far the strongest thing of all. Accordingly, it is as pleasant and welcome to us as it is fair and just that we should entrust every last thing to the Holy Scriptures, by which the truth is recognized, and to the church, which forms its judgment from the Spirit in accordance with those Scriptures. May the truth be victorious! In the year 1532."

I think it a good idea to insert these articles of Rothman's so that the pious reader may understand, first, in what regards they diverge from the doctrine of the Catholic Church, and, second, how far they differ from those which he later taught and defended after falling into the Anabaptist error. At first, to be sure, he fought quite vigorously against the Anabaptists, as he himself attests in a letter written by him to Busch on September 6, 1532, in which he states among other things, "Now my business is with the Anabaptists, who temporarily left us but threatened as they departed to return with greater force. On the other hand, if God is for us, who can be against us?"

190

The commons eagerly embraced these theses of Rothman's and petitioned the council to grant them permission to adhere to them safely. This petition was published under Rothman's authorization and sent to the surrounding small towns in order that the example of the local metropolis should entice the largest number of people possible to embrace a similar religion and profession of faith and that this religion should be spread as far as possible, resulting in the hatred or rather overthrow of the entire clergy.

The Catholic preachers in the city made no response to these articles, perhaps because they thought that all proper decisions had been made in the general councils and that the thieving commoners, who were plotting to defect from the authority of the ancient councils and from the official decisions, could not be prevailed upon to stop by the preachers' private response. Perhaps, they thought it inexpedient to bring upon themselves the anger of the commons, who favored Rothman's novel doctrines, with contentious argumentation and mutual recrimination, especially since they were enclosed within the walls of the same city and they saw that the power to pass judgment was in the hands of

191   the commons. | Accordingly, they judged it the safer course to keep silent rather than provoke the troublemakers under these circumstances, causing themselves to be killed and their possessions to be plundered. Hence, the spirits of the factious, Rothman's self-confidence, and the contempt in which the clergy were held all increased. The clergy came to be so hated that they scarcely dared to walk in public because of the impertinent rebukes of the troublemakers. All this happened because of the inopportune clemency, not to say indolence, laziness and neglect of the officials, who did not punish those responsible for the trouble-making at the start, when the situation was as yet lukewarm, and instead left them unpunished until their madness blazed forth more brightly. For the nature of rebellious troublemakers is such that if checked in the beginning they act less energetically, but if the start turns out well, they do not quiet down, and they do not end their rioting or in any way limit it unless they are made to plummet from top to bottom in such a way that they have no hope left of escaping. In this situation it is impossible that they should not also drag along with them to their doom the officials, who have been overcome through their longstanding toleration. So, the troublemakers in the city were neither checked nor crushed, and by an incremental process like climbing some stairway to the pinnacle of rebellion, they climbed up from crime to crime, from madness to madness, from rebellion to rebellion. It would not have been sufficient in their eyes merely to blacken the reputations of the opponents of their religion with insults, if they did not also make themselves and their supporters renowned with honors and exalted with offices. Since no church was available to Rothman for preaching either outside the city because of the prince's prohibition or inside it because of the opposition of the clergy, they undertook to open one through

192   force. Therefore, on January 23, a certain | Herman Bisping, who had severely offended both the prince and council in that it was said that he had forged letters and defrauded very many people with counterfeit money, Herman Tilbeck, Caspar Schrodercken, Arnold Belholt, a public judge and, as the story went, an adulterer, Bernard Knipperdolling the tailor and John Ummegrove, a pettifogger and defender of legal cases, were men who seemed prepared to risk not only their possessions but also their reputations and lives on behalf of Rothman if necessary, and on February 6 they brought Rothman to the cemetery of St. Lambert, accompanied by an escort of certain troublemakers and strengthened

with a guard of what was claimed to be certain leading men of the city. This was contrary to the decree of the prince and council, and not only did the main clergy resist but in the end all the good men and respectable matrons in the city shouted out in protest. When the church remained completely closed to him, they at first refrained from violence and listened to him as he preached from a wooden pulpit that stood before the repository for skulls.[33] This sermon, in which he preached about the extravagant evangelical freedom and the abolition of idolatry, inflamed everyone with such zealous ardor that they suddenly rushed to all the parish churches in the city, where they broke open the repositories for the Eucharist and pillaged the altar clothes, smashed the images, and destroyed all the ancient decorations and adornments of the churches, profaning everything sacred since they thought nothing sacred that conflicted with Rothman's dogma. In this way, all the churches in the city apart from the cathedral were exposed to the wantonness of the factious, and the pastor of St. Lambert's was removed to make a position available to Rothman. As a result of the troublemakers' impunity in this, the crowd was so increased and encouraged that it did not pay much attention to the prince's authority, the clergy's dignity or the council's warnings and decrees.

Now everything in the city was tending not only towards open rebellion but toward violence, random slaughter, the pillaging of both public and private property, and, in short, the overthrow of the entire state. | 193 After this turn of events was not punished appropriately by Frederick of Wede the bishop, he thought it better for himself to give up the bishopric than to get involved in calming these dangerous uproars and suppressing those responsible. Accordingly, on March 24 (Palm Sunday), in the sacristy of the parish church of a little town in the diocese called Werne he resigned from the bishopric that he had overseen well for more than nine years, placing it in the hands of the cathedral chapter and reserving for himself an income of 2000 florins per annum from its revenues. For the very circumspect prince foresaw the coming ruin of both the city and the entire diocese, and to avoid this he returned to Cologne, where he gave himself entirely over to repose and lived as a private individual until his death in 1549.

---

[33] Space in cemeteries being limited, the bones of older burials would be removed to make way for new ones and placed in a repository called a charnel house in expectation of the resurrection.

194   At this point, men weighty both by birth and by authority were
appointed in the customary way, being put in charge by public agreement. The job of administering the diocese is entrusted to them as
if during an interregnum, and they are called "vicars" in Latin and
"Stadtholders"[34] in the vernacular in that they exercise "vicariously" the
administrative functions in the absence of a bishop. Their administration
lasts not simply to the election of the new bishop but until the election
is confirmed and sanctioned by the pope. Once that happens, full legal
possession of the diocese is transferred to the new prince along with
the entire powers of administration.

Realizing that domestic dissension had arisen in the city because of
religion, these diocesan vicars resolved to send a precautionary letter to
the townsmen by their own authority, reminding them of the Imperial
decrees promulgated in 1530 at the Diet of Augsburg that prohibited
any innovation in religion or any rash change in ceremonial, and advised
that it was necessary to await the decision of an ecumenical council.
The vicars urged the towns to be mindful of their own salvation and
civil concord, obeying the council and refraining from all innovation,
especially in the matter of religion. For, they said, the example of many
cities had always shown such innovation to be dangerous, since it had
disturbed many cities in various areas and caused great uproars that
were accompanied by horrible revolution and lamentable destruction
not just in the distant cities to the southeast but also in the neighboring
cities of Westphalia. The townsmen should therefore take thought for
themselves and their wives and children and not let themselves be rashly
and contumaciously alienated from the other estates of the diocese.
Instead, they should free themselves from every suspicion of rebellion
to which they were subject, receiving a bad reputation from this. In
this way, the vicars said, they would receive from God not merely grace
and salvation but also unbroken tranquility in their state. This letter
was approved, but it could not placate the commons or call them back
from the course of madness upon which they had set.

195   After Frederick of Wied had resigned as bishop, the main clergy
who have the sole right to elect the bishop, on March 27 unanimously
chose Eric of Grubenhagen, the bishop of Osnabrück and Paderborn,
to put in charge of the Church of Münster. This choice displeased the
troublemakers to an unimaginable extent. Since he was born of the

---

[34] "Place holders" or "lieutenants."

illustrious and noble house of the dukes of Brunswick, and was related by blood to many of the most powerful princes in Germany who were particularly devoted to the Catholic religion, the troublemakers were especially afraid of his strength and power, being fully convinced that not only would all their most cherished endeavors collapse but they themselves would have to pay the price for all the trouble they had caused. Their aim, therefore, was to drive the commons in the city to join in their criminal behavior, implicating them in their evildoing and making it impossible to punish their own crime because of the large number of malefactors.

Therefore, at the urging of the commons, Rothman sent to Eric, who was now elected bishop, the articles of faith that he had stitched together (and are set out above), and promised that he would defend them at the risk of his own life before an audience of any right think-ing men, thinking that with these articles he would make the bishop more clement to himself and his followers. At the suggestion of Roth-man and his followers, the whole mob of the rabble and the workers made a petition to the aldermen and guild masters about maintaining religious concord in the city, though they appeared to approve and adopt Rothman's dogma and | to reject and oppose that of the other   196 priests. The following letter of petition was made public and presented on April 16.

"In the civil society of cities nothing there is better or more excellent than public concord and firmly established peace, and such a situation can be kept only if the burghers readily submit to a single religion and to a common justice and obedience to the laws. We have noticed to our great grief and lamentation that in the business of religion and the cause of the faith, which ought to be the chief element in our salvation, there have arisen in our city the most severe dissensions and the worst disputes, which will, unless merciful God should prevent this, violate the common rights, abrogate obedience to the laws, and cast the entire state headlong into the total and inevitable destruction. Therefore, in order to avert this calamity from ourselves and our wives and children and to avoid being justifiably considered obstinate rebels, as we are criticized by some, it seemed to us helpful and necessary to seek refuge as suppliants with you as our immediate ruler and to ask that you not deny us just protection and support before our city council. It has no doubt not escaped your notice that no little controversy and conten-tion has arisen among us in the business of the faith with reference to preaching. For those who would urge us with a single doctrine to one

faith, the fear of God and mutual concord disagree among themselves
in full warfare. On the one side, through the Word of God Bernard
Rothman has restored to the light from the filthy darkness the evangelical Truth that had up until now been overwhelmed by manifold abuses
and destructive errors, and he asserts that he will demonstrate this at
the risk of his own life both with the living voice in sermons and in
writings. On the other side, no one dares to oppose Rothman openly
by engaging him in battle with Scriptural quotations. Hence, we have
no doubt that his doctrine is in conformity with the Gospel and the
Truth. We do, however, notice that certain people oppose this doctrine,
both in private grumblings and in public sermons. Hence, in order
for all disputation to be dispelled in the state and concord nourished,
we ask you with great confidence and advise you earnestly that since
Rothman has offered to have his doctrine examined by the judgment
of all doctors or rather by the entire world, you should intercede with
the council and prevail upon them to force the priests of this city by
197   the government's authority | to prove Rothman guilty of error, if they
can, through manifest Scripture (in which case he would not only keep
quiet but also endure the punishment that he has voluntarily imposed
upon himself if defeated) or make themselves conform to his doctrine
and teach the Word of God in pure doctrine or themselves keep quiet
and no longer oppose the truth to the detriment of many souls in order
to avoid stirring up anew a further uproar in this state. For as long as
the preachers contend with each other in doctrine and cause division
among the people, there should be no expectation of either peace or
civil concord among us ever. Accordingly, since both sides disagree about
the same point and for this reason one side must be wickedly deviating
from the truth, our only wish, our only desire is to be freed from false
doctrine. For nothing more deleterious can happen to our souls than
that to be convinced of the correctness of false doctrine, since Christ
in particular, the sole restorer of our salvation, as well as the decrees of
his Imperial Majesty and the letter written by the vicars of this diocese,
order every one of us to keep our guard against false doctrine. In order,
then, that peace and tranquility should once more be sown, cherished,
nurtured and preserved among us, we think it fair and necessary that
the other preachers should, just like Rothman, make public a confession
of their own doctrine and of any solid complaint they have against
him, so that there should finally be an end to the disputes. There are
in fact very just reasons why we judge that Rothman's dogma is pure
and untainted by any of the filth of human tradition and that it instead

agrees with the Gospel. For he has promised of his own accord that he would, without any recourse to violence, demonstrate the correctness of his doctrine before uncorrupted judges, and, if it should turn out that he is defeated by the Word of God, he would readily yield to the truth and to the penalty that would be imposed upon him. It being the case, however, that they cite nothing from Holy Writings that seems to contradict Rothman, it is our view that their doctrine, however ancient and outwardly holy, is nonetheless contrived falsehood. Accordingly, we think it necessary to adhere to the Truth, the pure Word of God, until someone shows us better doctrines. Also, if learned men are to be summoned here from elsewhere for this purpose, it is our wish that this should be done at our expense and cost. Being Christians, we desire only that which is pious, respectable and salubrious, and would restore, nourish | and preserve our mutual concord. May God grant us His   198 grace plentifully, so that we may achieve these ends. Amen! We trust that you will not be remiss in pleading before the council our cause, or rather the common cause of everyone."

These requests were reported to the council by the aldermen and guild masters, and while the council was deliberating about the answer to be given, the following letter that Prince Eric dispatched to the council and all the estates of the city on April 17 was delivered.

"After we had, through the arrangement of divine providence, been chosen unanimously as bishop of the diocese of Münster, we received word of the following, by no means vain news. A certain Bernard Rothman, a priest who had the duty of preaching at St. Maurice's Outside-the-Walls, had, in specious preaching, made statements that seemed to bring the ancestral religion into contention and to lead the congregation into error. Therefore, our predecessor Frederick had for very just reasons forbidden Rothman to exercise the function of preaching and had, after Rothman had shown insufficient obedience to this decree, revoked and removed his safe conduct to live within the city. This Rothman took up residence within the walls in contempt of said bishop, and the protection of certain members of his faction allowed him to usurp a place in the parish church of St. Lambert in violation of the Imperial Edict promulgated at Augsburg and in contempt of his ruler. He then preached unaccustomed doctrines, introduced novel ceremonies and chants after abolishing the old ones, and by these acts stirred up a large part of the populace to such an extent that many men, having broken or shattered all the laws of civilized behavior, piety, obedience and concord, follow a sect of impious novelty, in violation both of the Christian concord that has been successfully maintained since the establishment of Christianity down to the present day and of the edicts and recesses[35] of the Imperial Diets. As a result of this, the thing first to be feared is sedition and the next is the eventual overthrow of all that is good. It is, in fact, impossible to state with what sadness we learned this news. For as far as we are concerned, nothing more welcome could happen to us than that mutual concord, Christian charity, and true peace should be restored to you by God's will. Therefore, we ask of you sincerely and warn you in a friendly way that | you should retain the traditional religion and the ancient ceremonies that have been bequeathed to us by our ancestors and maintained with true piety until the present day, that you should suppress the rioting of the commons and restrain them from every sort of criminal innovation until a permanent religious settlement is arranged. For our certainly favorable attitude towards you would be most grievously enraged if your rebellion called down upon us the outrage of the Emperor and brought upon us disfavor from him and punishment from the Empire. Let me point out to you the following point, which you should consider carefully. If, as I hardly expect, you are going to reject this very pious undertaking, this more than paternal attitude and this very friendly warning of ours, be advised that I will be obligated to fulfill what is demanded by my duty and the Imperial edict, namely preserve Christian charity and public tranquility among you. I leave you to think more deeply about all this. We expect a definite answer from you as to which among them you are going to do."

In response, the council wrote back on April 18 that they had, with the appropriate reverence, received, read and understood the letter sent by the prince to all the estates of the city specifically about the preacher Lord Bernard Rothman and others. Therefore, they said, they would make their burghers and other concerned parties aware of the letter at a suitable time and place. After that they would soon send a reply based in the traditional way on the common consultation of all the estates.

After Eric's letter had been read before the aldermen and guild masters and certain leading men among the commons and finally before the entire estate of the commons and they had made a copy of it for

---

[35] "Recess" is the technical term for the concluding resolution of an Imperial Diet.

Rothman, who was the man most concerned in this matter, they spent several days in prolonged deliberation. Impelled by his great confidence and impetuosity, Rothman forestalled the council by sending a response himself, writing to Prince Eric on April 19, as follows.

"At the start, I send grace from God the Father through Jesus Christ, His only Son, and the ready compliance of my innocence, most reverend and glorious prince! Although I could easily understand from the letter that you sent about me in particular to the council and all the estates of Münster | in what unjust ways my detractors have falsely denounced   200 me before you for sedition and rebellion, or rather for piety, I have nonetheless conceived the firm and confident hope that in light of the outstanding nobility of your birth and your exceptional love of fairness, you will be second only to God in not only patiently allowing me to clear myself against the false accusations of my enemies but also, after you are sure of my innocence, defend me, as befits a Christian prince, against all the defamation and injury inflicted on me by denouncers. For the fact that you have been divinely appointed as bishop of this diocese I rightly congratulate you and me and thank God, who does not so much set princes in charge of states as govern their hearts. And God will not, I am fairly sure, tolerate that after I have cleared myself, your heart should persist in such suspicion as a favor to these detractors, who happen to be the enemies of the Almighty no less than they are mine. For it is not my cause but that of God and His Truth that I uphold, for this reason receiving in large measure the greatest hatred and the most serious and savage insults.

"You write that you have learned through by no means false report that I have, in performing the office of preacher at St. Maurice's Outside-the-Walls, made in specious sermons statements that seemed to bring the ancestral religion into contention and to lead the congregation into error, and that therefore your predecessor Frederick had for very just reasons forbidden me to exercise the duty of preaching and had, after I had shown insufficient obedience to this decree, revoked and removed his safe conduct to live within the city. Most glorious prince, I ask you in supplication and for God's sake to follow your usual mercy and allow me to respond. From this it will easily become apparent in what a miserable way I am being treated and my reputation, such as it is, is being torn to shreds. It certainly is true that I have been called upon by divine providence (as I hope) and selected and appointed by the usual human ordination as the priest (chaplain) of St. Maurice's, as well as endowed with the ecclesiastical benefice that is attached to the position. With God's help I have carried out the duty entrusted to me with such faith that I have always been prepared to give an accounting of it before God and the entire world. I have not shirked the judgments of all good men, and if I have behaved badly in this duty, | I have made no excuse to avoid the penalty that the transgression deserves. Beyond all this, however, I suffered calamitous harm to my reputation through being accused before Frederick, and although I could never learn the charge or the name of the accuser, so that I would have been able to clear myself (a course to which I always offered myself), nonetheless, persuasion by my detractors led that good prince to forbid me to exercise the duty of preaching even though I had not been allowed to give an excuse, much less been convicted of any crime. I did not spit out his order with contempt, as they have persuaded you, or reject it at all. Although I knew myself to be innocent and yearned to see the face of the slanderer who dared to make up such lies about me, nonetheless I obeyed his command until such time as I would clear myself, to the extent that I could in writing since I was not granted a personal audience, by invoking the protection of justice and fairness against that lying whisperer. Later, however, when no account was taken of either justice or fairness and neither the accuser nor the charge were revealed to the light of day, I resumed the calling of the duty that I had undertaken, relying on my innocence and heeding the command of God, to which I owe priority if I mean to carry out the office of preacher. Therefore, most reverend prince, the man who not only obeys justice but invokes it in his defense as I have always done and am still doing, cannot be judged a contumacious rebel, as is the case with me. The reason that induced the prince to make a public declaration revoking the safe conduct for my wretched self (that is, the false denunciations of my enemies) I entrust to the Lord God and leave this matter for your more careful consideration, lest I cause you to become sick and tired of listening if at this point I verbosely count off one-by-one all the things that have undeservedly happened to me.

"Also, most gloriously prince, the accusation lodged before you against me that I took up residence within the walls in contempt of Frederick is completely contrary to the truth. Since one of his subordinates summoned me to him in the city and there in the name of the prince he took away my security from me, denying me the right of defense and all safe conduct, necessity compelled me in defense of my innocence to avail myself of the Imperial liberty of the city in which I was living.

201

"In addition, | you write that the protection of certain members of   202
my faction allowed me to usurp a place in the parish church of St.
Lambert without the lawful permission of the ruler, and that there I
preached unaccustomed doctrines and introduced novel ceremonies and
chants. If only my innocence were clear to you, most honored prince!
In that case, those defamers would certainly regret their false accusation
and poisonous tongue! For after I had been asked to preach in the time
of Frederick, I not only approached my ruler but also demonstrated with
the most weighty explanations that I ought not to fail divine providence
and the calling to preach (if he allows). I also requested that since I was
being pressed to preach from various quarters, the ruler should give an
indication of his will, since, I said, I would do nothing contrary to his
wishes. Hence, it is easy to see that I wished to satisfy my calling, not
with any help from the factious but with the faithful help of Almighty
God alone. When, then, I was called upon to preach, by the ruler's
permission I mounted the pulpit in the place where the congregation
yearning to hear the Word of God had gathered. Without injury or
harm to anyone and in mindfulness of my duty, I taught the Words of
Life, something that should in justice be denied to no Christian. For
by what right will one man be forbidden to teach another in doctrine,
especially in a spot intended for such teaching? After I was called and
sought nothing but the public good and civil tranquility, as the truth
attests, I did not think it necessary to ask of anyone permission to do
good, since this would be altogether contrary to praiseworthy custom
and Christian freedom. For it always has been permissible to do good
without anyone's leave, and it always will be. I at least would have been
right to have expected gratitude for a good deed from a ruler even if
I had done so without his authorization, though in fact I did nothing
without it. The reason why every Christian ruler has been appointed
by God is that he should of his own accord invite everyone to do good.
If, one the other hand, he gives some order that is hostile to God,
Scripture orders me to obey God rather than men.[36]

"Therefore, most glorious prince, since I have been accused by those
who slander me of disobedience and rebellion and of having preached
impious, erroneous and novel doctrines that are contrary to all the peace
and tranquility that has been maintained up until now and that have
resulted in nothing but dissension and horrendous sedition, I beg you

---

[36] Acts 5:29.

203   in the name of everything sacred and of divine and human justice |
to force my denouncer to demonstrate the truth of the charges laid
against me. If I am convicted with incontestable proofs, not only will I
refrain from the duty of preaching as the council, aldermen and guild
masters wish because of your prompting, but I will also be prepared to
undergo the penalty that the deeds deserve. However, since I know that
I am innocent of the crime of which I am accused, since the duty of
preaching has been laid upon me by God, who is owed more obedience
than is any man, and since very many pious people are asking for my
services, I neither can nor ought to refrain from carrying out the task
of preaching in public without risk to my eternal salvation. I therefore
have no doubt that you will lend me your support and defense, since
I have full confidence that you are an outstanding bulwark of God's
truth and glory. May you look upon this attempt of mine, such as it
is, to clear my name with a benevolent attitude, and with the noble
attitude worthy of a prince stop up your ears against the shameless lies
of those who defame me."

    After a prolonged deliberation back and forth about Eric's letter,
the commons explained their wish in an answer sent to the council on
April 28, and we set out the text of it as follows.

    "May the grace and peace of God acquired through Christ be with
you. Amen! Since, by God's will, you have been appointed by our votes
to the dignity of governing this city, we rightly owe you lawful obedience, but at the same time you owe us a just defense in a pious matter
relating to virtue, so that the body politic may enjoy better health when
all the sections of the state are kept safe. We understand the letter
that was sent by Eric, Bishop of Osnabrück and Paderborn and Duke
of Brunswick, who has been elected to this diocese as well, has been
presented, read and made known to our leaders, and that this letter
assails our priest Lord Bernard Rothman, a man outstanding in both
integrity and learning, and ourselves to some extent, treating us in an
unworthy manner. Since, however, Bernard has doubtless offered in his
own letter a sufficiently stout defense of himself against the slanderers
who wickedly reviled him before the prince, we are not going to plead
204   his case but our own, | so that the prince will not consider us to be the
kind of people we are said to be. We are therefore directing our petition
to you in particular, so that in your letter to the prince you should bear
witness to our innocence. It is not, however, the prince, whose honesty
and goodwill are very well known to us, that we consider responsible
for this defaming of us but those malevolent slanderers and accusers.

The revelation of our innocence will cast their lies into the dark, so that the truth will win out in the end, emerging triumphant and washing away every stain caused by our being defamed. To begin with, councilmen, we are accused of plotting sedition and revolution, and without any sense of shame our slanderers have convinced the prince of this. Since nothing can be safe against calumnies, we console ourselves with the example of Christ, Who was called seditious by His enemies even though He brought peace, or rather was Himself peace. Certainly as far as we are concerned, we think that nothing more better or preferable can happen to us than that peace and mutual concord, as well as the true, pure and evangelical doctrine, should flourish among us. This is perfectly clear from our previous letter and the confession that has been made public and offered for the whole world's criticism, as well as from the writing that we just showed you and that you still have fresh in your memory. With their lying these slanderers have inflicted the greatest injury on us despite our innocence, unless they consider it seditious that we do not cease to direct many requests to the ruler urging upon him matters that pertain to salvation, that we wish the Gospel's truth to be cleansed of every impurity by the action of the ruler and thereby rendered more gleaming, and that we yearn to retain the pure doctrine which Lord Bernard has been teaching, and think that we must not deviate from it if we wish to be Christians. For we have no doubt and know for a fact that this is the pure doctrine and the true Word of God, which he makes a public promise in virtually all his sermons to defend before anyone at all, even at the risk of his own life. Yet, no one on the other side dares to come forward, as is fitting. Also, in the prince's letter we are denounced for introducing innovation in the ancient religion in violation of Christian concord. If, however, the matter is assessed against the standard of the truth, it will never be possible to lodge this accusation against us rightly unless we pretend that Christian concord is violated by the fact that in accordance with the command of Scripture and of Paul especially, | we clearly and   205 concordantly sing psalms translated into the vernacular both before and after the sermon in order to increase the glory of God and to promote piety. Apart from this we do not admit that we are culpable in anything. If, however, you or any one else on earth demonstrates that any of us is guilty of any crime or violates Christian piety, we will not feel any reluctance in handing him over for punishment at your discretion, whatever his prestige or status. For we have decided to commit no act that we would be unwilling to have judged in the sight of God and of the entire world. We wish you now to bear witness to this fact too and to defend it before our prince and that our malevolent slanderers will be prevented from gaining a hearing with the prince when the truth is brought to light, which would put an end to the slanders."

After reading this submission from the estate of the commons by which they undertook to defend themselves, the council sent the following letter to the prince on May 2, including the commons' self-justification.

"A few days ago we received the letter you sent to the entire state and to all the estates of the city of Münster. In it we are warned to reject all religious innovation and civil sedition and to adhere to the traditional ceremonies and the ancient tranquility. After we had informed everyone concerned of this letter, they answered that they were devoted and genuinely inclined not to sedition but to retaining and preserving concord in the state. In addition to this response, we were offered a document from all the estates of the diocese, copy of which we send on appended to this letter so that you can learn everything more exactly. As far as Lord Bernard Rothman and his sermons are concerned, we informed him of your letter and strictly forbade him from preaching. To this he answered that he had written to you an explanation of his doctrine and bound himself to prove the correctness of everything, but that since he had not received any response, he would carry out his duty until the prince responded. Since we are expending a great deal of effort to preserve peace and tranquility among us and are very anxious, we leave everything to be considered more carefully by your 206 expeditious judgment, | so that you may give us your advice as to what must be done to calm the sedition."

After reading this, the prince realized, not just from the letter but also from the indications provided by many other things, that many councilmen favored the ancestral religion but were so stricken with fear that they dared not do anything against the rioting of the commons. On the other hand, he understood that others were tainted and were furthering the business of the commons. He also noted the commons' obstinacy from their earlier letter. For this reason, he was greatly offended and wrote back to the council as follows.

"I have received your response, with which was included a submission from the commons, and from it I have learned, among other things, that the burghers of the commons think that it was the suggestion of certain men who are ablaze with blind hatred against the townsfolk that impelled me to write since in my earlier letters they were assailed

for sedition, impiety and innovation in connection with ancient matters, contrary to all truth (as they claim). To this I respond that it is
not because of the disparaging of malevolent, lying enemies but of
my own accord and because of the outstanding zeal of my well-intentioned favor toward the city that I was roused to urge the council, the
aldermen, the guild masters and the entire estate of the commons in
writing to take steps that seemed to be salubrious for the city. For you
and your burghers have never been maliciously accused before me with
false accusations. General report and sure proofs provided by some
churchmen and burghers of yours have, however, brought you into
disrepute among men, and for this reason I thought it to be my duty
to give you and your citizens a friendly warning about the impending
calamity that will in the end burst forth from this situation. Therefore, in my letter of deterrence I tried to convince you that while the
innovation that you have undertaken should be done away with and
those who preach it abandoned, the ancient ceremonies and the kind
of church decoration inherited from antiquity should be retained. I
did this with great confidence that you would both give some consideration to my advice and send back an answer worthy of me and of
you. I was, however, unable to achieve either purpose with you, and
when I saw that a certain contumacious obstinacy was increasing your
burghers' resolve in their design as if they could not do without either
the preacher or his doctrine without risking their eternal salvation, | I   207
realized that the rash and ill-considered design of the preacher and his
faction had been undertaken under the guise of the Gospel. Now I have
also determined through more careful investigation that it is absolutely
true that through the assistance of the followers of his faction and in
particular of one Brixius of Norden this same preacher has, both in
the time of Frederick and now, said publicly from the pulpit many
things that violated the decision of the Catholic Church and the recent
Imperial Diet in connection with not just one but very many articles
of the faith, at the same time causing the ignorant commons to hate
the government and all the ceremonies maintained with praise from
antiquity until the present day. Accordingly, my predecessor had very
good reason to command him to refrain from this sort of unheard-of
doctrine and from the zeal to innovate. Although he has abstained from
such acts, he has contumaciously opposed that order with a certain
amount of insolence down to the present day, or rather he has more
and more indoctrinated the commons in the forbidden innovation and
its contentious doctrine, which is a breeding ground of every sort of

sedition, and has so fixed those doctrines in their minds that they have fallen headlong into dangerous errors, obstinately despising divine and human law and the Imperial edict. If this situation should be endured any longer, the surest destruction will result not just for you but for the entire diocese. I am striving to avert this with all my strength, and for this reason I am warning you sternly and asking you in a friendly way to oppose and remove Rothman, his colleague Brixius and the other preachers of this stripe, that you restore the ancient rites and ceremonies in the churches, abolishing all innovation, and that you give some consideration to my last letter, thereby protecting yourself from disaster. For if you and your fellow burghers pay no heed to my urgings and continue to press on with your novel contrivances, which I have no expectation that you will, I leave it to you to consider more carefully what it befits me to do by reason of my duty to uphold the edict of the Emperor and the Empire. It is my earnest wish to receive an answer soon as to which of these courses I should expect from you."

208   That this letter from the prince did not have much influence with the unintelligent commons can be gathered from the fact that they were not very worried about the answer to be given. After many days had slid by without the council writing back any answer, the delay in responding led to outraged astonishment on the part of the prince. Accordingly, he sent Berthold of Büren, a man who belonged to the knighthood and served as the bailiff of Iburg on an embassy to Münster. In a full session of the council he gave the following speech before the aldermen and guild masters in order to finish the matter. "First of all, the most reverend and glorious prince prays for salvation and tranquility for you and the entire city. Next, he commands me to inform you of the following. A few days ago he asked you in his letter to remove the preacher, who is protected by your walls, because he preached contentious doctrines by which he was able to impel the gullible commons first to error, which is the parent of strife, and then to the manifest insanity of sedition, in violation of the Imperial edict and the general peace. The prince was convinced that you would do this, particularly during these dangerous times, in order to avoid a greater calamity, but he has received nothing in the way of response from you. For this reason he once again strictly enjoins you with all the earnestness that he can summon to give a considered response within a few days as to what decision you have reached regarding the removal of the preacher."

The council promised that it would respond soon. At the instigation of certain people, however, the commons, who felt that they were being petitioned by the prince, became not only insolent but more savage, obstinate and impetuous. For even certain people of great reputation were enthusiastic with the desire to innovate and strove to spread this unheard-of doctrine throughout all the parishes of the city. Although Eberwin and John Droste, the council members from the Ward Across-the-River, were adherents of the ancient religion along with Herman Jonas, nonetheless on May 20 they were induced by the alderman Ludger tom Brincke, Herman Tilbeck and Michael Nording and by other followers of this stripe to ask the abbess of the Convent Across-the-River, who had legal control over that parish, | to remove a certain   209 Lord Martin, who was the chaplain and Catholic, and put in his place someone else who would teach the pure Word of God undefiled by human tradition and administer the sacrament of the Eucharist in both kinds according to the practice instituted by Christ. The abbess asked for a period of time to consider the matter, but since they were rather unenergetic in pressing their demands and the zealous desire to innovate was fading, none of the old ways was changed.

It is said that the prince deliberated day and night on the ways in which he could settle the disturbance in the business of the city. Certainly, that good prince would have achieved much in this matter through the assistance of his own authority and the support of his friends had he not been forestalled by a premature death. For some say that he fell ill while unusually happy in the stronghold of Fürstenau in the diocese of Osnabrück, though others say that he died suddenly on May 14 after drinking a large cup of wine.

Arnold Belholt, a judge in the city, was a man naturally inclined to sedition. We showed above that he was, along with certain other fol-lowers of his faction, responsible for the sedition, and in his lack of gravity he attributed the greatest authority and gravity to Rothman. At the death of the prince, this man thought that he was allowed to do anything at all with impunity, and for this reason he did not cease to do his utmost to stir up the commons against the chapter and council with his malicious plotting, but when he could not achieve his aim readily and feared for his wellbeing because of his guilty conscience, he left the city, though not with impunity. For he was arrested during his journey by the vicars of the diocese, into whose hands the administration is entrusted in the period between bishops. First jailed in the prison of Horstmar, he was transferred to Bevergern, where he was questioned under torture. | He confessed to being the instigator of many crimes   210 and revealed what he and his associates had had in mind. He would

certainly have paid the price for his rash activity if the vicars had not
forestalled the danger of greater uproar. Fined a great sum of money,
he was released from prison, and after returning to his associates he
was less energetic in pressing on with the business of sedition.

After the death of Eric, the main clergy wished to avoid any further
appearance that the government of the diocese was adrift without a
helmsman and met to elect a new prince in their stronghold at Lüd-
inghausen, thinking that they were no longer safe against the plots
of the seditious in the city. On June 1, they unanimously elected as
bishop of Münster the bold hero Francis, the bishop of Minden and
count of Waldeck, who was of the ancient and most noble lineage.
Immediately after the election, the main clergy handed over possession of some strongholds and castles to him, an unprecedented act
since this normally happened only after the public installation of the
new bishop. We have no doubt that the reason for this was to make
sure that no one thought there was no prince in the region, since it is
believed that everything is done by his authority. This was especially
necessary under the circumstances, since the city was ablaze within
because of great disturbances and horrible acts of sedition, and it would
have easily carried the entire region and all the smaller cities with it
over the edge to disaster if the troublemakers had not feared that the
chosen candidate already enjoyed the full power to command. When
211   he was freely elected bishop of Osnabrück too a few days later, | all
the seditious conceived a triple fear of him, shrinking from his powerful strength as if he were three-mouthed Cerberus.[37] It now remains
to say how much this good prince toiled against them to preserve the
general peace, true piety and the salvation of his flock without sparing
either himself or his resources.

The lower clergy complained to him secretly by letter[38] that their
duties, privileges and liberties were being violated by the faction
members, who did everything by their own caprice, that the Catholic
ceremonies were being abolished and new and unheard-of ones substituted, that good works were considered worthless, that the Catholic
preachers were being removed by force and replaced with Lutheran
ones, that the churches were being stripped, and that everything was

---

[37] Cerberus was the three-headed beast in mythology whose savage biting kept the
dead from re-emerging from the underworld.
[38] No such letter is extant, and Detmer thinks such a letter unlikely, since the letter
written by the lower clergy on August 24 sounds like their first.

being done capriciously. They asked him to deign to use his authority to get the townsmen to agree to a full restitution. This letter impelled the prince to write to the townsmen and to all the estates of the city on June 28, as follows.

"After we were elected as bishop of the diocese of Münster by divine providence, we learned through the report of trustworthy individuals and then through general rumor discovered it to be true, that Lutheran preachers have arrived in Münster, partly through their own bold daring and partly at the instigation of certain commoners, in particular the unreliable and rebellious adherents of their faction, and that they have not only despised the embassy and warning sent by my predecessor but also impetuously and contumaciously violated the edict by which their safe conduct was revoked, an act of remarkable insolence towards him. We hear that they remain there to the present day, and that without the permission of the secular government and contrary to the most recent Imperial edicts they have seized the main parish churches by their own authority, casting out the lawful pastors and chaplains along with the ancient rites | and replacing them with themselves, their own sermons and a doctrine concealed in the guise of unheard of ceremonies and novel rites. Finally, we hear that in disseminating this darkness of error they have imbued the commons in notions that clearly incite them more and more every day to sedition and every sort of rebellion, throw the political order into chaos, and completely overturn peace and tranquility. I would hardly have expected such unreliability, rebellion and impiety from you inasmuch as you were previously loyal and considered by all the neighboring cities to be highly devoted to every sort of piety and gravity. Accordingly, since Almighty God has divinely entrusted to our anxious care the rudder of this diocese, we have decided that the first thing that we should do by God's grace is make sure that the members of our flock should always live bound to each other by peace, tranquility, obedience and above all by religion, in order to uphold the Imperial edict. Thus, it is in your own interest that we beseech you to take the following steps. Under the circumstances, you should accommodate yourselves to the will and decision of the last Imperial Diet at Augsburg, which has been earnestly entrusted to our care, restore the ecclesiastical rites and the ceremonies that were instituted in antiquity and have been maintained down to our own time, cast out the preachers along with all the innovations and misuses introduced by them, and call the commons back to concord, tranquility and obedience, either until some final decision is made in the business of religion at the present Imperial

212

Diet by the estates of the Empire and our lawful ruler or until we are installed and attain full authority to administer this diocese. For at that time we will, if necessary, make sure that everything will be reformed by the standard of God's Word and that every opportunity for rioting will be done away with. For this reason, we have no doubt that you will take the Imperial edict and our paternal warning into consideration. If, however, you contumaciously spurn these suggestions, which we hardly expect you will do, we leave it to you to consider what steps we should take under the circumstances to make sure that we do not seem to be opposing the Empire and the Emperor's edicts whose enforcement was entrusted to us at the Diet of Ravensburg. | We yearn to receive from you a clear answer as to your attitude."

213

The people in Münster deliberated on this matter, arguing back and forth as to what they should respond. Finally, on July 13[39] they answered by merely saying that they had received the prince's letter touching upon the priests. They had, they said, heard the letter read and offered it to the aldermen and guild masters, but for certain reasons that it would take a long time to describe, they could not give a quick answer. For this they asked the prince's forgiveness, promising to answer by their public messenger as soon as they could and wishing him good health for a long time. The address on the letter almost exceeded its contents.

Meanwhile, Knipperdolling's obstinacy by no means softened and he prevailed upon the aldermen Henry Moderson the butcher and Henry Redeker the furrier to use their official authority to summon all the members of the guilds and the guild masters. On July 1 they obeyed the aldermen's order and entered the "*Schohaus*"[40] (guild hall) in droves. (This is the place in which all the guilds customarily meet when they are to deal with matters that concern the common good of the whole city.)[41] The dregs of the city gathered there, and—good God!— what commotion, what grumbling and shouting resounded not only in that house but in the neighboring ones on all sides, as some men bellowed one thing and others something else. Finally, when this initial uproar gradually died down, the aldermen and guild masters took the seats assigned to them in the customary way according to

---

[39] Actually July 10.
[40] The events narrated from this point until July 15 are not otherwise documented.
[41] For the *Schohaus*, see 77D.

their honor and prestige, and when they ordered silence, tranquility
suddenly prevailed. Then, John Windemoller, who had been coached
by the aldermen, Knipperdolling and other members of the faction, | 214
repeatedly said that the reason for the summons was hardly trivial, but
was one that concerned exalting the glory of God, the salvation of all
the burghers and the increase of peace and liberty. For, he went on,
the matter had to do with the evangelical doctrine and the life eternal:
in his doctrine Rothman clearly showed the true path to this life, cutting back the thorn-bushes of human enactments, and revealed how
the papist filth darkened this path with clever lies made up for its own
profit and blocked it with horrible confusions. Therefore, he said, they
should strike an agreement to protect Rothman and his doctrine, whose
truth they confessed. At this virtually the entire mob interrupted the
speech by shouting that they would defend Rothman and his evangelical
doctrine to the last breath and as long as the blood coursed in their
veins, both with arms, if necessary, and with all their resources. Some
peacemakers, however, opposed the seditious people, bearing witness
with open words that they did not like the innovation in religion, and
chief among them was John Menneman the tailor. (After the siege he
was raised up to the dignity of alderman by his outstanding gravity and
experience in many matters. He exercised the duties of this office to the
satisfaction of the commons down for many years down to 1570, and
then in 1573 was appointed as councilman.) At this point he publicly
shouted back at these innovators, bolstered by the greater confidence
he had compared to the others because of his sense of having the better cause. At these words, the crazed commons thronged around him
from all sides, hemming him in, and he was punished, rebuked and
punched. Some even bellowed that as a clamoring rebel against the
evangelical Truth and his government he should be removed, and if
good men had not intervened, he would have been stabbed with the
daggers that had been unsheathed in the midst of the dense crowd
of commoners. Certain other men who shared Menneman's attitude
and relied on his resolution were so terrified by this uproar that they
preferred keeping quiet to risking a similar danger. In the end, he was
dragged before the aldermen, who | ordered him to state his reason for 215
dissension. He said that this matter should be considered and decided
not with crazed shouts or ill-conceived rashness but with deliberation, clear thinking and timely reflection, since hurried, back-to-front
plans often bring along regret as their companion. If, therefore, they
wished to reach some laudable decision, he told them to conduct their

consultation in a calmer manner, with each man listening to the other with tolerance and good will. He said that if they separated the guilds and determined the opinion of each by vote, he too would support their decision if their votes all agreed. They would have followed this man's advice if it had not been the case that separate deliberation chambers were not available for the various guilds. Nonetheless, the aldermen decided to reduce the disorganized swarm of deliberators to a smaller number since it was difficult to have all the guilds participate in the various matters and in the midst of such human dregs to reach any sensible resolution given the importance of the debate. From all the guilds twenty-six men were chosen to inform the aldermen and guild masters of their plans whenever necessary and to harass the council, nothing being done by it without their authority. When Henry Iserman the goldsmith was appointed as one of the twenty-six, he left no stone unturned in resigning honorably from the post. He pointedly insisted that all the guilds should consider more carefully this civil tumult and the plans they had taken against the council, since it was seldom the case that those who opposed their government emerged successful. Such plans, he said, had almost always redounded to the misfortune of those responsible. He professed to having learned this from the memorable example of the sedition in the state of Cologne in 1513. There the men responsible for the sedition were penalized with beheading at the very time when they imagined that they were safe and successful. To these words the alderman Henry Redeker replied, "If with all this talk of cut-off heads you are showing your fear for yourself, you are not only useless in terms of implementing our intentions, but you are in fact a great obstruction." Thus, a bolder and more confident man who prattled on more resonantly about the Gospel was substituted in place of him.

216   After the men were appointed in this way, the authority of all the guilds was transferred to the aldermen and guild masters. The terms of this transfer were as follows. They were to deliberate in common and oppose the council in connection with advancing the cause of the evangelical movement, without, however, harming the state and the city's liberty. Their main aim in the council was to bring it about that a unanimous form of worship without any disagreement in any regard was to be taught throughout the city. This religion was to be nourished and cherished, and, along with all its accompaniments, defended to the last gasp and the last drop of blood. All false doctrine was to be uprooted like the most harmful plague, so that no impurity

that in any way opposes the evangelical truth was to be left. Finally, the general tranquility and liberty were to be procured, strengthened and preserved, being increased with daily additions. If, however, the council prevaricated in this cause, which was as pious and respectable as it was useful, and showed itself to be troublesome, this situation was to be remitted to the entire estate of the commons for its deliberation. After reaching these decisions, the men went their ways, chatting as they went in groups of two or three or four about the success of the Gospel and showing, in the manner of the apostles, more concern about this than about their own granaries.[42]

Later, on July 11, the aldermen and guild masters summoned the council to its chamber and laid before them the commons' requests, at the same time demanding that the council should protect the Word of God along with all its accompaniments and that full agreement in wishes and pursuits should exist between both the commons and council. To this the council responded that they would in no way oppose the Gospel and Word of God, but since it was not yet determined who was spreading the true doctrine of the Gospel, they would send an embassy to put before the prince a request that by his authority learned men should be sent for by the common counsel and expense. The power to judge the purity of worship would be entrusted to them, and it would be sinful to express opposition to the decision of their judgment. When this was achieved, said the council, it would be possible and appropriate to establish firm agreement in all wishes. The elected representatives of the commons were by no means satisfied with this answer, and at around 3 p.m. on July 12 they sent the aldermen and guild masters back to the council to get another answer, the main purpose being that the council should not obfuscate but state in so many words whether an agreement in all wishes on both sides was to be hoped for and whether the council wished and approved the resolutions of the commons. | To   217 this the council answered that they would never deviate the breadth of a fingernail from the Word of God, but would always adhere to it and defend all burghers devoted to it to the extent that their powers allowed. For this reason, they said, they asked the commons not to harass them any further.

The representatives of the commons were greatly offended and angered by this response from the council and sent the aldermen back

---

[42] Cf. Psalm 144:13.

to extract another response, saying that they were no longer willing to be
deceived with ambiguous, obscure and convoluted answers, and instead
the council should state clearly whether they were willing to agree to the
commons' wish and adopt common counsel in the business of religion.
Then, they said, they would plan their action more accurately in light
of the nature of the response and necessity of the situation. At about 9
a.m. on July 13, the aldermen and guild masters reported all this to the
burgher masters and certain other councilmen, who were deliberating
with the chapter in the cathedral about the Turkish tax.[43] They asked
the councilmen to be careful to give a specific response, since, they
explained, they could no longer keep the commons, who were ablaze
with love for the Gospel, from causing a disturbance and they feared
that unless a way to assuage and tame them was soon found, they would
begin to take energetic steps that would result in the destruction of all
the clergy and of many inhabitants. This statement from the aldermen
disturbed the burgher masters and councilmen so much that given this
emergency they had the attendants summon the full council at 2 p.m.
After once more explaining the desire of the commons, the aldermen
left. There was much debating back and forth as the council tried to
find ways to pacify the commons' anger, but no specific decision was
reached that day. Nightfall intervened and broke up the meeting, so
the vote was postponed until Monday, July 15. In the meanwhile, the
guild masters summoned their own individual guilds to the "*Schohaus*"
(guild hall) at 8 a.m. on that day, so that they could deliberate there
just as the council was doing in the council hall. When the councilmen
entered the council hall, the aldermen and guild masters were let in to
plead the case of the commons, as follows.

"First of all, wise and most honorable members of the council, the
commons, on whose behalf the necessity of our office has placed upon
us the duty of carrying out this embassy, publicly declare that in their
deliberations on the present matter | their sole aim is to procure the
glory of God, the salvation of their soul, and the common good. If,
on the other hand, the opposite can be ascertained by any judgment,

218

---

[43] A special tax voted periodically by the imperial diet (in this instance by the Diet
of Regensburg in the spring of 1532) and collected locally to help defray the heavy
expenses of the emperor's military operations against the Turks, who at this time
appeared to pose a serious risk to eastern Germany as a result of their decisive victory over the Hungarians at Mohács in 1526 (they had attempted to besiege Vienna
as recently as 1529).

they submit to their government, which they promise to obey readily in connection with all lawful and respectable acts, as is suitable and has always been the case before, and not to deviate the breadth of a fingernail from its orders. On the other hand, the commons demand that just as the ruler demands obedience from his subjects, so too should the government take up the guarding and defense of the subjects, maintaining the privileges and liberties with which the city of Münster has been endowed by many emperors and successive bishops, and, whenever necessity dictates, preserving, defending and protecting the advantages of each and every burgher, both within the walls and without. For without faith, defense on the part of the government, and true and lawful obedience on the part of the subjects in fear of God, no city and no state can long remain unharmed.

"As for the commons' not having ceased to demand these actions from the council in the humble manner of suppliants, they are eager to explain the reason and purpose of this when permission is graciously granted to give an account, so that with the removal of all the suspicion and disputation which is swelling up between the council and burghers, solid and by no means feigned concord can be restored in the state along with an honest way of living. For it is easy for the commons to perceive that when the subjects and the government are held in the thrall of suspecting the other of evil-doing and disagree with each other in concealed hatred, the state is enveloped in fatal dangers and buffeted about. Therefore, the commons, being subject to your power, are not too bashful to make known the reasons for their suspicion. On the contrary, it is their great yearning to learn from the senate what is displeasing in the commons. They promise either to undertake the defense of their innocence or, if they have acted badly, to live more correctly. Similarly, they ask the council to show to its subjects the kind of attitude that is demanded by their office.

"In order, then, that you, most honorable councilmen, may understand the reasons for the commons' suspicion and for their fear that they will be harmed by you, hear a few words. First, the council has for some time denied the opportunity for a meeting, and has instead shunned any discussion with the commons on a matter that is especially urgent and difficult. Second, the council, which is divided into factions, has avoided the customary location for deliberation in the council hall, and sometimes six, sometimes eight, sometimes ten councilmen have sought out little sessions, convening in various chapels and other hidden places. | The burghers were in no small way chagrined at this   219

practice, and since they were thereby denied the opportunity to speak
with the council, the commons began to hold the council's good faith
suspect. Third, on the advice of the aldermen and the guild masters,
the council promised to see to it that each parish should have sincere
heralds of the Gospel,[44] and whether it is through carelessness or for-
getfulness that this has been neglected down to the present time is not
known.[45] Fourth, although the estate of the commons has implored the
council's defense of all their laws and privileges, the council has not
cleared them of the accusation by writing to the prince. It is these and
other similar reasons that have led the anxious commons to suspect the
good faith of the council."

The matter was laid before the council in this way, so that the council
could more easily give answers to the individual points, and thereby
satisfy and assuage the commons, who would from then on trust their
government without any suspicion of evil-doing. After a short deliberation, the council gave the following response. They had never, they
said, averted their attention from the well-being of the commons and
had always devoted more concern to the burghers' advantages than to
their own, being well aware of the extent of the danger when limbs
of a single body are alienated against one another. For this reason the
council had avoided any grounds for disagreement and sought grounds
for concord. They had never, they said, kept away the aldermen or the
guild masters, who were the defenders of the commons, but only the
ignorant mob, who clamored in an unruly manner and did not plead
their case in the traditional manner through the aldermen.

"As for the fact that certain members of the council had occasionally
deliberated outside the council hall in rather secret locations, sometimes
about private matters, sometimes about public matters, but in any case
always about trivial ones, this had in no regard undermined the rights
or privileges of the city, the aim in these meetings being the public
good just as much as it was in the council hall.[46] It was only to avoid
the immoderate behavior of certain people that a lonely meeting place

---

[44] That is, preachers, the terminology being indicative of what was expected of
them.
[45] There is no external documentary evidence for such a promise on the part of
the council, but it is acknowledged in the council's reply.
[46] With this sentence, K. seems to shift to direct quotation, though this is clumsily
carried out at times and seems to be indirect discourse with the use of indicative verbs
after the fashion of German rather than the correct accusative-and-infinitive of Latin
(but note the use of the first person plural towards the end).

was chosen, it normally being the case that it is not through location but wisdom and reliability that a decision gains authority.

"As for the fact that the commons have lacked preachers down to the present time, this happened through neither the carelessness nor the forgetfulness of the council but through the lack of the kind of grave and learned men that the council wishes to entrust with the parishes, | it having proved impossible to acquire the services of such men on short notice. 220

"Finally, the council admits that they had not defended the impetuous acts of certain men before the prince, since they were under no obligation to defend acts which they had neither ordered nor authorized. On the other hand, acts carried out under a common plan had always received the council's protection. Therefore, let the commons stop harboring wicked suspicions about the council. Since one man could not do without the other's support, let us cast aside all suspicion and return to mutual affection. Let us be joined in mutual trust, being bound by oath to one another. Let us do each other favors, let us be ablaze with the zealous desire to help each other, let us conduct all our actions by each other's authority. Let the council love the commons, not disdain them, and seek to benefit them without harming anyone else. Let the commons be obedient to the council and not resist when the council issues proper warnings. If at times the commons deviate from the straight path, let them patiently allow themselves to be warned and think that they have won not through rebellion but through obedience. In this way it will happen that we will never fall into strife with one another and every kind of suspicion that may swell up on either side will be plucked out by the roots. In this way we are finally going to have a very firm state. If, therefore, the aldermen and guild masters promise that the commons will have this attitude regarding fairness and the council, the council in turn will promise that they will not fail the commons."

The aldermen and other representatives of the commons gave their assent to these words. After this agreement had been made by both sides, the aldermen and guild masters explained the commons' desire to the council in the following words.

"Now that the government and subjects of this city are tied to one another with the bounds of good will and obedience and every suspicion of disfavor and dissension has been removed, we think that in order to prevent any opportunity for sedition arising again in our state, it is above all necessary that a uniform religion consisting of the Gospel and pure doctrine should flourish throughout the entire city. For a varied

221 and impure doctrine | brings eternal death not only to the body but
also to souls. Since no doctrine works to achieve salvation as well as
the evangelical doctrine which Lord Bernard Rothman proclaims in
a pure and genuine manner through the enlightenment of God, the
entire estate of the commons embraces it as the route to salvation and
asks that they be allowed to profess it safely and unanimously, that
the council defend it and with their careful vigilance provide for the
individual parishes preachers who will spread the Word of God without mixing in falsehood and administer the sacraments in the manner
instituted by Christ, and that those preachers who opposed the Gospel
and Truth be deprived of the office of teaching doctrine. In addition,
since the estate of the commons, who have now been educated by the
Word of God, notice that abuses of many varieties have crept in, causing irrevocable harm to souls, they demand that through the council's
diligent action any ceremonies that diametrically contradict the Word
of God and cannot be retained without causing scandal be removed.
If the council perchance does not know which these are, it is easy for
them to perceive them on the basis of Lord Bernard's daily sermons
or Lord Bernard will be happy to define them at the council's request.
If, furthermore, anyone among the religious or the laity thinks he has
some means by which he hopes to overturn Rothman's doctrine through
Holy Scriptures and clear arguments, the estate of the commons ask
that by its own authority the council should command the clergy in
particular to make this public and to pay the penalty if refuted. Since
the commons have no doubt that Lord Bernard's doctrine is in agreement with the Gospel, they cannot deviate from it unless it is refuted
by Holy Scripture. He has often offered himself to such a contest and
comparison of Scriptures, but no one has dared to come forward against
him. Finally, since the burghers notice that everyday, alas, ancient and
praiseworthy customs, royal grants, and privileges are being broken
and that the failure to preserve them in their vigor results in harm
and damage to this city, the entire civil commonwealth[47] asks that the
council should, with the help of the aldermen and guild masters, take
strenuous steps to prevent the undermining of this city's ancient rights

222 and to see that they are instead restored. | In these matters, the council

---

[47] As opposed to the religious commonwealth. Medieval political theory held that
the state as a whole consisted of these two elements.

should present itself in the way that befits a Christian government, so that we may lead a way of life at once pious and peaceful. For just as nothing is more necessary for the collective body of burghers, so too do they seek nothing with greater ardor."

The council promised that they would do this and in a common compact under the signature of Henry Hoier the amanuensis of the council, they publicly associated themselves with the aldermen, guild masters and the commons, a copy of the compact being handed over to the aldermen. In addition, the council bound itself to announce to the pastors that within a prescribed period of time they should refute Bernard Rothman's dogma with legitimate arguments and scriptural passages, or else the council would, under the protection of the aldermen and guild masters, do what was demanded by considerations of justice and fairness.

On July 25, after the completion of the compact, the council by itself responded quite confidently, as follows, to the previous letter from the prince, even though it had been written to all the estates of the city.

"It was not only to us and the aldermen but also to the guild masters and the estate of the commons that you, most reverend prince, wrote in connection with a few preachers who partly through their own boldness and partly at the urging of certain commoners entered our city, taught their doctrines and spread unusual ceremonies among the public. You say that you were therefore requesting that we should preserve the longstanding ecclesiastical rites which had been established in ancient times, cast out the recently introduced preachers and ceremonies, and restrain the sedition of the commons. We have, most reverend prince, shown this letter to all the estates of our city and especially to Lord Bernard Rothman, whom it seems to concern most, and he has given us a response, a copy of which is being conveyed to you so that you may learn his intentions more fully. Furthermore, to remove any suspicion of rebellion as far as possible from us, you should be aware that neither this Rothman nor any other of the preachers was summoned by us to the city for the purpose of preaching, and that instead Derek of Merfelt the bailiff called Rothman to the city from the residence which he had at that time established in St. Maurice's, | and in the name of the prince he denied him any defense and revoked his safe conduct and immunity. Rothman conveyed various complaints about this matter to almost all the townsmen and promised that he would defend his cause with arguments based on justice. We too have in similar vows yearned for nothing other than Christian ecclesiastical rites. As you too, most

223

reverend prince, know, in our city there are a remarkably large number of clergy, including pastors, the members of the mendicant orders called "terminaries,"[48] and other learned men, and to them Lord Bernard has offered a confession of his faith and doctrine which is drawn up in articles and which he has, with good will, asked them to instruct and enlighten him if he has erred anywhere. Up until now, however, they have carelessly neglected to do so or to set out any objection to his writing, and for this reason the commons, who are devoted to the evangelical Truth, feel more confidence in adhering to the admonitions of the preachers. Also, we do not feel that we have tainted the ancient ceremonies in our city, much less abolished them. In addition, since our burghers have offered the obedience rightly owed by them and have adopted a single religion embraced by them in tranquility, it will be our task to strengthen the civil concord without violating the rights and ancient privileges of the city. Hence, we think that it will be easy for the prince to see how difficult it is to send away the preachers and to despoil our burghers of the saving Word of God. We therefore ask both that the prince too should consider this and that if he has some other thought which he thinks will be advantageous, he should advise us of it publicly. Please consider this a well-intentioned response to your request."

A copy of the letter from Rothman to the council which is mentioned above was attached to the council's letter to the prince, as follows.

"Grace and peace from God as well as ready compliance in my office I offer to you first, my lord councilmen! The prince elect sent you a letter concerning me in particular, and you showed it to me so that I could either rebut the charges against me or, as someone subject to your judgment, suffer the penalties that the prince commanded you to inflict. This letter I have carefully read and re-read, and in it I find that before the prince my innocence has been torn apart with abominable accusations of unspeakable crimes that are completely unacceptable among Christians, | as if the sole aim of my efforts has been that both my doctrine and my life should reflect nothing good or respectable. Hence, the prince has earnestly commanded that you should strip me of the office of preaching and cast me out of the city. Certainly, the crimes of which they accuse me before the prince are monstrous, and if they were shown to be true and not concocted with

224

---

[48] For "terminaries," see 71D.

hatred and a remarkable zeal to revile by enemies bent on destroying my reputation, it would not be surprising if the prince ordered that such an inveterate blackguard should be expelled from the boundaries of the diocese. Indeed, I would be worthy of having the earth split open and of plunging alive into the depths of hell along with Dathan and Abiron.[49] As it is, since I know that I am innocent and that I can absolve myself the more readily because of this, I have absolutely no doubt that so long as I am allowed a true response against these slanderous accusations, the fabrications of liars will harm me neither before the prince nor before you, councilmen. For my view is that Christian government is saintly and generous, and I am persuaded with a firm conviction that if I am both willing and able to defend myself with the truth, he will be so well disposed towards me that he will justly protect me against the lying fabricators of falsehoods, especially since the case concerns not me but that of God and His Word. The fact that my person, which is not of much importance since Christ Himself endured the same thing, is being torn to shreds with false reproaches and rent apart with the most impudent lies does not harm me. Rather, these afflictions are visited upon me by Satan, the instigator of every lie and slander, to overwhelm the noble, saving Word of God that He explains and distributes to His people through me as His servant. I would certainly respond in this letter to the individual accusations if I did not fear that I would exceed the limits of even a letter and if I thought that you were both officially and privately unaware of the charges against me, which are being falsely strewn about before the prince and have led him to write these things. Such verbosity on my part would cause disgusted boredom in you. Hence, I think that this general justification is sufficient for my defense at the present time. | If, on the other hand, 225 it should be thought necessary to respond to the individual charges and this is asked of me, I promise that I will do this so that if any lover of the truth wishes to examine everything more deeply, he will have the means to shut the mouths of the malicious. Therefore, I beseech you with my most ardent prayers in the name of all that is holy and for the sake of God that with good will you accept this response of mine and this offering of my office and that as much as possible you will help me in dealings with the prince. In the meanwhile, I promise you

---

[49] Numbers 16:30–33. The Lord attests to the wickedness of these two men by causing the earth to swallow them.

that without violence I will respond to anyone at all who thinks that he will cite against me anything that is contrary to Christian doctrine and piety. If I am refuted, I am prepared to suffer that penalty which Christian law imposes on those convicted on this account. Since these are the most stringent standards to which I can bind myself, I do not think that I should be oppressed with less tolerable conditions. If only one of my accusers would come forward so that either my innocence or my fault would be brought into the light of day! If it should be that I have done something wrong, I will not refuse to suffer a punishment worthy of the deeds. For it would be better for me to die than to plan anything against God and to stay alive while piling up God's outrage against me more and more. But God is the only just judge whom the thoughts of the heart do not escape. To Him I, too, readily submit the case involving my actions, so that He may, by His will and decision, direct all the matters between me and my enemies, and save me in my innocence from the hands of my oppressors. May God glorify His name for eternal ages. Amen!"

While this was going on, the leaders of the commons suggested that the council should strengthen their cause with external support, and accordingly the council sent an embassy in secret to the illustrious lord, Prince Philip of Hesse, whom they knew to support their Gospel. The
226   gist of this embassy was as follows. | Despite the opposition of the bishop and the clergy, the state of Münster had accepted the Truth spread by preachers both learned and pious, and for this reason the inhabitants were apprehensive about an attack from them, fearing that they would join forces and plot against the inhabitants and the preachers, particularly at the time of the bishop's installation. Hence, they entreated him to help them with the great influence he had among the evangelical princes and to send to the bishop a letter deterring him from overwhelming the Gospel, as he may have decided to do at the urging of the clergy. Philip promised that there was nothing that he would not do to defend the Gospel, and accordingly on July 30 he wrote to the council of Münster as follows.

"We are glad to hear that by Almighty God's favor you have been enlightened with the knowledge of the Truth and have, through certain evangelical preachers, successfully set out the Word of God before your burghers without any deceit or admixture of filth. Since you are apprehensive of your well-being, fearing that at his investiture your bishop will inflict a great harm on you by removing these preachers, you have asked us to deign to avert this dangerous eventuality by writing a letter. Wishing to gratify you in this matter, we have written to the bishop, and attach a copy of it to this letter. In addition, it seemed a wise idea to warn you to make sure with timely planning and careful diligence that your fellow burghers do not use the pretext of evangelical freedom to commit instances of contumely, rebellion and disobedience against their government or to seek and to lay false claim to license of the flesh, sedition, or some private advantage, which are all contrary to the Gospel. You should also take strict measures to oblige the cohorts of the factious to refrain from stealing Church property and unjustly seizing incomes. If you heed these admonitions of ours and just make sure that the Word of God is proclaimed sincerely to the people, we have no doubt | that the newly elected bishop will show favor and good will 227 in matters that involve exalting the glory of God, spreading the Gospel, and the common good of the state. If, however, it happens that apart from this some other dispute arises between him or the chapter and you, and our good offices are requested by both sides to settle it, we will strive through our councilors to achieve concord, so that you may live in piety and peace with one another after the remaining disagreement has been completely removed through God's help."

The council issued a short response on August 5, saying that they had, with due respect, received the letter delivered by the bearer of this letter and would inform their people of its content and do what fairness dictated.

Next there follows a copy of the letter that Prince Philip of Hesse sent to the bishop on July 30, which was mentioned in the previous letter from the landgrave.

"Reverend Lord in Christ! It is reported to me not by a burgher of Münster but by someone else whose name I will tell you in person, that the city of Münster is apprehensive of its well-being at the time of your installation, fearing that at the urging and instigation of the main clergy | you will force them to abandon their evangelical preachers. 228 The individual therefore entreated me to free the city of this fear by writing to you, and I was unwilling and unable to refuse his request, which came from a Christian heart. Although I have absolutely no doubt of your evangelical attitude, I ask you in a friendly way that if the chapter has urged you to expel the city's preachers, you conduct all your actions in a wise and circumspect manner so that neither side is left with any grounds for complaint, the clergy are not deprived of their fruits, revenues and annual incomes, and the burghers are not robbed of their evangelical preachers. In this way it will happen that both sides will live together in mutual tranquility and adapt themselves to your will and decision. If, on the other hand, you do not conduct yourself in a wise, circumspect and pious manner in the matter, you will offend the electoral duke of Saxony and other Christian princes and estates of the Empire and live with your people in discord and division. In addition, you can easily see from all the present circumstances that His Imperial Majesty is not as energetic in this matter as he used to be. Do not, then, act in such a way as to suggest that you have cast off the fear of the Lord, burdened your conscience and caused more discord than concord. If you are not much moved by such considerations, then be moved primarily by the glory of Almighty God and then by my requests that those poor, imprudent people not be robbed of the Word of God. If you do so and to some extent grant my wish, God will at the same time pour into you as if from the most plentiful spring salvation for your soul, health for your body, success for your administration, and His grace. I and all the other princes and estates in our turn promise to repay your kindness with all the obligations of friendship. Issued at Sababurg on the Tuesday after the feast of St. James,[50] 1532."

Next, on August 1 at around 11 a.m., the council members from the Parish Across-the-River called "*scabini*"[51] and certain guild masters approached the abbess of the Convent Across-the-River, who has legal control of that parish, and set out two requests in particular. | The first was that the parish priests and chaplains should refrain from preaching and that others should be put in their places and left alone by the previous incumbents unless the latter refuted them with clear arguments based on Holy Scripture. The other request was that they should allow the impious ceremonies which had previously been customary to be abolished. This was also announced throughout all the city's parishes at the urging of the commons but without the authorization of the council. Since this command was not given the council's authorization, it was by no means obeyed.

In any case, the prince took no small offense at the last response from the inhabitants of Münster and at Rothman's bold obstinacy, to such an extent that on both sides the situation now seemed to be leading to armed conflict. Nonetheless, the prince's innate clemency won out over his first inclination, and he preferred to try every effort

229

---

[50] July 30.
[51] For *scabini*, see 105D.

through forbearance before taking up arms in case the madness of the townsmen could be calmed through good will. Accordingly, on August 5 he wrote as follows.

"We have understood well enough the sense of the letter you wrote on behalf of your preacher. As for your response, your attempt to clear him, and all the other things that are decked out by you with some specious appearance of evangelical truth or other, although we find this to be quite divergent from the truth, as the general report attests, nonetheless we readily leave these matters to your judgment, though we make our own assessment. On the other hand, we relied on our more than paternal admonitions and requests and would have expected from you a more appropriate and solid answer regarding the banishment of the preachers, the abolition of the recent innovations, and the restoration of the ancient ceremonies. Be that as it may, we again ask and demand of you that you let these and earlier admonitions sink into your minds and not erase the memory of them, that you do away with the religion you have taken up and the innovation and misuse in ceremonies, that you restore and retain the traditional and praiseworthy rites that were instituted by the Church in ancient times, and that you exile your preachers. If, on the other hand, you again ignore these demands with contempt, as I expect you will not, then I leave it to you to consider more carefully what action it befits us, as a member and loyal prince of the Empire, to take against such disobedient rebels in order to preserve the general peace and tranquility and the law that was issued by the Emperor at the Diet of Regensburg and whose execution was entrusted to us, | though as God is our witness we shrink from this. We benevolently desired to send you these admonitions a second time, so that you should take thought for your salvation and give us a definite answer."

While this business was being conducted by correspondence, at the request of the aldermen and guild masters, the burgher masters convened the council on August 6 by virtue of their oath as councilmen. After the councilmen had taken their seats in the council chamber in the customary manner, the aldermen and guild masters gave the following explanation to the council. They had been sent by the guilds and the elected representatives of the commons, who had held a meeting in the guild hall, to ask the council to remember the earlier compact that had been signed by the council's amanuensis and to establish as their principle goal that once the papist preachers were removed, all the parishes should have pious evangelical preachers to whom the

230

council would, by its authority, entrust control over the parishes, just as had been recently promised in the council's registry.[52] As the council had a long debate about these requests, engaging in various conversations with the aldermen about the matter, it became obvious that the councilmen were prevaricating. Growing impatient at the delay, the aldermen reminded the council that the commons were gathered in the guildhall and expected from the council a serious answer without any procrastination. The aldermen said that if they could not get from the council a well-intentioned answer with which the commons' sense of outrage could be assuaged or at least satisfied in part, they would bring the entire crowd and the council could, with their customary prudence, negotiate directly with them.

When the council heard this, they began to be fearful of their safety, thinking it dangerous for them to deal with the unruly mob, who approved any impulse as if it derived from better reasoning. They therefore resolved that this matter deserved further consideration. After pondering everything long and hard, examining things this way and 231   that, up and down, the council decided that it was better for them | to make some concession to the raging commons and, given the exigency of the situation, derogate in some way from the rights of the Church rather than rashly put themselves in the greatest danger and risk their lives. It was therefore decreed that the judges ("*scabini*") and guild masters, as well as certain more respectable commoners, would, by virtue of the council's authority, proclaim to the pastors and chaplains in the various parishes that they should refrain from carrying out the office of preaching, admit the preachers established by the council until such time as they were convicted of error, and, finally, allow the abolition of the impious ceremonies that were diametrically opposed to the Word of God. Being satisfied with these decisions, the commons went their various ways.

After this, the townsmen did not give up the course of madness that they had undertaken, and since they yearned to spread their innovation as far as possible, on the feast of St. Laurence (August 10), by virtue of the authorization they had extorted from the council, and under the leadership of Bernard Rothman, Brixius of Norden, whose sermons had caused the people of Ahlen to lose their cows,[53] Bernard Knip-

---

[52] For the registry, see 76D.
[53] See 101K.

perdolling, Herman Tilbeck, Caspar Schrodercken, John Langerman, Peter Friese, Peter Mensing, John Windemoller, John Ummegrove and many other members of this faction, they rushed into the churches, where they abolished the old practice of the sacraments and the ancient ceremonies that still remained, broke up the altars and images that were still undamaged, threw the priests out of the churches, replacing them with effeminate, unlearned members of their faction who lacked gravity, prohibited the solemn celebration of the mass, and muttered psalms in German. In short, they barely kept their hands off of the cathedral and the Church Across-the-River, and in the other churches without any fear of punishment they threw everything sacred into confusion with the profane.

Escorted by followers of his faction, Brixius entered the unoccupied house | attached to the position of chaplain in St. Maurice's by remov-   232 ing the barricades in order to live there. After spending some weeks there, he eventually entered into a legal marriage with Rothman's sister, whose immoral company he had been enjoying for some time, thinking that he was making amends for the earlier immorality. When his previous wife arrived with two children, however, it is said that he repudiated the latest one. As a result a feud arose between Brixius and Rothman, but in the end their common zeal to spread the Gospel and their profession easily did away with it, so that those who professed with equal vows a unanimous faith in the evangelical truth would not seem to be in disagreement with one another, which would certainly have estranged many people from their preaching.

When the good men realized that they were exposed to the greatest danger by living among seditious men who seemed to hanker after the possessions of others, they secretly snatched away their titles to income and other wealth, which the factious men seemed to be plotting after. For they dared not have any confidence in a city that was thrown into confusion by the boundless authority of the commoners. On August 14, the nuns of the Convent Across-the-River also sent off a strongbox filled with sealed titles and certain other adornments of gold and silver, depositing them in a safer location outside of the city.

Who would ever have expected such a turn of events? Whereas in prior years the inhabitants of the diocese had, when faint with fear of hostile arms, had confidence in this city's fortifications and brought their property into it, now they thought that this same property was safer outside the walls. Certain more prominent members of the council and the patrician estate even abandoned their ancestral homes and

233   moved their residence elsewhere, such as Eberwin | Droste, Derek Münsterman, Wilbrand Plonies, Herman Schencking, a judge in the city, Herman Heerde, and other outstanding luminaries of this kind. Other good and peaceful men who had always proposed suppressing the sedition did the same, thinking that it was better for them to live among wild animals than among savage barbarians in a situation where they would endanger themselves and all their property. In order not to seem to be failing to support the state with their advice, the councilmen divided up among themselves their duties and the days fixed for council meetings, so that they would not all be present or all absent at the same time. No one doubts that it was an act of great prudence to adopt this practice in order to prevent the commons from assailing the entire council according to its own lights or extorting anything from it through the direct application of force. The burgher masters Eberwin Droste and Wilbrand Plonies did not return to the seditious inhabitants, resigning their office and hiding in voluntary exile. The commons were very chagrined at the absence of the burgher masters and their voluntary exile, particularly at this time, when the state of Münster was suffering from the lack of advice and public orators (the senior burgher master always served as the public orator on the council). Hence, the commons ordered the aldermen and guild masters to convene the now leaderless council at 7 o'clock on August 16. There the commons presented to them a bill of complaints, the text of which follows.

    "Most vigilant aldermen and guild masters, who are also most zealous for our interests! The commons and the entire multitude of burghers is worried, being moved by a suspicion of someone in that the senior burgher master, who possesses the leading position and the greatest influence on the council, has at this time in particular elected to go into voluntary exile and has in this way polluted his office and involved the city in critical danger. Also, it is rumored that the council has earnestly entreated this same burgher master by letter to return to his position as head of the council, and he might answer back to the council, so that the reason for his flight into exile would be made known. It is not without reason that the commons fear for themselves on account of this fugitive burgher master. Rather, the commons have many grounds for this, and they will reveal them at the appropriate moment. Although this city has been abandoned by the burgher masters, the commons nonetheless wish and consider it a matter of the greatest importance

234   that steps be taken | so that it should not receive any harm that would result in the destruction of all the inhabitants. Therefore, two things in

particular must be seen to. First, an orator must be procured at public expense to defend with great eloquence not so much our common rights as the rights of the city and the customs of the homeland. It is necessary to employ such an orator now in particular, since the senior burgher master, to whom the office of acting as an advocate belongs, is absent. Even if he were present, the advice and eloquence of an orator would still be needed, since the burgher master has openly stated that he is not up to the job because of the loss of his ability to memorize and that he would not bring down upon himself or his children the rancor and hatred of any man in order to benefit the city. The entire body of burghers thinks that no one is more suitable for undertaking the office of orator than John of Wieck, a man possessing an outstanding knowledge of the law. The commons therefore ask the council to strive with all its thoughts and diligence, and quickly too, in order to make sure that the city is not deprived of that man's services, however much it may cost the city's treasury. The second measure is that the strictest attention should be paid to this city's fortifications and weapons. The people make these requests of you and entrust them to your diligent good faith. If you have some other thought that you think will be beneficial to the city's interests or defense, the commons leave it to you to consider this by your judgment and to implement it in a timely manner."

After this statement had been handed over by the aldermen and read by the council, the councilmen promised that they would endeavor to the best of their abilities to make sure that the city would lack nothing that was necessary. An embassy was sent to Doctor John of Wieck, the orator of the city of Bremen, to offer him the position of orator for Münster. He declined on the grounds that he was so involved in the affairs of his own city that he could not abandon his people without violating his good faith, which he would do if he did not first extricate himself by performing his duties well.

After these events, on the same day (that is, August 16) at about 10 o'clock, the aldermen and guild masters reported to the council, which had not yet departed, that Bernard Rothman and the other evangelical preachers had drawn up certain articles about abuses which they wished to present to the council. They therefore wished to have these men admitted for discussion. The council, however, argued on various grounds that they should not be admitted, particularly since this matter belonged not to the council but to ecclesiastical judges. After much time had been spent in protracted debate without the aldermen putting any limit or end to their insistence, the men were eventually

235

admitted. At this point, Rothman and his people gave a document about ancient abuses to the council in the presence of the aldermen and guild masters. It was read out before a full session of the council, and a copy of it follows.

"Summary of certain abuses that have crept into the Church and been adopted over time composed for and presented to the council, aldermen and guild masters of the city of Münster by the servants of the Gospel.[54]

"We wish for you grace and peace from God the Father and the true and saving knowledge of Christ the only-begotten Son and our sole
236 savior | through the Holy Spirit, most wise and honored councilmen! For some time now, the Gospel of the Kingdom of Christ has been spread in your city by the grace of God, and through it, we hope, many people have acquired true knowledge and comfort for their souls, no one having impugned it, or been able to impugn it, with solid arguments down to the present day. For this reason, we think it obvious that from this doctrine the knowledge not only of our salvation but also of many impious abuses flows and becomes more manifest. The commons, therefore, being devoted to the Christian doctrine, recognize these horrible impious abuses and strenuously oppose them at the urging of the Holy Spirit in order not to lose both their bodies and souls, and thus they have, we gather, begged that by your authority you should cleanse the true doctrine of the Gospel, freeing it of all the blemishes caused by the impious abuses. In this matter you have readily shown the attitude towards your subjects that befits a Christian ruler, and for this reason it is easy to see that in your state you will tolerate no doctrine but the pure and untainted Gospel of Jesus Christ, having summoned us to spread it, though we are unworthy. We will, nonetheless, endeavor to satisfy our evangelical calling to some extent.
237 | May God bestow on us His grace! How faithfully and energetically we have toiled in the vineyard of the Lord is for others to judge, in particular you since you have discovered through experience whether our life has not corresponded to the doctrine presented by us. For it is necessary to conjoin these two elements, since anyone who teaches one thing as doctrine and lives another errs in one or the other. Hence, the magistrates are not only fully entitled to forbid the office of preaching to those who do not strengthen and express their doctrine with Holy Scriptures and their own way of life but obligated to order them to

---

[54] The original text is no longer extant.

refrain from all impious ceremonies, which cause no less harm in the
state than does false doctrine. Now, certain people complain that they
do not know which ceremonies are impious, and they claim that for
this reason they are unable to deviate from the traditional ceremonies
and the customary ecclesiastical rites unless the ones that are impious
are specified by name. This is stated well enough in our daily sermons,
and those who are uncertain in this matter should be referred to them,
but nonetheless, in order to facilitate their recognition of any kind of
impiety and abuse and to prevent them from being able to allege any
excuse for their obstinacy in maintaining these abuses, we wished to
bring forth for you from the shadows into the light of day a summary
of the abuses, which is, to the extent necessary at the present time,
corroborated with Holy Scriptures, so through this occasion those who
are surrounded by the fortifications of your city and remain ensnared
within these impious nets should at your command either be prevented
from following these practices or cite against the new ones some solid
argument by which they may legitimately defend their own customs. For
the abuses which have, up until now, been concealed under the specious
appearance of piety and will be revealed by us here are nothing but
blasphemy and slander against God, and what you should strive with
every resource and effort to avoid is that the holy name of God should
be befouled with any blasphemies by your subjects. For particular honor
is owed to God by everyone, especially the government, and if they are
insufficiently concerned about the glory of God, they also involve their
subjects in this same wicked carelessness. God will especially avenge
contempt for His glory at the hands of rulers. Since in our zeal to
honor God we are here explaining the abuse and blasphemy against
God's name, as the calling of our office demands, we beseech and pray
that you too remember the task imposed on you by God and act with
diligence in implementing what you will think relevant to the glory
of God and the salvation of souls. | For just as it is our duty to seek   238
God's glory and spread His Word, and to teach, exhort and console
Christians, so too does it befit you to restrain with lawful punishments
those obstinate rebels who blaspheme against God. For it is not for no
purpose that you ply the sword, but rather so that the wicked will fear
you to the glory of God and the good will love you. For what has not
been planted by the Heavenly Father will be uprooted,[55] and what this
is we will explain in an orderly and brief way. May the will of God

[55] Matthew 15:13.

work in us, and to His protection we commend you. Issued at Münster on the feast of the Assumption,[56] 1532.

> Zealous for your Reputation,
> Bernard Rothman, Brixius of Norden,
> John Glandorp, Henry Rolle,
> Peter Wirtheim, Godfrey Nienhove of Stralen

"1) The mass, which has been stitched together piece by piece by men, is the destruction of the Lord's Supper and is blasphemy against His death.

"2) The Lord's Supper will be taken in the manner instituted by Christ, whereby Christians meet and proclaim the death of the Lord.

"3) On the other hand, in the mass one man eats and drinks contrary to the manner instituted by Christ, presuming to do so on behalf of another person and, what is more abominable, making of it an offering that is to be Christ Himself, Who is again to be offered by the officiant on behalf of the living and the dead, which is a derisive insult to the Passion of Christ. In addition, almost all masses are paid for with money in just the way that the Jews bought Christ from Judas the traitor.

"4) Just as it is impious for one man to usurp the Lord's Supper on behalf of many, so too is it impious to distribute it in only one kind (bread).[57] For the Lord's Supper is a testament to the Son of God that no one ought to change.

"5) The sacrament (as they call it) that is placed in patens, carried around and worshipped is blatant idolatry. For the Lord God alone, Whose seat is the heaven and the earth His footstool,[58] | Who is neither able nor willing to be enclosed within temples wrought by the hands of men, is to be worshipped. What is carried around in patens, invoked and worshipped is nothing but mere bread, and it cannot be a sacrament.

"6) Since the bread and wine are shared in the Lord's Supper as a commemoration of Him, it is indeed a sacrament. Otherwise, the bread

239

---

[56] August 15.
[57] This refers to the development of late medieval liturgical practice whereby the parishioners received only bread in communion and the wine was reserved for the priest (wine and bread being referred to as the two *species* or "kinds" of communion).
[58] Isaiah 66:1.

is and remains bread, and the wine is and remains wine.[59] As for their saying that through the action of the five words "For this is my body" they make the sacrament or body of Christ, this is an impious lie.

"7) Masses for souls, vigils and other rites for the dead have no basis in the Scripture and Truth of God.[60] Rather, they are derisive insults to the blood of Christ. For it is thought that they can cancel sins, but this should be attributed only to the blood of Christ. Such masses are deceitful tricks with which to gut the wallets of the ignorant commoners.

"8) For these and many other reasons it follows that the papists' masses, in which they place the host in a paten, carry it around, worship it, and distribute it in one kind, are pure slanders and blasphemies against God and contrary to Divine Scripture.

"9) Since everything in the Church, that is, the congregation of the faithful, should be done for the purpose of educating and correcting it, it is also necessary that we should understand the things that are being done, since there can be no correction on the basis of what is not understood.

"10) It is therefore wrong if among the congregation of the faithful in church we use a different tongue from the one that can be understood by everyone.

"11) Thus it is also fitting for baptism to be practiced in the vernacular tongue, since it is in everyone's interest to understand the method of the baptism.

"12) Also, all ecclesiastical rites, chants and anything else encompassed under the rubric of divine worship that has become traditional for the sake of presents or money, whether this is the main or a secondary intention and whether principally or co-incidentally, are useless.[61]

---

[59] An attack on transubstantiation (the notion that the bread and wine are literally converted into the flesh and blood of Christ).

[60] An attack on the institution of purgatory.

[61] Two notions are combined in this article. First, it is assumed that certain rites were instituted for the monetary benefit of the priests, who refused to carry them out without some form of recompense. The statement about the primary or coincidental purpose of the payments is added to dispose of any counterarguments from defenders of traditional practice to the effect that the payment was neither the reason for the original institution of the rite nor an integral element of it (thereby deflecting the assertion that the payment invalidates the practice). Second, all such rites are to be abolished as pointless (whatever the origin).

"13) Chants by which the benefit of the intercessor or advocate is attributed to anyone other than Christ, like the *"Salve, Regina"*[62] and the similar chants, are impious blasphemies.

240   "14) To bless water, candles, plants, boughs, statues, bells, salt, oil and the such like with formulas for the benefit of our salvation smacks of paganism, shuts out true faith and opens the path to eternal damnation.[63]

"15) To anoint the sick with oil for any purpose other than to revive their limbs and bodies and to restore their strength, but as if the soul's salvation depended on this, is impious blasphemy.

"16) To invoke, honor and carry around images of the saints is manifest idolatry.

"The reason why we have selected these abuses among many to list here is so that those who are fattened by them may not cite as an excuse that they do not know which abuses have crept into God's churches. Thus, they can grasp here in a few words that the feigned worship of God is the greatest blasphemy against God (even though they also learned this from our early writing). From these writings and the reasons cited it is indisputably true that these abuses not only do not correspond to Holy Scriptures but are in diametrical opposition to them and reopen the wounds of Christ. Second, we have noted these abuses all the more readily in order for the son of perdition, who exalts himself above everything that is called God, sitting in the church of God and setting himself forth as God, to be revealed,[64] so that those men who usurp God's power and publicly declare that they represent God or rather that they are the vicars of Christ and possess the authority to absolve souls and remit sins should be betrayed through the removal of their covering. For with these abuses that lurk under the specious guise of religion they slaughter souls just as brigands slaughter unwary men in their lairs. There is a general clamor, and the princes also write,

---

[62] Known as "Hail, Holy Queen" in English, this is far and away the most famous of the four breviary anthems to the Virgin Mary. Its authorship is unclear (it was attributed to a number of individuals), but seems to have been composed ca. 1000. It was adopted in the late medieval period by a number of monastic orders for evening services, and chantries were established specifically for performing it. Both Erasmus and Luther objected to the emphasis placed in the work on the role of Mary in salvation, and while the sentiment in it was not doctrinally offensive to Protestants, the anthem became strongly associated with the Catholic Mariology promoted during the Counter Reformation.

[63] Attack on the widespread use of exorcized objects in traditional worship.

[64] 2 Thessalonians 2:3–4 (the text was taken as referring to the Antichrist).

that the ancient, Christian and praiseworthy rites of the Church should be retained, it being impossible ever to deviate from them. If only in obeying the commands of princes we learned with outstanding zeal which rites are to be considered ancient, Christian and praiseworthy, and which sinful and impious! Without a doubt we would not in that case so readily embrace the abuses that have been betrayed by us, since they have been introduced and accepted in violation of Scripture, of ancient Christian custom, and indeed of Christ Himself, for the sake of profit. In your presence, then, we will defend what we have written here against anyone. Accordingly, if any sinning in connection with such blasphemies takes place later in this city, | we consider ourselves   241 to be innocent before God. It will be your task to ponder carefully what the considerations of the office entrusted to you by God demand of you in this matter."

After these statements were read in the council, the council noted that they pertained not to themselves but to ecclesiastical judgment, since it was not the city's liberty but the clergy's that was at issue. Therefore, in order to give an opportunity for defense, they sent a copy of the document to the clergy, so that they could defend their own cause by rebutting the arguments of the preachers. When these articles about abuses were handed over to the clergy, they sent them to Cologne and awaited a solid refutation of them by the theologians.[65]

On the same day (August 16) the council deliberated about the response they should give to the previous letter[66] from the prince. In the end, they issued the following statement by decree. They had, in the customary manner, shown the letter from the prince to the aldermen and guild masters, and from it these men had learned that the prince had not, as they had expected, been pleased by the council's previous response. In that response, the council had written that the preacher Lord Bernard Rothman, who had not been summoned to the city by the council, had offered to submit a document containing articles outlining his faith to the pastors, terminary monks and other men outstanding in learning, earnestly requesting correction from them if he erred in any regard, but they had given no response as if the matter were no concern of theirs and instead slept peacefully on either ear.[67] For this

---

[65] The theology faculty of the University of Cologne was a hotbed of reactionary scholasticism and a staunch defender of orthodoxy.

[66] That of August 5 (see 229–230D).

[67] A Latin expression signifying a lack of worry.

reason, they had written, the commons, being devoted to the Gospel and the Word of God, had been more confident in following Rothman. They also requested of the prince in that same response that he should, in order to protect civil society, deliberate about what measures seemed suitable to calm the uproar without violating the ancient rights and privileges of the city. They had hoped that the prince would not

242   spurn a respectable request but would hear it graciously, | but since they found the contrary to be the case, they asked that the prince should, if so inclined, send to the city council some of his own councilors who were foremost in learning and authority, so that by their common counsel they could deal with all the uproars in the city in such a way that when all error and discord was done away with, an opportunity would be given to truth and concord.

To this the prince responded on August 17 as follows. He had expected to receive from the council and the entire city of Münster a very different answer to his previous request, imagining that the inhabitants of the city would have obeyed by banishing the priests. Since, however, he saw that they had done nothing of the kind, a matter that caused him no little distress, he again requested that being mindful of their own salvation, they should finally, particularly under the present circumstances, consider the whole matter as carefully as possible, returning to a more sincere frame of mind: they should not introduce or allow to be introduced any innovation or any ecclesiastical rites different from those which existed in ancient times and should instead retain in use the ancient ceremonies and ancestral rites of the Catholic Church. As for their having asked him to send councilors, they were at the present time occupied with a different and necessary embassy, but upon their return he would take up this matter for deliberation and quickly write back the decisions of his council and make known what was considered appropriate in this situation.

While this was going on, news reached Charles V, the most august emperor of the Romans, who was at that time engaged in business in Regensburg, about the innovations that had arisen in Münster and resulted in changing the form of religion and the ancient ecclesiastical rites. Realizing that this was a matter that could brook no delay, he immediately sent a letter to Bishop Francis of Münster, the text of which follows.

"We, Charles V, by the grace of God the ever august emperor of the Romans and so on, wish our grace and everything good for our prince Francis, the most reverend bishop of Minden and nominee

for the sees of Münster and Osnabrück. | Most reverend and pious   243
prince, we have gathered through hearing by no means false accounts
that many citizens and inhabitants of Münster have welcomed into
their city certain Lutheran preachers in violation of our pious and
beneficial edict that was issued at Worms in 1521[68] as well as of our
law that was promulgated at the last Imperial Diet in Regensburg in
1530, and that these preachers are leading the ignorant and unwary
commons from the true Word of God with their monstrous views and
self-serving doctrine and do not cease to cause hatred, enmity and
sedition among the religious and the laity, who are still devoted to the
ancestral religion, as a result of which nothing but public disorder and
bloodshed is to be feared if the opportunity is not quickly removed. It
will be our task to obviate this misfortune with the appropriate remedy
of timely planning. Accordingly, we command you, earnestly enjoin
and resolve that you should as bishop examine the deeds in the city,
not only remove from office the seditious preachers along with their
following but also drive them out of the city, and restrain the factious
burghers with lawful punishments and compel them with specific laws
to obey their government, so that the clergy, as well as the city council
and the other townsmen, may live together within the city walls in
tranquility and full peace. Be advised that if you take these steps you
will have complied with our will."

The prince had a copy of this Imperial letter that was checked
against the original sent to the city council, and he attached it to his
own letter of August 21, as follows.

"That his Imperial Majesty has written a strict command to us that
particularly concerns you and the inhabitants of our city you will learn
from the copy that we have checked against the original and attached
to this letter. Therefore, by virtue of the authority of this Imperial letter, we ask you with our devoutest wish and faithfully advise you under
the impulse of our good will towards your city that you should disown
the innovation that you have undertaken in the business of religion,
cast out the seditious Lutheran preachers and restore the ancient and
accepted ceremonies of the Catholic Church, | so that you will not   244
seem to be violating the edict of his Imperial Majesty and the Estates
of the Empire and contumaciously despising our frequent warnings.

---

[68] The manuscript erroneously has "1530" but the correct date appears in the
original of the Imperial letter.

We are certain that you will take these steps as obedient subjects of the Empire. Otherwise, we will be obliged to proceed to carry out, as we have been ordered, the Imperial order commanding the repression of the rebellion with lawful remedies, though in our devotion to you we shrink from these. We wish you to send through the bearer of this letter a response stating what you are going to do."

To this the council gave the following response on August 28. They had received the letter from the prince along with the copy of the Imperial command that had been sent to the prince. They had shown the letter to the aldermen and guild masters in the customary manner and received from the burghers the answer that they had done nothing in violation of the Imperial decree, to which they declare they owe all obedience. For the fact that they had summoned and admitted preachers to teach the Gospel and Word of God in a pure and sincere manner without pollution from any stain of heresy was in complete and express agreement with the Emperor's edict issued at Worms, so far was it from violating the edict. Also, the council had found that it was indisputably true that these preachers had shown the pastors and chaplains of the parishes certain articles about doing away with abuse in certain ecclesiastical rites, and that the pastors and chaplains had as yet given no response to these articles, just as had been the case with Rothman's. From these responses and others given previously, the prince could easily assess how impossible it was for the council to keep their burghers from the Word of God and to drive the preachers from the city. If, then, the prince did not cease to be oppressive and burdensome, the council and their people would invoke the city's rights and in particular the privilege of the diocese, because of which they did not expect that they would be in any way oppressed or afflicted by the prince with insufferable savagery.

They seem to be referring to the following article, which is included among the privileges of the diocese: "Item. The bishop will admit every single one of his subjects to their rights, privileges and reasonable customs, and he will defend those so admitted." There are also other articles among the privileges which the burghers thought supported their position. For instance, "Item. If one of the subjects contends that he has some legal action or | case against the bishop, it should be settled amicably by the chapter or decided according to justice and custom, and the Lord should acquiesce in the decision" and "Item. His appointees will not execute 'koslach' against the members of the knighthood or the city of Münster and its towns," though here the burghers

245

incorrectly read "*toslach*" ("arrest") as if the bishop were forbidden the right of arrest among his subjects.[69]

On August 29, the prince responded as follows to the townsmen's letter of August 16, in which they asked for councilors of the prince to be sent to settle the sedition. He had been quite prepared, he said, to send the councilors in order to preserve the tranquility and well-being of the state, but it had become quite clear to him that in recent days, and in particular on August 10, the townsmen had done what he had by no means expected. In violation of the Imperial edicts and in derisive contempt of the Imperial decrees promulgated in various Diets, in the parish and other churches they had, by their own authority and in the manner of seditious rebels, altogether abolished and done away with all the pious ceremonies and worship of God that were ancient and traditional. Accordingly, by his own council it had been decided that he would not send members of his council to waste their time in negotiations with people who are constantly consumed with the zealous desire to innovate, unless, that is, all the innovation in religion and ecclesiastical rites that had also been forbidden by the Emperor was first cast out of their territory and then the rites now in exile were recalled. In that case, he would negotiate with the townsmen either in Münster or in any other place, and if any sort of feud, hatred, abuse or error was discovered in either the ecclesiastical or secular order, he would do away with it by his authority and substitute practices that were conducive to unbroken peace, a tranquil life and public well-being. Hence, he had no doubt that the townsmen would be mindful of the obedience they owed and of their duty.

The lower clergy were upset at this miserable situation and unheard-   246
of turn of events, and since they were unable to oppose the commons' uproar and their seditious and violent machinations with their own strength, they begged for the prince's help in the following words.

"Most reverend and glorious prince! We have no doubt that you have learned through the general report that certain lowly men unknown to us have, without the permission of the secular government but at the

---

[69] It is hard to make sense of K.'s argument because while K. is apparently denying to *koslach* the meaning "arrest" (in the sense of "seize"), which he restricts to the word *toslach*, *koslach* does in fact share this sense with *toslach* (and also signifies "driving cattle from a meadow"). K. apparently gives this incorrectly restrictive meaning to *koslach* in order to deny the burghers' interpretation, but he does not explain what he takes *koslach* to mean or what he thinks the bishop's officials are actually supposed to refrain from doing.

command of certain councilmen, aldermen and guild masters and of certain people of commoner status, intruded into the parish churches, throwing the pastors and chaplains out of their positions and taking over their offices, that they have disseminated many innovations and unheard-of propositions among the common folk, that they have rejected as destructive, impious blasphemy the ancient rites in the churches and the worship of God that were established many centuries ago and have been accepted since then, and that they have drawn up their doctrine under a few headings, claiming that these matters will remain valid until they are refuted by Catholic preachers with legitimate arguments based on Holy Scriptures. All these matters have caused us the greatest grief, and under these most distressing circumstances we take refuge in no one (after God) other than you, our prince, defender, protector and future bishop, expecting advice, help and support from you. As a result of such disorderly, violent and forbidden enactments and undertakings on the part of seditious men not only all good and pious ceremonies but also the worship of God, peace and tranquility are smashed, cast to the winds, and despised, and the commons are not roused to mutual affection but instead are made to be so angry against us that we can scarcely be confident of the peaceful possession of our property for a single day or conceive what we should do and expect in the end amidst such vicissitudes and constant innovation. Consequently, most reverend prince, we implore you, we beseech you, to help us with your authority. May the frightfulness of the present time,

247   our pale worries and anxieties, | the risk of death with which we are threatened every day, or rather every hour, and finally consideration of your office impel you to succour us with your advice and help amidst these distressing and perplexing difficulties and bring it about that with the ancestral rites and ceremonies retained in churches we may be reconciled with the council and commons and live in peace as we have up until now. If you do this, you will make us obliged, or rather most obliged, to you. We are eager for you to answer back what your attitude toward us is."

The prince gave the following response. "I am compelled to endure with great distress your afflictions and the death of the ancestral ceremonies and holy rites at the hands of the people of Münster. At the present time I cannot aid or succour you with definite advice given my situation or with sufficiently strong protection compared to the importance of the matter. Let us, therefore, put up with this joint misfortune for the time being. With God's help, however, steps will be taken to ensure the swift suppression of the rebellion rashly undertaken by the people of Münster, so that all your afflictions will be done away with and you yourselves will be restored to your former status."

On the same day (August 30), the prince responded as follows to the letter sent by the council on August 28 concerning the Imperial edict. "You responded to our previous letter, to which we attached and conveyed to you a copy of the Imperial letter, by stating that your burghers did not feel that they had violated the Imperial edict by calling to them preachers who would declare the Word of God to the people in a pure and sincere manner just as was ordained by the Imperial edict promulgated at Worms. In addition to this, we have also noted how frivolously, stupidly, pointlessly and without any justification you have invoked the rights and privileges of this diocese. That neither you nor the other inhabitants of Münster have brought yourselves into compliance with the edict of Worms is not only demonstrated everyday with your manifest and very well-known deeds but also manifestly proven by a comparison of your innovation with that edict and other edicts and recesses from various diets. | We would never have expected that 248 you and your burghers would so obstinately persevere in the course of rebellious sedition that you have undertaken in contempt of the Imperial edict and our pious warning or that you would invoke the privileges of this diocese in specious defense of your case, there being, in our opinion, no occasion for you to invoke it in this case in particular. Accordingly, it would have been fitting and right for you to have considered these matters differently and to have arranged your affairs more prudently. Hence, by this letter we advise and exhort again and again, to the point of excess, that you and your burghers should obey the command of his Imperial Majesty and give due consideration to our pious prayers and friendly admonitions that you should not call down the Emperor's outrage upon you and your townsmen, thereby putting yourselves at great risk through your own fault."

The people of Münster could not, however, be deterred from the obstinate course of rebellion that they had undertaken by any warnings from the prince, however pious and extremely beneficial. Instead, his good willed clemency made them not only bolder in their innovating but even more precipitous, since they were confident of the city's fortifications. This situation had partly offended the prince and the good men and partly terrified them to such an extent that nothing more was needed for the future overthrow of the city. But to avoid it being said of him that by his own authority he was making any overly harsh decision against the city or imposing more burdensome sanctions than was fair, the prince wished to refer everything first to the public consideration and deliberation of the entire nobility, and the time and place established for this deliberation was September 17 in Bilderbeck (this is a little town in the diocese of Münster that is particularly celebrated as the place of death of St. Ludger, the founding bishop). After the nobles had assembled there, the prince, through his orator, praised the nobility, noting their ready compliance with his wishes, and at the same time indicated his own frame of mind and his gratitude towards them in turn. Next, the orator revealed the reason for the assembly and continued as follows.

249   "The nobles summoned here know on the basis of sure and manifest proofs that with their doctrine certain preachers in the city of Münster have in recent days led the ignorant and unwary commons astray from the Word of God and cast them headlong into the most baneful views, and after abolishing the ancient Catholic ceremonies that have been accepted for many centuries, they have, by their own authority, replaced them with new ones which violate the edict of the Emperor and the decisions of the Imperial Diets. They also know that unless this innovation is promptly opposed with their advice and assistance, in many towns and country districts of this excellent diocese error, faction, discord, sedition and disobedience on the part of the subjects and the destruction of the good men, or rather the complete dissolution of the nobility, are to be feared as a result of contamination. Having been elected by God's ordinance as bishop of this diocese, the noble and high-born Francis of Waldeck honestly declares that it is his duty to cure these evils to the best of his ability, and he has down to the present time attempted to achieve this end in many ways, asking of the people of Münster that they remove their preachers and refrain from any innovation until he attains full authority to administer the diocese, at which point he promised that he would look after the interests of all his people on the basis of fairness, so that no one could justly complain. In order that this request should have greater authority, he passed on to the city a copy of the Imperial order forbidding innovation that had been checked against the original. Yet, the people of Münster neglect and spurn all of this, keep their seditious preachers, do away with the customary ecclesiastical rites, substitute uncustomary ones, and exceed the limits of their jurisdiction by seizing the prince's prerogatives, which they usurp for themselves. The prince thinks that these acts should by no means be tolerated by him. Relying, instead, on the help of God

and his friends, he intends to beat down, as far as possible, both the townsmen's impious beliefs and their impudent wantonness in doing whatever they want, so that he may satisfy the command given to him strictly both verbally and in writing by the Emperor at the most recent diet at Regensburg. Since this insolent rebellion of the townsmen | has by no means been checked but will result in the destruction of the whole nobility of this diocese, whom they involve in a disaster similar to their own, the prince asks, nay begs, that you be on your guard for the common honor and benefit of the diocese, consider everything quite carefully, help your prince in a cause both pious and respectable, and save yourselves and your children from the threatening disaster, so that the townsmen's rebellion, sedition, impiety and lusting after every crimes will not break out anew to your destruction and after making the entire diocese, which has always been remarkable for its noblemen, into the laughingstock of foreign populations along with them, and eventually destroy you. Rather, as a warning to others their crimes should be quickly restrained, so that this region may maintain its ancient reputation unharmed, intact and uncontaminated and pass it on to your descendants. What, I ask, is the benefit from this false pretext of religion used by the townsmen? What is the use of specious piety? In this, the Word of God is cleverly stitched together as a concealing cloak for every sort of rebellion, insolence and impunity in malfeasance, so that hatred and enmity, disobedience and rebellion, every sort of contempt for both the ecclesiastical and the secular government, dissension and sedition, slaughter and bloodshed are covered over and concealed, out of which the most certain disaster will in the end burst forth against the city. Let it serve as an example to us that in past years it is mostly for these same reasons that noteworthy disaster has befallen other cities. Accordingly, the prince has no doubt that in this matter you will, of your own accord, do what Christian piety and obedience, the honor of the homeland and, finally, the well-being of yourselves and your children seem to demand. He will not fail to recompense you in turn for carrying out these meritorious duties. The prince desires to receive a reply indicating which of these steps he can expect from you."

To this the nobility responded as follows. The townsmen could not be deterred with any warnings from their obstinate rebellion, religious undertakings and unheard-of innovation in ceremonies, but were all the more zealously pressing on with their business, | neglecting the laws of the faith and of the common compact and becoming alienated from the rest of the other orders of the diocese. Although the prince would

250

251

have been completely within his rights if he had attacked them more fiercely and bitterly—and in that case, the nobility declared that they were obliged to help the prince with advice and assistance—nonetheless, the one thing that they demanded from him for the sake of the general peace was that in his mercy he should temporarily postpone carrying out any more severe punishment that he had in mind for the townsmen. This would avoid causing bitter feelings on both sides as a result of a sudden onslaught, and otherwise the townsmen, being reinforced with the protection of many cities on the pretext of religion and rendered more precipitous because of the fortifications of the city, would drag all the clergy, the whole nobility and the entire diocese down with them into the fullest disaster and permanent ruin. For if they are provoked, they would mix everything up topsy-turvy, confusing the sacred and the secular, so that they could have as many allies as possible in their rashness and downfall, and they were so deranged on account of their religion that they would prefer to endure anything at all rather than give it up. Hence, every effort involving clemency must be taken before resorting to a step as a result of which the downfall of the good men was to be feared. The good men should be considered more than the wicked. The tares should not be pulled up to the detriment of the wheat. The wicked should be temporarily tolerated in the meanwhile, so that when the wicked are restrained with more severe penalties and with great fear, the innocent will not be included in their downfall. Accordingly, let the prince not blaze forth with excessive anger because of the townsmen's impudence and insolence, and the passage of time would recommend a method of punishment that would restrain them without harming the good men. According to the dictates of necessity, the nobles would, if at all possible, bring it about that the townsmen should, after casting off the seditious preachers and bringing back the ancient ceremonies, be reconciled with the prince. If, on the other hand, this could not be achieved, they would join forces with the prince to execute whatever kind of penalty he wished."

This response from the nobility was heard by the prince with good will and brought the townsmen a delay in punishment until the last measures that seemed conducive to restoring peace had been tried. Lest this difficult matter that was replete with trouble should be conducted with insufficient gravity, eight prestigious noblemen whose authority was respected by almost everyone were chosen to give counsel to the vicars of the diocese, receiving from the knighthood the official authorization to make decisions and pronouncements on the understanding that

whatever they decided would be considered valid. Their names were |
John of Münster, bailiff of Steinfurt, Bernard of Westerholt, Godfrey
of Schedelich, Caspar Smising, John of Asbeck, John of Büren, John
of Merfelt the younger, and Henry of Merfelt the bailiff. After choosing
these men to negotiate with the people of Münster in the assembly at
Bilderbeck, the knighthood sent a letter to the council and leaders of
the commons on the same day (September 17), as follows.

"We have unanimously decided that since we are busy, the vicars of
this diocese and other men of outstanding influence who have been
chosen by us from the knighthood should negotiate with you for your
own sake about important matters that concern the well-being of the
diocese, and for this reason we ask that at 8 a.m. on the Monday after
the Feast of Matthew[70] you come without prevarication to Wolbeck to
hear the logic underlying our advice and to deliberate in light of this
with the vicars and with our representatives about the clear demands
of necessity in order that on that basis peace and tranquility will be
established and strengthened in the state. We have no doubt that since
this is in your interest, you will readily comply with our requests."

Having also received authorization for this from the knighthood,
on September 18 the representatives wrote to the council and the
other estates of the city, in the following words. It was with the greatest distress, they said, that they had learned within the last few days
that the prince and the people of Münster were disaffected from one
another because of a change in religion and ceremonies. As a lack
of peacefulness swelled up among certain people, this could lead to
certain acts, which, if they were not calmed through the intervention
of peace-makers, could cause the destruction not only of those who
were party to the dispute but also of all those who were caught in the
middle. For nothing is more detrimental to a state than for its heads
to disagree among themselves, since if both sides are inflamed with
the desire to cause harm, they squeeze the members, who are caught
in the middle, and entangle them in great misfortunes.[71] Therefore, to
avoid a situation where the entire diocese would be cast headlong into
such perils, the representatives had been entrusted by the knighthood

---

[70] September 23.
[71] This sentence is based on a play on words in Latin. *Membrum* signifies both literally a "limb" of the body and metaphorically the "member" of a group of people.
Medieval political thought compared the government and members of the body politic
to the head and limbs of the human body.

253   with the task | of cutting short this destructive disaffection and then, if possible, of resolving and dispelling it without harm to this homeland. The representatives promised that they would readily do this, since these matters concerned the well-being and general peace not of one person but of everyone. Accordingly, by the authority of the entire nobility, at whose command they were carrying out this embassy, they entreated and beseeched the estates of the city to be mindful of their own well-being and to send plenipotentiary representatives on September 23 to Wolbeck (a little town located about one mile from Münster). In that place there would be deliberation on a matter that would cleanse the diocese of all factions and internal disturbances and, after restoring, with God's help, the diocese to its former tranquility, keep it in that state for the longest period of time possible.

It was not without reason that neither the main clergy nor the burgher masters of the other towns were invited to this day of deliberation in the customary way. First, the people of Münster would have considered the main clergy, whom they did not allow to be named, to be responsible for everything that they imagined to be directed against them at that meeting, and as a result the clergy would have incurred even greater enmity among the townsmen. As for the second point, since a certain number of towns in the diocese had adopted the same innovation, their presence would have made the people of Münster even more bold and impetuous. Accordingly, it was better for those whose presence would have been more a hindrance than help in the matter at hand to be absent.

The representatives of the people of Münster arrived on the appointed time and place, and after they had been brought into the presence of the noble delegates for the discussion, the official given the vernacular title "marshal" spoke as follows. The council, aldermen and guild masters had been summoned by letter to this assembly in a friendly way, but neither of the burgher masters was present and instead some foreign orator was to be seen among the representatives. Accordingly, the vicars of the diocese and the delegates chosen by the knighthood to convene this meeting wished to receive a declaration as to whether the people of Münster had come there with the intention

254   of listening to the delegation from the nobility with good will, | and after receiving an answer they would consider more fully what needed to be done. For it was the accepted practice of ancestral custom that in meetings to discuss the common well-being at least one if not both burgher masters should be present.

Understanding that he was viewed as a foreign member of the delegation from Münster, Goswin of Velmede, the orator for the people of Münster, answered as follows. A few days ago he had come to Münster to complete some business, and at that time the council had asked him to undertake the job of orator and act on behalf of the burghers at this meeting. If, however, he came to the conclusion that this business was acting against the interests of the prince, nobility or diocese, he would voluntarily dissociate himself from the people of Münster.

The people of Münster also responded to the marshal's statement, as follows. The burgher masters had not been in town when the nobility's letter had arrived, and the council relayed it to them. The reply from them was that one was gravely ill and the other had been seriously injured when his grazing horse suffered a fall, and accordingly neither of them could be present at the appointed time. The aldermen, guild masters and other representatives of the city, on the other hand, were present in order to hear with good will the words that the delegates were instructed to say. At this point, the marshal of the diocese thanked the people of Münster for having readily attended this meeting when summoned by the knighthood's letter, and he gave the following report.

A few days ago, he said, the prince had summoned the knighthood of the entire diocese to Bilderbeck and laid out the following points. After having been elected as bishop of the diocese of Münster, he found out through sure indications and factual proofs that recently certain lowly and insignificant fellows who were Lutheran preachers had crept into the city of Münster. They perceived that the pliable commons were devoted to their preaching, and being protected by their advice and help, they had ill-advisedly seized the city's parish churches without the permission of the lawful secular government, being carried away by their own authority. | They deposed the lawfully appointed pastors and   255
chaplains, substituting themselves in their place, and in their sermons they disseminated among the ignorant and unwary commoners very many erroneous, divisive and baneful innovations and views, inciting them to every sort of rebellion, impudence and insolence and increasing the hatred felt for the order of presbyters[72] in particular in order to bring about the destruction of the entire clergy. As a result of this contempt for all rulers, both secular and ecclesiastical, was to be feared. They not only had thrown out all the pious rites that were Catholic

---

[72] The context suggests that this signifies the main clergy.

and traditional along with tranquility, unity and obedience but had changed, nay altogether abolished, them in violation of the Emperor's edict and the decisions of the Imperial Diets and in derision or contempt of their secular government. The prince, on the other hand, having noted with the greatest distress this seditious insurrection mounted by the burghers against the Church within the city's walls, had often, by virtue of the Imperial edict, whose execution had been entrusted to him by an Imperial letter, as he demonstrated to the nobility, written to the people of Münster to warn them in a friendly way to refrain from their divisive sedition, give up their preachers, unanimously embrace the ancestral Catholic religion, and cherish peace and mutual concord until the abuses were done away with in a general reformation.[73] Ignoring all this advice, however, the preachers, along with their following of the same stripe and the seditious dregs of the commoners' faction, had persisted in this rebellion, casting to the winds and altogether despising the edict of his Imperial Majesty and the prince's friendly warnings. They had completely abolished and done away with all the ecclesiastical rites and the worship of God that rouses the people with a passion for the duties of piety, and had by their own caprice replaced them with an immoral, impious and schismatic way of life. Up until the present they had been devoted to this terrible example in which they wallowed, though in the end nothing was to be expected of it but a deplorable look in the city, the destruction of general tranquility, the neglect of obedience, the overthrow of the government, mutual civil slaughter, the shedding of kindred blood, and the most certain downfall of the entire diocese. "Since[74] the prince has also noted that the people of Münster are obstinately clinging to their impious faction and the undertaking of rebellion, and could not be pacified with any warnings, however friendly, he thought that it was his duty and role | to ward off and avert from his subjects any misfortune through the help of God and the assistance of his friends, and to check and restrain the burghers because of the rebellion they have set in motion with the obstacle of lawful penalties to avoid the eventuality that they would become more and more insolent through long-standing impunity, and, as often happens, drag down the innocent precipitously into the same disaster by infecting them. Instead,

256

---

[73] Here "reformation" refers to internal attempts at reform within the Catholic Church, a common meaning in the years before Luther.

[74] Here K. suddenly begins to translate the response in direct quotation.

his aim is to restore civil peace, religious unity and obedience towards the government and after restoring them preserve them for as long as possible. In this matter the prince earnestly asks for advice and assistance from us. The knighthood is deliberating about this affair, and the more deeply considered opinion of its timely reflection is that this innovation rashly undertaken by the people of Münster will bring an exceptional revolution and destruction not only to the burghers and the city but also to the entire diocese, and that as a result, after the bonds by which this city was, by the grace of God, always tied in loyalty to the prince and the other estates of the diocese are broken asunder, the city will in the end collapse in unending disaster and drag down with it into this calamity the largest number of people possible. The threat of these misfortunes is such that the nobility and the other estates of the diocese will not refrain from using the most careful diligence and the highest zeal to forestall them as far as is possible." Accordingly, in a friendly and familiar way the knighthood offered for their salvation the carefully considered and serious advice and request that the council, aldermen and guild masters, and indeed the entire state, should examine the matter from all the best perspectives, carefully consider it and reconsider it, putting both their own and the city's salvation and destruction in the balance, obey the edict and command of his Imperial Majesty and the frequent written warnings of our prince, abandon the preachers, reject all the uncustomary rites and innovations introduced by their own authority, restoring the ancient ceremonies now hallowed by age and the original decoration of the churches to their previous position of dignity and respect, and willingly allow themselves to be penalized with the punishment for rebellion that they deserved for violating the Imperial edict. If the people of Münster would accede to this, there was no doubt that given his inherent mercy, the prince would, without any admonition and of his own accord, make sure that if there existed within the city any abuse, any disturbance or any dispute between the religious and the laity concerning religion and ceremonies, he would do away with it with his advice and assistance | and restore the longed   257 for tranquility with fine or fair terms. Consequently, the prince, the city and its inhabitants, and the entire diocese would thus live together for the longest period of time possible in mutual concord and the Christian religion, as had been the case up until then. If the knighthood had any influence with the prince in this matter because of their advice and assistance, they would not fail the city in using all their waking efforts to cast out discord and restore peace. If, on the other hand, the people of Münster did not acknowledge the Imperial edict, the prince's very frequent and friendly warnings and the great favor and beneficial counsels of the knighthood, and instead went on with their obstinacy, impiety, rash presumptuousness, and zealous pursuit of disagreement, which was not to be expected, the knighthood of the entire diocese would not fail to give the prince their advice, assistance and action, but would, in their adherence to him, join their forces with his in order to free the city and the whole region from the Emperor's outrage and punishment. The knighthood expressed its great desire to be informed as to which of these courses the people of Münster would take.

After the marshal brought his speech to an end, the representatives of the townsmen gave the following response after holding a consultation. They would be eternally grateful to the knighthood for the present good turn, favor and outstanding goodwill that they had shown to the city of Münster in removing their disadvantageous situation. But the vicars and the delegates chosen by the knighthood to settle the dispute in the present case could easily realize with their great wisdom that it was not within the power of representatives, especially ones not granted full authority, to agree that the townsmen would give up and oppose their factious rebellion and plotting of revolution, and that instead they had to report for the entire city's deliberation the terms that had been laid out before them, though certainly in the confident expectation that the disagreement would be settled. They said that being in particular need of the nobility's advice in this matter they asked them not to fail to give it, so that the rebellion of the commoners, which all good men had always opposed and for which the commons and not the government were responsible, should be halted and uprooted. Hence, they asked to be given fourteen days to deliberate with all the estates of the city.

258   To this the vicars and the delegation of the nobility gave the following response. It was not in their power to grant them such a long period of time to take counsel, and they dared not exceed their instructions, since they had been strictly and officially enjoined to demand a firm and unalterable decision from the representatives of the townsmen without delay. Although this situation did not allow private modification, they would nonetheless grant them one day to consult with their people. And if the people of Münster were willing to comply with and obey the terms set out, the knighthood would not fail to give them advice and assistance, so that the city, the nobility and the other estates of the

diocese would remain bound together in tranquility and full peace, as had been the case until then.

The people of Münster persisted in their request to be granted a fourteen-day period for deliberation, and although the vicars and the noble representatives produced the instructions in which the knighthood and the prince specified that a very short period of time was to be granted to the people of Münster for deliberation, the representatives of Münster complained to the contrary that the innovation in religion and ceremonies had taken such hold of the minds of the burghers and set down such deep roots that it was impossible to eradicate it quickly. Therefore, they said, they again and again asked that the vicars and representatives of the knighthood should in their mercy grant the amount of time asked for, promising that in that case they would zealously strive to the best of their abilities to restore the peace. In the end, they managed with difficulty to get a grant of two days, on the understanding that within this time they would give the knighthood a serious answer as to what they were going to do in order to avoid the possibility that the prince might, if they gave a different sort of answer, give vent more bitterly to the sense of outrage that he had conceived against the city because of the rebellion, something that the knighthood would strive with all its might to prevent. The representatives from Münster, however, did not budge from their request for fourteen days, since the undertaking of sedition could not be settled so quickly. For, they said, if the burghers' activities were suddenly checked, the council feared the worst consequences for itself in its innocence,[75] since a sudden change in the city's affairs had always been a source of danger and had never been achieved without great uproar. In order for them to avoid being responsible for many deaths, they entreated the vicars and the representatives of the knighthood to use the wisdom with which they were endowed to consider and reflect upon this matter more deeply | and not to deny them such a small period of time for deliberation,   259 promising that within that time they would bring a definite answer to Wolbeck or any other place determined by the knighthood.

---

[75] This is apparently a mistranslation on K.'s part. The original seems to state that the representatives feared for their own safety: "they would be killed by the council like the innocent" (*se vam rade als de unschuldigen umb de halsse komen*). (It is not clear why the "innocent" should be killed, and perhaps this is itself a mistake for *als de schuldigen*, i.e., "as those responsible.")

When the vicars and the noble delegation neither wished nor dared to give an extension of more than two days, the representatives of Münster gave the following answer. Since such an uproar and sedition in the city could in no way be settled suddenly and the small amount they had in supplication requested for deliberation was rashly denied to them, if, then, the matter unexpectedly turned out badly, the vicars and nobles should remember this day on which the representatives of Münster had both invoked the privileges of the diocese and in supplication asked for a mere fourteen days to deliberate on a matter involving the life and salvation of the innocent. To this the vicars answered as follows. It was not within their power to grant an extension. As for the invocation of the privileges of the homeland, they were not relevant in the present case and could not be twisted to suit it. Nonetheless, said the vicars, they would tenaciously remember the statements made by the representatives of Münster, so that if the occasion arose in the future, they would not seem to have forgotten. They in turn asked that if the beneficial warnings and peaceable advice of the knighthood were ignored, the representatives of Münster should recall the good turn, goodwill and favor that had been discarded contrary to the homeland's privileges.

Since the representatives could not get the fourteen days, they asked that they should at least be given eight, promising that within that time they would give a definite answer in the name of the city of Münster. After a short deliberation, the vicars and the nobles granted the eight days, expecting that the prince would not take it amiss if all the strife and the calamity of the impending disaster was prevented. They did so on the condition that the people of Münster would follow the warnings and advice of the knighthood, and otherwise be mindful of the goodwill shown them. Next, after all the negotiations had been carefully drawn up by both sides as a protocol, the meeting was ended and the participants went their separate ways.

After returning to the city, the representatives of Münster copied out the protocol in the form of a letter of information and showed it to Rothman. While they engaged in private and public deliberation and consultation, on September 25, Rothman spewed out the responses that 260 they had written against the terms laid out by the marshal | and offered them to the assembled council, aldermen and guild masters with the intention that in the coming meeting the council should relay these to the knighthood as their official response, as if the council were in need of someone else's advice and of Rothman's services as a wordsmith.

Copy of Rothman's response

"Response to the instruction set out by the vicars and knighthood of the diocese of Münster to the city's representatives on September 23 at Wolbeck.

"First, the vicars and the representatives of the knighthood will be thanked for their loyal warning, for the offered support and consolatory promise of their good services. Even if these had not been offered, the city of Münster considers that they would not be missed because of the superiority of their case and because of their privileges. Since a definite response was asked for by the knighthood at the meeting at Wolbeck, they should receive this one with good will and discretion.

"As for the first item (that the bishop elect has discovered through reliable indications that certain lowly and insignificant fellows and Lutheran preachers have crept into the city, and after making the people devoted to them, seized the churches of the city with their help and without the authority of the government, casting out the lawful pastors and preaching impious and seditious doctrines, and so on) our response is this. If anything that is impious or incompatible with the true office has been introduced in the business of religion, so that anyone could justly complain about it, it did not arise from us or from the commons but from the preachers, who promise that they will give a perfectly justifiable defense of their doctrine without any recourse to violence. If, then, there is anyone who can lodge any accusation against them or our burghers, we will not shut the courts of our city to him, but we allow what will be just in our tribunal to be carried out (this procedure will prevent the violation of the privileges and royal rights of our city being violated).

"Second, as for the claim that by the Emperor's command we have been ordered by the prince in writing to oppose the impious, seditious and forbidden doctrine by expelling the preachers but instead have unalterably persisted in this rebellion in contemptuous derision of the Imperial edict and the prince's well-intentioned warning, | our   261
response is this. If anyone censures our preachers or burghers for a fault of which they cannot clear themselves with legitimate arguments, or if, as is fair, he proves the criticism made of us, not only will we give up our plan and remove the preachers but we will also inflict the due penalties on those convicted of criminal wrongdoing. For we have always opposed what is impious, unrighteous and false, and pursued what is pious, righteous and true. Thus, the matter has been referred to the parish priests and those in other positions, so that if they think

of any complaint against the doctrine of the preachers, they should bring it to the light of day. But no one has come forward. We have also written in supplication to our prince with the request that he turn this dispute over to fair arbitrators for judgment, so that it should be revealed who defends the more righteous case. Since the commons are convinced of the truth of the doctrines that they have heard from their preachers, who do promise that they will defend these doctrines, but no one among the parish priests or other curates of our souls or anyone else overwhelms these doctrines with more solid arguments from Holy Scripture, it is difficult, nay impossible, to drag the commons away from the truth.

"Third, since we are criticized for having completely abolished and removed from the parish churches the worship of God and all praise-worthy ceremonies, we are necessarily compelled to note how each act was carried out. It so happens that everyday now the commoners seek to know the true God through being educated in Holy Scripture in order to do away with every dispute between the ecclesiastical order and the laity (one preacher says one thing and the next another), and that at their request the government of Münster announced to the parish priests and chaplains that they should teach the Word of God without the admixture of falsity and refrain from teaching falsity as doctrine. When, however, these priests and chaplains declared that they knew no abuses, the preachers wrote them up in a list and offered it to us. We therefore convened a meeting of our pastors and curates of souls, laying these abuses before them so that they should either overwhelm them with arguments or refrain from their own ceremonies if they are impious. But to the present day nothing has been alleged against the abuses compiled by the preachers, and the priests and chaplains have instead allowed their own ceremonies to fall into abeyance and die out. For our own part, we could have allowed everything that was not contrary to true piety, but since neither our clergy nor anyone on 262   their behalf | is able or willing to defend their position and refute the preachers' list, we can in no way make the commoners return to the ancients rites in the churches before the propriety of such practices is demonstrated and the doctrine of the preachers refuted. If, on the other hand, the doctrine of the preachers is refuted with legitimate arguments, we will readily obey you in this matter, as we always do otherwise. Therefore, we ask that the vicars and the knighthood strive to convince the prince that he should, with the assistance of all the estates of this diocese and at our expense (since this is in the interest of all the inhabitants of the diocese, as the marshal stated), summon from elsewhere learned men of great authority. To them both sides will entrust the right to assess and decide the matter, and if in their judgment the preachers are convicted of erring and of teaching impious doctrines, they should be sentenced to their deserved punishments. For as long as they are not found guilty of error, and instead publicly profess their doctrine in writing and speech and invoke the protection of the truth without anyone coming forward to dare to prove them guilty of error, there is no opportunity to expel the preachers, this being the only kind of force we can apply. However, in order that the vicars, the representatives and the entire knighthood should know that we, along with the entire citizenry of this city, are zealous in our pursuit of the truth and of fairness and are not plotting any rebellion against anyone, we have ordered the preachers to refrain temporarily from giving sermons. If their doctrine will, in the meanwhile, be proven to be impious by anyone, they will not escape the lawful penalty. If in the meanwhile the prince too organizes the matter of religion into a pious, Christian order, we will very readily embrace it unasked."

Rothman stitched together this document for delivery as the response to the vicars and the knighthood, doing so in the name of the council but without any authorization from it. The council, however, quashed it in order not to be dependent upon his advice and suggestions and to avoid offending the knighthood with this emotive document, which was full of irony and sarcasm and seemed to be a pleading on behalf of the preachers. After deliberating, they told the representatives what response they should give in the name of the city. The representatives returned to Wolbeck to give this response on the eighth day granted to them (September 30). There they found at the meeting the noblemen Gerard of Recke, a golden knight,[76] Gerard Morrien the marshal, Arnold of Raesfeld, Godfrey of Schedelich and Bernard of Westerholt, | and the scribe Master Eberhard Aelius. These men declared that they   263 had the authority to act on behalf of the count of Bentheim and the rest of the absent nobility, and to them the representatives of Münster relayed the following message.

---

[76] This is a technical expression for a knight who received his knighthood through being dubbed personally rather than through inheritance. Comparatively uncommon, this status was indicated by the privilege of using golden spurs and stirrups, which gave rise to the title.

They said that they had, on September 23, received the requests that
had been made by the knighthood assembled at Wolbeck in written and
oral form concerning the city's preachers and the rites in its churches,
and they had laid these requests out to the council, aldermen and guild
masters and to all the estates of the city whose interests were involved.
Since after many entreaties and much suppliant begging eight days for
deliberation had been granted to them only with the greatest difficulty by
the vicars and the noble delegation, accordingly, in light of the amount
of time given them they had left no stone unturned every day in their
efforts at advising, requesting and beseeching now the commons and
now the leaders to whom the commons harkened most. Day after day,
they had expected a definite answer about restoring the ceremonies in
the churches and removing the new preachers, but down to the present
time they had been unable to manage this. Therefore, it was not in
their power to give any definite answer in the name of the city to the
items laid before them, and thus they asked the vicars and the noble
delegation that being mindful of the dangerous toil undertaken by the
representatives in an attempt to lessen the commons' madness, they
should not suspect them of malfeasance but should argue earnestly for
their innocence before the prince. Since the clergy had, through the
assistance of learned men, come up with a counter-argument against
Rothman's articles, the prince should turn over this case for decision
by fair arbitrators, so that the preachers would be convicted of error
and acquiesce in Holy Scripture. If this request was granted, there
was no doubt that the commons would accept different doctrine and
thus easily allow the ancestral religion to be restored. If, on the other
hand, the prince could not be persuaded to adopt this course of action,
which they hardly expected, they were sure that the prince's concern,
civility and fairness were such that he would certainly not inflexibly
force upon the city of Münster's council, aldermen and guild masters
actions that they could not perform. The representatives also invoked
the assistance of the regular law and of the Imperial edict promulgated
at Regensburg on August 3 and made known in Münster on September
264   9 and in different cities of the Empire | at various intervals, expecting
that neither the council or any individual would be oppressed or treated
inappropriately in violation of these measures.

To this the nobles responded that they wished to report the negotia-
tion to the prince in the exact form in which it was conducted.

This is the gist of the Imperial edict mentioned above. It was
clear that many seditions and various dangerous situations had arisen

throughout the Empire in the name of the faith and of religion, and
it was to be feared that the result of this would be very bitter uproars,
dissensions, wars and irreparable devastation and damage to assorted
populations, and in the end, unless timely counsel prevented this,
the destruction, downfall and lamentable demise of all of Germany,
particularly at that time, when the Turk was considering a campaign
against Hungary, Austria and the other regions of Germany. Therefore,
in order to provide for tranquility in Germany, the Emperor Charles
V ordered that a general peace was to be maintained, intending that
no one was to use the excuse of the faith and of religion or any other
matter to harass someone else with arms, plundering, stealing, burning
or taking captives, to attack or suppress him with violence either by
himself or through another, and that no one was to harbor the violators of this edict until the dispute about religion was settled either in
a general council[77] or by the Imperial Diet.

Knipperdolling and certain members of his faction imagined that
they were being oppressed by the bishop and clergy, and they also
sent to the Imperial Chamber Court[78] a complaint in the name of the
council and city of Münster, though without the council's authorization or even its knowledge. On September 23 they begged for and
received an injunction against the bishop and clergy that would, they
imagined, help them. The gist of the injunction was as follows. The
burgher masters, council and the entire city | of Münster explained   265
to the Chamber Court with their sad complaints that in recent times
they and the lower clergy had, without the participation of the bishop,
reached an agreement that certain intolerable ceremonies should be
abolished and the Word of God announced to the people in a pure
manner without any additions made by human enactments, just as was
very reasonably provided for at the Diet of Nuremberg, and that it was
not right to deprive anyone of his possessions undeservedly, whether he
belonged to the religious or the laity. The bishop, however, had been
incited at the suggestion and urging (as was suspected) of the main clergy
to terrify the townsmen with frequent threatening letters. Indeed, he
had led off certain men under arrest and committed other acts which
would have long since caused a noteworthy sedition and the shedding

---

[77] I.e., an ecumenical council of the Catholic Church.
[78] German *Reichskammergericht*. This court was established at the Diet of Worms in
1495 as a venue in which the estates of the Empire could settle their disputes through
legal adjudication rather than by resorting to force.

of human blood if thoughtful planning had not forestalled this. What was worse, the canons, who were responsible for this misfortune, would have driven the townsmen headlong into disaster with their clever and under-handed schemes if the crime they had resolved upon had not been providentially checked by God. Since these townsmen were eager to avoid sedition, calamity and the destruction of their city, they had invoked the common rights of the Empire and received an injunction against the bishop and the main clergy, the Emperor thereby commanding that they should not inflict any violence upon the burgher masters, council and city of Münster and on its inhabitants under any excuse of wrong doing. Otherwise, they would themselves pay the penalty for violating the peace and the Empire's outrage.

In the presence of Peter Mensing, Herman Krampe, Bernard Bontorpen, Ludger Mumme and Henry Xanten,[79] who were the elected representatives of the commons, Bernard Knipperdolling handed this injunction over to the aldermen so that in the name of all the guilds they would deliver it to the council for them to announce it to the bishop and main clergy. After reading it, however, the council refused to carry out this task, since it had been gotten not by the authority of the burgher masters, who were in exile, or of the council, but | by that of a few individuals. Thus it was sent back to Knipperdolling through the aldermen, so that he could make use of it as he wished.

266

Being unwilling to be made a fool of by the townsmen any more, the prince ordered his bailiffs and stewards throughout the diocese of Münster to sequester the property of those men in particular whom he understood to be the leaders of the sedition. In obedience of this order, at Werne at around 8 o'clock on October 8, they halted the cattle of Caspar Judefeld and of other burghers that were being driven to Cologne, and then detained them by virtue of the chief judge's authority and the prince's order. (Werne is a little town of the diocese of Münster about four miles from the town itself.) Next, on October 9 the prince wrote to the council, aldermen and guild masters in the following words.

"We thought that you would have set higher value on our friendly and clearly fatherly warnings and on your well-being and the safety of

---

[79] There is much confusion over this man's last name. Dorp calls him Santes, but K. gives the forms Xantus, Xantis and Sanctus. The initial "x" perhaps suggests that K. associated it with the town of Xanten.

the entire homeland than on your rash pursuits, and we would not have expected that in derision of our reputation and in defiance of the obedience that you owe to us as your ruler you would be so concerned about the divisive innovation introduced into your city and of the preachers who are responsible for all the sedition in the city, much less that you would be such impetuous defenders and supporters. Having discovered that the opposite is the case, however, we would long since have been perfectly within our rights to have taken more severe and harsh steps against you and the other inhabitants of the city of Münster, as the best reasoning and the emperor's command, a copy of which we have relayed to you, dictate. In our mercy, however, we have up until now given you the favor of not doing so in the hope that you would become mindful of the common well-being and would restore the institutions you rashly abolished and remove the preachers you foolishly let in, so that we will not pile up the emperor's outrage and the Empire's penalty to the detriment of ourselves and our diocese. Being unable, however, to attain either of these aims from you, we ordered that the goods of certain burghers who were notable in pressing on with the business of sedition should be sequestered, | deciding to exercise our rights against   267
them, by virtue of the chief judge's authority. We therefore earnestly warn you that you should not take them under your protection and custody to the extent of removing them from our jurisdiction and the punishment they deserve. Otherwise, with the assistance of God and of all the estates of the diocese, we shall try out against you the steps demanded by justice and the emperor's edict. If, however, any of you is innocent or now regrets the sedition and wishes to return to obedience, we will, if his name is made known to us, adopt the same attitude towards him as we have towards you, and he will not be bereft of our good will and grace. We desire to be informed of which of these courses of action you have in mind."

After the ominous story about the seizure of the burghers' cattle had become widely disseminated, incredibly fearsome fulminations were uttered by the seditious men and resounded throughout the whole city at the beginning of the madness, as is usually the case. They reviled the bishop with pointless curses and imprecations, some calling him a tyrant, others their oppressor. Some referred to him as the meagre, paltry count (though he was actually corpulent), others bellowed that he was unworthy of his position. Some accused him of lacking wisdom and prudence for daring to provoke such a well-fortified city, others held the main clergy responsible for the misfortune since these were all happening at their urging. Some advised that the cattle should be reclaimed physically, others that the prince himself should be sought out. If they had not lacked confidence in their ability to return, their blind rage would have urged many other steps. Some, being terrified by the start of the misfortunes, lamented to themselves in their anxiety about the future, others who had invested almost all their fortune in purchasing cattle feared for their cattle that were still in pasture. Some secretly took their cattle from the pastures at night and successfully drove them away over long and circuitous paths, but others unwarily fell into the hands of the bishop's stewards.

268   During these events, those who had lost cattle complained to the council that their property had been wrongfully and violently taken away from them by the bishop's stewards, and for this reason on October 11 the council sent the prince a written supplication to secure the return of the cattle, as follows. Certain of their citizens who had been about to drive off their fattened cattle to sell them in Cologne had complained to the council that certain of their cattle had been stopped on the journey while still in this diocese and sequestered by the bishop's bailiffs and stewards. The council did not know the reason why this had been done, since the owners owed the bailiffs and stewards nothing as a debt or surety. Accordingly, the council was roused by the burghers' complaints to inform the prince of this in writing and to ask at the same time that since such property would naturally decline in value as a result of long sequestration, the bailiffs should, at the prince's command, release the cattle from the pens and restore them to the burghers, and that they should in future refrain from this sort of seizure and sequestration of burghers' goods. If, on the other hand, the prince, chapter, nobility and diocese of Münster as a whole imposed just burdens that did not conflict with the diocese's privileges, the council would not take this amiss. They asked the prince to write back what reward the burghers could hope for from this supplication.

The council sent a letter of virtually the same content to the dean and the main chapter, asking that they plead before the prince the case of the burghers whose property had been stripped from them, and that once the sequestration was cancelled, the burghers should go about their business activities without harm or fear. If, on the other hand, the prince or anyone else thought that they had a complaint against the council or their citizens, the council said that they should pursue the matter legally.

On October 12, the prince responded to the letter sent to him as follows. He had several times been led by his very great grace and good will to write to the people of Münster to ask of them in a friendly manner that they should cast away the impious, divisive and seditious innovations rashly allowed in violation of the emperor's edict and the Empire's decree and in contempt of both the ecclesiastical and the secular government, and that they should return to the original religion and concordant mode of living, just as the knighthood had constantly, with equal zeal and concern, warned and asked them to do in the name of all the estates of the diocese. | All these efforts, however, had been   269
endured fruitlessly, and as the people of Münster cast everything to the winds, it was impossible to sway them with any warnings or entreaties. The bishop, then, had long had the most just grounds, given the dictates of the emperor's edict, to take more severe steps against the people of Münster (especially those responsible for the innovation) and their property in connection with stamping out their obstinate sedition and to suppress their undertakings in the same way that the seditious had pressed on with them. He had indicated this in earlier letters, but as a favor to them he had postponed action until the present time. Now, however, since they were not bringing their tumultuous behavior to an end, the circumstances demanded that he should resort to this legal step, and he thought that he should henceforth persevere in it. Since it was in violation not only of the city's privileges but also of the emperor's edict, the decisions of princes and all the magistrates that the people of Münster had begun the establishment of their seditious schism and were protecting it and illegally maintaining it within their walls to the present day, it was pointless and contrary to legal reasoning that they should invoke the protection of those privileges, and this invocation would not be recognized by him. For he who had violated the law was unworthy of its help. He would shun the sight of no one, but would publicly give an account of his action before any princes of the Empire or any other men of good sense. Accordingly, he again advised and urged them, as he had done so often, to be mindful of their own and the whole diocese's well-being and obey the emperor's edict and the prince's very frequent warnings by casting down the seditious preachers and restoring the ecclesiastical ceremonies and all the adornment of the churches to their original place of dignity, and by keeping those guilty of sedition in their own custody without protecting them from justice and the penalty for law-breaking and handing

them over for punishment once they were convicted. If this was denied to the prince, as had been the case up until then, he would, with the help of the Almighty and the assistance of the princes and his friends, justly suppress the seditious, schismatic, impious plotting of the people of Münster until they repent of their sedition, becoming peaceful and obeying the Imperial edict. They should consider this the response that they had asked for.

270   Henry Hake, the dean of the main chapter, also answered, as follows. He had received the letter from the council about the cattle of certain burghers that had been put under sequester while in transit by the stewards and bailiffs of the most reverend bishop. Since he represented only one person among the members of the chapter and knew that it was not in his power to make a decision by himself without the votes of the others, he would find out the views of the other lords who lived in reasonably close proximity. Whatever they decided he would send on as a well-intentioned answer. Dispatched at Schönebeck on the Saturday after the feast of Sts. Gereon and Victor.[80]

After holding a consultation with a few noble canons, the dean wrote a petition to the prince on the same day on behalf of the burghers whose property had been sequestered. The prince for his part wrote that he had responded to the council's petition seeking the cancellation of the sequestration and restitution of the cattle, including a copy of his response with his letter to the chapter. He did not think that he should change his course of action under the circumstances. On October 14 the dean passed this answer from the prince on to council so that they could learn of the zeal and care with which he had pled the case of the people of Münster before the prince.

On October 12, the prince also wrote to the individual guilds letters of virtually the same content as he had to the council, now warning, now entreating them not to pollute themselves and their children with impious schism and voluntarily plunge them into destruction. He asked them to banish the madness from the city by their own authority just as they had introduced it by their own authority, and to embrace tranquility, cultivate mutual peace and revere their government. He gave them this and other well-intentioned advice.

Both burgher masters and certain other members of the council had resigned their office, going into voluntary exile, and although they had

---

[80] October 12.

often been summoned back to duty, they refused to make themselves available to the city. It was therefore decided that the council should be restored to its full membership by replacing them, especially now that the city was tied up in rather complicated entanglements. Accordingly, on the Monday after the feast of Sts. Gereon and Victor (October 14), an assembly for electing the government was held in the commons' hall. | After the aldermen and the guild masters along with all the guild members had gathered there, everyone voted to fill the council by election. From there, then, they proceeded to the council hall in the customary way, though at a different time, and they voted for the electors by ward. Peter Mensing and Herman Krampe were returned from St. Martin's Ward, John Baggel and Master John in der Bade the smith from St. Lambert's, Herman Wedemhave and John Wechler from St. Ludger's, Gerard Kibbenbrock and Herman Redeker from St. Giles', Anthony Grotevader from the Ward Across-the-River, and Henry Roede the goldsmith from the Jews' Field Ward. After giving their oath, these men entered the council chamber, and in the place of the four men who had defected (Wilbrand Plonies, Eberwin Droste, Bernard of Tinnen, and Herman Heerde) they freely elected Anthony Jonas, John Bastert, Henry Fridagh and John Palck the iron smith.

271

A few days later, on October 18, the council responded to the prince as follows. A few days ago, they said, they had received the prince's letter concerning the legal halting and detention of their burghers' cattle. As their well-intentioned response they did not wish to conceal from the prince the fact that in recent days representatives of the council, aldermen and guild masters had been sent to Wolbeck to give to the vicars of the diocese and the delegation of the nobility the response that the council had striven with all its zealous industry to bring it about, namely that the priests should be removed and the ceremonies restored to the churches to avoid offending his Imperial Majesty in any regard, but that the council had hardly been able to achieve this. The main reason for this was that Lord Bernard Rothman had offered to the pastors, chaplains and other heads of churches in Münster, first, articles about his doctrine and, then, with the advice and assistance of his people, further articles about the abuses that had for some time taken over the Church, but these men had not yet given any response to the articles or refuted them with Holy Scripture, although the council was aware that the clergy of Münster had received a retort to those articles from learned men. Since, therefore, the council and all the burghers had always invoked the rights and privileges of the diocese as they were doing at present, the council begged with all the energy it could muster that in light of his mercy the prince should put the better interpretation on everything and let this case involving the preachers and ceremonies come before fair judges, that the articles should be generally distributed among them and examined to be refuted with manifest passages of Scripture, and that in the business of religion a specific formulation be established that it would be fair for both clergy and laity to obey. The council also asked that | the sequestration be cancelled so that the burghers could get their cattle back, and that they not in future be harassed in violation of their invocation of justice and privilege, but that they be protected against all violence and daily harm. The council asked to receive a response as to which of these courses was to be expected from the prince.

272

To this letter was attached a sheet, the text of which was as follows. "Also, most reverend prince, since you have written to the individual guilds of our city, the response to your letter, which was presented to us by them in the customary manner, we pass on to you with our own letter. We are sure that you will take this action reasonably. You will readily perceive the attitude of the burghers from the response. Dated as above."

The response of the guilds to the prince sent on October 18: "We have, most reverend and glorious prince, received with suitable veneration your letter that was brought to us. Having read it, we learned to our very great distress that we had fallen under suspicion in your eyes of having instigated sedition and rebellion and that we were judged and considered to be despisers of your warning and rebels against the council. The reason for our distress is not that we admit to being guilty of the accusations lodged against us and therefore rightly fear suppression and disaster. Rather, we grieve because we see that you are being carried away by the immoderate language of certain men and (if it is no sin to say so) that you are being compelled by our evil-minded detractors to pile up such charges against us without allowing any defense on our part. We do know, since you are a prince with a benign and Christian heart, that you never cobbled together these charges through the impulse of your own mind, | but to the contrary you were brought to this by suggestion, urging and exhortation of malicious men. We ask, then, that in your mercy you allow us a defense against impudent slanders and false complaints and cease to have evil suspicions about us until the case is properly examined on both sides. For if our case should be assessed by the standard of truth and justice, you will see that we are

273

not only free of any grounds for suspicion but are totally cleared of the charges. If, on the other hand, we lose our case in court, we will not give excuses not to suffer the penalties worthy of our deeds. Since the accusation lodged before you (which is also the source of the suspicion of our criminality) is that we have impetuously undertaken schism and divisive scheming in our city of Münster and have spread this scheming as far as possible and so on, we are quite amazed as to the right or reasoning by which these charges are made against us, since those men do not deserve to be called seditious or schismatics who subordinate all these actions to the judgment of Holy Scripture and the decision of the written law and who indeed assert that they will demonstrate that their undertakings are in conformity with Holy Scripture, promising that if they cannot succeed in this, they will adhere to the judgment of those with better sense and readily undergo the chastisement of condign penalty. Those men are seditious and schismatic who begin some business on their own authority, ignoring divine, natural and human laws, and impetuously and obstinately defend their undertaking. We, on the other hand, have never had the intention of committing any act that was opposed to God, respectability and justice. Therefore, it is not without reason that we have very often, both orally and in writing, invoked the phrase "justice and fairness," not secretly but in a published document, and that in this case we seek and have always sought the judgment not of one or two men but of all the princes of all the nations and of the entire world. If someone had proven us guilty of sedition and schism and we had nonetheless obstinately persisted in our view and our course of action without accepting any salutary warnings, we would not be free of the suspicion and fault alleged. As it is, we are entangled in suspicion without being convicted, indeed without being heard. But we are sustained by the confident expectation that what we have undertaken is not only in agreement with fairness and justice | but also an extremely necessary act that we cannot give   274 up without showing contempt for God's majesty and losing our own salvation. For when the Word of God is not preached, His glory goes unheeded, is cast into darkness and gradually becomes erased from the hearts of men, so that they cease to be Christians. It is therefore better for Christians to lose all their possessions and, if necessary, their lives through violence than to separate themselves from the Word of God and allow anything as a concession to any man in violation of God and the dictate of their own consciences. Hence, most glorious prince, you can easily recognize what compels us to hold our course in the matter undertaken by us, which we maintained even before the dignity of prince in Münster was bestowed upon you. You will not therefore rely on the urgings of malicious men and believe that we have undertaken this matter in contempt of you and our council, to whom, after God, we have as far as possible, as God bears witness, given our primary obedience, judging, as we have said, that the matter is pious, fair, respectable and necessary for salvation. Hence, we ask you, after God, that you reconsider this business and in your mercy break it off, and then let it come before fair judges, so that we may be granted permission to defend ourselves justly against the slanders of those malicious men who accuse us of sedition and schism. For justice enjoins that a man should not be condemned for any suspicions or presumptions but should first be shown to be guilty of the charge through manifest proofs. If, on the other hand you, most reverend prince, or someone else clearly demonstrates that the dogma of our priests that we have ordained as our own is opposed to true religion, piety and respectability, we are prepared to dispose of it immediately. For the only reason for us to defend it is that we judge it to be pious and salutary. Since, then, we are not going to act against you in a contumacious or in an impetuous or obstinate manner but are invoking the decision of justice and fairness, we are certain that you possess such mercy that you are unwilling to overwhelm and condemn us without hearing the case. Also, most glorious prince, you write that you will proceed against us on account of our disobedience, as the most recent decree of the Diet dictates, in order to avoid incurring the Empire's outrage against you and the entire diocese, and that this is the reason why you halted the goods of our fellow burghers in transit and detained them in sequestration, | although we have not yet been declared rebels in sedition and whatever has been done among us is a matter of the faith and religion, which is freely granted to anyone in the emperor's edict and the Empire's command under pain of the penalty for violating the general peace. According to the Imperial edict, then, we think that you have no grounds to overwhelm us without hearing the case, and accordingly we ask that you not let us and our fellow burghers be oppressed in violation of the general peace of the Empire, and that you order the restitution of our goods. Whatever sentence is justly passed against us or for us by a suitable judge we are prepared to obey."

Next, on October 21, when twelve councilmen (no more were present), namely Henry Rotgers, Melius Herte, Bernard Gruter, Gerard Averhagen, Anthony Jonas, John Langerman, Herman Tilbeck, Caspar

Schrodercken, Henry Fridagh, John Palck, Caspar Judefeld and Henry Moderson, convened in the council chamber for deliberation, at about 9 o'clock the aldermen, guild masters and certain elected representatives of the commons approached them to complain about the shortage of preachers in a city with such a large population and the fact that the agreement signed by the council's amanuensis on July 15 had not been fulfilled. The commons, they said, therefore asked the council not to neglect the provisions of that agreement. To this the councilmen present responded that once they had entered into an agreement, they would not violate it in even the least respect, but would carry out the provisions that were pious and just before God and the world. Satisfied with this response, the aldermen, guild masters and representatives departed.

But in its constant hankering after new schemes, the commons once again devised new ones, and their representatives recounted them in the council on October 25, as follows. First, they said, the commons took it very badly that the Lord's Lords had without any just cause become the most hostile enemies of the city of Münster and had together left the city because of the doctrine auspiciously spread by Lord Bernard Rothman, | though the council and virtually the entire city of Münster   276 had undertaken in a general compact to defend and protect it until such time as Rothman would lapse into silence when refuted with Holy Scripture and the truth. Also, the lower clergy had churlishly put its snarling eloquence to use before the prince, and in recent months had without warning impiously, basely and bitterly reviled, slandered and accused the commons, though the commons did not knowingly deserve this but promised that they would always do whatever was urged by considerations of justice and fairness. The commons did not believe that the burgher masters, Eberwin Droste and Wilbrand Plonies, were free of fault in this suspicion; and it could be easily perceived from the following fact that they favored the side of the clergy and the shaven crowd.[81] They had recently been warned by certain councilmen in the country district called Bösensell to remember the common good and the oath that they had given and return to their city, to carry out the duties that they had been offered and had accepted, to exercise their office without the fault of being held suspect, not to oppose the calling of God and to protect themselves and their descendants against disgrace and any other detriment, being told that if they had not reached

---

[81] Meaning "monks," because of their tonsure.

a final decision in this matter and thought this course unsuitable, they should take a month to consider what they would do. It was said that to this they had given the response that within a month the people of Münster would have new views. Since, then, the burgher masters had put off their return until the present day and a few days after they gave this answer, the bishop had seized the cattle under sequestration during their journey, there could be no doubt that the burgher masters were joined to the clergy and the shaven crowd in a common compact and were aware of the harm inflicted on the burghers. For another thing, Derek of Merfelt, the bailiff of Wolbeck had dragged burghers before a foreign tribunal on the pretence of the sequestration, and although the burghers had availed themselves of their just right of refusal and their immunity from trial elsewhere, nonetheless he got his way in that court through violence and not through justice. For another thing, the

277 council | had promised to the aldermen and the guild masters that they would, with full zeal and effort, protect the city's rights, privileges and burghers, but now that the burghers were involved in foreign lawsuits and were being harassed with various difficulties, they were finding out that quite the opposite was the case. What the commons discovered from this was the powerlessness of the government, even if it did genuinely yearn for the burghers' advantages. Now, in order that the city should avoid destruction and downfall, the commons was asking the council to immediately enroll five hundred veteran infantrymen to protect the city against violent assault from clergy and the shaven crowd. For this was more tolerable for the commons than being harassed by their hostile foes within the walls at the latter's discretion as much as they pleased, being stripped of their property and finally being plunged by them into the extreme risk of death. If, on the other hand, these requests from the commons seemed to the council burdensome and difficult, the public treasury having been drained through the erection of the city's excellent fortifications, then the commons would see to their pay, even if this exceeded their abilities. And since the commons noticed that the city's resources were exhausted and that there was not much public money left, they thought it appropriate for the city's situation that the council should strike for the soldiers' pay copper money worth two thousand gold coins, which would be used only within the city until timely planning could acquire money from some other source. For the commons had definitely decided that they would in no way put up with the injury inflicted on them and their property, but would avenge it, even at the cost of the blood of many.

This matter was left for the council's deeper consideration. The commons also requested of the council that the clergy should be restrained from leaving the city gates by the public watch and should instead share the common lot, and finally that the council should issue a strict decree to the clergy and their allies commanding them that since they were, as the accusers, responsible for the commons' misfortunes, they should pay 4000 florins every month until they removed all the injuries done to the burghers and also made good their expenses. For the commons wished the clergy, whom they not only tolerated but even protected within their walls, to take these actions, and would defend themselves against their enemies to the extent permitted by the Almighty.

After a short deliberation, the council answered that they would take every step on behalf of the common good. But in order to avoid oppressing the less wealthy with unbearable burdens, the council thought that at first only three hundred soldiers were sufficient for the city. They enlisted them within a few days | and put them under the command of George of Kyll, a man of great experience in warfare, minted the copper coinage, and elected four important councilmen to act in place of the absent burgher masters. They advised that the other proposals made by the commons' representatives should receive further consideration, to make sure that it did not seem that any decision had been taken rashly.

Then, when the prince realized that he was being deceived by the intricacies of the townsmen's various letters, that they were nonetheless attacking and violating his jurisdiction by their own authority and with a certain violence, and that even after his warnings they were not restoring anything to its original status, he thought that he could avail himself of the same. Therefore, wishing to break the bolder spirits among the factious and to lay their arrogance low without bloodshed or fighting, he had his cavalry take possession of the public roads and cut off access to the city, and throughout the diocese he forbade any food supplies to be transported into the city and any revenues or income to be paid to the burghers. His intention was that the lack of necessities would force them to recognize their prince, to learn to obey, to confine themselves to the limits set for them, not to overstep their boundaries, not to rashly intrude on someone else's jurisdiction, to make use of what was theirs without injuring anyone else, to restore what had been removed and torn down, and to call back and restore to their original status those who had been removed from their offices without the authorization of those whom this concerned.

278

Taking this action badly, the people of Münster wrote on October 30 to the vicars and the representatives of the diocese gathered at Wolbeck in the absence of the prince, as follows. They understood that the public roads were being kept under guard by certain cuirassed cavalrymen everyday, so that no supply of necessities was being brought to the city for sale, and that this was being conducted from the city of Wolbeck in particular. That small town was serving as a place of refuge for those who were returning with plunder, | something which the people of Münster had hardly expected since they were endowed with the same liberty and privileges as the other inhabitants of the diocese and perhaps with greater ones. They therefore asked that these violators of the public roads be restrained lest any occasion for complaint or attacking them be thrust upon the people of Münster. They requested a response as to which of these steps would be taken.

To this the vicars and the nobles responded as follows. If the cuirassed cavalrymen had committed any act on the public roads at which the people of Münster could take offence, they were unaware of it. If, on the other hand, such an act and the circumstances surrounding it were described to them, they would give a legitimate response. If, however, the prince had legally begun any action against the burghers of Münster and their property, they had no doubt that they would learn of the cause of this in a letter from him, and in the absence of the prince they could not change the situation. The people of Münster were to consider this the response that they had asked for.

Next, by order of the prince the burghers Caspar Judefeld, Peter Friese, John Rotermunt the elder and the younger, John of Deventer, Bernard Menneken, Bernard Schomacker, Henry Redeker, and Albert Bodeker were summoned by various judges (those of Wolbeck, Sendenhorst, Bokenfeld, Telgte and Aschenberg) to assorted tribunals on the grounds of being leaders of the sedition and of having acted in violation of the edict of his Imperial Majesty issued at Worms in 1521 and of the recesses (laws) promulgated at Augsburg by receiving Lutheran preachers. These men entreated the council on November 2 not to let them be dragged before foreign courts contrary to the burghers' ancient liberty, adding that they would respond to any adversaries before their proper judge. | On November 3, the council wrote to these judges to say that they should let the cases drawn up and lodged against their burghers lapse in order to avoid stirring up a cause for greater misfortune. The judges wrote back to say that they had to obey the prince, and that if the council got relief from him, they, the judges, could put up with this.

The townsmen were made more impetuous by this response, and in frequent armed raids they carried back to the city from the surrounding country districts the necessities that they lacked. At the same time, they ordered the peasants to have no fear in bringing grain, wood and the other necessities just as they had before, stating that otherwise they, the raiders, would take them without payment. Whatever else the raiders found on the roads, they brought back with them. The entire situation was now one of hostility and aggression, everything pointing the way to violence, and as a result there was such trepidation among the inhabitants of the neighboring countryside that they even quivered at the arrival of a single mouse from the city and thought that the enemy was at hand to steal all their possessions. Thus, fear of enemy raiding broke the prince's command.

While these men were engaged in frequent raids outside the gates, others strove to further the affairs of their faith as widely as possible within the city. On November 3, which was the Sunday after All Saints' Day, Ludger tom Brincke, Michael Nording, Herman Foecke the tailor, Paul Busch and Anthony Guldenarm approached Ida of Merfelt the abbess in the name of the Parish Across-the-River, asking that as a favor to the parish she should remove the present chaplains and replace them with Dionysius Vinne of Diest and Godfrey Stralen, men outstanding for their learning and eloquence on the one hand and for good character and piety on the other. The petitioners stated that they wished to be always deserving of this favor through their good will and dutifulness. The abbess replied in the name of the nuns | that they had been forbidden by letter by the prince and the dean, 281 their lord John tor Mollen the doctor, to receive either new preachers or the new doctrine which smacked of sedition in any way, and were instead commanded to avoid and reject them. Thus, she said, they did not dare to implement any innovation unadvisedly in the dean's absence. If, on the other hand, any violence or insult was inflicted on them by anyone on this account, they would not only leave it to God and His blood to avenge this but also make it known to foreign princes and to the entire world with their tearful laments, "and from this all good men will understand with what piety you attempt to spread your religion." To this, Ludger tom Brincke replied, "Be advised that however the matter will turn out, the parish has decided to support the two preachers at their own expense for the time being." In the meanwhile, he said, the nuns should remember the answer they gave on this day. Thus, by their own authority they hired these preachers with the money contributed, and after conducting them to the church with a foul crowd of members of the faction, they entrusted the pulpit to them after removing the Catholic priests. After the abbess refused to support them (she customarily maintained her chaplains) or provide them with the daily necessities, they sowed together cone-shaped sacks out of blue-colored linen, and after attaching them to the end of long prongs, Lubbert Lenting and Reiner Stell, two men who surpassed the others in being convulsed with the evangelical spirit, carried these sacks around in the crowd at sermons, with this contrivance begging for money to support the preachers. Since most people were so ardently focused on the evangelical doctrine that their zealous obsession caused them to become virtually stupefied, chimes were fixed to the inverted or dangling sack strings, | so that when the chimes struck the audience, the jingle would rouse them to make a contribution. Some womenfolk also became inspired with the evangelical spirit, and chief among them were the wives of Lenting and Severinus, who would beg from the adherents of their faction throughout the parish and gathered such a supply of meat, grain, butter, candles, smoked and wind-dried fish, linen, cheese, mushrooms, wood and other necessities that they quite luxuriously and daintily fattened up the one preacher, who had a wife and five children, and the other, who was an unmarried celibate. For they considered it a sin to deny anything for the bodily maintenance of those who would spread the glory of God and nourish the souls of the many with evangelical food.

    Lacking its chiefs, the council was reduced to the most dire distress and was completely at a loss as to what they should do about the general peace and the cancellation of the sequestration. For the sense of feuding and resentment was growing on both sides, the people of Münster accepting no warnings or terms for peace, however tolerable, from the prince or the nobility, and the prince, though importuned by the city's letters and reminded of the Imperial edict and the homeland's privileges, not allowing the sequestration to be cancelled. Accordingly, there were many sorts of deliberation, and attempts were made to find reasons to oppose the prince and void the sequestration. In the end, it was decided to get a specific injunction against the prince and clergy from the Imperial Chamber Court, and so on October 23 the following letter was written to Francis of Werne, a lawyer then working in

282

the Imperial Court who was in the employ of the council and who became the council's amanuensis after the siege.

"You are not unaware of the efforts undertaken by the bishop of Münster to have the preachers removed and banished and cast out ceremonies restored in the city's parish churches. The vicars and the knighthood of the city of Münster also summoned the council, aldermen and guild masters to set out these proposals before them and gave them a written copy of these. To this the council also responded through envoys, and at the same time invoked the authority of the general law, fairness and the Imperial edict recently made known throughout Germany, turning over a copy of this edict that had been checked against the original. | Yet, the prince despised this sort of Imperial   283 edict and our invocation of the law, and through his stewards he had the cattle and property of certain burghers put under sequestration while in transit. We wrote to him that he should let the sequestration lapse, and at the same time invoked the privilege of this homeland and other rights, but he cast all this to the winds to destroy the burghers. Therefore, since we cannot dissuade him from his undertakings either with our friendly letters or any means other than the Emperor's edict and that of the Imperial Chamber, we are sending you copies of all the documents so that you may see what action is necessitated by the facts, and after employing the counsel of learned men and especially of John Helfman the licentiate[82] in law, may, in the name of the council, aldermen, guild masters and of all the burghers and inhabitants of Münster (since we lack burgher masters), procure against the bishop, dean and chapter, and the knighthood and all the estates and classes of the diocese of Münster an order that no one should use violence against the city of Münster and its inhabitants on account of religion, ceremonies and preachers. By virtue of this order, authority over the seized cattle and all other sequestered property would be taken away from all courts and a proclamation issued to our adversaries through the official herald of the Imperial Chamber. Issued on the feast day of Severinus,[83] 1532."

---

[82] A licentiate was someone who had completed all the requirements for a university degree (and was therefore "licensed" to teach) but had not made the (not inconsiderable) expenditures necessary to receive the degree.

[83] Surprisingly enough, three Sts. Severinus share October 23 as their feast day: Severinus Bishop of Cologne (born in Bordeaux and martyred in 403), Severinus Bishop of Bordeaux († ca. 420), and Severinus Boethius, the literary figure more commonly known simply as Boethius († 524).

The leaderless council sent the same message to Helfman, asking him not to fail to provide Francis of Werne with his help and assistance as a favor to the city, and if Werne happened to be absent, to reseal the sealed letter written to him and expedite the entire business.

In accordance with their instructions, then, these two men pressed on urgently with the petition, but since that most august panel of judges recalled that on September 23 of the same year they had issued an order against the same defendants in the same case, they thought that the city should avail itself of the earlier order until there was need of a stricter one against disobedience.

284   Meanwhile, the people of Münster applied their vigilant and strenuous efforts in gaining as many supporters as possible for their faction, strengthening themselves with defenses in all directions and stirring up many people to hate and resent the bishop. Thus, the leaderless council wrote to various princes, counts, lords and cities. On October 24 they wrote to the most reverend Archbishop Herman of Cologne as follows. "Most reverend bishop in Christ and most illustrious prince! We wish you to know that for some time a man named Bernard Rothman has proclaimed the Word of God to the people at St. Maurice's, a church located within sight of this city, and that a large crowd of burghers and other men has followed him to hear his preaching. When he was no longer tolerated there and the hope for official protection and peace had been taken away from him, he was summoned to our city by the people and brought in to assume the office of preaching. After drawing up his doctrine in the form of articles and offering these to the pastors, chaplains, terminaries and monks and to other learned men among the clergy, he asked to be corrected by them if he had committed an error in any regard, but as if deaf they have ignored this and given no answer. Being devoted to the Word of God, the commoners have embraced his doctrine more zealously and summoned to them more preachers, who, after abolishing certain ceremonies, have taught pious hymns. They too have offered to the pastors and chaplains instances of abusive ceremonies, but have not yet received any response. For this reason, we have allowed the abolition of the ancient ceremonies. Our prince has therefore written to us and to the aldermen and guild masters that we should remove these preachers and restore the abolished ceremonies. We have spent much effort in obeying him, but since the articles about Rothman's doctrine and the ancient abuses have not been refuted by anyone with Holy Scripture, it has been impossible to

implement the requests made of us by the prince. We therefore asked the prince to have this case involving the preachers and ceremonies entrusted to fair judges for settlement and the articles presented to pastors for a decision on the basis of Holy Scripture. We have also invoked the argument of fairness on the basis of the general law and this homeland's privileges, but the prince has ignored all this, and contrary to everyone's expectation he seized the burghers' property in transit and put it under sequestration. These are the acts, most reverend prince, that we wished you to know, and at the same time we beseech you to remedy this sequestration either by letter or by any other means and to cause the fairness of this case to be examined by just judges, | so   285 that we will not be denied the right that we have invoked."

On October 31, the archbishop replied as follows. "We have received you letter, and since, contrary to your ancestral custom, it bears the name of only the council, excluding that of the burgher masters, it declares that you are in dissension, something that usually causes nothing but baneful sedition and unassuageable hatred against the government on the part of the subjects. Given the remarkable amount of favor that I have always bestowed on you and that I thought would be long-lasting, this situation has caused me the greatest distress, and I leave it to you to consider more deeply what sorts of benefit and harm are going to arise from it. It would be unpleasant for me to hear such things about my own subjects. As for the preachers who have proclaimed the Word of God to the people and issued certain articles, I do not think that this has been done in accordance with the established practice of the Catholic Church. To the contrary, it is in violation of the Imperial edict, of the decision of the Empire and its Diet, and of the ancient, praiseworthy custom inherited by the Christian Church from our ancestors that you have, by your own authority, tolerated this preacher in your city and lent your wanton ears to him. You say that you allowed the abolition of the ceremonies after the articles were laid out without getting any response, but if you gauge the matter with the better half of your minds, you will easily conclude that neither you nor anyone else is allowed to take such steps. Accordingly, it is not unreasonable, in my opinion at least, for your prince to have been roused to oppose your undertakings. Be that as it may, since you are invoking my assistance and perhaps place confident expectations in me, our advice to you is that you should give up any inclination to sedition that you may have conceived against your ruler, and that whatever you do in connection with

the activities of preaching, changing ceremonies or any other matters should be in conformity with the emperor's edict, the decisions of the
286 Diets and the rites of the Catholic Church, | so that every sort of civil disturbance that could arise from this will be avoided. Nonetheless, I will send a copy of your letter to your prince and indicate to you whatever he sends back as a reply."

Since the archbishop did not seem to have understood their letter, the council wrote back on November 8. "We have received, read and understood your response to our previous letter about the preacher and the sequestration inflicted on us by our prince. We ask that in your mercy you receive the following words for your information about the case pertaining to the preacher. When Lord Bernard Rothman was preaching the Word of God as chaplain at St. Maurice's outside the walls of our city and the people would go in large numbers to hear him, eventually Derek of Merfelt, the bailiff of Wolbeck, summoned him to our city and revoked and took away from him the safe conduct officially allowing him security. Rothman was therefore terrified by this decree and dared not return to the parish of St. Maurice, and instead kept within our walls, relying on the protection of our city's liberty. Since he was guilty of no capital offence, we could not deny him the rights of our city, and thus he was impelled to preach by the people, as we indicated in our previous letter. As for your writing that our letter, being uncustomarily written in the name of only the council without the names of the burgher masters, smacked of sedition and hatred against the government, we reply that we have not driven off our burgher masters. Instead, when they left, we left no stone unturned and spared no effort, sending now councilmen as envoys, now letters, to get them to return to their positions among us, but all the trouble we have hitherto taken has been in vain. Accordingly, what we could find no cure for had to be endured, and we do not expect that you will cast this in our teeth for smacking of sedition and discord. We therefore ask you again and again in supplication that you intervene with the prince for us and our burghers and ask him not to be offended by the invocation of rights and privileges that we made in our previous letter and instead to give
287 that invocation a more favorable interpretation, | and not to continue with the sequestration and the cases begun in other courts against our burghers and instead to allow them to lapse in his mercy. If any dispute arises on account of the preachers and the ceremonies, let him refer it to peaceable arbitrators, and at the same time let some definite decision be made in the matter of religion that both sides will obey."

A sheet with the following text was attached to this letter. "Also, most reverend prince, we have no doubt that it is still fresh in your memory that the edict of his Imperial Majesty concerning religion that was issued at Regensburg has been proclaimed to everyone all over in Germany, including this city. We therefore ask that you deign for our sake to write to our prince to bring it about that we and our burghers will not be harassed in violation of this edict."

To this the archbishop replied on November 13 as follows. "I have received the reply that you have made to my most recent letter concerning the sequestration and dispute arising between you and your prince. To satisfy your requests I have sent on to your prince a copy of your earlier letter. Since he has not replied, there is no reason why you should expect an answer from me at this time. But to repeat my previous letter, I genuinely advise you again and again that you should give up your bold and presumptuous authorization that opposes praiseworthy ancestral custom and acquiesce in my warnings, lest you plunge into disaster both yourselves and your fellow burghers, who have always rendered to me and my subjects the mutual good turns urged by neighborliness. If in this matter you indulge one who is giving you good advice, you will pile in large amounts pleasure for me and countless benefits for yourselves and your fellow burghers."

On October 24, the leaderless council wrote to Prince Philip of Hesse as follows. "Illustrious Prince! On July 30 you wrote to us about the preachers | who expound the Word of God to the people in our   288
city, and we have received a copy of the original document sent to our prince in connection with this matter. Our burghers have therefore placed such confident expectations in your letter that they have no fear for their own well-being and instead think that they may in safety retain those preachers and press on with and adhere to their doctrine. Our prince, however, has ordered us by letter to banish the preachers and restore the ancient ceremonies in the churches to their prior state of honor. Since this command has not yet been obeyed, the cattle and property of certain burghers, and indeed the burghers themselves, have been seized in transit and sequestered by the prince's authority. After the burghers had brought their complaints about this action to us, we earnestly pleaded with the prince by letter to cancel the sequestration and invoked the rights of public and private privilege, but he contemptuously ignores all this, and in fact, contrary to our expectation, the cases are being proceeded with under even stricter sequestration. We are therefore impelled by our burghers to reveal our wounds to

you and to beseech that in order for us to feel that your letter was influential with our prince, we should recover our previous liberty in movement through the cancellation of the sequestration, and that the case involving the preachers, the ceremonies and the articles drawn up by the preachers should be decided by fair judges, in particular those who serve on your council. For it is our particular hope that if by your permission they bring their presence, advice and wisdom to this case, we may finally enjoy general peace."

On November 3, the Prince of Hesse replied to the council as follows. "I have received the letter conveyed to me from you in which you complain about the harm inflicted on your citizens by the Bishop of Münster because of the Word of God and your preachers, contrary to the confident hopes you conceived as a result of our previous letter. Your letter was immediately delivered to your prince attached to a letter from me. I have no doubt that he will readily accept the entreaties for

289 peace | and in his mercy will in the meanwhile suspend the sequestration and the legal actions he has undertaken. When he replies, I will, under the inducement of the love of peace, cut this dispute short, burdensome though this may be. I will soon fix a date for a council and will send important and wise men who serve on my council so that they may spare no efforts in case they can, with the assistance of God's favor, restore peace between you. Meanwhile, in a friendly way I ask you and your fellow burghers not to stir up against yourselves a fresh case involving new disturbances."

To this the council replied as follows on November 8. "When it was brought to us, we embraced your letter with the appropriate reverence. In light of the good turn you have done us, we offer you the greatest thanks possible and in turn declare publicly that we are under the greatest obligation to you. We will not conceal from you the fact that while our messenger was en route, the prince's stewards and gaugrafs[84] have, though provoked by no fresh offences, inflicted the greatest harm on our burghers, and we once more complain of this to you, a prince of the Empire in whom we place our hopes, beseeching in supplication that you be moved by this wretched situation in which we find ourselves and that on our behalf you approach our prince either with your entreaties or, if this is not burdensome for you, with your own

---

[84] The overseers of country districts. This term seems to refer to the officials whom K. otherwise calls "bailiffs" ("satraps" in K.'s Latin).

presence, so that he will in his mercy let the sequestration and the cases undertaken either lapse or be temporarily suspended and the case be referred to arbitrators for judgment."

When Prince Philip of Hesse received from the bishop of Münster the reply that he had asked for several times, he wrote back as follows to the council on November 20, attaching to his own letter a copy of the reply sent to him by the bishop. "Because of my love for the general peace, I would have dearly wished to halt the dispute between you and the bishop. As it is, the bishop writes that the estates of the diocese have made the same request of him with their most ardent entreaties, as the attached copy of the bishop's reply shows, and so I have no doubt that the inhabitants of the diocese, to whom the case is better known than to me, will, with less hard work and diligence, settle the disturbed affairs of their diocese. Wishing to gratify you too, I have on your behalf asked the bishop to let the sequestration lapse."

Here is the copy of the bishop's reply that was attached to the previ-   290
ous letter.[85] "You asked me in your letter that I should, at your urging, allow the dispute that is being pursued between me and the city of Münster to lapse, but since the entire diocese of Münster has for a long time been making the same demand of me with great earnestness and I could not rightly deny them this, I have allowed them to be parties to this dispute. If, however, I can gratify you in some other, indeed greater, matters, I will not fail to oblige you."

The council also wrote to the noble and well-born Count Arnold of Bentheim and Steinfurt, who was the leader and orator of the knighthood in the diocese of Münster, and to the entire knighthood, to urge them to favor the council. They complained that they were being injured, especially given that the articles of the preachers had not been refuted and the council wished to have the case brought before arbitrators, invoking public and private rights and the privileges of the diocese. Ignoring all of this, the prince had, they said, seized burghers' property in transit and undermined the fourth estate in the diocese, the city of Münster. The council, therefore, asked, that the knighthood should intercede with the prince to assuage him and to persuade him to cancel the sequestration and entrust the decision in the case involving the ceremonies and preachers to arbitrators.

---

[85] The original gives the date as November 11.

On October 24, the council sent a letter to the main clergy. "In our previous letter[86] to you we indicated that the prince had had his bailiffs seize burghers' cattle while in transit in the diocese and sequestered them, and we availed ourselves of your services as intermediaries in this case. Having received from the prince a reply that will hardly be helpful to us, | we wrote back to him that in this case involving the preachers and ceremonies we were invoking the privileges of this homeland and the common judgment of all the other estates. We have found, however, that we have achieved nothing, since every day not only the goods of our burghers but also the burghers themselves are being constrained with further, ever tighter sequestrations, prohibitions and seizures. Constituting as we do the fourth estate of this diocese, we would hardly have expected such treatment. Since, therefore, you have not been offended by our burghers and you agree that on several occasions we, as the fourth estate of the diocese, have at great cost to ourselves protected subjects of this diocese who were invoking the privileges of the diocese (one example of this which took place a few years ago is still fresh in the memory of men), we wished to point this out to you in a friendly way. At the same time, we entreat you to obstruct the prince's sequestration, so that the invocation and protection of the law will not be denied to us, the articles of the preachers will be demolished through Holy Scripture, and a definite order to which both the religious and the laity should adhere will be ordained in the business of religion."

To this Henry Hake, the dean of the main clergy, responded on October 27, saying that he and his college would faithfully plead the case of the people of Münster before the prince when he returned. For he had suddenly left the diocese and his return was to be expected.

The others to whom the leaderless council had written each promised their efforts in persuading the prince by entreaty.

In order to have imitators and adherents in the other cities, the guilds of Münster also wrote to the individual guilds of the smaller cities, advising, urging and beseeching them to follow their own example, even if their magistrates objected, by casting away all the superstitions, additions and frauds of the pope's followers | and embracing the Word of God and to protect themselves with mutual assistance against the persecutors of the Gospel and the whole papist crew. With these and

291

292

---

[86] See 268D.

similar words they provided the commons in certain towns, particularly those in the eastern half of the diocese, with heavy weaponry against their own councils. In the western half, on the other hand, where the leading men of the cities were not given over to factions, the business proceeded more slowly. It made a great difference that a peaceable government was in charge.

To make sure that they would not be stripped of the favor and protection of the allied cities, the council also called upon them to provide assistance through intervention. Accordingly, they first wrote to the people of Coesfeld on October 23. "We have no doubt that you have learned through general report that a man named Bernard Rothman, a priest and chaplain in the parish of St. Maurice outside the walls of our city who was summoned to our city, has for some time taught the Word of God to the people in both locations and summoned to him a certain number of colleagues in his avowed beliefs, and that as a result of this the prince was upset and sent us an earnest letter bidding us to drive away these preachers and restore to their previous status in the churches the ceremonies which had been abolished through their doctrine and articles. We, on the other hand, have rightly, as we see it, invoked our public and private rights, that is, the privileges of our homeland. The prince, however, has cast all this to the winds and had his bailiffs seize the cattle and other property of our burghers, and indeed the burghers themselves, during transit, putting them in sequestration. Since the states represented by our own and your cities constitute the fourth estate of this diocese, we would never have expected this to happen. Hence, we have requested in writing that the articles of the preachers be refuted by Holy Scripture. It was our wish that you should not be unaware of these events, and at the same time we ask you to explain them to the cities near you and to persuade the prince through entreaty to cancel the sequestration and not to deny us the invocation of the law, to refer the case to fair arbitrators who are by no means suspect, and to have the articles demolished through Holy Scripture."

A letter of virtually the same content was written to the people of Warendorf bidding them convene a meeting of their towns in the eastern half of the diocese and consult with them about a response. | Being attached to the people of Münster with remarkable favor and   293
having at the same time been long since initiated in the faction through a certain contagion as a result of proximity, the people of Warendorf immediately convened the meeting, read out the letter from the people of Münster, and discussed the matter back and forth in deliberation.

On October 26, they decided upon a response. They said that they would not violate their common treaties or separate at all from their metropolis, having no doubt about the fairness of the case, since what was at stake was the business of the Gospel, the glory of God, the true faith that had hitherto been polluted through enactments, and eternal salvation. Accordingly, they earnestly promised their efforts before the prince.

On October 26, the council of Coesfeld gave the following response to the council of Münster. They said that they had already learned through the general report the matters contained in the previous letter, and as requested they would summon the other towns to the customary location to set out these matters to them and to tell them of the decision of the people of Münster. This location in which the western towns customarily meet to discuss important matters is between Ramsdorf and the public inn called Hulschen's house. Hence, the people of Coesfeld, the chief town in the western half, summoned the people of Bocholt, Borken, Dülmen, Haltern and Vreden to meet for deliberation on October 30, and after advice was proffered there, a decision was reached as to the response that should be given to the people of Münster.

This is the reply sent to the council of Münster by the Hammonic (Bramian) towns.[87] "To satisfy your wish, the council of Coesfeld summoned the leaders of the other towns to the customary place and laid your letter before them. Accordingly, we, the plenipotentiary representatives of the towns, deliberated with timely judgment about giving an answer and at the same time compared our views. Consider this, then, as the response that you requested. In the first place, we have long since learned that the preacher has given sermons for some time outside your walls and then inside, that he called others to him as colleagues, and so on. We would not have expected that you, in whose hands lies the governance of the city, | would tolerate this but that you would have halted their extravagant freedom in the beginning before they progressed in rashness to the point where they thought that they were allowed to do anything. As for the prince having written for this reason that you should cast out those preachers and restore to their original position the ceremonies abolished by their articles and so on, it seemed to us fair that you should, as obedient subjects, obey the prince in this. If, after everything had been restored to its original state, some

294

---

[87] I.e., those of the western Münsterland.

dispute had remained on either side, then there would have been in this regard, as far as we can see, an opportunity to invoke privileges and rights. Also, you write that after casting your invocations of the law to the winds, the prince had used sequestration and seizure to restrain burghers' cattle and other property as well as the burghers themselves, contrary to your expectation since the cities have hitherto constituted the fourth estate and so on. We do admit that we are allied with each other in the firm and specific bond of a treaty just like the limbs of a single body, but since in the records of the treaty an exception is made for the decisions of the pope, our mother the Church, the Roman King,[88] and our prince, all of whom we must obey under all circumstances without the possibility of prejudicing their prerogatives in our own treaties, we did not feel that we had violated the treaty if we did not give our sanction to or approve the innovations that you have undertaken without consulting us. For the religious obligation to adhere to the treaty remains equally inviolate. Be that as it may, if you are prepared to become reconciled with the burgher masters and the councilmen who have withdrawn from you and to remove every unheard of innovation that you have for some time tolerated in your city, then after your representatives come to the assembly to be convened at Dülmen, we will, to the extent possible, endeavor to have your dispute halted in accordance with the agreement entered into in the past by the entire diocese and brought to adjudication. Since we have always lived together in full peace because of our mutual treaty since ancient times, we also ask you not to violate the obedience that you owe the prince, | so that we will not become involved in common risk and danger and in the end be plunged with you into inevitable disaster. We send this to you as our well-intentioned reply."

On November 4, the council of Münster replied to the towns individually as follows. "We have read the letter you sent as a reply, and from it we note your benevolent favor towards us and your helpful advice (as you thought). We leave all this to its own devices, though we will remember it at the appropriate time. As for your warning us in that letter to become reconciled with the burgher masters and the councilmen who have withdrawn from us and so on, we respond that we have expended great efforts, now through envoys from the council, now through letters, beseeching them to deign to return to us and the

---

[88] The Holy Roman Emperor also held the title of Roman King.

duties entrusted to them, and when we realized that these entreaties had no influence on them, we thought that this should be taken in an indulgent, if unhappy, spirit. We convey this information to you as a reply, so that you may understand the facts."

On November 4, the council of Münster also sent a letter to the estate of the commons in each city to stir them up against their government, and its text follows. "In recent days we wrote to the council of Coesfeld about matters of no little import, so that after summoning the magistrates of the other cities to a meeting, they should set this letter before them and satisfy our requests. But in our judgment at least we find that the reply sent to us by the burgher masters and representatives of all the towns, a copy of which we are conveying to you, is ill-considered and undutiful if the religious obligation to adhere to the treaty and consideration of neighborliness are taken into account. We would by no means have expected such a reply from them since we have received a more tolerable and reasonable response from the other towns in the east. We did not, as they perchance imagine, drive out the burgher masters and councilmen. To the contrary, we have in a friendly way invited these men, who wrenched themselves away of their own accord, to return by sending embassies and letters. We did not wish to conceal this matter from you in the confident expectation that you would plead with your burgher masters and council that they should not rashly cast off treaties entered into in ancient days."

To this the estate of the commons in the various cities replied as follows on November 8. They said that they had read a copy of the letter sent by the towns but could find in it nothing ill-advised | or contrary to the obligations of civilized behavior. Thus, after the burgher masters and councilmen compared advice and gave an answer as to what seemed fair, honorable, pious and peaceable, the commons would not reject and would instead approve the decisions of their magistrates in order to avoid being tarred with the suspicion of sedition. If, on the other hand, the council of Münster deigned to acquiesce in the warnings of the towns and allowed themselves to be turned from their seditious undertakings back to obedience, the commoners would always act on behalf of the city of Münster to bring about what fairness urged, the religious necessity of the treaty demanded, the consideration of the general peace dictated, and the obligations of civilized behavior suggested.

The people of Münster had no hope of assistance from the main clergy or the knighthood or the leaders of the towns or the estate of the commons in those towns, but would not allow themselves to be led away from their obstinacy, so they first strengthened themselves as far as possible through their own resources and then decided to seek refuge in the advice of foreigners. Hence, the two aldermen summoned all the burghers of the city and the inhabitants residing outside the walls to a meeting on November 6, and one of them addressed the burghers as follows. "The Word of God and the pure doctrine of Christ has been spread for some time in our city through God's propitiousness, and it has not only brought many people to a true knowledge of the faith but confirmed them in it to such an extent that the guilds and archers of the entire city publicly avow that it and no other is the doctrine of heaven. For this reason, these people have agreed among themselves that it is impossible to deviate from this doctrine through fear of some danger, thinking that instead it is necessary to fight on behalf of it to the last breath of life until such time as it is demolished through Holy Scripture. Also, though we have invoked both public and private rights in defense of ourselves, nonetheless we are being harassed. Therefore, all the guilds and the archers demand of you, their fellow burghers and the inhabitants of this city, that all those who voluntarily wish to adhere to the Word of God (no one should be forced) and who are prepared to defend it, even at risk of their lives if need be, should move to one side of this building."

At these words, some people, being devoted to Rothman's faction, which they were convinced was in accord with the Word of God, obeyed the alderman, while others, being uncertain of the outcome of this matter, departed. After their departure, the alderman said, "It is rightly fitting that when their fellow burgher and neighbor invokes the common privilege, every single one of the burghers should protect and defend him against violence and injury, even to the loss of his life and property. If, then, we invoke right and fairness for the sake of the Gospel and yet not only we ourselves but the entire city is harassed in violation of this right, would you be prepared, as fellow burghers and inhabitants in the faith, to ward off this injury at the risk of your lives and property?" Everyone answered together that because of their love of the Gospel they would undergo the most extreme dangers.

Thus, as the alderman recited the formula of the oath for them to repeat, a formal union was established. After this was finished, the aldermen, guild masters and elected representatives of the commons accosted the council with the following words. "In the cause of the Gospel and religion, because of which we are being afflicted by our prince, we have often sent letters to our prince, the main clergy, the

knighthood, the towns and certain princes, vainly invoking the general
law, the homeland's privileges, and the ancient liberties, immunities and
customs of this city of ours, and in derisive contempt of privilege, law,
custom and the edict of his Imperial Majesty we have been unable to
get any protection from any estate or class. Indeed, contrary to our
expectation, we are being oppressed with unfair sequestrations by our
own people rather than by foreigners, entangled in foreign courts, and
defrauded with unjust legal decisions under the specious pretence of
law and fairness. We accordingly ask in the most dutiful terms possible
and remind you in a friendly way on behalf of the commons, that you
should devise other ways to stop this unjust use of force and implore
other princes of higher rank to keep this city from being stripped of its
liberties and privileges and shoved over a cliff from which there can be
no hope of return. Hence, since no assistance is to be expected from
those by whom we could not be justly abandoned, and we are instead
being increasingly overwhelmed with unjust force in violation of the
edict of his Imperial Majesty and the Empire that was promulgated
throughout the provinces of Germany, it seemed expeditious to us,
provided this could happen with your authorization and consent, to
set out this case of ours before certain electors, princes, counts and
other leading men and estates of the Empire who are going to hold a
298   meeting[89] at Brunswick on the feast of St. Martin[90] | and to implore
their advice and assistance to keep our prince from shattering this city
and throwing it into chaos contrary to public and private rights and
in violation of the Imperial edict. It is on the best of grounds that we
seek refuge in the help and assistance of these princes and estates. First,
they are Christians and with outstanding zeal pursue the evangelical
Truth for the sake of which we are being afflicted. Second, they are
members of the Empire, and the edict in violation of which we are
being harassed was drawn up and promulgated on their advice and by
their authority. There is therefore no doubt that they will uphold this
edict in light of their very weighty authority and undertake to defend
us. We protest, however, that we will take no action against our prince
except to the extent necessary against the unjust use of force."

The council embraced this advice from the aldermen, and on
November 7 sent a letter to John of Wieck, doctor of law and syndic

---

[89] This refers to a proposed meeting of the Schmalkaldic League.
[90] November 11.

of the city of Bremen, asking him | to plead their case faithfully before   299
the princes in that assembly. The text of the letter was as follows.
"You must be reasonably sure from general report, most learned sir,
that certain inhabitants of our city have earnestly received evangelical
preachers who adhere to the Word of God and that because of the
sermons and articles made public by these preachers on the subject of
doing away with abuses the hitherto customary ceremonies have been
removed from the parish churches. For this reason, our prince Francis,
the confirmed bishop of the diocese of Münster and Osnabrück and
administrator of the church in Minden, has demanded of the council,
aldermen and guild masters that we should drive out the preachers
and restore the ceremonies to their prior position of honor, but since
the estate of the commons insists that they will not allow this unless
the preachers are convicted of error and their published articles are
demolished through the testimony of Holy Scripture, we replied that
we were invoking the fair usage of the privileges of this homeland
and the dictates of general law, or rather the common judgment and
decision of all the estates of this diocese. By no means satisfied with
this response, the prince seized our burghers and their cattle en route
and sequestered them, and after dragging them before foreign courts,
he plunged some of them into constant disaster, and being heedless of
the Imperial edict recently promulgated in connection with the faith
and religion, he inflicted irremediable harm on others. We offer this
narrative to you, most erudite sire, for your deeper consideration with
the wisdom and experience in which you are surpassing. At the same
time, having learned that you are going to attend the assembly that
certain princes, counts, leading men and estates have called to meet
at Brunswick, we ask you to plead this case of ours faithfully before
the princes so that they will bring it about by writing letters or sending embassies or some other more convenient means that the prince
will let the sequestrations and legal cases against our burghers lapse,
make no use of violence, and remit the matter of the ceremonies and
preachers to fair arbitrators, so that there should be some consideration
of our invocation of the law. We are confident that you will not fail to
oblige us in this matter." An additional sheet said, "Also, most prudent
sir, we would have sent representatives to you from the council, but
we understand that the public roads are occupied in such a way that
virtually no one is able to leave the city in safety."

Having learned from the council's letter that the Word of God was   300
taking root in his own homeland too, this syndic for Bremen, who was

ablaze with the common zeal for religion, undertook to carry out in quite good faith the task entrusted to him, and for a few days he detained the messenger sent to him by the council so that he would not lack one after successfully completing the business. On November 18, then, he wrote back via this messenger with news of what he had achieved at the assembly on behalf of the city. Having taken letters from the syndic for Celle, however, the messenger roamed through other places to make a greater profit before returning to Münster, and he arrived there rather late because of the distraction of delivering the other letters. Having expected but not gotten some response on November 30, the council took this delay on the part of the messenger very badly and sent another one to Bremen with a letter from the council to ask for a reply. In this letter, the council asked for two things from Syndic Wieck. First, since the messenger through whom he was to write back about what had been done on behalf of the city of Münster in the most recent assembly of princes had not returned, they wished him to write back via the second messenger about the progress of the mission entrusted to him. Second, they wished him not to begrudge coming to them on the feast of Mary's Conception,[91] adding that if his activities did not allow this and he preferred to postpone it to another, more convenient time when he could stay a while in Münster without great harm and detriment to himself and others, this course was acceptable to the council, so that a longer period of time would be available for mutual deliberation on very important matters. Finally, if he did not think that it was permissible for him to do so without consulting the people of Bremen, he was to order the messenger to deliver a letter he had written to the council of Bremen. The text of this letter was the following. "We have written to the most learned John of Wieck and asked him to assist us in person for a while in connection with some difficult matters which are necessary for us. We therefore ask that you grant your permission for this to happen. We will repay you with a similar or greater favor."

While this was going on, Eberhard Fabri,[92] the long expected messenger, suddenly showed up with the letter from Wieck. The council 301 would certainly | have made him pay for his long delay with prison if he had not cited many plausible reasons to excuse him and the council

---

[91] December 8.
[92] Presumably, a Latinized version of Schmidt.

and aldermen had not been delighted with the newly brought letter. A copy of it follows.

"John of Wieck, doctor of laws and syndic of the city of Bremen, to the council of Münster. As soon as your letter was delivered to me in Brunswick, I went before the deliberative meeting of Ernest and Francis, the Dukes of Brunswick and Lunenburg, the councilors of John Frederick, the electoral Duke of Saxony, and of Philip, the Prince of Hesse, and the representatives of other cities. In the presence of all these men, I delivered a speech with all the faithfulness and care I could, pleading the case of your distressed and extraordinarily harassed city. At the same time, I presented the written judgment for contumely issued by the bishop's judges against Caspar Judefeld, and I indicated that other burghers were being overwhelmed with similar legal decisions. The letter of Master John Ummegrove that contained in exact detail all the circumstances of the case was also read out along with the instructions given to you by the knighthood and your response, so that it would be clear that nothing that was relevant to a detailed explanation of the case had been passed over. The whole matter was opened for discussion, and they considered the means by which you could be provided with assistance, and at that point the councilors of the landgrave reported that you and their prince had exchanged letters about this matter and that permission had been granted by the bishop elect to settle the dispute, and that he would soon send a delegation to your city to bring about a restoration of peace. The princes and the representatives of the princes and cities not only asked that this be done promptly but also gave an order in some fashion in the name of the Schmalkaldic League that the landgrave should negotiate with your prince elect in such a way that the unfortunate situation would be done away with and that you would be restored to your former liberty without being stripped of the Christian truth and the salvation- and life-giving Word of God. The landgrave's councilors promised in the name of their prince that all these things would soon take place. | As   302 far as I could gather from the councilors and representatives, I have no doubts about the loyalty, favor and good will in which you are held by him and the other princes and cities. When certain among them expressed uncertainty as to whether your doctrine agrees with the Confession of Augsburg, which very many cities have embraced, and you desire to be admitted to the League, in which many princes and cities are bound in alliance, I replied that on the basis of many indications and factual demonstrations I was sure that your city was

keeping itself resolutely in the truth without any adulteration and had
not become tainted with the impious errors of the Sacramentarians[93]
and Anabaptists. I said that for a long time it had been your genuine
wish to join the Christian League but you did not know the best way
for you to become signatories to it since you had lost the ability to
send representatives here through the blockading of the public roads,
as I indicated by reading your letter before the general meeting. I also
reported that after the landgrave had intervened to settle the dispute,
your prince elect had seized burghers' goods in transit and blockaded
the public roads contrary to the landgrave's confident expectation, and
that those who hate the Truth and Word of God have in the feigned
desire for peace allowed the landgrave to act as an arbitrator, so that
in the meanwhile they could run riot at their own discretion, oppress
the city and strip the burghers of their property, their intention being
that once the public roads were occupied, the burghers would labor
under an extreme dearth of necessities and in the end be robbed of
all movement. When the councilors retorted that the prince elect had
indicated to their prince by letter that he would not oppress the city
with sequestrations or any other annoyance, I replied that after sending that letter he had nonetheless dragged Caspar Judefeld before a
foreign court, despoiled burghers, driven off cattle, and plundered
the burghers' possessions not only in areas close to the city but also
in Vechta. Then, after a consultation was held, I received the following answer. They said that since the landgrave had brought about a
suspension of this dispute, since he now had a specific mandate from
the evangelical princes to finish this matter, and since his councilors
had promised to expedite the matter, they wished to refrain from writing in order to prevent the prince elect from being able to say that he
had been accused while the task undertaken by the landgrave was still
pending. My advice, therefore, is that you should urge the landgrave
303   by writing to complete the matter quickly. There is no doubt | that he
will take the steps that befit a pious, Christian prince. In addition, it is
the vehement wish of all the cities of Saxony and the coast, which are
very eager for your salvation, that the city of Münster should join the
Christian alliance, so that it may be saved from tyranny and preserved

---

[93] Those who, contrary to the apparent sense of the term, deemphasized or altogether denied the importance of the traditional sacraments, in particular the eucharist
and baptism.

in the true evangelical doctrine. Though distracted by having been appointed as the commander of the forces defending this league, the landgrave will nonetheless not fail you in this matter. I too will deny you no duty, however burdensome, when the retention of the true doctrine and Christian liberty are involved in it."

After this letter from Wieck had been read out in a full meeting of the council in the presence of the aldermen and guild masters, they were heartened by the hope of assistance from abroad, which made them much more impetuous, and they thought that now they should not retreat from their undertakings, since they understood that they had been strengthened through foreign favor. Hence, they decided that the opportunity presented by the offer to join the league was not to be turned down rashly. The representatives of the commons entrusted the swift completion of this matter to the thoughtful care of the council.

In addition, when Wieck received the council's letter complaining about the messenger's delay, he immediately wrote back that he had sent Eberhard Fabri from Celle on November 18 with the expectation that he would return directly to Münster as he had promised to do and would deliver the letter entrusted to him to the council and Umme-grove. He said that he did not know what the reason for the delay was but he suspected that the man was unreliable since in disregard of his word he pretended one thing for the sake of profit and did another. Hence, he would send a second copy of his earlier letter, from which the council would learn what had been done for the city of Münster at the assembly in Brunswick. He also noted that the tyranny by which the city was being oppressed because it had embraced the evangelical Truth and rejected the papist abuses had not yet been done away with and no date had been fixed for a meeting to make peace and restore tranquility, and that instead everything was being done as a pretense by the prince. Accordingly, his advice was that they should approach the landgrave with the request that he should deign to accept into the alliance of the Christian League the city of Münster, which was devoted to the Confession of Augsburg and would also adhere to the self-justification, protestations and | appeals submitted in the name of the princes and the other cities, and that this city should enjoy the same privileges and defenses as the others, which were contained in greater detail in the letter of Ummegrove. Finally, he said that he would have come to Münster at the council's summons on the day requested, but his distractions had not at all allowed this. For the people of Bremen, whose syndic he was, had undertaken a suit against their clergy who

304

were in voluntary exile since the people of Bremen would not tolerate them within their walls along with their impious ceremonies and foul abuses, and the articles for the defense had to be worked out for presentation in the Court of the Imperial Chamber. There were also, he said, many other reasons that prevented him from coming, especially the dangers caused by the blockade of the public roads, but he would come once he had taken care of his burdens and the fear of dangers had been removed.

Later, on December 12, Wieck wrote the same thing to the council. He said that at his own expense he had laid out the case of the people of Münster before Duke Ernest of Brunswick, and asked the duke what he thought Wieck should do in connection with this matter. The duke replied that he had gathered at the previous assembly held in Brunswick that the landgrave had cut the dispute short, and for this reason it seemed useful to him that the landgrave should arrange the settlement of the case, which could be done most conveniently at the next assembly of the allied princes and cities, which was to be held at Höxter on January 1. He said that he would by no means fail the people of Münster at this meeting. In the same letter, Wieck also advised the people of Münster not to reject joining the Christian League.

The council introduced Wieck's advice about joining the alliance of the Schmalkaldic League as a topic for discussion, and after rather careful deliberation it was decided to keep the city free from participation in other people's factions. The purpose of this was to avoid the possibility that if the council made the city an ally of the Christian League, 305 | the council would turn liberty into slavery, multiply the number of lords, get itself involved in new taxes and exactions, violate the bishop's jurisdiction and derogate from his rights, in which case it would be said that the council had subordinated rule over the city to foreign control. Nonetheless, on December 13 it was decided to send a delegation in the name of the city to the illustrious princes, the brothers Ernest and Francis, the Dukes of Lunenburg, to Prince Philip of Hesse, and to Count Philip of Waldeck, the bishop's brother. John of Wieck the doctor, Caspar Schrodercken, a council member, and John Ummegrove, a very clever pettifogger, were appointed to carry out this embassy. The gist of the mission's pleading was as follows. The city of Münster had received the Word of God from men no less pious than learned, who had criticized and rejected the ancient ceremonies in the churches not only from the pulpit but also in writings which they had made public. These writings had been offered to the pastors and chaplains, and when the latter had given no response to them, the ceremonies had fallen into abeyance. Various discussions about this matter had taken place between the council and the other estates of the diocese. After the council had not, as the bishop and the other estates desired, cast out the preachers or restored the abolished ceremonies to their previous place of honor, the bishop had not only seized the burghers' goods and the burghers themselves in transit, placing them under sequestration, but dragged them before foreign courts, cut off the burghers by blockading movement on the public roads, and forbidden the payment of incomes, so that they should be subdued by the dire lack of necessities and stripped of their privileges. Although the council had invoked public and private rights, this had not helped the council at all. The council therefore demanded advice and assistance against these acts in the name of the entire city, so that as a result of the princes' writing the prince should at least concede the cancellation of the sequestrations, the rescinding of the suits, and the abrogation of the harsher decisions and decrees, mercifully allowing the dispute about the preachers and ceremonies to be halted and settled by fair arbitrators.

After accepting the task of carrying out this mission and receiving a letter to prove that they had been sent with plenipotentiary power, | the representatives Schrodercken and Ummegrove hastened to Bremen. After being greatly impeded by inclement weather and the blockaded roads, they arrived on December 24. Wieck read the letter in which he was graciously invited to undertake this mission and expressed his great willingness to take on not only the mission but any efforts that would gratify the city of Münster. After he learned that his advice had been ignored, however, and that for certain reasons the council would not join the Christian League, he seemed to get annoyed and was exceedingly amazed at the carelessness of the people of Münster, who had involved themselves in the business of the Gospel and received the Word of God without first acquiring for themselves the protection and defense of the princes or striving to do so even now, when they perceived that the clever and crafty plotting of malicious men and the wars started by them aimed at oppressing the city of Münster with never-ending enslavement to the papists. He said that it was now becoming doubtful whether permission could be gotten under present circumstances for the city of Münster, which was in dissension with its prince, to be admitted to that general alliance. For the princes and cities would hardly make a city from which disturbances and wars were to be feared an allied member of their League, nor would they take up

306

a war on behalf of someone else at a time when they themselves now enjoyed full peace in the business of religion and the faith. In addition, he said, the lack of substance to the arguments and urgings which had deterred the council from joining the League was clear from two facts. First, this alliance of princes and cities had been formed not to inflict but to ward off harm and to protect liberty and not to multiply servitude, as the people of Münster persuaded themselves to be the case. Second, the members of the alliance were not worn down with any exactions and burdened with any contributions unless considerations of the Gospel and of eternal salvation so dictate, and this salvation ought to be protected not only by those bound by this treaty but by all those who boast the designation "Christian," even at the cost of their fleeting possessions, indeed at the risk of life itself. Next, that this treaty did not violate anyone's jurisdiction or the Empire or diminish the authority of any ruler was obvious from the fact that the electoral Duke of Saxony and the other princes and Imperial cities[94] were not shaking off or violating the obedience by which they were bound to
307   the Emperor more | than the people of Münster were to their prince. Also, membership in the League was held by certain cities that were subordinate to archbishops and to bishops of greater dignity, authority, power and wealth than was the bishop elect of Münster. Finally, he argued, it would be the height of folly to doubt the respectability of the League, as if so many princes and cities had done away with their obedience through membership, had violated anyone else's jurisdiction, and had imposed slavery and new exactions upon themselves and their people. For the treaty was a part of the Christian religion and the evangelical liberty, in no way derogating from municipal authority or undercutting anyone's governance or office. Furthermore, if the people of Münster were terrified of joining the alliance, then it was pointless to send the delegation to the princes, from whom they would get no hope, advice or assistance apart from sending a friendly letter to the bishop, which they could have gotten at less expense. If, on the other hand, they changed their mind and decided that the attitude of the princes should be sounded out with a view toward joining, he told them to send authorization to negotiate without any delay to Höxter

---

[94] Free Imperial cities had no intervening overlord and were directly granted self-government by the Emperor.

on January 1, since the princes and cities belonging to the Christian League had summoned an assembly to meet there.

After Schrodercken and Ummegrove dispatched on December 25 a swift messenger who told the council of Wieck's agitated frame of mind, these arguments moved the council to change its mind, and it immediately sent the delegation members a document authorizing them to negotiate on the day specified. The text of this document follows.

"We, the council of the city of Münster, proclaim to each and every one and publicly declare by this document of ours that we have appointed the most honored and learned John of Wieck, doctor of law and syndic of the city of Bremen, as well as Caspar Schrodercken, member of our council, and Master John Ummegrove, burgher, as agents or representatives in our affairs, and that in granting them pleni-potentiary authority individually and collectively, we have ordained that in the name of the council and of the entire city they should, given a suitable opportunity, principally aim to have this city enrolled by the princes, cities | and other estates in that Christian League in which   308 the members were bound in mutual alliance, being incorporated and united within that League under the same terms as are the other cities. Whichever of these actions said delegates take in our name we promise without chicanery or deceit to consider valid, fixed and unchangeable. As a sign of good faith and truthfulness, we have certified the present document with the official seal of our city. Issued December 29, A.D. 1532."

This document of appointment as representatives was sent to the members of the delegation, and in a letter to Schrodercken and Umme-grove the council asked them to carry out everything faithfully and to bring Wieck back with them to Münster after finishing the mission, since there was a very difficult matter that the council would discuss with him. The mission was hindered by news of the capture of Telgte that spread in the assembly at Höxter. The town had been captured on December 26, as will be related below.

While these events were going on in Münster, the bishop recognized the zealous efforts with which they were striving to acquire both external and internal protection against him, particularly when they schemed to win over the favor of the lesser cities by writing now to their leaders and now to the estates of the commons in them. Fearing the defection of the towns, he summoned a general assembly to be held in Dülmen on the Tuesday after the feast of St. Martin, which was on November 12. The prince, the chapter, the nobility and the burgher masters of the lesser cities arrived on the appointed day, and after they had dealt with the Turkish tax[95] and other public matters for a few days, the representatives of Münster were summoned on November 15, not by the prince to take part in this general assembly but by the estates of the diocese for private discussion. They presented a document from their council in which it complained that while the council had not been summoned to the assembly in the customary way, it did not know the reason for this. They also said that the estates of the diocese were well aware that the cattle of burghers had been seized in transit and sequestered by the bishop's bailiffs and stewards, that burghers had been dragged before foreign courts to which they were not subject and oppressed with intolerable decisions, as a result of which harsher steps were to be feared, this despite the fact that the burghers had always, but vainly, appealed to their own court to which | they were subject. The council, the document went on, could easily and justly be excused for not coming to this assembly, but it did have one request to make. Those in attendance should remember the letters most recently sent by the council and accost the prince with entreaties, asking him to allow the council's invocation of the rights and privileges of this homeland, to forget the sequestration and the suits lodged in foreign courts against the burghers, to refer the case involving the ceremonies and preachers to fair judges, to have those preachers' articles refuted through the manifest testimony of Holy Scripture, and then to have a definite order and arrangement instituted in the business of religion, which both the religious and the laity would embrace and maintain jointly in pursuit of peace and obedience. If the grant of these requests could be achieved in good grace, then the council said that it would not be unmindful of its obligation.

309

This document from the council was offered by certain representatives of the estates of the diocese to the prince, and they energetically strove both to make him placated toward the city and to remove all resentment from his mind. On November 16, they made a report in the assembly of all the estates still in attendance in Dülmen as to what their plea to the prince had been and what concessions they had gotten.

Here is a copy of the items set out by the estates of the diocese to the representatives of Münster at the assembly at Dülmen.

---

[95] See n. 43.

First, the estates said that they had offered to the prince in the most careful and dutiful way possible the document from the council of Münster and its request. It was with the greatest distress that they pondered the discord that had arisen between the prince and the city, and in considering this disagreement in the better half of their minds they definitely foresaw that when feelings were embittered on both sides, it would result in a huge disagreement that would drag the entire city and a large part of the diocese with it into inevitable downfall. All the estates of the diocese were inspired with the equal and concordant desire to forestall this disaster, and have approached the prince with frequent entreaties. Relying in their pleadings before him | upon the claims of law and fairness to which the people of Münster   310 always showed themselves ready to submit, they insistently asked that he mercifully allow the disagreement between him and the city to be halted by the estates.

The prince thought that he should not allow this for many reasons, and particularly because they had always contemptuously cast aside both his own and the knighthood's many warnings. There was no doubt, he thought, that the good services offered by the estates would, if granted, be wasted fruitlessly and bring nothing but new annoyances. In addition, the prince had definitely decided that he would use the aid and assistance of certain princes and his friends in a serious attempt to stamp out the rebellious undertakings of the people of Münster, having also found through their advice a specific method and way in which they could be easily brought back to the obedience they owed and to a fairer frame of mind. The vicars of the diocese spoke about this matter at some length in the name of the prince.

When the representatives of the estates would not stop insistently urging and entreating the prince to allow them to halt the dispute, they eventually won this concession from him with the greatest difficulty. Indeed, it seemed that they almost wrestled this from him. They said that the people of Münster had been summoned there to hear with good will the views and deliberation of the estates concerning this matter. The actions that the people of Münster had allowed without any hearing but by their own authority in violation of the edict of his Imperial Majesty, of the decision of the Holy Roman Empire, and of the prince's friendly warnings and jurisdiction as ordinary bishop were, they said, considered inappropriate, impious and seditious not only by all the estates of the diocese but also by all right-thinking men, and if these actions were not soon done away with or put to rest through the intervention of good men, it would result in irreparable damage, a lamentable downfall and, in the end, the general destruction of the city, which would be fatal to the inhabitants in particular. The estates therefore gave as their general advice and in a friendly way urged the people of Münster again and again that they should arrange their affairs in a different way than had hitherto been the case, and recognize the Emperor's edict, the Empire's decree, the prince's frequent well-intentioned warnings, the letters from the knighthood, and the salubrious advice of the towns of this diocese. They should above all set their salvation and death before their own eyes at the same time and consider them more accurately, so that they would abandon the preachers and innovations, revive the rites and ceremonies abolished in the parish

311   churches, | replace the objects unjustly plundered and removed from the churches by force, and restore those who had been removed from their offices to their previous state. If these steps were taken, the estates would, with all the zeal they could muster, readily halt the dissension which had arisen between the prince and the people of Münster and, after doing so, get rid of it, and then restore the good will and friendship that used to prevail. If any minor offense had crept into religious practice through the passage of time, the estates would, to the extent possible, plead strenuously with the prince to institute a cleansing and purification of that practice through the removal of the offence and a settlement of the status of the government, and then get him to suspend for the time being the sequestration under which the halted goods of the burghers were being detained and to return the cattle once surety was given. If, on the other hand, the people of Münster ignored this faithful advice from the leading men of the diocese and persisted in their obstinate schism, which was hardly expected, then all the estates had, at the urging of their prince, officially decided as loyal subjects to offer their advice, aid and assistance in this just case and unite their forces against the people of Münster.

These declarations were to be set out before the representatives of Münster in the name of the leading men and estates who had authority over the diocese, so that the representative would report them in accurate detail to the council and to the other towns concerned and make no delay in giving a response. A written copy of the declarations was left for the representatives to present to the council, aldermen and other estates in the city for deeper consideration, so that they could learn with greater certainty and clarity both the estates' severe criticism and their decision, in case the representatives reported the course of their mission in overly mild and relaxed terms.

After these events, the representatives of Münster first bandied about ambiguous statements that were sometimes coaxing and relevant, sometimes harsher and uncouth, and then demanded of the delegates from the diocese that they deign to lay out before the prince the following requests in the name of the city and to secure his agreement to them. If this was denied to them on the first approach, they should still not stop asking. The oak is not, they said, felled with one chop but many, and in the end God Himself could be swayed by prayers. Although | the delegates for the diocese took that statement about   312
the oak very badly, since on account of his remarkable stature and height the representatives of Münster seemed to be referring to the prince, they nonetheless thought that the public peace deserved more consideration than did a private insult. They did, however, carry out this mission rather unenergetically.

The articles to which the prince's agreement was to be gotten were the following.

1) The prince should graciously grant a delay to the people of Münster in replying to the demands set before them on November 25 at the assembly at Dülmen. For the representatives needed to seek out a suitable occasion on which to deal with the commons. As for the reply, if they were first given a public guarantee of safety in coming and going, they would bring it to Wolbeck at 9 a.m. on the appointed day.

2) Within the period of time requested for deliberation, the sequestration should be relaxed and abated, so that everyone would be allowed permission to travel safely and freely with his merchandise and cargo.

3) After the production of sureties to give the prince a guarantee for their value, the burghers' cattle should be released and returned to their owners, since they were deteriorating and losing value as a result of the long detention.

Meanwhile, a letter was presented to the representatives of Münster asking them in the name of all the estates of the diocese to attend the new assembly to be held at Wolbeck on December 9 and to come there with plenipotentiary authority. After reading this letter, the representatives used crafty verbal ambiguities redolent with suspicions. Daring to speak openly rather than reservedly, they said that they would prevail upon their people to send plenipotentiary representatives. The later capture of Telgte made it reasonably clear what they had meant with

313 these words. They instilled such fear and trepidation in the hearts of the burgher masters of the lesser cities | that they demanded from the representatives of Münster permission to travel safely through their city and were immediately granted it. Though their other impetuous, ill-advised blatherings and demands prove their rashness, it is better to pass them over in silence.

The delegates for the diocese delivered these demands to the prince in the most careful way possible, though they suppressed those whose utterance could only have annoyed him. Then, on November 17, they reported to the council the concessions which they had been granted in the following words. They said that before their most reverend prince, the bishop elect of Münster and Osnabrück and the administrator of the Church of Minden they had both verbally and in writing set out in order the proceedings between the members of the diocese and the people of Münster at the assembly at Dülmen and the requests made of the former by the latter. To the first article the prince had replied that for the purpose of responding he would grant both a delay for the period of time requested and safe conduct. The second one he had said he had to deny for very just reasons. The third one concerning the release of the burghers' cattle he had granted to the extent that reliable guarantors were provided for paying the value of the cattle. These, then, were, they said, the concessions which they had been able to get from the prince at the present time as a favor to the city.

After learning of the prince's frame of mind, the townsmen deliberated and consulted about everything, turning it this way and that in their minds. Finally, after comparing their views, on November 25 they gave the following reply to the assembly of the vicars at Wolbeck through their representatives. On November 12,[96] the estates of the

314 diocese | had given for presentation to the council and the other estates in the city a copy of the demands that had been set out in the assembly at Dülmen specifically regarding the preachers and ceremonies in the churches, so that after a short deliberation they should reply as to what they were going to do, and thus in the name of the city they gave the response that they had often given. Since the articles of the preachers had not been refuted by anyone, they could not yet get any particular answer from their people about repudiating the preachers. If, however, this dispute could be halted through salubrious advice,

---

[96] Rather on November 16 (see 309D).

the council, aldermen, guild masters and the entire estate of the commons could tolerate that the priests should establish and practice in the parish churches the ceremonies which did not smack of superstition but savored of true piety, and that the preachers should proclaim to the people the Word of God uncontaminated with human filth and dispense the sacraments in the way ordained by Christ until the decision of a general Christian council. The vicars should consider this the townsmen's well-intentioned reply and report it to the other estates of the diocese. If the townsmen changed their view, they said they would deliver this at the coming assembly to be held at Wolbeck on December 9. In addition, all the estates of the city asked that an attempt be made in a friendly way to persuade the prince through entreaty not to inflexibly pursue the legal action undertaken against the burghers and their property and instead graciously allow anyone to use the public roads in safety and without any fear.

To this the prince gave the following response. He had hardly expected such a reply from the people of Münster. Noting their obstinacy, which was the companion of rebellion, he was obligated to entrust the entire matter to the patient passage of time. For if he lent his authority to their acts in violation of the Emperor's edict and granted what they wanted, they could always shift the blame to him by alleging this as an excuse for their deeds, which would in no small way lessen and diminish his reputation in the eyes of his Imperial Majesty and of the estates of the Empire | and give rise to a suspicion of fickleness.　315 Also, this permission desired by them would produce not peace and tranquility in the city but a desire to disagree, argue and dispute. For some people would think one thing pious and evangelical and other people something else.

After a brief deliberation, the estates responded to this as follows. They could not give a better answer than the prince's or give any other suggestion under the circumstances. The prince was aware, they said, that the estates of the diocese had been summoned to an assembly at Wolbeck on December 9 for consultation about the sum of money imposed on the inhabitants of the diocese for the Turkish campaign, and on November 25 the people of Münster had added to their last reply the statement that if the townsmen changed their mind and made another decision, they would report this at the coming assembly to be held on December 9, it having proven impossible at that time, given the short period of time granted to them for deliberation, for them to extract another response from their people. Accordingly, to avoid any complaints on their own part about being undeservedly oppressed, the estates asked of the prince that they be graciously granted a delay in giving a more specific answer at the coming assembly in case they could, after considering these matters more fully, give responses that would quash and suppress any reason or motive for later disturbance.

When the prince replied to this that it was with the greatest reluctance that he would grant this extension since it would be pointless, and such delay would instead greatly hinder him when he was ready to implement other courses of action, the estates of the diocese pressed on with their demands more eagerly. In the end, the prince was prevailed upon to acquiesce in their requests. He would not, however, cancel the sequestration, which was reported to the people of Münster in a reply directed to them specifically. At the same time, they were warned not to play games with the prince and the estates any longer and instead to come on the appointed day with instructions for a definite reply. They were to give definitive answers that they thought to be honorable, pious and peaceable and not to be obstructive of their interests. Otherwise, they would be accused of rashness and fickleness before foreign populations.

On the same day that these events were going on, that is, on the feast of St. Catherine the Virgin, which is November 25, in the Church of St. Maurice a certain monk was giving to the people the customary sermon about the martyrdom of St. Catherine. | From the pulpit he described the tortures inflicted on the young virgin for the sake of Christ and how she was put to death in a terrible and unworthy manner. At the end, the women folk offered small coins at the altar for the support of the monks as the organs soothed their ears with sweet harmony. In their midst not only could Brixius, the priest of the factious, be seen wearing an expression of derision, but he even kept saying overtly with quite confident emphasis that the tale just read out by the monk had been thought up for papist profit. The women folk were upset at this and suddenly surrounded him. Soundly beaten with fists, sandals, slippers and pew benches, he received such a drubbing that the only thing he took away from that sermon about the martyrdom was a martyrdom for himself and bruises on the face that he showed to the council the next day as proof of the event. He complained about the injury and demanded vengeance, but the council thought the whole crowd of women could not very well be summoned for punishment, since the person responsible for the deed could not be discovered amid such a

large number. This injury was thus punished with connivance by the
council, laughter by the Catholics, and curses by the factious.

Next, on November 28, the theologians of Cologne, who had been
consulted,[97] sent back a retort against the articles which Rothman had
made public as an attack on the Catholic ceremonies and handed over
to the clergy for refutation. After learning of this, the council sent its
amanuensis, Master Derek Hoier, to fetch this retort from the lower
clergy. On November 29, four representatives of the lower clergy
(the canons Master Gerard Schrodercken, John Vogelsang of the Old
Church, John of Meschede, and the chaplain from the Parish Across-
the-River) presented it to the council and aldermen in the council hall,
with Rothman in attendance along with the membership of his faction.
The council asked if they were prepared to defend the book offered by
them before anyone. Schrodercken answered that its author would no
doubt defend it. (This author was John of Deventer, the provincial[98] of
the Minorite Brothers in Cologne.) | Having received three copies of   317
the retort, which was entitled "Catapult of the Faith," the council gave
two to the aldermen and Rothman, keeping the third for itself. At this
point, Rothman gave in the council chamber a solemn speech in which
he seemed to embrace this retort with good will. He repeatedly stated
that he now had no doubt that as a result of the comparison of many
passages of Holy Scripture, the Word of God would recover from the
dirty filth of human traditions and from every counterfeit admixture,
to regain the pristine splendor of its integrity for the salvation of many
souls. After leaving the council hall at the end of the speech, however,
he was immediately received by a great crowd of his people, who kept
asking about the attitude and hopes he had about the progress of the
evangelical business. He confidently told them to be of good cheer, for
the squared stone could not be undermined by any battering rams of the
papists, however mighty, and no theologians' darkness could cast the
light of the Gospel into shadows.

Next, after news of the handing over of the retort spread quickly
throughout the city, the factious rushed back and forth in swarms for
the sake of the innovations and wore themselves out with various conversations and discussions among themselves. Some people gave the

---

[97] See 241D.
[98] I.e., head of the local province of the order.

palm to the clergy, others to Rothman. Since Brother John of Deventer, the provincial mentioned above, has rebutted Rothman's articles about abuses at the end of the book entitled "Spear of the Christian Truth, or Catapult of the Faith, a Treatise against many pseudo-prophets and in particular against Bernard Rothman of Münster, a Misleader of the People" and so on, I do not think it worthwhile for me to spend more effort in demolishing those articles than is expedient. I refer the reader to that book in order to avoid interrupting the flow of the present work.

    After Rothman's departure, the aldermen and guild masters, being worried about the burghers' benefit (as they put it), remained with the council in the council chamber to deliberate more carefully. | There they once again, just as they had before, used many verbal contortions to misrepresent the cause of all the sedition stirred up between the prince and burghers as being the fault of the lower clergy. For, they said, as the result of the complaints made public by the clergy in recent months, in which the clergy had also made up many accusations, the prince had first been made annoyed at the townsmen and then become so upset that he seized the burghers' property in transit, blockaded the public roads, forbade the transport of supplies into the city, entangled the burghers whose cattle had been taken from them in foreign lawsuits, and exhausted the city's wealth in paying for the soldiers' wages. The city would have no need for foreign protection if the burghers did not see the enemy roaming within the city walls, or fear betrayal at the hands of the clergy, or dread being suddenly overwhelmed by the prince now that they had been cut off from the transportation of supplies at the clergy's instigation. It was also at the clergy's urging that the knighthood had been incited to hate the city. Therefore, since the clergy were tormenting the burghers to their heart's content and were the cause of all misfortune, calamity, dispute, enmity and anger, it would be just for them to be stripped of all their possessions and then either driven from the city or compelled to make good all the burghers' losses suffered in connection with this case, give a guarantee about future losses by providing real estate and bondsmen as surety, or immediately prevail upon the prince to cancel the sequestration of all the burghers' property, to stop blockading the public roads, and to allow anyone free movement. In addition, the clergy should pay the wages for the soldiers enlisted by the council to protect the city.

    Realizing that these actions could not be taken without causing a great disturbance, the council advised that they should be postponed

318

till the coming assembly. The officials of the commons, however, urged their implementation all the more keenly and fiercely, arguing that if they were not implemented, they, the officials, could not in any way maintain the commons' concordant attitude or keep the people, who were already gnashing their teeth against the clergy, from attacking them. They left it to the council to consider what would happen at such a perilous moment to those who protected the clergy. Finally, to elude the madness feared from the people, the decree against the clergy was passed by the council according to the wishes of the officials of the commons. After 11 a.m., then, four members of the council were sent to the dean of the Old Church, who was the head of the lesser clergy and their orator. Finding him alone, they commanded him | to convene   319 a few members of his order. For their important mission, which had, they said, been entrusted to them by the council, concerned the lesser clergy. After these men had been summoned, the councilmen related the decree of the council and their own mission in the following words. "The council, aldermen and guild masters and the officials chosen from among the entire estate of the commons of the city of Münster order that the lesser clergy should, within two days, persuade the prince to stop seizing the burghers' property during transit, to cancel his prohibition against transporting supplies into the city, to lift the blockade of the public roads and grant anyone permission to move freely, and to return everything to its original state of liberty. Next, they order that within the prescribed period of time the clergy should contribute a sufficient sum of money to pay the first month's wages to the soldiers hired to guard and defend the city. If the clergy disregard and ignore these commands, let this happen at their own risk."

This decree of the council instilled unbelievable terror in the lower clergy. No delay or postponement was allowed, and all of a sudden the council, aldermen and elected representatives of the commons compelled them to send a petition to the main clergy before they would consent to end the meeting and leave the council hall. The lower clergy thought that they had to yield to necessity, and on the vigil of St. Andrew, which was November 29, they wrote the following letter to the main clergy in terms that were less harsh than the proceedings before the council had been. On the present day, the council, aldermen, guild masters and elected representatives of the city of Münster met and argued in the most urgent manner about ending the sequestration and oppression of the burghers and unblocking the public roads, so that all fear would be done away with and anyone allowed to travel back and forth. In the end, the council advised the colleges that if they wished to escape the fear of danger, they should write earnestly to the main clergy, by whose help and assistance the prince could easily be prevailed upon to grant the previous liberty for the burghers' goods. The lesser clergy said that they thought that the reason why these demands were being made of them in particular and the burden of writing was thrust upon them was the petition sent by them in recent months to the prince in which they had asked for the restoration of the abolished ceremonies and of the worship of God, which had been cast out of the churches. Hence the story that they had denounced the burghers before the prince, | and hence the reason for the lower clergy having offended the burghers and incurred their hatred. For this reason, they said, the commoners were stirring up plans to set upon the property of the clergy both within the city walls and without and to keep it for themselves until all the afflictions imposed on the burghers were done away with and their expenses repaid. The council, aldermen and guild masters, however, had intervened earnestly and asked for a delay until the next assembly of the diocese on the grounds that they would strive at that time to prevail upon the prince to grant their requests, but they had not been able to attain such a small delay from the commoners, who were now bent on plunder. The lower clergy said that with importunate entreaties they had barely been able to extract the concession of a single day on the condition that both the council and colleges would write to the main clergy before those who were pleading the case of the commons departed. Also, certain councilmen as well as guild members and commoners hostile to the lower clergy had come and rather forcefully set out the decision of their will. Hence it was, said the lower clergy, that they had promised to write. Therefore, since the main clergy could understand well enough from this the great size of the perilous risks in which the colleges were ensnared, the lower clergy asked as emphatically as they could that the main clergy should restore the lower clergy, who were now almost faint with fear, to good spirits and prevail upon the prince to do away with the sequestration and reinstate in all regards the previous situation of security in travel. Otherwise, they thought that they would not be free of fear or safe from being oppressed by the commons. They said they were eager to hear which of these courses of action the main clergy would grant.

The council also added the following letter to the main clergy. Certain members of the lower clergy of the city of Münster had handed over to the council certain articles which they had devised over a long period of time. In these they strove to demolish the articles made public some months before by the preachers regarding abuse in the ceremonies. The council had immediately presented these articles to the preachers, who promised that they would respond to them. The council informed the main clergy that these actions had been taken in the council because the prince had, as a result of this case concerning the preachers and ceremonies, detained burghers and their property under sequestration and entangled them in foreign courts, as well as issuing a prohibition against transporting supplies into the city. At the same time, the council requested that the main clergy should prevail upon the prince to let the sequestration, the suits lodged against the burghers, and the prohibition of transporting supplies into the city | lapse into abeyance. If, on the   321 other hand, it was not possible to secure this concession, and any other act that the council could not oppose was taken in the meanwhile on account of this case, the council left this to the chapter for more careful consideration. The main clergy were to be quick in responding as to what fruit this petition from the council would bear.

On December 2, the main clergy gave the following response to the lower clergy. They said they had been pained to learn from the college's last letter of their grievous circumstances. They had immediately sent this letter on to the prince, and at the same time entreated him by letter and delegation to be mindful of the very diseased nature of the times and of the general peace and to give his gracious permission for the sequestration, the suits and the edict about not transporting supplies into the city to lapse. There was, they said, no doubt that the prince would soon give an answer to this petition.

On the same day the main clergy also sent the following response to the council. They had, they said, been induced by the letters of the council and of the lower clergy to send the prince a humble supplication about restoring mutual concord, and they would leave no stone unturned in striving to get the prince to grant their requests if this was in any way possible. Since, however, they noted from both the council's and the clergy's letter that the clergy was not unreasonably fearful of the worst from the burghers, they, the main clergy, therefore entreated the council, aldermen and guild masters to halt this decision of the commons and keep them from resorting to violence and bloodshed. For if the commons did not refrain from unbridled criminal violence and instead stained their hands with either plundering or killing, | 322 this action would not only anger the prince and overturn the plans for future peace but also pile for them outrage among many people and the occasion for countless disasters. All of these things were matters to be avoided with great and diligent efforts.

At the end of his sermon on the feast of St. Andrew, which was November 30, Rothman invited the people to his sermon on the following day. He said that he would speak at 3 p.m. in the Church of St. Lambert and show by Holy Scripture how much rash stupidity was contained in the book which the lower clergy had bought from the theologians of Cologne for two hundred florins. On the next day, December 1, which was also the first day of Advent, such a large number of various people arrived that the church could barely hold them though it was very big. Some of those who thronged together there were inspired by evangelical spirit, and others were excited by the novelty of the event. Some were eager to learn and others to hear the arguments that Rothman would use in demolishing the articles. Some were enticed by the sweetness of singing hymns and others were attracted by the familiar companionship of their neighbors. After they sang a few hymns in German, Rothman began his sermon with the statement of St. Paul in Romans 13: "Night has passed and the day is approaching" and so on.[99] From this text he took the opportunity to flog the pope and all those who support him. At mind-numbing length, he inveighed against the papist kingdom, calling it darkness and the blackest night of errors and ignorance in that for many years now it had, with the filth of human traditions and the invention of impious ceremonies, polluted the light of day, that is, the knowledge of the true God, and cast such shadow over it that no one was able to see the true light of the Gospel in the midst of so much haze. The pope had never allowed even a spark of true knowledge to emerge into the very bright light. Though it was true that this spark had sometimes shone forth in a few pious men, it had always been smothered by the pope's tyranny. "Oh, three and four times blessed are we to whom the true light has returned, now that the papal dungeon is broken open! Up until now covered in the foulness imposed by the papists, this light has finally burst forth and escaped the tyrannical chains in which it used to be held fast, becoming much more bright for us. Now, therefore, the night has passed and the day is approaching. The very sweet light of the Gospel has dawned! We now know what God demands of us.

323 | We now recognize what the traps and snares used by the pope and

---

[99] Romans 13:12.

the devil are. Let us, then, shake off the very clever nets of the papal supporters in which they even now strive to ensnare the unwary among us with the help of the sophists in Cologne! Let us beware of that leaven of the Pharisees,[100] and flee the papist blathering! Let us shun the erroneous articles stitched together by the people in Cologne in defense of the papists' hallucinations by which they are, in disregard of the true light of the Gospel, thrusting upon us the darkness of idolatry by means of human enactments and impious ceremonies!" He used these and many other statements to revile the theologians in Cologne and the clergy of Münster, vanquishing the articles not so much with solid arguments as with clumsy aspersions. The ignorant commoners, however, who cannot distinguish eloquence from bombast, thought that he had spoken excellently.

On December 4, John of Raesfeld, who had earned the rank of commander through long experience in war, Caspar Smising and Jodocus Korf, noblemen of great influence with the prince, came to Münster. They did so at the urging and instigation of certain leading men of the diocese and the city, and in particular at the suggestion of the main clergy, as was reported at the time, in order to do a favor for the colleges and lower clergy, who they had learned were suffering savage oppression at the hands of the seditious. After these men had been received with very great courtesy by the council, a discussion began about the dissension between the prince and the city. These men made a promise to the council to do what they could before the prince if certain patricians who were acceptable to the prince were sent along with them. Herman Schencking the judge, William Clevorn and Herman Buck were therefore brought in, and after undertaking the mission they negotiated with the prince for two days about the terms for peace. They discussed back and forth everything that seemed to contribute to peace. Without a doubt, a way to settle the sedition would have been found if the people of Münster had pulled back a little bit from their obstinate undertaking. Instead, they clung to their position with such impetuous persistence that they made not the least concession to the prince, and in fact Knipperdolling and Kibbenbrock, the heads of the sedition who controlled the entire commons and were viewed by them as gods on earth, said openly in front of certain people that they preferred killing their own children and cooking them into food to abandoning

---

[100] See Matthew 16:6, 11; Mark 8:15; Luke 12:1.

324   the preachers or changing any of the practices which they had started. |Accordingly, the whole effort was undertaken in vain.

After this, the prince consulted with the representatives of the chapter and of the knighthood, who had come when summoned to take counsel. The topic was what they thought should be done if the people of Münster remained obstinate, as he expected, in their undertakings and if recourse to violence was necessary. The expenses for this he could not bear alone, he said, since he had to pay off the debt contracted by his dead predecessor, and his own confirmation as bishop had to be bought from the pope at a high price. He would very readily and of his own accord expend the strength of his own body and funds on this matter if necessary.

To this the representatives (the provost, the school master, the dean of Osnabrück, the suffragan,[101] and Bodeswing on behalf of the chapter, and Gerard of Recke the golden knight, Bernard of Westerholt and Godfrey Schedelich on behalf on the knighthood) gave the following answer. It was ancient practice, they said, that under such circumstances the prince should first bear such expenses if his resources allowed. Otherwise, he should mortgage a castle or collect a land tax and extract assistance from his subjects. Since they were now being worn down by the Turkish and the congratulatory[102] taxes, however, they ought not to be oppressed with a third burden.

The prince thought that the collection of a land tax would hardly be helpful for the reasons already stated. He noted that the mortgaging of a castle to creditors would represent no small detriment to his interests since the revenues acquired by his predecessors for the bishop's maintenance would be thereby reduced. He said that he would not allow this willingly, since in addition to the disadvantages already related he had to pay two thousand florins every year to Frederick of Wiede, the bishop who had resigned, and virtually nothing was left for daily needs in the episcopal strongholds throughout the diocese. He said that he had, however, found another way to see to this exigency. Since the Turkish expedition had been cancelled, so that it was not necessary to spend

325   all the money that had been collected for military needs, | the people of the diocese could divert to this purpose the remainder that had not

---

[101] That is, the man who acted in place of the bishop during the latter's absence.

[102] That is, an obligatory payment to be made upon the installation of the new bishop as a supposed form of congratulations. Such payments were then used to pay off the pope for confirming the appointment.

yet been distributed among the soldiery. He left this to be considered and decided at the discretion of the whole diocese.

These and many other topics that were thought to concern the general interest and concord of the entire diocese were put off for determination at the coming assembly. It was also considered useful for the prince to deign to grace that assembly with his own presence and for all the leadership of both the religious and lay estates to be summoned, since this would lend no little authority to the proceedings.

The people of Münster did not dare attend this assembly without an official guarantee. When they therefore requested this from the prince by letter on December 6, he wrote back on the next day that he was graciously granting to the representatives of Münster an official guarantee of safe conduct in coming and going.

All the estates gathered on the prescribed day and place, and the people of Münster came forward to give their response as they had promised in the previous assembly. First, they thanked the estates for having striven with much effort to halt and then end the dispute between the prince and the city. With great distress, they said, they marveled at the prince's having repudiated the supplications of the estates and their own submissions and invocations of law and privilege, which had given rise to such outrage. As for his writing that the townsmen had contemptuously cast aside his own and the knighthood's frequent warnings, they were unaware of ever having contemptuously rejected his and the knighthood's clement and well-intentioned urgings. Quite to the contrary, they had always accepted and extolled those urgings, just as they were doing now, and as obedient subjects had been prepared to embrace them to the extent that they were in conformity with piety and fairness. In the end, they said, the estates had, after many petitions and with the greatest difficulty, gotten the prince's consent to halt the dispute on the following terms. All the estates | held the view that the townsmen's undertaking violated the Emperor's edict, the decision of the Holy Roman Empire, and the prince's well-intentioned warnings and his jurisdiction. Therefore, if the townsmen followed the estates' advice by arranging their affairs in a different, more sensible manner, obeyed the Emperor's and the Empire's decisions, and considered more carefully the prince's and the knighthood's frequent written warnings and their own salvation by driving the preachers out, by rejecting the innovations, by restoring the abolished ceremonies and rites in the churches, and by reinstating those who had been removed with unjust violence and restoring them to their previous state, then the estates

326

would intervene in the dispute between the prince and townsmen and negotiate about terms for peace with the greatest care. To this the representatives said they responded as follows. If the townsmen whose mission they were carrying out were allowed to defend themselves and were then convicted of their purported crime by anyone, they would willingly follow the advice of others and take a different route. But since they had not been convicted of and sentenced for the crime of which they were falsely accused, what reason did they have to arrange their affairs in a different, more sensible manner? For the townsmen were convinced of this: what they had undertaken was not impious or seditious, and it would not in the least undermine, much less overthrow, the majesty of the Emperor or the jurisdiction of the prince or the authority of anyone. Instead, they would easily defend it before anyone not only through human justice and reason but also by the laws of God. They therefore asked the estates in the most earnest terms possible to prevail upon the prince to convene within one month another assembly in which the matters under dispute would be set out by both sides before the estates and the leading men of the diocese and then examined in such a way that the reasoning behind each side's case would be judged according to the truth, and the right or wrong of which each side availed itself would become obvious. If it was perceived and decided in this assembly that the people of Münster had wandered into error and done wrong, they would of their own accord return to the old way and deprecate their fault. Furthermore, since no one accused of brigandry or stealing or any sort of felony is executed unless he is convicted with manifest proofs that are too great for any exception, did it not also seem unfair and unseemly to afflict the accused townsmen with injuries without hearing the case? Therefore, the representatives also demanded that the estates should prevail upon the prince to sus-

327 pend the sequestration and whatever other harm | had been thought up against the burghers until the date (assembly) that they had asked for. The representatives said that they would get the townsmen to make the preachers keep silent about the disputed articles in the interim, so that each side would be able to attend the requested assembly freely after setting aside all annoyance and apprehension. In the meanwhile, since with the help of the council, the prince should also aim to bring it about that since the confession of both the clergy and the preachers was about to be issued, men who are weighty in learning and wisdom should calm and settle the tempestuous contention between them after examining it. Since the people of Münster did not know what more

they could or should do, they hoped that when this response of theirs was brought to the prince by the leading men of the diocese, it would soothe his currently offended ears. If, on the other hand, this could not be gotten from the prince, which they did not expect, then they had no doubt that their manifold invocations of the law, privilege and all honorable behavior would at least win for them the favor that the estates would refrain from all injury and would not assault the innocent townsmen either with secret plans or open contrivances. Finally, they also requested that the prince should be persuaded with the following reasoning. First, apart from the detriment that both he and his people would have to expect, he should also consider the calamity, the expenditure, the profanation, the losses, the deaths and in sum the destruction that would break loose to the detriment of both those within the city walls and those who reside in various locations outside if the matter turned out badly. Second, he should reflect upon the fact that in the edict issued at the Diet of Regensburg and promulgated throughout the diocese, the emperor commanded that no one of either the highest or the lowest rank was to be robbed or in any other way afflicted because of religion, since everything was to be remitted to the decision of a general council or to the diet. Third, he should ponder the fact that a similar religion had been accepted in certain kingdoms, principalities, provinces, and regions and in very many Imperial cities, including ones where the Emperor himself was active in person, and yet no such disturbance and no such penalty ensued.

After this proceeding, since no specific decision was reached about the dispute between the prince and the city, a deliberation was held about calling a later assembly | to which all hope of concord would be   328
referred. In the end, December 21 was fixed as the date by everyone's agreement. In the meanwhile, the people of Münster were told to deliberate about giving a fairer and more tolerable answer. In this way the assembly was dismissed without any great success.

Then, since they found hostility and unfriendliness virtually everywhere, the people of Münster trained their soldiers and burghers with frequent raids, so that they would not lose heart through long inaction or, being prone to mutiny, plot worse acts within the city. On December 13, six hundred foot and fifteen horse were sent out on a raid, and they brought back with them some carts of flour and fifteen wagons loaded with wood (though they paid for them) and two prisoners, one the servant of the marshal and the other that of Bernard of Tinnen, who had been captured near Sonnenbrunn.[103] On December 16, a similar raid took place in which armed townsmen intercepted and captured Henry Schencking, who was carrying out an official mission, along with three servants and Arnold Torck, a burgher of Wolbeck, and then brought them into the city.

On December 17, the lower clergy were summoned by the council to its chamber, but when only four members of it showed up, the council put off their wishes until the next day, ordering them in strict terms to be present at that time. Thus, on December 18, Master Gerard Schrodercken, the deacon of the Old Church and orator of the lower clergy, Gerard Provesting and John Vogelsang, canons of the Old Church of St. Paul, Reiner Judefeld of St. Ludger's, John Tulen, the school master of St. Martin's, John of Meschede and Conrad Boland, canons of St. Martin's, Master Timan Kemner, pastor of St. Martin's, and Gerard Tonsoris, chaplain of St. Giles', came to the council hall. The council, aldermen and guild masters gave them the order that one month's pay for the soldiers | was to be contributed by both the absent and the present clergy. Otherwise, they would have to be gravely apprehensive of their own and their property's safety. At first they were terrified by these words, but after moving off a small distance they regained their spirit. Then they deliberated and gave the following reply. Although they did think that they would not be hostile to a contribution that was necessary for the general good, nonetheless, they had no doubt that given the prudence with which it was endowed, the council would take very just reasoning into consideration and graciously exempt the clergy from this contribution at least for two reasons. First, their resources had been exceedingly strained by the Turkish tax, and each clergyman's means were so exhausted that they had no money left. Next, under the circumstances they could not extract income and payments from anyone, and they barely had anything left to support themselves with, living a wretched and miserable life within the city walls. Finally, they could in no way force the absent clergy, who were more powerful and more wealthy, to contribute. Accordingly, since there were few clergymen in the city, and these the poorer ones, they were certain that they would find the council well-disposed and gracious, especially since they

329

---

[103] Or so one might guess the German equivalent of K.'s *Solisfons* to be (Detmer does not list this location in his geographical index, so presumably he too was puzzled by it).

would not abscond from adversity and instead would experience and endure the common misfortunes in the city with their people.

These words did sway the council, but the commons, being incensed with a murderous and more than prophetic hatred against the clergy, clamored that the clergy would not be free from payment since they were the cause of all the burghers' afflictions and troubles. In the end, the council, aldermen and guild masters decided that the clergy present in the city should pay five hundred copper marks within one month for the benefit of the soldiers, and the names of any who shirked contributing should be reported to the council. In the meanwhile, the clergy were to urge the prince to cancel the sequestration and the prohibition against transporting supplies into the city.

On the same day, the council feared that since the commons were enraged at the clergy, they would riot savagely if not prevented by being kept occupied with some activity, and so the council decided to keep them busy with a raid so that they would put uproar and their hatred of the clergy out of their minds. Not even an egg was to be taken without payment. For the next few days, bad weather and deep snow kept the townsmen from their raid. The matter was not very pressing since the nearby peasants, who were terrified by their raiding, disregarded the prince's prohibition and of their own accord brought in wheat, flour, barley, wood and other daily necessities.

On December 19, the lower clergy, being worried about the contribution imposed by the council, summoned all the members of their estate to the chapters' meeting room in the Old Church, but neither the Knights of St. George, nor the Knights of St. John, nor the monks across the river, nor the father of the nuns of Nitzing convent came at the time and place prescribed. Thus, the meeting was ended without any specific decision being reached, though it was resolved that if necessary, they would report the rebellion of others to the council. Not only this contribution imposed on the clergy but many other plans thought up to ruin many people were cut short by a great disturbance, as will be related, and fell into oblivion. 330

Meanwhile, as these events were going on, Bernard Rothman, the chief among the priests in the city, was determined to make good his name,[104] and strove not only to spread his faction but to increase its

---

[104] Reference to the pun by which the name Rothman was taken to signify "trouble maker"; see 160D.

numbers with new innovations. It was not enough for him to bring back into practice communion in both kinds if he did not also abolish the Catholics' custom of having a communion in fasting. By Christ's example, he would summon people in the evening, sometimes to church and sometimes to private homes, to have communion. There, after reading out a public confession, he would pick off as many pieces as he wished from a loaf made of flour, then put them into gaping mouths, and offer a cup to be quaffed, paying no attention to whether the people had come sober or drunk. Furthermore, if someone was prevented by illness or some other reason from coming to this public gathering to take communion, he would console this person after his own fashion, bringing with him the flour bread in his rather large sleeve (it also handily contained mushrooms, wedges of cheese, and other such gifts from matrons). As a result, people throughout the city began to call him "Stutenbernard" after the bread made of wheat or flour that the Westphalians call "ein Stute" in their dialect.

331   Then, step by step, this sacrament of the Eucharist gradually began to be devalued among the factious schismatics. | It now reached the point that those taking communion would not allow the bread to be placed in their mouth by Rothman but would take as much as they wanted, washing it down with a full cup. It is said that in the end they would crumble white loaves onto a platter and pour wine over it, and then the people standing around would take it out with knives or spoons and in this way gulp down the wine together with the bread. I leave it to all good men to judge how much piety and reverence there was for the Salutary Name. Things eventually reached the stage that they began not only to depreciate this sacrament and consider it of very little import but also to revile and curse it with foul language and with words insulting to God, calling it Baal[105] and Satan.

     This Rothman was often warned by many men, and in particular by Philip Melanchthon, that he should keep within the boundaries of the Confession of Augsburg and not usurp an excessive amount of license or personal authority, as Melanchthon himself bears witness in the following letter, which he wrote to Otto Beckman, a licentiate in law. "I often warned Bernard of Münster, but he was clearly subject to very many impulses." The nature and accuracy of Philip's

---

[105] Chief god of the Canaanites, who often figures as the competitor for the Hebrews' affections in the Old Testament.

judgment is known by those who were not only stripped of all their property but had their lives placed at the greatest risk on account of Rothman. For he labored under such a mental illness that the more he was warned of his error, the more obstinately would he devote his efforts to his faction.

Philip Melanchthon also wrote to Rothman | in the following words.[106] "Nothing so unexpected has ever happened to me as my hearing that you condemn and prohibit the baptism of children, which no one among the learned has done hitherto, although many practices have been disputed. Certainly, it has been the opinion of all of them that the baptism of children is either permissible or even obligatory. Hence, I ask you again and again for the sake of Christ to take thought for the tranquility of the Church and not to abolish the baptism of children. For there is no reason why it is necessary to abolish it. This being so, what sense does it make to stir up both scandals and the greatest disturbances for no reason? You have my judgment, and although I can guess what value you will put on it, nonetheless I wished to write it out for you, particularly since I was also writing the same thing to others. If only we could, by our joint efforts, polish up and illuminate those passages which are necessary for the Church, Bernard! We have enemies enough, as you see. For them no sight is more pleasant than that we should die as a result of being done in by mutual disagreements like the Cadmean brothers.[107] May Christ steer your mind to the glory of the Gospel! It seems to be the main aim of certain people to bend what is in Holy Scripture into agreement with the views of burghers, which is not only dangerous but also not very pious. Although I am not the kind of man who is very delighted by ridiculous opinions, nonetheless I see that clever men are sometimes deceived when they wish to transform spiritual views into the views of burghers. I have written this to you with the best good will, desiring that the interests of both you and the Church should be looked after in the best way. Farewell!"

---

[106] This letter is not preserved elsewhere, and clearly comes from a later period, since at this point in the narrative Rothman had not yet come out against child baptism.

[107] An esoteric allusion to ancient Greek mythology. Eteocles and Polynices, the two sons of Oedipus, killed each other while disputing about control of the city of Thebes after Oedipus' departure. The adjective "Cadmean" refers to Cadmus, who founded the citadel of Thebes, and thus simply means "Theban."

Martin Luther also wrote to the government of this city in the follow-
333   ing words. "Grace and peace in Christ, our Lord | and Savior! Prudent
and circumspect gentlemen, we give you our sincere congratulations
and thank God that God, the father of grace, has mercifully infused
into you His loving Word and the knowledge of His Son, our Lord
Jesus Christ, rousing you with His Spirit and illuminating your minds
so that you would resolutely and joyously embrace that knowledge. For
this reason, since the ancient foe is always laying traps for the pure
Word, we are not unreasonably apprehensive about you, fearing that
the crafty lying spirit is creeping into your undertakings, as St. Paul
warned the Corinthians and Galatians. Accordingly, we earnestly ask
you for the sake of the fresh knowledge of Christ that you keep on your
guard carefully and with all diligence and protect yourselves against
unwarily falling into the false doctrine about the sacrament held by the
Zwinglians and other Schwärmer.[108] God has punished this doctrine
with fearsome penalties in the cases of Thomas Müntzer,[109] Tilman
Heshaus,[110] John Hut,[111] Balthazar Hubmaier[112] and, more recently,

---

[108] K. leaves this German term in his text in a superficially Latinized form, so I have
retained it in the original German form. The word literally means "swarmer" and is
a term used by Luther to refer to reformers who he felt went too far in rejecting the
traditions of the medieval Church (i.e., who went further than he himself was willing
to go). Thus, it can be rendered as "fanatic" or "radical."

[109] A very prominent proponent of the "Radical Reformation," he both disseminated
views that led to the outbreak of the Peasants' War (1524–25) and actively participated
in the uprising at Mühlhausen. Captured by Landgrave Philip of Hesse, Müntzer
recanted and took Catholic communion before being beheaded.

[110] A peculiar error. The original text read "Hetzer," meaning Louis Hätzer, who
was a learned proponent of Anabaptism. Active in various localities, he was beheaded
in 1529 for adultery. The Heshaus with whom K. replaced Hätzer died in 1588 and
was born only in 1527, so he could hardly have been referred to by Luther in 1532,
and in any case was a staunch proponent of Lutheranism.

[111] Another prominent Anabaptist proselytizer of apocalyptic views (normally known
by the less formal name Hans), he was arrested in Augsburg in 1527 and examined
under torture. He was accidentally killed when a candle left in his cell ignited the pal-
let on which he lay prostrate as a result of his sufferings. The corpse was nonetheless
tried and condemned to be burned at the stake.

[112] Yet another Anabaptist proselytizer of apocalyptic views. Active among the many
Anabaptists in Austria, in 1527 he was handed over by a noble patron to Ferdinand,
the brother of the Emperor Charles V whom the emperor had placed in charge of the
Austrian realms of the Habsburg inheritance. As a result of his Spanish upbringing,
Ferdinand was a fanatical Catholic and had instituted a fearsome suppression of the
Anabaptists. Hubmaier was burned alive in January 1528 and his wife was soon after
cast into the Danube with a rock tied around her neck.

Zwingli himself,[113] thereby showing Himself to be the enemy of so monstrous a doctrine. Nonetheless, there are some flighty, incorrigible spirits who despise such punishments and warnings from God and rush back and forth leading the people astray by spewing forth their poison. God has, I gather, bestowed upon you splendid preachers, in particular Master Bernard. It is, however, necessary to take into account the devil's trickery, especially at this perilous time, so that all the preachers would be warned and impelled not to sleep and instead to keep watch and fortify the people entrusted to their care against the monstrosities of such doctrine. | The Devil is a hardened criminal who sometimes   334 ensnares pious and learned preachers, and the examples of this fact now exist in unfortunately large numbers. Be, therefore, advised by the examples of those who have defected from the pure Word of God to the Zwinglians, Müntzerites or Anabaptists, who, being prone to acts of sedition, always involve themselves in the political order and rashly seize control of it, just as Zwingli himself did. Things cannot happen any other way, since the devil is a lying spirit and a murderer (John 8[114]). So whoever falls into lying must necessarily eventually fall into murder. Therefore, if you love both spiritual and temporal peace, flee the traps of these sorts of spirits! We have given the same counsel to very many cities, and experience has shown well enough what happened to those cities which rejected it. As far as we are concerned, it is our sincere wish to avert the dangers and losses to both body and soul. May our God and Savior preserve the faith uncontaminated through His pure Word until His glorious arrival! Amen!

"Wittenberg, on the feast of Thomas the Apostle,[115] 1532.

> "Martin Luther
> in his own hand."

Although the council, aldermen and guild masters showed this letter from Luther to Rothman and the other preachers, adding a stern

---

[113] At first a supporter of Luther, Ulrich Zwingli soon became disaffected. He advocated a more radical form of magisterial reformation among the Swiss cantons, and his activity in the secular government of Zurich was strongly censured by Luther. In 1531, Zwingli served in the army of Zurich in the battle of Kappel against the forces of some Catholic cantons. Left seriously wounded on the battle field after the defeat and withdrawal of the army of Zurich, he was recognized by Catholic troops, who killed him. His body was then quartered for treason and burned for heresy.

[114] John 8:44.

[115] The traditional date is December 21 (the feast was later transferred to July 3).

warning, he nonetheless continued to be no less energetic in increasing, defending and strengthening the number of the seditious and their cause. This stock of factious people was increased in particular from the following sources:[116]

- those who had squandered their parents' wealth and could not acquire any more for themselves through their own efforts;
- those who were unable to maintain their own property through entanglement in other people's business affairs;
- those who had used up their own plentiful resources for banquets and were plotting to seize other people's;
- those who, after learning idleness in their first years, got trapped in the account books of creditors;
- those who were offended by the clergy on account not so much of religion as of money, and by the example of the Apostles hankered after common possession of goods;
- those who were sick of their own poverty and were scheming to plunder, sack and pillage the clergy and the wealthier burghers;
- those who rejected good works and thought that they were allowed to do everything with impunity; and
- those who learned to despise other people's things and to extol their own.

After disobedience had, for some months, conceived this useless filth of commoners and nurtured it in its womb with the warmth of rebellion, it eventually gave birth to a spawn that was horrible to look

---

[116] This is one of K.'s few interpretive passages. This analysis is framed in terms of the moralizing categories used in antiquity to explain attempts to overthrow the social order in the Late Roman Republic, especially in Cicero's *Catilinarian Orations* and Sallust's monograph *The Conspiracy of Catiline*. The general idea was that those who wished to attack the social and political order were motivated by greed. Although some of these "revolutionaries" came from the lower orders of society, the emphasis was placed on leaders who belonged to the upper class. These leaders were considered degenerates who had squandered their resources in high living and sought to recoup their losses through plundering the wealth of respectable society. This analysis is at the root of all the subsequent categories here, which mostly ignores the religious issues that motivated the men (and women) of sixteenth-century Münster, who rejected the traditional *ecclesiastical* order and in order to change the ecclesiastical order had to change the political order (i.e., the powers of the prince/bishop). Only the fifth and the penultimate categories (respectively, the desire to revive a putatively Apostolic community of property and the rejection of the validity of good works) have a religious motive, but even these are considered to be pretenses to conceal the desire to seize other people's wealth.

upon. | Suckled on the milk of wantonness, it soon grew up into the   335
loathsome monster of Anabaptism, which terrified the entire Holy
Roman Empire with its movements and wailings.

In order to obstruct the countless disasters that they foresaw with
sure conjecture would emerge from the birth of the new spawn, the
estates of the diocese strove with great energy and zeal to constrain
and quash the spawn while it was still in the womb, so that it would
not appear in the light of day and grow up to overturn and destroy
the entire homeland. Accordingly, on December 20 they gathered in
Wolbeck to hold the assembly the next day, and there they awaited the
arrival of the representatives of Münster and the solid reply from the
whole city, just as had been agreed at the previous assembly. It was
not, however, a delegation that was sent on December 21, even though
they had received a safe conduct fairly far in advance (on December
12), but a letter delivered by a doorkeeper and by John Schuttorp, the
attendant of the council, which went as follows. It was true that they
had promised at the last assembly in Wolbeck that they would, after
public deliberation, send back to Wolbeck at 8 o'clock on the feast of
St. Thomas (which is December 21) plenipotentiary representatives who
would, in the name of the entire city of Münster, deliver to the estates
a report on the decisions reached in the deliberation. It was also true
that they had been quite willing to comply with the resolutions of the
assembly, but an interruption caused by an event of unexpected and
extreme importance had prevented the sending of a delegation. Nonetheless, they had dutifully had discussions with their people about the
terms for peace and about changing their previous reply, but from the
start they had been unable to extract a different one. They therefore
asked the estates not to take badly this absence on their part and the
reply that their view was unchanged. In any case, to do away with the
whole dispute, they asked, just as they had done several times in earlier
assemblies, that in this case the bishop should allow the appointment
by joint agreement of two princes as arbitrators who would halt the
dissension, then examine it, then try it, then settle it with fair terms and
decisions. They also asked that in the meanwhile | he should allow the   336
sequestration and cases lodged against burghers in foreign courts and
the prohibition against transporting supplies into the city to lapse.

The representatives of the main clergy, the knighthood and lesser
cities of the diocese assembled in Wolbeck gave the following reply on
December 21. They had no doubt that on the basis of many proofs
provided by actions, accurate indications, and the various terms for

peace suggested for this dispute they understood well enough how displeasing they found this disagreement which had arise between the prince and the townsmen. In this matter they would in future spare no active and diligent efforts until they halted and then settled the dispute with God's help. They would immediately tell the council which of these courses of action was granted to them by the prince, whose arrival they were awaiting.

Meanwhile, since the birth of our Savior was fast approaching, many men adhering to the ancestral religion and very respectable matrons were getting themselves ready to share in the sacrosanct Eucharist with fasts, alms giving and the other duties of piety. Since in the parish churches seized by new preachers the participants were only given communion in both kinds, they decided to take just the one kind in the Lords' Church, where four chaplains from St. Lambert's and the Parish Across-the-River were also kept very busy hearing the confessions of the Catholics. When this came to the attention of the council, on December 23 they asked the individual burghers and matrons by herald that particularly under present circumstances they and their people should refrain from holy communion in order to avoid the risk of rioting. At the same time, the council forbade anyone to allow infants of his who should have been baptized in the parish churches to be taken to the Lords' Church. This request and this edict were complied with.

On the same day, the prince arrived in Telgte from Lübbecke with a modest escort of cavalry. After entering he bound the townsmen to him by oath and then celebrated his day of installation with a fair amount 337 of solemnity given the resources of the town. | Lübbecke is a large town in the diocese of Minden situated on the banks of the river Weser ten Westphalian (long) miles from Münster, while Telgte is a town of the diocese of Münster situated on the banks of the Ems about one mile from Münster.[117] In this place, the vicars of the diocese, the other estates, and the men of greater age and dignity of whose advice the prince was accustomed to avail himself on an intimate basis in connection with difficult matters assembled. After earnestly pleading the case of the people of Münster before the prince and trying everything that they thought conducive to restoring peace, on the same day they asked the people of Münster to deign to send a delegation to them in Telgte

---

[117] A "common German mile" was much larger than the corresponding English unit, equaling 4.6 of the latter (and 7.42 kilometers).

on the next day (December 25) at 8 a.m. The purpose, they said, was
that these representatives should first hear what concession the estates
had been able to prevail upon the prince to grant as a favor to the city
and then negotiate with him in person about the terms for peace. The
estates promised that they would not fail to work for peace.

The people of Münster wrote back on December 24 as follows. They
had received the letter from the estates by which they were summoned
to Telgte and understood their frame of mind from reading it. They
gave them this response. Since they were not allowed to negotiate officially without the consent and agreement of their people, it was not
unreasonable to forgive them for not having come when summoned
by the estates. Moreover, they asked for a response to their previous
letter in which the request had been made that each side should by
agreement appoint one of two princes to whose arbitration the matter
would be entrusted for an honest decision, so that they would end the
sequestration and the prohibition against transporting supplies into the
city. The people of Münster would then be able to bring their plans and
pursuits into conformity with such a response. Also, they had gathered
through reliable report that certain cavalrymen were keeping the public
roads under guard, pulling down bridges and blocking travel, which
they had hardly expected since the negotiations about the terms for
peace were even now going on. They were informing the estates of
this so that they would not be unaware of it.

To this response the estates wrote back on this same day, December
24, on which the prince also moved on to Iburg after having lunch.
This letter was delivered at Münster on December 25, that is on the
very Nativity of Christ, by a servant of the marshal, the text was as
follows. "You responded to our previous letter requesting | that you   338
send a delegation to us in Telgte with the reply that it was not right
for you to do so without public permission and authorization to send
them, and at the end of your letter concerning the selection of two
princes by agreement and the sequestration and closing of access to
the city you asked for a response from us so that you could bring your
plans and pursuits into conformity with it. Having read and understood these requests, we give as our response to them that we have
certainly eagerly awaited the arrival of your delegation for the purpose
of restoring peace, and we did not think that we would deny you the
smallest services on our part though the matter concerns you primarily.
For it was our intention and inclination to plead with you in person in
a friendly way about this appointment of the two princes and about

all the other burdens on the city, in the confident expectation that the whole dispute would be done away with when it was referred to the two arbitrators. Be that as it may, since you wished to learn from us what proceedings were transacted by us before the prince in connection with this case, we, who seek nothing in connection with this case but the well-being and benefit of you and of all of us in common, will conceal none of these matters from you. With the greatest effort we strove to get the prince to graciously agree to your requests, and although from the start he denied them to us by adducing the fairest rationales, we nonetheless did not give up. In the end we prevailed upon him with insistent prayers to be prepared to transfer the dispute between you and him for decision by two princes of the Empire, one to be chosen by him and one by you, and to make the appropriate agreement for this. In the meanwhile, the sequestration and the suits lodged against your burghers, and the prohibition against transporting supplies into the city are to lapse on the condition that the ceremonies and the ancient rites in the churches which were abolished by you are to be celebrated in the customary way during the same period of time, the preachers are to refrain from giving sermons and from other innovations, and the captives (Henry Schencking and the others captured by you) are to be set at liberty under fair terms and restored to their previous state without any inconvenience. Since it was only with difficulty that we managed to get the prince to make these concessions, which also
339   seem to be in partial agreement with your petition | and under the present circumstances cannot bring any disadvantage to you and your burghers, it is our advice and request that you judge them all by the standard of fairness and assess more carefully among yourselves the well-being of the city of Münster and of the whole diocese, in this matter conducting yourselves with an eye to keeping the peace and tranquility, so that once all dispute, contention and discord are done away with, good will and concord may be put on a permanent foot-ing. We are fully confident that given present circumstances and your constraints you will implement these measures. Nonetheless, we wish to receive through the bearer of this letter a response as to which of these steps you are going to take. If, on the other hand, you send a delegation to us here, which we think would provide no small help to the present case, we grant them free and safe conduct in coming and going by virtue of this letter with the prince's agreement."

After the townsmen received this letter, they cleverly held the mes-senger back for that entire day, persuading him that since it was the Nativity of Christ, they could not deal with profane matters because of

the festivities and that the council and the representatives of the commons could not gather to deliberate about giving a reply on account
of the particular reverence felt for this day, upon which the whole
city's attention was focused. He should, therefore, let this day pass. By
this trick the man was kept in the city unaware of the deceit. Even
if a suspicion of future misfortune had perchance induced him to be
inclined to leave the city, this would hardly have been allowed. For all
the gates of the city were kept under close guard by the burghers, so
that while no one was permitted to leave, everyone was permitted to
enter. As the shadows of dusk were falling, however, the council summoned the aldermen and guild masters, deliberating on the future until
9 o'clock. In the end they voted for a raid at night, and for this reason
heralds hurriedly rushed from door to door ordering the burghers to
present themselves in arms at the council hall at midnight. As a result,
the city was seized by a terrifying dread, which was magnified by the
darkness of the night.

Being ignorant of everything, the lower clergy began to tremble and
looked for hiding places, | fearing that immediate destruction was being   340
prepared for them and lamenting that they had not paid the money
asked of them. The Catholics thought that an attack was being mounted
on themselves and their property. The matrons bewailed the coming
disasters, feared the death of the ancient religion, and prophesied that
everything would be unlucky, unsuccessful and disastrous. In the end,
apart from the dregs of the blackguards, there was no one who did
not fear a remarkable disturbance in the city, an internal conflagration, and the downfall of the city. Meanwhile, the council ordered that
weapons of every kind, the more maneuverable cannons that could be
transported on four-wheeled wagons, and the other material considered
suitable for this raid be brought out. A certain number of carts were
also filled, some with poles, some with lighter-weight ladders and some
with gunpowder and iron shot. Some could also be seen empty, from
which it was easy to surmise what was being planned.

Next, men suddenly thronged together at the prescribed time and
place from all corners of the city, some equipped with short matchlocks,

some with arquebuses,[118] some with pikes, some with battle-axes, some with halberds, some with grappling hooks, some with crow-bars, some with stakes and other things useful for raiding. Such large numbers streamed together that the council hall and the neighboring marketplace could scarcely hold the multitude. Only six hundred were chosen from them to take part in that raid on Telgte, and to them were added the three hundred soldiers hired by the council as protection and a few armed cavalrymen. The rest were left behind to guard the city in the meanwhile.

On there other hand, the estates of the diocese and all the other leading men who were assembled in Telgte noticed that the people of Münster were not sending an answer and were instead detaining their messenger in the city, and keeping such watch on the city gates, as they had learned through scouts, that no one was allowed to leave, with the purpose of preventing the assembly from learning their intention and plan from anyone. They therefore harbored the suspicion that the people of Münster were rearing some sort of monster and setting some deceit in motion, and sent out a few cavalrymen at nightfall to reconnoître. Reaching the bridge over the River Weser on the road from Telgte to
341 Münster, they removed a few planks from the bridge, | thereby preventing the townsmen from crossing. Sensing no offensive movement on the part of the townsmen and fearing nothing untoward, they prepared to return home since they were tired of the bitter cold.

---

[118] In the early fifteenth century it was common practice to equip infantry with two sorts of hand-held guns: shorter ones ("matchlocks") three to four feet long and longer ones up to five feet long. The former could be carried around by the soldier, but the latter were a bit too cumbersome and had a hook to assist in handling during battle (they were carried in wagons at other times). In some languages, both types were called arquebuses, but Italian distinguished the two, calling the smaller ones *sciopetti* and reserving the term arquebus for the latter, a practice followed by K. (who uses a Latinized version of *sciopetti*).